PUBLIC AND
PRIVATE INVESTMENTS

PUBLIC AND PRIVATE INVESTMENTS

SOCIOECONOMIC ANALYSIS

Henry Malcolm Steiner

The George Washington University

A RONALD PRESS PUBLICATION

JOHN WILEY & SONS

New York • Chichester • Brisbane • Toronto

Library of Congress Cataloging in Publication Data:

Steiner, Henry Malcolm.
  Public and private investments.

  "A Ronald Press Publication."
  Includes index.
  1. Capital investments—Evaluation. 2. Economic development
projects—Evaluation. I. Title.

HG4028.C4S713   332'.0415   79-26036
ISBN 0-471-01625-X

Printed in the United States of America

10 9 8 7 6 5 4 3 2

To my teachers and to my family

Preface

I wrote this book because I believe there is a gap separating the analysts who perform economic analysis in government and business and the economists themselves. This separation of the theorists and the practitioners shows itself in many ways—and in one all-important way—the acceptance of prices unquestioningly as though the allocation mechanism of the price system were working perfectly. Much of the time it is not. Therefore, the practitioner must know when it is inoperative and by how much. Disastrous decisions are made if the analyst is unaware of the immense difference the idea of opportunity cost makes. This work seeks to close the heady subject of economics with those more mundane disciplines of engineering economy, management accounting, capital budgeting, and operations research.

The first part of the book deals with decision making when the price system is assumed to be working perfectly. Discounted cash flow methods are reviewed here, along with the major issues regarding this type of analysis. The second part deals with the meaning of resource allocation under the price system, particularly when—as is usually the case—the price system is not working for one reason or another. Here the social aspects of economic decisions are explored. The third part of the book deals with socioeconomic analysis in the development of nations. A number of factual cases are presented here with a commentary on the issues brought up by each situation.

My audience I imagine to be composed of economists, engineers, accountants, management specialists, financiers, operations researchers, or in fact, anyone who finds himself making decisions on socioeconomic matters. Analysts in engineering and economic consulting firms and in government agencies on the local, state, and national levels, I trust, will form an important section of my readers. I also direct my argument to those persons, be they accountants, engineers, economists, architects, financiers, managers, or planners, who make decisions in regard to investment in private industry. The book may be used in courses in economic analysis, engineering economy, capital budgeting, and operations research in universities in schools of business, engineering, architecture, and planning. It may be used in executive development courses in private industry or government. It may be employed as a handbook.

The presentation is as concise as I can make it. It is directed toward the essentials of using the methods of economic analysis for investment. The theory included is limited to that necessary for an understanding of the application. The first examples presented in a new topic are purposely made simple and are designed to give the reader a chance to see the methods in action exposed to view. These are usually followed by factual studies which are much more realistic and complicated, like the cases familiar to students of law and business administration that attempt to approximate real-life situations. The book contains no homework problems.

A semester's course for beginners should cover all of Part I, Chapter 1 through 16. A second semester should include the remainder of the book, Parts II and III, Chapters 17 through 26.

My deep appreciation goes to Maria Cecilia Steiner, Jessie Aileen Steiner, Raj Chopra, Yvette Shelton, Betty Fink, and Marian Pierson.

HENRY MALCOLM STEINER

Washington, D. C.
March 1980

Contents

PART III SOCIOECONOMIC ANALYSIS IN THE DEVELOP-MENT OF NATIONS

1
Introduction

This book is concerned with an aspect of socioeconomic planning—that is, the selection of capital investments. But this is such a broad subject that it may at times touch on all facets of socioeconomic planning. In the context of this book *socioeconomic planning* is the consideration of alternative solutions to a problem with a view to deciding on a course of action in the future. Alternative solutions are those that will to some extent solve the problem. These solutions may be one, or all, of three types. First, they may be mutually exclusive, as in the case of different alternative highway locations to connect two cities. Under normal circumstances we would not build a highway in more than one location, and thus one alternative excludes the others. Second, they may be independent, as in the case of a priority list of highways to be constructed by an agency. In this situation the number of possibilities for highway construction that exist is more than the amount of resources available to build them all. A list of projects whose total construction cost falls within the budget must be made up. The alternatives are then examined and evaluated according to some methodology in order to make a decision on a course of action that will answer the question: "Which of these projects shall we build and in what order?" Third, projects may be interdependent—that is, we may not build one without building the other.

Socioeconomic planning is concerned with the future, since we can do nothing to change the past. A study of the past is not useless, however, because it may give us a hint as to what will happen in the future. This is its only use to us. We must be careful not to let it influence us in illogical ways.

Planning is concerned with the possibility of change in an existing situation and how to deal with that change. An investigation may show that no change is to be expected. It is more likely, however, that some change in the future is inevitable. This change may be characterized

1

by growth or its opposite. For example, it is practically a certainty that over the next five years potable water use in the United States will increase. It is almost equally certain that the miles of railroad track in service in the United States will decrease.

INVESTMENT

Investment means an addition to the supply of facilities provided to satisfy a demand. For example, new subway cars are bought over 10 years in order to supply the mounting demand for urban passenger transport, as well as to replace cars going out of service. Supply implies cost, both construction (or first cost), and operation and maintenance cost to keep the facility running. Demand implies that someone receives some satisfaction from the investment and its up-keep. A stockbroker reads the morning paper on his way to his downtown office aboard a comfortable subway car. Another way of saying that someone receives satisfaction is to say that someone benefits from the investment. It seems logical to require that the cost of an investment be somehow related to the benefit expected from it. Some method or rule must therefore be formulated to prescribe the relation between cost and benefit to tell us whether the investment should be made.

The rule that has evolved over many years is that the benefits must exceed the costs of an investment in order to justify making the investment. (A number of other ways of formulating this rule exist, but in this introduction we concern ourselves with the simplest of them.) To describe benefits and costs, since we are not dealing with invest-ments whose economic lives are instantaneous, we must imagine the future. Benefits and costs, as they will be experienced over the eco-nomic life of the investment, must be pictured. Comparison takes place between a stream of benefits and costs spread out over a number of years.

The advisability of making an investment implies choice, how-ever, and choice implies that we choose between at least two alterna-tives. Choosing a course of action in investment means that we must compare one stream of benefits and costs with at least one other stream of benefits and costs. This other stream of benefits and costs is often nothing more than the effects of continuing the status quo—that is, not doing anything at all. To compare and thus decide which alternative will be best, it is necessary (1) to define "best," (2) to develop the costs and benefits of each alternative over its lifetime, (3) to allow for the fact that these benefits and costs will appear over time, and (4) to compare the alternatives according to some methodology. All these matters are treated in Part I of this book.

PUBLIC AND PRIVATE INVESTMENTS

This book is concerned with investments in both the public and private sectors. Public investments are largely infrastructural—that is, they provide some necessary service to industry and the public such as power, drinking water, or rail transport. Examples of private sector investment are largely industry or real estate. The private sector investments, since they are normally analyzed from the private point of view, accept the workings of the price system as a proper indicator of costs and benefits. Public sector investments, since they are made from the viewpoint of the society as a whole, sometimes require adjustments to the prices indicated by the price system. This system and the adjustments to it are discussed in Part II.

In addition, public sector projects are usually subject to some sort of political judgment. This matter is touched on somewhat tangentially, but this does not mean that the political process is considered unimportant in public project decisions. It is all-important. Indeed, the public project analysis is often made only to support political decisions with logic.

Part III contains applications of the matter of Parts I and II to problems of national development.

SOCIAL BENEFITS AND COSTS

It might be assumed from the previous discussion that the benefits and costs referred to were in terms of money and money only. This is not necessarily true. Other consequences of a course of action exist that are not usually conceived of in money terms. One of the best known examples of this is the air pollution that came as a cost of the urban freeways in many cities. These types of consequences, known as *externalities*, may be recreational, social, political, or aesthetic in nature.

A road where none has existed before from a main highway into a remote village brings benefits that can only be called socioeconomic. A road built into a Mexican village brings educational benefits with it, among many others. It is easier to retain a teacher in a community where he is not completely cut off from his former life, friends, and family. How difficult to express this benefit in a study except in words! But we will see that it is necessary to express it in other than words if it is to be given its proper place and importance.

A new road makes it easier to get from San Francisco to Santa Cruz for those city dwellers seeking recreation at the beach on a Sunday. The trip is faster and less dangerous. There are less traffic fumes and fewer long lines of cars with bored drivers and passengers waiting to get where they are going. These are benefits on a number of counts.

A political benefit of a road is fairly obvious in a developing nation where a road may connect a number of communities to the rest of the country by four-wheeled traffic for the first time. Better communication begins, including increased awareness of belonging to a larger society than the village. The nation is that much more integrated, less a collection of towns and villages, and more a single unit. Not all the consequences of building a road of this kind are benefits. There are costs. Children leave home and families are broken up with much more ease than before. And the cities themselves suffer from having to accommodate new waves of untrained people.

Aesthetic benefits are easy to describe but difficult to evaluate. A road up the Northern California coast may owe a good part of its existence to the joy that travelers receive in looking at a series of magnificent views of forest and ocean. Aesthetic benefits are quite real. And so are aesthetic costs. The Embarcadero Freeway in San Francisco is the now-classic example of a highway that cost a good deal more than construction, maintenance, and operation. It cost San Franciscans a landmark—the Ferry Building—which was not erased, but diminished by being hidden behind the massive double-decked freeway. The freeway was never completed because of the protests of the citizenry, who were moved by aesthetic outrage. In partial use, the Embarcadero Freeway stands as a warning to analysts who would disregard benefits and costs that are not readily reduced to money terms.

These matters are dealt with, through factual studies and comments on them, in Part III of this book.

In conclusion, it must never be forgotten among all the numbers, graphs, and tables, that what is being predicted in investment analysis is *change over time*. Very often, especially in public projects, human reaction to change must also be predicted. For example, when demand for an urban subway project—and thus revenue, which is a most important part of the benefits of the project—is being projected over 20 years, we are attempting to forecast how human beings are going to react to the project itself, and more, how they are going to react to many other effects that have nothing to do with the project itself. One of the important factors that will affect subway use is the population of the city, which is itself affected by the rate of growth of the population of the area of the country as a whole, by migration from rural to urban areas, and by a great number of other variables. Could anything be more discouraging to the analyst than to attempt to predict all this? Yet it must be attempted if we are to avoid the greater mistakes that will surely accompany a surrender to despair and no analysis at all. How to analyze such matters, while recognizing their difficulty, and how to handle the difficulties themselves are the subject of the chapters that follow this introduction.

I
WHEN THE PRICE SYSTEM IS WORKING

2

Economic Decisions

This chapter addresses certain aspects of logical decision making in economic matters, particularly investment in capital goods. A number of topics discussed here are often forgotten in the maze of detail that usually accompanies an economic study. But the mistakes attributable to lack of logical thinking about such matters as sunk costs, depreciation, differential consequences, and the other points of logical decision making are usually of the most important kind, the kind on which a study depends for its success.

CRITERIA FOR DECISIONS

Need it even be stated that certain clearly understood criteria are necessary in order to make decisions about alternative courses of action? Evidently the answer is, "Yes." Yet such criteria as, "The greatest good for the greatest number" have been seriously proposed as logical rules of choice. Such a statement gives no method for deciding between two alternatives, each costing the same amount of money but benefiting different numbers of people. In this example, if we choose the alternative involving the greatest number of people benefited, we are left wondering how to interpret "the greatest good." If we choose the alternative involving the greater sum of money per person, we have difficulty explaining why we are choosing to benefit a lesser number of people. Unfortunately, such self-contradictory criteria are not rare.

It is clear that the criterion for deciding among alternative courses of action ought to be the effect of each course of action on the future. In other words, we should ask, "What will be the future effect of alternative A as opposed to alternative B?" Evidently, we must ask this question in a more precise manner for it to have meaning. We must establish a situation or series of situations that will be affected by the alternatives, and the ways these situations change with respect to each alternative course of action will be our criteria. Another way of saying this is that we must define relevant objectives and then predict the effect of each alternative course of action on these objectives. The alternative that affects these objectives best—and we must also define what we consider "best"—is the one chosen.

For example, say we are trying to decide between two types of passenger buses for an urban transport company. The alternative courses of action are to buy one type or the other. The objective of the company may simply be to make the largest profit possible each year. The criterion of choice between the two buses is then the effect of buying one type or the other on the future profits of the company over the economic life of the equipment.

Needless to say, objectives may be multiple, alternatives many and not necessarily mutually exclusive, and consequences difficult to predict. Nevertheless, the criterion of choice as described above seems not only logical but the only logical approach that can be taken.

RECOGNIZING ALL ALTERNATIVES

Unhappy the analyst who, after making an exhaustive study of a situation and recommending a course of action, discovers that the best alternative had not even entered his mind! The population of second-guessers in the world is indeed large, as the analyst soon finds out. It suddenly becomes incredible that anyone studying the situation would not have thought of this most obvious solution. Embarrassment, apologies, loss of professional standing, and perhaps much more serious results, such as the waste of a large amount of society's resources, ensue.

The rule that the best alternative cannot be chosen if it has never even been considered is fundamental. The application of the rule is difficult. Perhaps the best advice to the analyst is to remember it, with the result that considering all possible alternatives, even the most farfetched, will be given a place of primary importance at the beginning of every study that is undertaken. Nothing in this phase of the study will be left to chance or to the policy of hoping for the best. At the beginning of the final report, a discussion of possible alternatives and the reasons for including some and not others will be prominent. Clearly, this requires that some preliminary study be done on many alternatives, and only those alternatives that survive this test will be studied in depth. In this area, judgment and experience count.

To illustrate: A construction company working on the bank of the Columbia river found it necessary to carry fill from a small island several hundred feet from the bank in order to complete a railroad embankment. Some million cubic yards were needed. The question was: "How can we best reach the island?" The project engineer immediately decided on a bridge and began the design. The bridge was to cost about $50,000, which was expensive for a temporary structure at that time and place.

When the design was almost done, the engineer arrived at work one morning to discover that the night shift had completed a causeway to the island at a cost of a few thousand dollars. The engineer had not thought it possible to thus dam even a small arm of the mighty Columbia river. The effect of the causeway had simply been to divert the flow to the other side of the island. True, there had been some tricky moments when the final gap in the causeway was being closed by bulldozers, but the night shift superintendent had been successful in his gamble.

What had seemed impossible, out of the question, an alternative not to be thought of, had turned out to be by far the best and cheapest solution. We will not dwell on the sensations experienced by the engineer over the succeeding weeks.

DECISIONS BASED ON CONSEQUENCES OF ALTERNATIVES

Decisions should be based on the consequences of alternatives over a certain period. The alternatives with the best results are the ones preferred. But how are these consequences to be expressed? Certainly, they have no meaning unless expressed in terms of objectives. Even when objectives are known—for example, the simple one of profit—it is possible to make a decision based on a hunch—that is, a decision made without considering any consequences whatever.

Typical of such decisions is the hope that all will be well. For example, one can have a hunch that a small airline between two cities not previously served by air will turn out to be a gold mine. The next step is to buy the airplanes, hire the pilots, ground crew, agents, and proceed. Decisions based on hunches sometimes turn out to be all that was hoped for. More often, however, the result of such decisions is failure, as so many airline projects have shown.

VIEWPOINT

As soon as one begins to consider the consequences of an investment, the question immediately arises—or should arise—"Consequences to whom?"

For example, if an investor is considering buying a small dump truck and operating it for profit, the consequences he will consider are those referring to himself. The truck will cost its first cost and operation, and it will bring in a certain amount. The point of view the investor will take is strictly his own, and this viewpoint defines what costs and benefits he will consider. Gasoline will be a cost, but he will not consider the extra wear and tear on the streets of the city in which he will operate, although these are also costs caused by his truck.

Now change the point of view in the matter from that of the individual investor about to take a flyer in a dump truck to that of the city in which he will operate. When he applies for a permit to operate his truck, the city considers a completely different set of costs arising from his operation, such as the extra wear and tear on the streets, as well as the increased air contamination, the increased street congestion, and a different set of benefits such as the increase in employment in the area. These distinctly different costs and benefits may well determine whether or not the permit is issued at all, and if it is issued, how much it will cost.

In other words, the point of view taken by the analyst determines the costs and benefits to be considered as consequences of a course of action, and these may and probably will differ depending on the point of view taken. This subject is treated at length in the following chapter.

CONSEQUENCES OVER TIME

Consequences imply the future. It is the consequence of a course of action during some future period that we must be concerned with. We are immediately confronted with another question: "How can we take these time differences in consequences into account in our decision?" There is no doubt that we should take them into account, on the theory that a good thing that occurs today is better than a good thing that will occur a year from now when both are equally certain to happen. If we defer a trip to Europe from this summer to the next, we feel as though we have made a sacrifice. As a matter of fact, if we invest the money we would have spent on the trip in a savings and loan association, we will receive more than our money back at the end of a year. The extra money that we will receive is known as *interest*. This interest is really payment for satisfaction deferred.

In the same way, we would all prefer to defer an unpleasant experience until later—and the later the better. For example, a serious illness is better borne 10 years from now than tomorrow. Death would be deferred indefinitely if we could only manage it. We will defer paying for many years a heavy debt that will prevent our taking any trips at all, but we will pay more when the debt finally comes due. And we will pay more by the amount of interest that our creditor has stipulated.

In some way, we must be able to equalize the good and bad effects of a course of action that will occur—we believe—two years from now with those that will occur 10 years from now. These effects must be algebraically additive. And here we leave the accountant's way of thinking about such matters. To him, a payment of $1000 tomorrow or $1000 10 years from now is entered in his books at exactly the same rate: $1000. Thus, his calculations relative to the consequences of a course of action differ profoundly from those of an economic analyst. Arguments ensue, but in the end there is no doubt that both the accountant and the economic analyst proceed correctly if they are always guided by their individual purposes. These purposes are different. Nevertheless, great care should be taken by the economic analyst in order to recognize that his purposes and methods are different from those of the accountant. Most important, the economic analyst recognizes the time value of money and consequences in general. Just how he does this is explained in Chapter 4.

TRACING CONSEQUENCES AND SYSTEMS ANALYSIS

Consequences—especially economic ones—can be far-reaching. Tracing them so that they may be included in an analysis is an immense, sometimes an impossible, job. It is somewhat like the much easier physical problem of tracing the sources of a great river back from its mouth to all the other rivers, streams, brooks, rills, and springs that supply it. For example, a decision to rebuild the railroads of Ecuador has immediate consequences such as direct labor costs, secondary consequences on the labor supply of the country, and tertiary effects on consumer buying power. It means that rails must be bought abroad; thus, there will be balance-of-payments effects, which in turn means that other uses of foreign exchange must be forgone. The effects of such an action are multitudinous. And how are we to delimit these effects? At what point do we stop the search? This must be determined by the point of view we are taking. For example, if I am a private investor thinking about buying a Mercedes-Benz for my limousine service, I will give little or no thought to the effect this purchase will have on the balance of payments of the United States. First cost, maintenance, and operation are as far as the investor goes in following the train of effects of his decision to purchase the Mercedes-Benz, and rightly so. A federal government economist, concerned with reviewing the effects of many such purchases, goes much farther—and again rightly so.

This tracing of consequences is partly what systems analysis is all about. We outline the limits of a system and trace the effects and interdependencies of a course of action. Neglect of this system viewpoint has caused innumerable problems in transportation. The city of Los Angeles went ahead and built its urban freeways without really worrying about system effects. The result was immediate congestion, uncontrolled urban growth, air pollution, and other undesirable effects. Whether such effects are desirable is not the question here, however. The point is that it is mandatory to trace all effects relevant to the point of view of the analyst.

SECONDARY CRITERIA—CERTAINTY, RISK, AND UNCERTAINTY

Because the analyst must base his decisions on the different consequences in the future of the alternatives he is considering and because the future cannot be predicted with certainty, he must in some way be concerned with the fact that his decision is a probable one. He must be concerned with the mathematics of probability in some way, perhaps only to the extent of realizing the existence of the matter and consciously rejecting any change in his calculations because of it.

If he rejects any inclusion of the notion of probability in his calculations, he is said to be acting under certainty, by definition. Risk means, in the usual technical parlance, that the probability distribution of possible consequences or outcomes of a course of action is known. If not precisely known, it may be guessed at. Or even if it cannot be guessed at, it may be worthwhile to assume very roughly extreme values for the probability of certain outcomes. Uncertainty means that nothing can be said, and no guesses are made as to the probabilities of the consequences of a course of action. These considerations of certainty, risk, and uncertainty we call *secondary criteria*, and they are applied at some point in the analysis to the primary criteria of the best use of scarce resources.

We deal largely with certainty and risk situations. And we do this by means of so-called *expected value*. All this is discussed at length in Chapter 12. For the moment, it is important to recognize that the threat of future consequences' not turning out as we have described them must be taken into account somehow. The analyst may not act as if the future were certain without making such an assumption explicit.

PLANNING HORIZONS

It is obvious that if one talks about the future, he needs to state how far into the future he intends to look. He must establish a planning horizon (*time horizon*). How to do this?

A planning horizon in reference to investments must be based in some way on the time the investments will be in use. Their possible life, in the sense of technical possibility, is termed *technical life*. A road conceived under the conditions of construction, location, and use in the second half of the twentieth century has an unlimited technical life. There is no reason why, with proper maintenance, it cannot last forever. Indeed, some Roman roads are still in use as to their location and subbase. Their original wearing surface is acting as a subbase in some cases. Many Roman bridges are still in use, practically as they were built. But usually a road has a much shorter life. Parts of it are abandoned, or it is completely relocated on being widened.

Technical life is normally much longer than economic life. *Economic life* is defined as the period over which society or some portion of it experiences either benefits or costs from an investment. Even a railroad that should be abandoned in favor of a highway, for example, is still considered to be in economic existence. An abandoned stretch of highway, if no one objects to it or gains from it, is considered to be economically dead.

Of interest to the analyst, therefore, is the possible economic life of an alternative. Economic life is sometimes the same as technical life, sometimes lesser, never greater. It is in this kind of determination that historical records of investments become of use. What is the average economic life of highways in the United States? About 20 years. And that is the period over which their consequences are usually investigated.

DIFFERENTIAL CONSEQUENCES

A logical rule of decision making is that it is only the differences in alternative courses of action that are relevant to a decision between them. Aspects of alternative courses of action that are the same do not enter into the decision because they are disregarded automatically, almost subconsciously. For example, a traveler is trying to decide how best to fly to Cleveland from San Francisco. Two airlines each run a flight. The traveler notes that the elapsed flying times of the two flights are the same, and the equipment is also. The differences between the two flights are in the hours of departure. The traveler makes his decision on the basis of the difference between the two alternatives—the hour of departure—and completely ignores the elapsed flying times and the equipment used, often without recognizing that he is applying the major decision rule stated here.

Another important example of this rule is worthy of considerable discussion on its own merits—which it receives in later sections of this chapter. Anything that has happened before the moment a decision is made is not a difference between alternatives and should not be considered. As Grant and Ireson put it, "... the past is common to all alternatives for the future." [1]

WITH–WITHOUT CRITERION

Some time ago, in an Asian country, a new high-speed freeway between two cities of over 2 million persons each was being analyzed. It was decided that the benefits exceeded the costs by no great margin.

The method used by the analyst was to compare the stream of costs and benefits of the new freeway over the next 20 years with the costs and benefits of the present road, which had become congested. Specifically, he took the net present worth of the stream of benefits from the new road and compared that amount with the net annual cost of the present road *at the present time* multiplied by 20. In doing this, he violated the with–without criterion.

The analyst should have predicted the costs and benefits of the new freeway over the next 20 years—the "with" part of the with–without criterion. Then he should have predicted the costs and benefits of the existing road over the next 20 years—the "without" part of the with–without criterion. He would have found that the relative benefits of the new facility were greatly increased as the existing road became more and more congested in the future. The new freeway would thus have appeared much more attractive.

Defining: The with–without criterion requires that any new alternative be compared with the existing alternative. Changes in both these alternatives, over the time horizon selected, must be included in the comparison. The mistake in this connection is to assume that the benefits and costs of the existing alternative continue unchanged over the life of the project, which is what multiplying the net annual cost of the road in the example above by 20 does.

COMMENSURABILITY

If we are to measure future consequences—and this is implied in a choice between them—we must have some unit of measurement

---

[1] E. L. Grant, and W. G. Ireson, *Principles of Engineering Economy*, 5th ed, New York, Ronald, 1970, p. 13.

common to all alternatives. If we are to measure apples against oranges, we can do so only by converting both the number of apples and the number of oranges to some common measure, usually money. If things have a price and a cost in the market, or if they can somehow logically be assigned a price and a cost, then consequences can be reduced to dollars and cents. When effects are thus measurable, they are said to be *commensurable*.

In the private sector, effects of interest to the analyst taking the private point of view are usually stated monetarily, although not always. The effect of a certain new product on the image of the company, although an important effect, may be expressible in monetary terms. A new machine may have an effect on worker morale that is not expressible in money.

In the public sector, matters are much more difficult. Many of the effects may be expressible in terms of words only, or if in numbers, then not in terms of commensurable numbers. These effects are called *irreducibles*. However, it can be argued that all effects must be measured in common terms if a decision is to be made logically. If this cannot be done, or is not accepted by the organizers of the study, then to the extent that the important effects cannot be expressed in common terms, the decision may be incorrect.

SUNK COST

As was stated previously, "The past is common to all alternatives." Certainly, we cannot re-do the past. No matter what we do in the future, the past remains unaffected. All this seems patent, but the conclusions that follow from it are not so obvious.

For example, if we buy a piece of transport equipment, say, a city bus, and discover that it is costing far more than was expected, we must not say, "Well, we'll just have to hold on to this until we get our money's worth out of it." This course would allow the past, and now evidently incorrect, decision to rule our behavior in the future. The cost of the buses is sunk. Nothing can "get our money's worth" out of that decision. What we can do is look to the future. We can compare, say, two alternatives: selling the buses for what they will bring on the used vehicle market and buying new buses with better operating costs, against keeping the present buses operating, remembering that only the present worth of the buses (what they will bring on the used market) is to be considered. In other words, the past is dead and with it our money. All we can do now is to forget what the buses originally cost (a sunk cost) and concentrate on what they are worth now, for that is how much money we have in them.

Sunk costs are costs incurred in the past. The only value such costs have is a historical one. They may help to predict the future, and then again they may not.

DEPRECIATION

Is depreciation a cost or not? Should it be included in an economic analysis? These questions are frequently asked. Most questioners find the answer difficult to accept.

Depreciation should not be included as a cost in a before-tax economic analysis. Depreciation is simply a reflection of a sunk cost that appears on the accountant's books. Accounting practice decrees that investments in fixed assets be depreciated over an assumed life of the asset. Dutifully, the accountant complies. But this accountant's convention has nothing to do with economic analysis. The fact is that once the asset is bought, its cost, and any reflection of it, becomes a sunk cost which should not be included in a before-tax economic analysis. Another approach to answering the question that began this section is to ask ourselves if depreciation involves a flow of cash out of the enterprise. If the answer to that is, "No," then it is sure that depreciation is not a real cost but only an accountant's way of describing the situation in which his company finds itself.

The reason the words "before-tax" appeared in some of the sentences of the foregoing paragraph is that in after-tax analysis an effect of depreciation must be considered, although not the amount of the depreciation itself. Depreciation, according to the tax laws of the United States and other countries, is an expense that may be deducted from taxable income. Therefore, to the extent that its effect is to cause a reduction in taxes, depreciation does have an effect on future costs. For example, if a company is in the 50 percent tax bracket and its profits are $2 million, it pays taxes of $1 million. Say that a certain forklift truck is being depreciated on a straight-line basis of $1000 per year and that it has been mistakenly left out of the tax analysis. Its inclusion affects the tax bill as follows:

Profits	$2,000,000
Less depreciation	1,000
Revised profits	1,999,000
Revised taxes at 50%	999,500
Original taxes	$1,000,000
Revised taxes	999,500
Difference	$ 500

Depreciation makes a difference of $500 in the tax bill. This reduction in taxes of 50 percent of the amount allowed for depreciation is an important saving and must be considered in an after-tax analysis on the advisability of making an investment for this company.

Public sector analysis excludes depreciation completely because public agencies do not normally pay taxes.

It follows from the foregoing discussion that the book value of an asset may or may not represent its value in the market place. Value in the market place is all the economic analyst is interested in when considering the value of a used asset. Book value is best ignored, except in after-tax analysis when it has an effect on taxes paid because of book loss or book gain.

INCREMENTAL ANALYSIS

Most readers who have taken a course in microeconomics remember the well-known rule concerning the optimum production quantity of a good: "Produce until the marginal cost of production is equal to the marginal revenue when the good is sold." In other words, the company should continue production until the extra cost incurred in producing a unit of a good is just equal to the extra revenue to be gained from the sale of that extra unit. The rule in general economic analysis is similar: "The size of an investment is increased until the extra benefit gained from each increase becomes equal to the extra cost incurred to realize that benefit." Neglect of this rule has led to many an error.

Just as the rule in microeconomics does *not* say, "Produce until total cost equals total revenue," so the rule in investment analysis *must not* say, "Size the investment up to the point where total benefits equal total costs." The latter erroneous rule has been followed in many analyses and has led to the waste of respectable sums of money.

As an example of correct analysis, which is explained in depth at a later point, imagine the analyst attempting to decide how many docking spaces a new port should have. If he conducts the analysis correctly, he increases the number of docks until the extra benefit from the last dock built just equals its extra cost.

OPPORTUNITY COST

Opportunity cost is the benefit lost by choosing one alternative rather than another. It is the cost of a lost opportunity. When mutually exclusive alternatives are being considered, an opportunity cost must be incurred because by definition one alternative excludes the other. Opportunity cost must be included in a managerial analysis in order to make a decision. It is typical of opportunity costs that they are never included in a bookkeeper's summary of costs.

If I should decide to go to Japan rather than Europe for my summer vacation, the opportunity cost of the decision to go to Japan is the pleasure I would have received had I gone to Europe. I cannot go both places at the same time, so these are mutually exclusive alternatives. If a city decides to continue to operate its own water supply system rather than to contract it out, the opportunity cost of that decision is the loss of funds resulting from the sale of the facilities involved in supplying its own water.

This concept of lost opportunity is one of the most important in economic analysis.

THE DIFFERENCE BETWEEN THE ACCOUNTANT'S AND THE ECONOMIST'S ANALYSIS

By now it is evident that accountants and managers (or economists) abide by different rules when analyzing decisions.

The accountant ignores the value of money over time. A $1000 now or a $1000 a year from now are treated in exactly the same way in the accountant's books.

The accountant applies costs to cost centers, that is, to the area where costs arise. The economist applies costs to a decision, no matter where differences in costs or benefits may occur in an organization or a society.

The accountant includes items such as depreciation, allocated costs, and overheads in his cost schedule. The economist in a before-tax analysis excludes all these items as nondifferential, which is the normal situation. When costs are differential, he includes the differences.

A FACTUAL STUDY: JASON MOWERS

Jason Mowers, producing an expensive powered lawnmower, considered closing down the portion of its plant producing axles and instead buying them from a company specializing in that kind of machined product. The accountant for Jason prepared the following annual cost figures for the axle department:

Direct costs	
Materials	$ 52,000
Labor	108,000
Department overhead	
Manager's salary	20,000
Rent	6,000
Machinery maintenance	5,000
Machinery depreciation	15,000
Expenses	16,000
Administrative overhead	24,000
	$246,000

The Tuohy Axle Company offered to make the required 5000 axles per year for $210,000 per year, delivered at Jason's, on a two-year contract.

Steel rod, from which the axles were made, was sufficient for the next two years. It had cost $20,000, could be disposed of for $16,000, and would cost, if bought in today's market, $22,000. The machinery had a book value of $30,000 and a salvage value of $20,000.

What should be Jason's decision? Do a before-tax analysis. The accountant's figures should be scrutinized one by one.

Materials presumably include the cost of axle stock. Yet the axle stock has already been bought and thus constitutes a sunk cost. The annual cost of materials should be reduced by half of $20,000 if we assume that equal use will take place per year.

Labor is a real annual cost, as is the manager's salary. Both of these are direct labor costs for the economist.

Rent, however, is normally an allocated cost for consolidated operations in one building and not a differential cost. Thus, rent should not be included since the rent paid by the company will remain the same no matter what use the company makes of its space.

Machinery maintenance will continue.

Machinery depreciation is not a cash flow but simply a reflection of a sunk cost, that is, its purchase price. Do not include it.

Miscellaneous expenses will no doubt continue.

Administrative overhead is normally an allocated cost. It covers the salaries of secretaries, accountants, and managers, the cost of paper, typewriters, and filing cabinets—in fact everything that cannot be assigned to a particular production operation. It is usually not affected by production decisions and thus should be excluded.

Revised Annual Costs

Materials	$ 42,000
Labor	108,000
Department manager's salary	20,000
Machinery maintenance	5,000
Miscellaneous expenses	16,000
	$191,000

If the machinery and axle stock are sold, they will bring in their salvage or resale value. We ignore book value, original cost, and replacement cost because we are concerned solely with cash flow.

Axle stock	$16,000
Machinery	20,000
	$36,000

The resale value of the machinery and axle stock is a lump sum payment that will occur only once. It is the opportunity cost of continuing with production. It must be included as an addition to the revised annual costs. But how to include a lump sum payment in an annual cost?

The method that might occur to a bookkeeper is to divide the sum by 2, since we are concerned with a two-year contract and a two-year supply on hand. He would thus arrive at $18,000. This approach ignores the possibility of investing the $36,000 at our opportunity cost of capital and proceeding to subtract from the resulting principal plus interest an equal sum at the end of each year such that the fund will be left with zero at the end of two years. Let us say that the before-tax opportunity cost of capital to this firm is 20 percent. At the end of the first year the $36,000 will have accumulated to:

$$36,000 + 0.20 \,(36,000) = \$43,200$$

If we now remove $23,564, we have:

$$43,200 - 23,564 = \$19,636$$

At the end of the second year we will have accumulated:

$$19,636 + (0.20) \,(19,636) = \$23,564,$$

which can then be removed, leaving nothing in the account. (How we chose $23,564 is explained in Chapter 6.)

The cost of continuing with the plant axle production is $23,564 more than is included in the revised annual costs, or $214,564. Thus, the difference between making and buying the axles is reduced to only $4,564, a sum so small that irreducibles must be considered by Jason as decisive. Irreducibles are such considerations as inflation of wages and materials, quality control, Tuohy's reliability, the contract price two years hence, and so forth. In order to include some of these items, the analyst may lengthen the time horizon from two years to four, or more.

This study shows the treatment of opportunity cost, allocated cost, time horizon, depreciation, book value, and salvage value. It also illustrates the difference between the accountant's and the manager's or economist's attitude toward analysis in economic decisions.

3

The Analyst's Viewpoint
and Its Effect on Relevance

Viewpoint is the institutional position that the analyst takes in relation to the project under consideration. The word *institutional* is used here in its social sense in which elements of the public and private sectors of society are considered to be institutions. For example, if the analyst is working for a city government, he may be expected to judge the consequences of the project he is considering in relation to their effect on that government. Costs are therefore costs to the city, and benefits are benefits to the city. In effect, he draws a line around the city and says, "Any adverse consequences that cross the line in any outward direction, I will count as costs, and any favorable consequences that come in across that line I will count as benefits of this project." For the very same project, the same analyst may be imagined as working for a higher unit of government, say, the national government. Here the institutional line he draws will include the entire society of the country. However, he will make exactly the same statement he made previously, but now some of the costs and benefits of the proposed project will not cross the new line and will become transfer payments from one portion of the national society to another. They will thus be neither costs or benefits in the new institutional context. Other consequences will cross both lines and will remain costs and benefits. A glance at Figure 3.1 clarifies this important notion. Arrow 1 is, say, a mass transit subsidy by the national to the city government. From the city government's viewpoint, it is a benefit, but from the national government's viewpoint, it is a transfer of funds within the society and does not enter into the analysis. Arrow 2 represents an increase in the welfare of the citizens of the city because, say, the pollution level will be reduced by this project. It is not

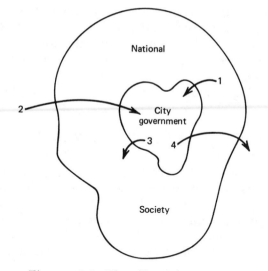

Figure 3.1 The effect of viewpoint.

just an exchange of funds from the national society to the local society;
it is a true increase in the joy that the people of the community take in
life. Thus, it is an increase in the total well-being of the national
society—if the well-being of society is thought of as a vast sum to
which all the satisfactions of each individual member of the populace
are added. Arrow 3 represents taxes that will be paid by the city to the
national government, and they are thus transfer payments in the national context. Arrow 4 represents the labor of an electrician who will
be paid by the city and whose labor is thus lost to any other use in the
society. It is a true cost in social resources.

Evidently, favorable and adverse consequences of courses of action appear and disappear depending on whose viewpoint the analyst
takes. It is therefore important that the analyst have a clear idea of
exactly where he stands in the economy, for his position determines
the costs and benefits he will consider, not only as to whether or not
they exist, but even their amount.

It can be argued that the analyst who takes the viewpoint of his
own organization is being selfish, if not actually antisocial. He should
really, it is said, take consequences to everyone into account as much
as possible. Unfortunately, this attitude would probably be considered overly altruistic by those for whom he is working for "charity
begins at home" in most institutions in both the public and private
sectors.

Finally, the reader should remember throughout this chapter two
ideas to be further developed in Chapter 19: the Pareto optimum and
opportunity cost. According to the *Pareto principle,* to undertake a

given course of action, everyone concerned with the course of action will have to be made better off than he would have been had the action not been taken. *Opportunity cost* is that loss in the benefits that would accrue to one when one chooses one opportunity over another. It is the loss incurred by not choosing the next best opportunity. And, in fact, the notion of opportunity cost underlies everything said here.

THE PRIVATE SECTOR VIEWPOINT

The viewpoint of private sector enterprises presents few problems. The line is drawn around the business itself. Benefits are consequences of a course of action that are favorable to the company in some way. Costs are unfavorable consequences. The owners of the business are presumed to set the criteria for judging what consequences are to be considered favorable and what unfavorable.

The last statement is open to some doubt. What if the owners of the business are thousands of scattered stockholders and the actual decision-making power is in the hands of those managing the business? Can it always be presumed that these two groups have the same view of what consequences are to be considered favorable and what unfavorable? Take the example of the decision to purchase a company airplane or a resort house for the use of executives of the company. The management may well consider the benefits of both these conveniences to exceed their costs whereas the stockholders may not because their standards of what is favorable and unfavorable are different. The management may be concerned with the prestige and image of the company whereas the stockholder is concerned solely with profit.

The idea that all companies are run to make a profit for their owners is oversimplified. Other goals exist, such as expansion of the business and the accumulation of power, or the preservation of the salaries of the management. Many a company, especially in regulated industry, tots up a loss year after year while its executives continue to make large salaries.

In big companies it often happens that a smaller unit than the entire company is taken as having an institutional position. One department (for instance, the traffic department) may make decisions on investment purely on the basis of its own budget and its own well-being. It will come as no surprise to the reader that fiefdoms tend to be set up in large companies, and in them the rule is, "We will look after ourselves and our budget. What happens to the rest of the company—that's the worry of top management." In such cases, inter-departmental charges become costs to the department, and inter-departmental credits become benefits instead of what they really are—a transfer of funds from one pocket of the company's trousers to another and nothing more. Use of such figures in economic analysis causes much confusion. The study of company operations and investments from the viewpoint of the entire company instead of individual departments is one aspect of systems analysis. Among other advantages, such studies avoid the problem of interdepartmental transfer payments and draw the analyst's line around the company as a whole.

Taxes for a company are real costs and should be treated as such.

THE PUBLIC SECTOR VIEWPOINT

In the United States, the economic analysis of public projects was given a viewpoint by Congress in the Flood Control Act of 1936. In that act it was stated that ". . . if the benefits to whomsoever they may accrue are in excess of the estimated costs . . ." the federal government should participate in such public works. The key phrase on viewpoint is "to whomsoever they may accrue," which implies that the viewpoint of the whole of society is to be taken in such projects. This attitude was extended to the economic analysis of many other types of projects, including highways, air pollution control, forest conservation, and so on. It is a reflection of the ideas of Pareto and Kaldor, particularly the latter, who held that public projects are justified if the total sum of individual benefits exceeds the total sum of individual costs, providing that the government make up the losses of individuals whose personal balance shows the costs to exceed the benefits. (Chapter 19 discusses these matters at length.)

It is possible for an analyst to take the societal viewpoint but to restrict the area of society that he takes into account. For example, an analyst working for a state highway department may well take the viewpoint of the state in his consideration of costs and benefits. For him it would be perfectly possible to include as a benefit the 90 percent subsidy that the federal government supplies on highways belonging to the interstate system. His analysis of a particular stretch of proposed highway belonging to that system would show a high benefit/cost ratio in the documents to be shown to his superiors. It would show a much lower benefit/cost ratio in the documents to be shown to the federal authorities whose viewpoint would be that of the country as a whole and for whom the total cost of the project would be exactly that.

Subsidies ideally should be treated as transfer payments, no matter what unit of government the analyst takes as his viewpoint. If this is laid down as a general rule for governmental entities within a nation—city, county, state, and national—what are we to say of world viewpoints? The United Nations, for example, should take this viewpoint in its recommendations for investment. Therefore, international transfer of resources should be considered transfer payments and thus not enter into the analysis. Only costs that represent actual use of world resources or real decrease in well-being for the persons affected by the project and benefits that represent real increases in well-being should enter into the analysis. Needless to say, it would be difficult to convince an analyst whose duties demand absolute loyalty to his country that a subsidy from an international organization should not be taken as a direct benefit of the project he is analyzing.

Taxes are analogous to subsidies. Although local governments do not pay taxes as institutional entities, still the citizenry they govern do. If the viewpoint of the people of a community and not just the governmental agency associated with them is taken, as would be normal, then taxes edge into the analysis. For example, imagine that a city government is considering a new bus system one of the benefits of which is an increase in income of a part of the population of the city. This implies an increase in the federal income taxes that this part of the population will pay each year. Should this increase in taxes be considered a cost of the project? The answer is, "No." The taxes are simply a transfer payment from one part of the population of the country to another.

Ideally, therefore, subsidies and taxes should be excluded from the analysis of a project. As has been indicated in this section, however, difficult questions of loyalty to one group or another in a society present themselves. How these difficulties are resolved depend on the individual situation in which each analyst finds himself.

UNEMPLOYED RESOURCES AND VIEWPOINT

An example best explains the thorny point of unused resources. Imagine an oil company operating in the Amazon jungle just east of the Andes. After the exploration has ended and the first well has been brought in, the company decides to build a road to supply the oil field. Exploration teams, equipment for survey of the site, and finally the drilling rig, casing, and pipe for the first well have been brought by air. Now many hundreds of tons of supplies will be needed in the field, and these will be trucked in across the Andes. The crude oil that the field produces will be trucked out in tankers. The company decides to do a cost study along with the engineering design of the road. The benefits are so obvious that no benefits study will be undertaken.

Among the important costs is that of local labor. Converting the cost of the labor per hour from the currency of the country into dollars, a laborer will receive $1.00 per hour. This cost is correctly entered as the unit cost of local labor by the company's economist. It is multiplied by the number of laborers needed, by the number of hours needed to complete the job, and this total enters the cost breakdown for the entire project under the heading "Local Labor." The company's economist has, of course, taken the company's viewpoint.

The project proposal is taken to the government of the country for approval. The road, even though constructed with private funds, will enter the national system of roads, bridges, and highways. It will be numbered as a national highway. When the company leaves the country, as it may eventually, the road will be maintained by the government through the public works department. An engineer in the department of public works is asked to analyze the costs of the project from the point of view of the country. In his consideration of the cost items, he encounters "Local Labor" at $1.00 per hour. He notes, however, that the laborers will be drawn from tribes of Indians in the area who have heretofore been unconnected with the national economy. They have been unemployed in the sense that they produced nothing but their own food and just enough of that for subsistence. The engineer asks himself, "What cost to the country should I put down for these laborers?" He concludes that the cost of the labor should be the value of the food they produced as hunters.

He reasons like this: "The laborers produced nothing except food which they ate when they worked as hunters. As laborers they will produce, along with other inputs, a road. The opportunity cost of their labor to the country is therefore $0.02 per hour, the cost of the food they produced as hunters. It costs the country nothing for them to give up their jobs as hunters except the food they produced for their own subsistence." He writes two statements to clarify for himself the effect of the shifting of this labor from hunting to road building:

Contribution to national income as hunters per hour = $0.02

Contribution to national income as road builders per hour = $1.00

It is now clear that the nation loses the opportunity for food when these hunters shift from hunting to road building. That is, it loses the opportunity to employ them as hunters when they become road builders. The cost—the opportunity cost—to the nation is therefore $0.02 per hour, and this is the cost that should be placed after the item in the cost breakdown entitled "Local Labor."

Notice the immense difference in labor costs that viewpoint has made for the very same workers on the very same project, yet both costs are perfectly correct: $1.00 per hour from the private viewpoint and $0.02 per hour from the public viewpoint.

What has been said about workers' wages is true also of other resources. The private viewpoint is straightforward, but the public sector analyst must ask himself: "What is this resource costing the nation in its next best use? What is the opportunity cost of this resource?"

In the example given earlier of the hunters who become road builders there is a hidden assumption. It is that the local laborers put no value on their former occupation as hunters except the value of the production that sprang from it—the $0.02 per hour. The example assumes that they are just as happy as road builders as they were as hunters. If they valued their time as hunters at a larger figure than the simple value of the production they received from it—say, at $0.10 per hour extra, which is the value they placed on their enjoyment of the chase—then the value that must be assigned as an opportunity cost is $0.12, the sum of the value of production and the value of the hunter's recreation.

If, on the other hand, the hunters were happy to be relieved of the boredom of hunting tree squirrels with blowguns, then it is logical to assign a negative value to their occupation as hunters if they would have been willing to pay something in order to give up their jungle tasks. Say this amount was $0.05 per hour. The opportunity cost to the nation of shifting them from their jobs as hunters to their new jobs as road builders would then be $0.02 − $0.05 or −$0.03. In other words, the nation would gain in production plus satisfaction an amount $1.00 + $0.03 or $1.03.

The previous two paragraphs depend on the assumption of the Pareto criterion. Everyone gains by shifting the hunters from a jungle village to a construction camp, thus fulfilling the Pareto criterion. The rest of the society gains their production of $1.00 per hour. They themselves are either indifferent between building roads and hunting, put a value on hunting as compared to road building, or put a value on road building as compared to hunting. The point is that their individual gains and losses must also be totted up if we are undertaking a social analysis and are not concerned merely with national production as a measure of benefit.

The question of how long a hunter-turned-road-builder is likely to feel about the switch the way he originally did when he took the road-building job needs to be answered. If after a year of road building, he longs to be a hunter again, his opportunity cost to society will ascend by the amount that he now values his old occupation above the value he placed on it when he left it. This new opportunity cost must be included if the road job goes on for more than a year, and successive changes need to be made as the ex-hunter changes his estimation of his present versus his past life. The implications of this statement for the Amazon are fundamental enough without considering what happens when we shift the example to an industrialized country. How workers feel about their jobs becomes important and thus, too, the ways of measuring those feelings.

In conclusion—and it is perhaps an obvious point to the reader who has reached this far in the discussion—transfer payments to workers should also be excluded from the analysis of a project in which workers are taken off relief and idleness and sent back to regular employment. The fact that one portion of a society passed money to another portion has made no difference in the production of the nation, always assuming that the worker was not encouraged to be idle by the unemployment checks he received.

REFERENCES

Grant, E. L., and W. Grant Ireson, *Principles of Engineering Economy*, 5th ed. New York: Ronald, 1970, pp. 456–493.

Mishan, E. J., *Cost-Benefit Analysis*. New York: Praeger, 1971, pp. 67–78.

4

Consequences Over Time

Benefits and costs appear in the future at various dates. Some way, therefore, must be found to compare sums that make their appearance at different times. It is a fact recognized by all economists that money is really a reflection of two attributes: (1) a face value, and (2) a value according to when one receives it. If you were offered $1000 now or $1000 a year from now, it is evident that you should accept the $1000 now rather than a $1000 a year from now because the $1000 now can be invested at some rate of interest (at least a safe 5 percent at the time of this writing in savings and loans associations, and thus be worth $1050 a year from now).[1]

Inflation is not involved in any of this. A common misconception is to think that the time value of money exists because of inflationary tendencies in the economy. Although these tendencies may very well exist, the following discussion does not refer to them. Money is not discounted because of inflation but because of its time value. Nor are other economic concepts, such as diminishing returns, in point here. Discounting sums received or disbursed in the future has nothing to do with that famous law.

Furthermore, for the moment we make one important assumption: We assume that the alternatives we analyze are all mutually exclusive. By this is meant, as mentioned previously, that selecting one alternative as the solution to a problem precludes a person from choosing a second or third. For example, one highway location, and one only, will be chosen out of the two or six or 20 proposed as routes from Ghent to Aix. Only one, and its selection makes impossible the choice of an-

---

[1] For an excellent discussion of the economic rationale behind the time value of money, see Paul A. Samuelson, *Economics*, 5th ed. New York: McGraw-Hill, 1961, pp. 644–650.

other. We are yet discussing in what order we will build nonexclusive alternatives: the road from Ghent to Aix, from Antwerp to Brussels, from Ypres to Menin.

Another important assumption, which we adhere to throughout the remainder of this book, is that all transactions during a certain year may be accumulated to a single sum at the end of the year without seriously affecting our calculations.

In the following chapters we look into some methods of comparing money and time and thus of comparing benefits and costs. The methods are as follows:

1. Present worth or benefit minus cost
2. Annual worth
3. Benefit/cost ratio
4. Internal rate of return

THE TIME VALUE OF MONEY

A simple example serves to make clear what is meant by the time value of money. Imagine that it is possible to invest money at 10 percent and that you have $1000 available. Let us call "P" the principal—in this case $1000. Lowercase "$i$" is the rate of interest—in this case 10 percent. "F" is a sum in the future to be received after "N" periods. In benefit/cost analysis the periods are usually years. Table 4.1 shows how your $1000 increases by years if the interest is left to accumulate in the bank and if interest is compounded annually.

Table 4.1 was derived in the following way. At the end of year one, you will have received $100 in interest, and the money accumulated in your account will be, therefore, the original $1000 that you had plus the $100 of interest, or $1100. At the end of the second year, you will receive another 10 percent worth of interest on the amount that was in the account at the beginning of the second year ($1100). Ten percent

TABLE 4.1

	Payment at Interest		
N (Year)	P	i	F_N
0	1000		
1		100	1100
2		110	1210
3		121	1331

of \$1100 is \$110, which added to the amount of money in the account at the beginning of the year, \$1100, is \$1210. It should now be obvious how \$1331 was accumulated.

Now, if we substitute letters for the numbers given in the preceding paragraph and follow through with the same mechanics of multiplication and addition, we can derive the following equations:

$$F_1 = P + Pi = P(1 + i)$$
$$F_2 = P(1 + i) + iP(1 + i) = P(1 + i)(1 + i) = P(1 + i)^2$$
$$F_3 = P(1 + i)^2 + iP(1 + i)^2 = P(1 + i)^2(1 + i) = P(1 + i)^3$$

We could continue like this, but it now appears that what we are doing can be reduced to the following expression:

$$F_N = P(1 + i)^N = P(F/P, i, N) \tag{1}$$

The factor $(1 + i)^N$ is called the compound amount factor for a single payment of P. It is designated symbolically as $(F/P, i, N)$.

The Appendix contains a series of tables by interest rate and factor. The left column shows the *single-payment compound amount factor* for various interest rates and for various periods.

DERIVATION OF OTHER FORMULAS

Using equation (1) given earlier we can easily derive the present worth equation for any future payment.

Since $F_N = P(1 + i)^N$, and since we may divide both sides of this equation by $(1 + i)^N$, then:

$$\frac{F_N}{(1 + i)^N} = P \frac{(1 + i)^N}{(1 + i)^N}$$

Therefore, $P = F_N \left(\dfrac{1}{1 + i}\right)^N = F_N(P/F, i, N)$ \hfill (2)

Thus, any single payment in the future may be discounted to its present worth if we know what i we should use. The factor $\left(\dfrac{1}{1 + i}\right)^N$ is known as the *single-payment present worth factor*. It is symbolized by $(P/F, i, N)$.

Two formulas concern the relation between the uniform annual payment, A, and the single payment at some future period, F. Both of these formulas can be derived from the single-payment formula with which we started this section—$F_N = P(1 + i)^N$.

Suppose we have the following problem: Determine the future amount, F_N, we will receive if we invest P_1 at the end of period one, P_2 at the end of period two, P_3 at the end of period 3, and so on until we invest P_N at the end of period N, all at interest rate i. Applying equation (1):

$$F_N = P_1(1 + i)^{N-1} + P_2(1 + i)^{N-2} \ldots + P_{N-1}(1 + i)^{N-(N-1)} + P_N(1 + i)^{N-N}$$
$$= P_1(1 + i)^{N-1} + P_2(1 + i)^{N-2} \ldots + P_{N-1}(1 + i)^{1} + P_N$$

Now let us say that:

$$P_1 = P_2 = P_3 \ldots = P_{N-1} = P_N = A$$

Then, substituting A for all the Ps in the preceding equation:

$$F_N = A(1 + i)^{N-1} + A(1 + i)^{N-2} \ldots + A(1 + i) + A$$
$$= A[1 + (1 + i) \ldots + (1 + i)^{N-2} + (1 + i)^{N-1}] \qquad (3)$$

Multiplying both sides of the preceding equation by $(1 + i)$:

$$(1 + i)F_N = A[(1 + i) + (1 + i)^2 \ldots + (1 + i)^{N-1} + (1 + i)^{N}] \qquad (4)$$

Subtracting equation (3) from equation (4):

$$(1 + i)F_N - F_N = -A + A(1 + i)^N$$
$$iF_N = A[(1 + i)^N - 1]$$
$$F_N = A\left[\frac{(1 + i)^N - 1}{i}\right] \qquad (5)$$

The expression within the parentheses is called the *series compound amount factor* and is designated by its symbol $(F/A, i, N)$.

Now suppose we are given the following problem: Determine how much money we must invest, A, at the end of each period, to arrive at a certain sum in the future, F, at the end of period N. Since equation (5) gives the relation between A and F_N, we need merely divide both sides of the equation by $\dfrac{(1 + i)^N - 1}{i}$:

$$\frac{F_N}{\dfrac{(1 + i)^N - 1}{i}} = A$$

and:

$$A = F_N\left[\frac{i}{(1 + i)^N - 1}\right] \qquad (6)$$

The expression within the brackets is called the *sinking fund factor* and is designated by $(A/F, i, N)$.

If a series of future payments exists, all equal to each other and therefore to A, then

$$F_1 = F_2 = F_3 = \ldots F_N = A$$

Applying the single payment present worth factor to each of the future sums individually, we discover that the present worth of all of them may be indicated by the following expression:

$$P = F_1\left(\frac{1}{1+i}\right)^1 + F_2\left(\frac{1}{1+i}\right)^2 + F_3\left(\frac{1}{1+i}\right)^3 + \ldots + F_N\left(\frac{1}{1+i}\right)^N$$

and since all these Fs are each equal to A, we may then replace them by A and factor out the A. Factoring gives us the following equation:

$$P = A\left[\left(\frac{1}{1+i}\right)^1 + \left(\frac{1}{1+i}\right)^2 + \left(\frac{1}{1+i}\right)^3 + \ldots + \left(\frac{1}{1+i}\right)^N\right]$$

$$= A\left[\frac{(1+i)^N - 1}{i(1+i)^N}\right] \tag{7}$$

and the expression within the brackets of equation (7) is known as the *series present worth factor,* or $(P/A, i, N)$. The reader is invited to perform the algebra necessary to make the last step to equation (7).

To convert a present payment into a series of equal future payments, it is necessary only to divide both sides of the preceding equation by the series present worth factor. The following equation results:

$$A = \frac{P}{\left(\frac{1}{1+i}\right)^1 + \left(\frac{1}{1+i}\right)^2 + \left(\frac{1}{1+i}\right)^3 + \ldots + \left(\frac{1}{1+i}\right)^N}$$

$$= P\left[\frac{1}{\left(\frac{1}{1+i}\right)^1 + \left(\frac{1}{1+i}\right)^2 + \left(\frac{1}{1+i}\right)^3 + \ldots + \left(\frac{1}{1+i}\right)^N}\right]$$

$$= P\left[\frac{i(1+i)^N}{(1+i)^N - 1}\right] \tag{8}$$

The expression within the brackets of equation (8) is designated as the *capital recovery factor* or $(A/P, i, N)$.

All the foregoing factors appear in the Appendix by period, N, and interest rate, i.

Finally, note that:

$$(F/P, i, N) = \frac{1}{(P/F, i, N)}, \quad (A/P, i, N) = \frac{1}{(P/A, i, N)},$$

$$\text{and } (F/A, i, N) = \frac{1}{(A/F, i, N)}$$

CONVENTIONS

The usual convention in the representation of the flow of benefits and costs over a number of periods is to represent the periods on a horizontal axis, the benefits at each period by arrows pointing upward, and the costs by arrows pointing downward. Both benefit and cost arrows may be drawn to scale. The stream shown in Figure 4.1 illustrates the convention. In words, it says that a cost of 10 is associated with benefits of 8 at the end of year 3, and 2 at the end of years 4, 5, 6, 7, and 8. Sometimes a line is drawn at the arrow tips of uniform periodic payments as in Figure 4.2, example 3.

All payments, no matter how made during the period, are assumed to be accumulated to the *end* of the period.

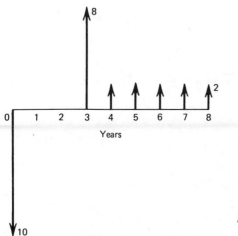

Figure 4.1 Conventional cash flow portrayal.

Examples 4.1 to 4.6

1. If 100 is invested now at 4 percent per year, how much will be accumulated by the end of the tenth year? (See Figure 4.2 for the cash flow diagrams for examples 1 through 6.)

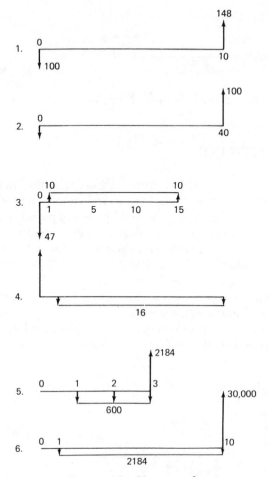

Figure 4.2   Six examples.

$$F_{10} = P(F/P, 4, 10)$$
$$= 100 \ (1.4802)$$
$$= 148$$

2. What is the present worth of a benefit of 100 that will be realized 40 years from now if an opportunity cost of funds of 12 percent is considered justifiable?

$$P_B = 100(P/F, 12, 40)$$
$$= 100 \ (0.0107)$$
$$= 1$$

3. If a benefit of 10 is received at the end of each year for 15 years,

what is the present value of the benefits if the discount rate is 20 percent?

$$P_B = 10(P/A, 20, 15)$$
$$= 10(4.675)$$
$$= 47$$

4. If an enterprise borrows 100 now at 10 percent, what equal end-of-year payment must it make to its creditor in order to pay off the debt in 10 years if interest is computed annually?

$$A = 100(A/P, 10, 10)$$
$$= 100(0.16275)$$
$$= 16$$

5. If the best rate of return I can get anywhere else at the same risk is 20 percent before taxes, how much overhaul expenses at the end of three years will I be justified in avoiding if I spend 600 per year for maintenance on my car?

$$F = 600(F/A, 20, 3)$$
$$= 600(3.640)$$
$$= 2184$$

6. A couple with a child now eight years old wish to guarantee his college education by having 30,000 ready when he reaches 18. If they can deposit at 8 percent interest compounded annually, how much should they deposit each year?

$$A = 30,000(A/F, 8, 10)$$
$$= 30,000(0.06903)$$
$$= 2071$$

In the preceding examples, the figures could be in dollars, pounds, francs, pesos, or any other currency.

SEPARATION OF INTEREST AND PRINCIPAL

Frequently, investors are interested in the principal and interest to be paid in any one year because interest is an income tax deductible item and principal is not. As a loan is paid off, the individual interest payments decrease at the same time as the individual principal payments increase, for equal periodic payments. To see this clearly, let us imagine a loan of $1000 to be paid off at 10 percent interest over three years. An up arrow of $1000 at time zero is followed by down arrows at the end of each of three years. These down arrows are each equal to

$$A = P(A/P, i, N)$$
$$= 1000(A/P, 10, 3)$$
$$= 1000(0.40211)$$
$$= \$402.11$$

according to equation (8), which uses the capital recovery factor. (This cash flow is shown in Figure 4.3.)

Each payment is composed of principal and interest. Notice that the interest is always applied to the remaining balance, as can be seen in Table 4.2. The remaining balance at year zero is the loan itself of $1000. At the end of the first year a payment of $402.11 is made. We can calculate what part is interest simply by taking 10 percent of $1000, which is $100. The interest paid is subtracted from the payment of $402.11, leaving the payment on principal of $302.11. Subtracting this from $1000 leaves the remaining—sometimes called *declining*—balance of $697.89, of which 10 percent is $69.79, the interest payment for year 2. The principal payment is computed in the same way as before. Finally, the last principal payment is determined

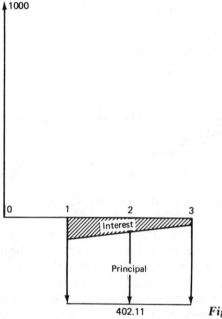

Figure 4.3 Repaying $1000.

to be $365.55, just 2 cents less than the remaining balance at the end of year 2. The difference is caused by the errors of rounding in the capital recovery factor table. Figure 4.3 shows the interest portion of the payment as a crosshatched area. Principal payments are shown as clear. Notice that the interest payment decreases each year, while the principal payment increases—not linearly, as we see later.

It is easy to make the calculation of Table 4.2, but let us see if we cannot formulate an expression for the principal and interest payment for any year, Y. Start by considering the remaining balance for any year Y. Is it not simply the present worth of the remaining payments on the loan? The remaining balance when Y = 0 is the loan itself—and it is also the present worth of the three yearly payments of $402.11 because

$$P = A(P/A, \ 10, \ 3)$$
$$= 402.11(2.487)$$
$$= \$1,000.05$$

This occurs because the series present worth factor is the reciprocal of the capital recovery factor. Figure 4.3 may be viewed as $402.11 paying back $1000 or as payments having a present worth of $1000. The remaining balance at the end of one year may be viewed as the present worth of two payments of 402.11 each:

$$P = 402.11(P/A, \ 10, \ 3 - 1)$$
$$= 402.11(1.736)$$
$$= 698.06$$

Evidently, to find the remaining balance to begin a year $Y + 1$, after the payment at the end of a year Y, I must apply the series present worth factor at the given interest rate with a period set at $N - Y$.

To find the principal payment, R, at the end of any year, Y, I

TABLE 4.2 Interest Is Paid on the Remaining Balance

Year	Payment A	Interest payment	Principal payment	Remaining balance
0				$1,000 = P
1	$402.11	$100.00	$302.11	697.89
2	402.11	69.79	332.32	365.57
3	402.11	36.56	365.55	0

$i = 10\%$

subtract the remaining balance at $Y - 1$ from the remaining balance at Y:

$$R = A(P/A,i,N - Y + 1) - A(P/A,i,N - Y)$$
$$= A[(P/A,i,N - Y + 1) - (P/A,i, N - Y)].$$

In our case, for year 2, this is:

$$R_2 = 402.11[(P/A, 10, 2) - (P/A, 10, 1)]$$
$$= 402.11(1.736 - 0.909)$$
$$= 402.11(0.827)$$
$$= \$332.55$$

which is as close as the tables allow us to get. Notice, however, that the difference between any two entries in the series present worth factor column of the tables is the same as the single payment present worth factor for the later period, thus:

$$(P/A, i, N - Y + 1) - (P/A, i, N - Y) = (P/F, i, N - Y + 1)$$

In our case

$$1.736 - 0.909 = 0.827 \approx 0.8264$$

So that

$$R_Y = A(P/F, i, N - Y + 1)$$

The reader is invited to determine the truth of this equation by using the mathematical expressions for $(P/A,i,N)$, which I have derived in this chapter.

Also notice that

$$(P/A, i, N) = \sum_{N=1}^{N}(P/F, i, N),$$

which is no more than another way of describing how the series present worth factor was derived from the single payment present worth factor.

The interest, I, paid in any year, Y, is simply:

$$I_Y = A - R_Y$$
$$= A - A(P/F, i, N - Y + 1)$$
$$I_Y = A[1 - (P/F, i, N - Y + 1)] \tag{9}$$

This has great practical use as Example 4.7 demonstrates.

Example 4.7

A real estate developer wishes to know at what point his interest payments, which are deductible from taxable income, will equal his principal payments, which are not deductible. The answer to this question will be a factor in determining when he will sell the apartment building he has invested in. He borrowed $950,000 at 9 percent annually for 20 years to finance the building. His yearly payments are:

$$A = \$950,000(A/P, 9, 20)$$
$$= 950,000(0.10955)$$
$$= \$104,072.50$$

Since, $I + R_Y = A$ and, in this example, $I = R_Y$, then $\dfrac{R_Y}{A} = \dfrac{1}{2}$. The question becomes:

$$\frac{R_Y}{A} = 0.5 = (P/F, 9, 20 - Y + 1)$$

On the 9 percent table this is at about 8 years. Therefore:

$$20 - Y + 1 = 8$$
$$Y = 13 \text{ years}$$

Checking this answer by equation (9):

$$I_Y = A[1 - (P/F, i, N - Y + 1)]$$
$$I_{13} = 104,072.50[1 - (P/F, 9, 20 - 13 + 1)]$$
$$= 104,072.50(1 - 0.5019)$$
$$= 104,072.50(0.4981)$$
$$= \$51,838.51$$

which is as close as we will get to half of A, which is 52,036.25. The investor should hold the property 13 years if he wishes to wait until principal and interest payments are equal.

GRADIENT FACTORS

Figure 4.4 illustrates a gradient series in which each succeeding cash flow exceeds its predecessor by the amount G. G begins at period 2, not 1, as might be expected. The series is defined in this way so that the formulas for the present worth of a gradient series and the equivalent periodic worth of a gradient series will use the same number of periods, N, as the other cash flows with which they may be associated in the same cash flow diagram.

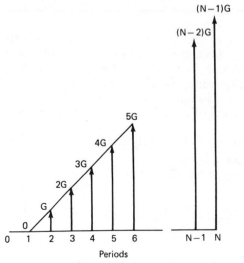

Figure 4.4   Gradient series.

Gradient flows are useful in many problems in which a cash flow increases by a constant increment each period. The growth curve of the benefits of an agricultural investment by a government is often approximated by such a curve. The increasing maintenance costs of machinery is also an example.

Two formulations are sufficient. The first is for the equivalent periodic worth, A, of a gradient series:

$$A = G(A/G, i, N)$$

Let us formulate $(A/G, i, N)$ by imagining that the payments of the series will sum to an amount, F, at period N. For example, the annual payment, G, considered alone will amount at period N to:

$$F_N = G(F/A, i, N - 2)$$

$$= G\left[\frac{(1 + i)^{N-2} - 1}{i}\right]$$

Thus, for all the Gs, referring to Figure 4.4:

$$F_N = G\left[\frac{(1 + i)^{N-2} - 1}{i} + \frac{(1 + i)^{N-3} - 1}{i} \ldots\right.$$

$$\left. + \frac{(1 + i)^1 - 1}{i} + \frac{(1 + i)^0 - 1}{i}\right]$$

$$= \frac{G}{i}[(1 + i)^{N-2} + (1 + i)^{N-3} \ldots + (1 + i)^1 + (1 + i)^0 - (N - 1)]$$

$$= \frac{G}{i}[(1 + i)^{N-2} + (1 + i)^{N-3} \ldots + (1 + i)^1 + 1 + 1] - \frac{NG}{i}$$

but at $N = 1$, in the definition of Figure 4.4:

$$(1 + i)^{N-1} = 1$$

Substituting this for a 1 in the preceding equation:

$$F_N = \frac{G}{i}[(1 + i)^{N-1} + (1 + i)^{N-2} \ldots (1 + i)^1 + 1] - \frac{NG}{i}$$

The brackets contain the expression for the compound amount factor. Therefore

$$F_N = \frac{G}{i}\left[\frac{(1 + i)^N - 1}{i}\right] - \frac{NG}{i} \tag{10}$$

To find P, given F, we must multiply by the single payment present worth factor:

$$P = F_N\left(\frac{1}{1 + i}\right)^N$$

$$= \frac{G}{i(1 + i)^N}\left[\frac{(1 + i)^N - 1}{i}\right] - \frac{NG}{i(1 + i)^N}$$

This is the present worth of any gradient series.

The factor for converting a gradient series to a series to equivalent periodic payments, A, is obtained by multiplying the value of F_N of equation (10) by the sinking fund factor, because

$$A = F(A/F, i, N)$$

The gradient factors appear in the Appendix, designated $(P/G, i, N)$ for the present worth of a gradient series and $(A/G, i, N)$ for the equivalent uniform periodic payment of a gradient series.

Example 4.8

Maintenance costs for the transmissions of a standard truck, representing large numbers of similar trucks of a fleet, are expected to experience increasing maintenance costs according to the following schedule. (The transmissions will be maintenance-free during their first year of life.)

Year	Maintenance costs
0	
1	0
2	20
3	40
4	60
5	80
6	100

At the end of the sixth year the trucks will be sold. What is the equivalent annual cost of transmission maintenance during six years if the company uses a 12 percent discount rate?

The gradient is 20. Therefore

$$A = G(A/G, 12, 6)$$
$$= 20(2.17)$$
$$= 43 \text{ annually.}$$

The present worth of the maintenance costs is

$$P = G(P/G, 12, 6)$$
$$= 20(8.9302)$$
$$= 179.$$

A factual study using gradients is at the end of the chapter entitled "Sensitivity Analysis."

NOMINAL AND EFFECTIVE RATES OF INTEREST

Example 4.9 ───

A car you intend to buy can be financed at your bank at 12 percent interest, compounded annually, for two years. The purchase price of the car is $5000. How much need you pay at the end of each year if the bank is willing to finance the total cost of the car?

$$P = \$5,000$$
$$i = 12\%$$
$$N = 2$$
$$A = ?$$

$$A = P(A/P, 12, 2)$$
$$= \$5000(0.59170)$$
$$= \$2,958.50$$

What if in the previous example you had wished to pay the principal and interest payments on a monthly basis rather than a yearly basis? How would you calculate the cost to you per month of the loan? A common error would be made if you divided the yearly payment, or $2,958.50, by 12, yielding $246.54. In performing such a calculation, the neglected point was that money has value over time. Instead of paying a sum at the end of the year, you would have paid a sum at the end of each month during the year. This means that the bank would have had the monthly payments available to it at an earlier date than they would have had the full payment been made at the end of the year. Therefore, the monthly payment must be something less than the number arrived at by dividing the yearly payment by 12. To calculate this properly, we must analyze the relationship between periodic and yearly payments and periodic and yearly rates of interest. Let

i_Y = the effective rate of interest per year,
i_M = the effective rate of interest per period,
M = number of compounding periods per year, and
r = nominal interest rate per year.

Many installment loan contracts, such as the one mentioned above on an automobile, or a mortgage loan on a house, stipulate an interest rate per year and a money payment per month. When this is done, the interest per year is called the *nominal* interest rate, r. The effective interest rate per year, i_Y, is the rate that would correspond to the effective rate per month, i_M. The relation between the nominal rate per year, r, and the effective rate of interest per period, i_M, is

$$i_M = \frac{r}{M} \tag{11}$$

The relationship between the effective rate per year and the effective rate per period is found by imagining that a sum of 1 is borrowed at the beginning of the year. We know that the sum that will be due at the end of the year equals 1 multiplied by $(1 + i)$. If the 1 is to be accumulated on a periodic basis, the amount at the end of the year will be 1 multiplied by $(1 + \frac{r}{M})$ raised to the Mth power. Symbolically,

$$(1 + i)^1 = (1 + i_M)^M$$

Therefore,

$$i_Y \text{ per year} = (1 + i_M)^M - 1 \tag{12}$$

$$\text{and } i_M = (1 + i_Y)^{\frac{1}{M}} - 1 \tag{13}$$

We are now in a position to calculate the effective interest rate per month that corresponds to an effective interest rate of 12 percent per year:

$$i_M \text{ per month} = (1.12)^{\frac{1}{12}} - 1$$
$$= 0.00948$$
$$= 0.95\%$$

Using this effective interest rate per month of 0.95 percent, now calculate the amount of the monthly payment that would correspond to a 12 percent effective interest rate per year:

$$P = \$5000$$
$$i = 0.95\% \text{ per month}$$
$$N = 24 \text{ months}$$
$$A = ?$$

$$A = P\left[\frac{i(1+i)^N}{(1+i)^N - 1}\right]$$

$$= 5{,}000\left[\frac{0.0095(1.0095)^{24}}{(1.0095)^{24} - 1}\right]$$

$$= \$233.97$$

Finally, notice that if the interest rate had been quoted as a 12 percent *nominal* rate of interest per year, the effective interest rate per month would then have been the nominal rate of interest per year divided by the number of months, or an effective rate of interest per month of 1 percent.

Example 4.10 ───

A house you are interested in is offered at \$74,000. If a down payment of 20 percent is required, what yearly payment will be necessary to amortize principal and interest at 12 percent for 30 years?

$$P = \$74{,}000 - (0.20)(\$74{,}000)$$
$$= \$59{,}200$$
$$i = 12\%$$
$$N = 30 \text{ years}$$
$$A = ?$$

$$A = P(A/P, 12, 30)$$
$$= \$59{,}200\,(0.12414)$$
$$= \$7349.09 \text{ annually}$$

What monthly payment will be required if a 12 percent *nominal* interest rate per year is quoted?

$$P = \$59{,}200$$
$$r = 12\%$$
$$N = 30 \text{ years} = 360 \text{ months}$$
$$A = ?$$

$$i_M = \frac{r}{M} = \frac{12\%}{12} = 1\% \text{ per month}$$

$$A = P \left[\frac{i\,(1+i)^N}{(1+i)^N - 1} \right]$$

$$= \$59{,}200 \left[\frac{0.01(1.01)^{360}}{(1.01)^{360} - 1} \right]$$

$$= \$608.94 \text{ monthly.}$$

What monthly payment will be required if a 12 percent *effective* annual interest rate is given?

$$P = 59{,}200$$
$$i = 12\% \text{ per year}$$
$$N = 360$$
$$A = ?$$

$$A = P \left[\frac{i(1+i)^N}{(1+i)^N - 1} \right]$$

I have already calculated in Example 4.9 the effective monthly interest rate that corresponds to 12 percent annually—0.95 percent.

$$A = \$59{,}200 \left[\frac{0.0095\,(1.0095)^{360}}{(1.0095)^{360} - 1} \right]$$

$$= \$581.75$$

Example 4.11 ————————————————————————————————

A savings and loan company offers 6 percent on regular passbook savings, compounded quarterly. A small note adds that this is equal to 6.14 percent annual yield. Can you check this?

$$r = 6\%$$
$$M = 4$$
$$i_M = \frac{6}{4} = 1.5\%$$

From equation (12):

$$
\begin{aligned}
i_Y &= (1 + i_M)^M - 1 \\
&= (1 + 0.015)^4 - 1 \\
&= 0.06136 \\
&= 6.14\%
\end{aligned}
$$

Notice that $(1 + 0.015)^4 = (F/P, 1\frac{1}{2}, 4)$.

___

5

Comparing Benefits and Costs: Present Worth

There are four ways in which costs and benefits of alternatives can be compared:

1. Present worth,
2. Annual worth,
3. Benefit/cost ratio,
4. Internal rate of return.

The first of these methods is widely thought to be the most nearly foolproof. The present worth method has long been favored by operations research investigators because they believe that it presents the easiest technique to use in a technical sense. No ratios are involved, and no trial and error solutions searching for a rate of return are necessary.

The annual worth is a method familiar to engineers, particularly to those in administrative positions. This method is suited to the kind of cost and revenue figures that are reported on an annual basis. It has none of the anomalies associated with the benefit/cost ratio or the internal rate of return method. In this and following chapters, each of these methods is explained in detail.

The benefit/cost ratio came into being as a result of federal legislation passed in the 1930s that was related to dam construction. It is the method most used in engineering studies. There are some difficulties connected with its use, however, that I treat in subsequent pages.

The internal rate of return method is associated with finance and banking. Groups such as the International Bank for Reconstruction and Development (World Bank) and the Interamerican Development

Bank find the internal rate of return method congenial. There are difficulties in its use that are explained in later pages.

PRESENT WORTH

The criterion of choice in the present worth method—sometimes called *benefit minus cost* or *net present value*—is that the present worth must be zero or larger for the project or alternative under investigation to be considered feasible. In other words, the discounted benefits minus the discounted costs must be greater than or equal to zero as follows:

$$B - C \geqslant 0 \tag{1}$$

where B is equal to the discounted benefits and C is equal to the discounted costs. Put in terms of the symbols seen previously, the equation becomes

$$\sum^{N} (B_N - C_N)\, (P/F, i, N) \geqslant 0 \tag{2}$$

where B_N and C_N mean the benefit and cost at the end of period N, $(P/F, i, N)$ is the single payment present worth factor at discount rate i for period N. This equation serves to qualify or disqualify the first alternative considered.

For the moment, only the case of two possible alternatives will be treated. We leave to a succeeding chapter the multiple—more than two—alternatives problem.

As mentioned previously, a good deal of economics is based on the logic of the rule that each increase in production or investment must carry its own weight. Each extra cost must be balanced by an extra benefit at least equal to it. (*Marginal* and *incremental* mean the same as *extra*.) For example, if a new facility is to be built and two alternative locations are proposed, one costing more than the other, it is logical to test the alternative with the lower first cost to see if it will qualify. Then it will be necessary to test the second alternative against the first by measuring the increase in cost and comparing that increase with the increase in benefits that the second alternative will bring about. With the usual cash flows, I emphasize that the two projects are ranked for comparison on the basis of their first cost, or construction cost, the lower cost alternative first.

The foregoing procedure resembles an application of the rule noted before that it is only the difference between alternatives that is relevant to their comparison. And this is so—with the added idea that the projects are qualified in ascending order of first costs and that we are concerned with the difference—the increment, now—in those first costs and the differential consequences flow that follows from them. The equation that expresses this idea is

$$\sum_{}^{N} [(B_N - C_N)_2 - (B_N - C_N)_1] (P/F, 1, N) \geqslant 0 \qquad (3)$$

where the symbols mean the same as in equation (2) and the subscript numbers refer to alternatives 1 and 2. Should the left side of equation (3) result in a value equal to or greater than zero, alternative 2 wins out over alternative 1.

When the benefit and costs are a series of equal payments, the series present worth factor $(P/A, i, N)$ may be used to shorten the calculations. Example 5.1 uses this factor.

Example 5.1

Two possible sewage disposal plants are being considered for adoption by a city. The first alternative is a system that will have a first cost of $1,000,000 and that will return a net benefit for 20 years of $100,000 per year. There will be no salvage value at the end of 20 years. The

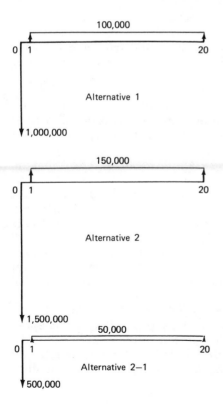

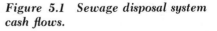

Figure 5.1   Sewage disposal system cash flows.

second alternative involves an expenditure of $1,500,000 and an annual net benefit of $150,000 for the next 20 years. This alternative also lacks a salvage value. Which course of action should the city take if the discount rate used for the city is 4 percent? Figure 5.1 shows the cash flows.

For alternative 1:

$$\sum_{}^{N} (B_N - C_N) \, (P/F, i, N)$$
$$= (0 - 1,000,000) \, (P/F, 4, 0) + 100,000 \, (P/A, 4, 20)$$
$$= -1,000,000 + 1,359,000$$
$$= +359,000$$

Therefore, alternative 1 qualifies because substitution in equation (2) gives an amount greater than zero.

For alternative 2 − alternative 1:

$$\sum_{}^{N} [(B_N - C_N)_2 - (B_N - C_N)](P/F, i, N)$$
$$= [(0 - 1,500,000) - (0 - 1,000,000)](P/F, 4, 0)$$
$$\quad + [(150,000 - 0) - (100,000 - 0)](P/A, 4, 20)$$
$$= (-500,000) \, (1.000) + (50,000) \, (13.590)$$
$$= +179,000$$

And therefore alternative 2 should be accepted over alternative 1 because substitution in equation (3) has resulted in an amount greater than zero.

The example was performed meticulously with substitutions of zero where required. With practice such rigidity becomes unnecessary. In addition, it was constructed in a simple proportional manner so that the reader can arrive at the correct decision by observation only.

What, in plain language, does the example mean? It means that the first alternative will result in a positive net benefit, even after discounting the future. The benefit is $359,000. The city should at least approve of this project if no better one is available. Is alternative 2 better than alternative 1? This question must be put more exactly. Is the extra investment in alternative 2 justified by the extra amount of benefits that will be received as a result of the extra investment? Application of equation 2 reveals that choosing alternative 2 rather than 1 will result in an extra $179,000 in the city's treasury at the time the project is begun.

At least two questions arise from this example. Why, since the net present value of alternative 1 is $359,000, should not it be accepted over alternative 2, which shows a net present value of only $179,000. The answer to this question is that the $179,000 is the incremental net benefit of alternative 2 over alternative 1, not the net benefit of alternative 2.

The second question is this: Why not simply apply equation 2 to both alternatives and choose the alternative with the highest net present value? The answer is a pedagogical one. Incremental analysis is the only correct method of analyzing mutually exclusive alternatives. Therefore, incremental analysis is used to explain all methods of comparing consequences over time. It so happens that in the benefit minus cost method the correct answer will appear even if total, rather than incremental, analysis is used. But this is because of the mathematical operation involved, which is algebraic summation. Nonetheless, total analysis of each alternative is often used because it is sometimes easier to compute. For that reason, the same example will be performed by total analysis, as follows:

Alternative 1 is treated totally in either the incremental or the total analysis. We have seen that a benefit of $359,000 results. Therefore, we should accept alternative 1 rather than do nothing. "Doing nothing" means investing the $1,000,000 of alternative 1 at 4 percent, the opportunity cost of capital. The procedure amounts to comparing alternative 1 incrementally to the status quo or "do nothing" alternative, which is the same as treating alternative 1 totally.

Alternative 2:

$$\sum_{N}^{N} (B_N - C_N) (P/F, i, N)$$
$$= -1,500,000 + 150,000 (P/A, 4, 20)$$
$$= -1,500,000 + 150,000 (13.590)$$
$$= -1,500,000 + 2,039,000$$
$$= +539,000$$

It is not surprising to discover that this result, $539,000, is the sum of the net benefit of alternative 1 and the net benefit of alternative 2 minus alternative 1, $359,000 + $179,000, taking rounding off into account.

Example 5.2

Two alternatives have the consequence flows shown in Figure 5.2. The discount rate is 10 percent.

For alternative 1:

$$\sum_{N}^{N} (B_N - C_N) (P/F, i, N)$$
$$= (0 - 1000) (P/F, 10, 0) + (300 - 100) (P/F, 10, 1)$$
$$\quad + (900 - 400) (P/F, 10, 2) + (1500 - 600) (P/F, 10, 3)$$
$$= (-1000) (1.000) + (200) (0.909) + (500) (0.826)$$
$$\quad + (900) (0.751)$$
$$= +271$$

Thus, alternative 1 passes the test.

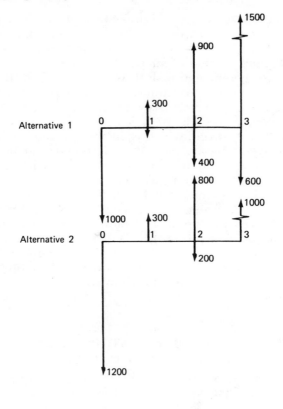

Figure 5.2   Example 2 cash flows.

For alternative 2 − alternative 1:

$$\overset{N}{\Sigma} \; [(B_N - C_N)_2 - (B_N - C_N)_1] \, (P/F, i, N)$$
$$[(0 - 1200) - (0 - 1000)] \, (P/F, \, 10, \, 0)$$
$$+ \, [(300 - 0) - (300 - 100)] \, (P/F, \, 10, \, 1)$$
$$+ \, [(800 - 200) - (900 - 400)] \, (P/F, \, 10, \, 2)$$
$$+ \, [(1000 - 0) - (1500 - 600)] \, (P/F, \, 10, \, 3)$$

It now appears that the incremental cash flow between alternative 2 and alternative 1 is as shown in the bottom sketch of Figure 5.2. The net present value of this cash flow is:

$$(-200) \ (P/F, \ 10\%, \ 0) + (100) \ (P/A, \ 10\%, \ 3)$$
$$= (-200) \ (1.000) - (100) \ (2.487)$$
$$= +49$$

Therefore, alternative 2 should be chosen instead of alternative 1.

Example 5.3 ───────────────────────────────────

Two alternative plans for electrical switching gear are estimated to have the following features:

	Plan I	Plan II
First cost	$28,000	$50,000
Life	10 years	20 years
Salvage value	$ 3,000	none
Annual cost	$ 5,500	$ 2,600

Figure 5.3 shows the cash flow for the plans, along with the incremental cash flow.

One of these plans is certain to be chosen. The opportunity cost of capital, before taxes, for this firm is 15 percent. Using the net present worth method, choose between the plans, assuming that all replace-

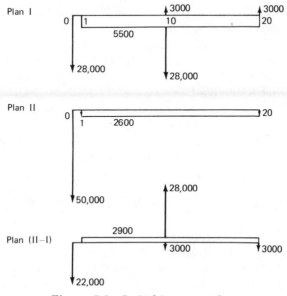

Figure 5.3 Switching gear plans.

ments have the same first cost, lives, salvage values, and annual costs as the initial facilities.

The present worth of the incremental cash flow is:

$$
\begin{aligned}
PW_{(\text{II}-\text{I})} &= -22{,}000 + 2900\ (P/A,\ 15,\ 20) \\
&\quad + (28{,}000 - 3000)\ (P/F,\ 15,\ 10) \\
&\quad -3000\ (P/F,\ 15,\ 20) \\
&= -22{,}000 + 29{,}000\ (6.259) \\
&\quad +25{,}000\ (0.2472) \\
&\quad -3000\ (0.0611) \\
&= -22{,}000 + 18{,}151 + 6180 - 183 \\
&= +2148
\end{aligned}
$$

Therefore, accept plan II rather than plan I.

UNEQUAL LIVES

In Example 5.3, the lives of the assets were unequal although technically they served the same purpose equally well. However, they must serve not only technically but for equal periods of time in order that a fair comparison between them can be made. Thus, the lives must be equalized, which requires that a further investment of $28,000 be made at the end of 10 years, that $3000 in salvage value be indicated at the end of 20 years, and that the cost of $5500 be continued through the twentieth year for plan I. The general rule is that lives must be equalized in present worth analysis by selecting the least common multiple of the lives. For lives of 10 and 11 years, say, the least common multiple is 110 years, and we must compare on the basis of the basis of that time span!

To do so thinking that the analyst actually plans ahead 110 years would be ludicrous. The period is chosen only for the logical reason that equal lives give a fair basis of comparison. We are actually planning only for the period of the longer-lived alternative.

THE NULL ALTERNATIVE DISREGARDED

Example 5.3 also illustrates that, because one of the two plans is sure to be chosen, it is not necessary to compare plan I with the null alternative. We need only ask ourselves, "Is the extra investment in plan II justified by the extra benefits to be derived from it?" The answer must be, "Yes," because the present worth of the cash flow is positive.

How can two almost totally negative cash flows result in an incremental cash flow with both benefits and costs? The key word is *incremental*. The benefits should be thought of as saving brought about by choosing plan I rather than plan II.

Example 5.4

A $1000 tax-free bond offers interest at a nominal 8 percent compounded semiannually. The term of the bond is 15 years. It is offered at $950. Your personal opportunity cost of capital for investments of equal risk is a nominal 12 percent annually after taxes. Should you buy the bond if the first interest payment will be received six months after the bond is purchased? Figure 5.4 shows the cash flow.

$$i = \frac{r}{m} = \frac{0.12}{2} = 0.06 \text{ per period}$$

$$N = 30 \text{ periods}$$

$$
\begin{aligned}
PW &= -950 + 40 \ (P/A, 6, 30) + 1000 \ (P/F, 6, 30) \\
&= -950 + 40 \ (13.765) + 1000 \ (0.1741) \\
&= -950 + 551 + 174 \\
&= -225
\end{aligned}
$$

The bond should not be purchased.

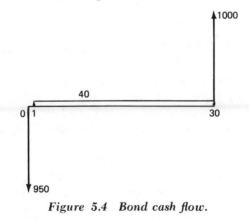

Figure 5.4 Bond cash flow.

Example 5.5

A university chair is proposed in economic analysis. The prospective donor wishes to know the cost of the endowment if the chair expenses are estimated to be $40,000 per year. The endowment can safely be invested at 6 percent compounded annually.

$$PW = 40{,}000 \ (P/A, \ 6, \ \infty)$$
$$= 40{,}000 \left(\frac{1}{0.06}\right)$$
$$= 40{,}000 \ (16.667)$$
$$= \$666{,}667$$

PERPETUAL LIVED INVESTMENTS

The previous example illustrates the problem of perpetual lived investments. The use of the factors—and their numerical value—may be simply illustrated by observing that a perpetual investment will return periodically its amount multiplied by the interest rate at which it is invested:

$$A = Pi$$

and therefore

$$P = \frac{A}{i} = A\left(\frac{1}{i}\right)$$

The investment rate acts as the compound amount factor (F/P) and its inverse as the series present worth factor (P/A).

A FACTUAL STUDY: ELECTRIC VEHICLES

Electric vehicles have become a subject of increasing interest in automotive circles because of greatly increased gasoline prices as a result of the petroleum price rises of 1973 and 1979 (and the prospect of further increases) and because of the identification of the automobile as the chief polluter of the urban atmosphere. This study undertakes to explore the potential of the electric vehicle in the near future. The point of view taken is that of a large United States manufacturer of automobiles. This company is assumed to have a primary goal of maximizing profit. Secondary goals are to maintain or expand the company's obligation to the community to offer a better product.

Electric Vehicles

Since their inception in the early 1900s, electric vehicles have never ceased to be manufactured throughout the world. In the United States they have appeared as passenger cars, trucks, buses, golf carts, and materials-handling vehicles. There are over 100,000 electric materials-handling vehicles in the United States alone.

The reason there are not more electric vehicles on the roads of the United States is a technical one stemming from a characteristic of the society. The electric vehicle runs on a lead-acid battery. Besides being extremely heavy, such batteries provide only enough power for short-range travel at relatively low speeds. The American driver is accustomed to fast, long-range travel. Thus, most of the technical research is aimed at finding a replacement for the conventional battery, decreasing its weight, or increasing its power capacity. The marketing research is aimed at discovering consumer preferences in an electric vehicle. As of 1978, neither type of research had proved fruitful enough to persuade a major automobile manufacturer to enter the field of electric vehicles on anywhere near the scale which this study imagines.

Research has been sponsored by the United States government in over 100 studies. Private industry has spent and continues to spend millions on electric vehicle or component research. (The component research focuses on lighter body materials and improved body design.) Everyone agrees that a place for the battery-powered vehicle exists, but everyone doesn't agree on how large that place is or at what particular year in the future it will arrive. Optimists believe that the electric car's time will come in five to 10 years, but they have been predicting that for some time now.

Electric automobiles range in weight from about 1500 to over 4000 pounds, in top speed from 32 to 70 miles per hour, in range from 25 to 150 miles, in cost from $1000 on up. All are powered by 6-volt or 12-volt batteries. Batteries are lead-acid, zinc-air, silver-zinc, lead-cobalt, or some combination of these. All have one or more direct-current motors, some of which act as generators during the braking portions of the trip to regenerate the battery. Passenger capacity is normally two adults. Electric automobiles are produced in the United States, Europe, and Japan.

In Europe and Japan, the incentive to develop electric vehicles has been greater than in the United States because of generally higher prices of gasoline. For example, four or five models have been introduced in England but without significant success. However, many small urban delivery vans are electric. Over 40,000 such vehicles are in operation in England, mostly as milk delivery trucks. In Japan, the problems of air pollution, congestion, and fuel cost have caused increased interest in electric vehicles.

Nowhere in the world has the electric vehicle achieved the measure of acceptance that its supporters believe is possible.

Estimating Market Potential

The market potential for the electric car rests on its advantages for urban and suburban use. No one supposes that it will be used for long trips. Apart from its fuel savings, it has other important advantages: It is virtually noiseless when running and completely silent when standing still. It is simple to operate, and it has a longer life and needs less maintenance than do cars with internal combustion engines. The motor does not run while the vehicle is standing; therefore, there is greater economy in stop-and-go driving. It is highly maneuverable because it is so small.

Polls taken by Gallup, the Opinion Research Corporation, and others indicate that the regions in which greatest interest in buying an electric car exists is the northeastern cities with populations greater than 100,000. At 1978 prices, people would be interested in a car costing less than $3000. Something around a third of those persons polled answered that they would buy a vehicle with a top speed of 40 miles per hour, with a range of 140 miles, whose batteries could be recharged at home.

The speeds and ranges of an electric car appear to cover a great portion of the driving done today with much larger vehicles. Sixty percent of car trips are less than 5 miles; 92 percent are less than 20 miles. About 80 percent of commuters use autos, and 56 percent of these persons carry no passengers. The average trip is between 6 and 10 miles. Average speed is also within the range of the electric car. Off-peak traffic speeds vary from 12 to 42 miles per hour; peak hour speeds vary between 8 and 24 miles per hour.

The acceleration of an electric car averages about zero to 30 miles per hour in 10 seconds. A fast sports car will go from zero to 60 miles per hour in 10 seconds. In city driving, especially for impatient drivers, the relatively slow acceleration of electric cars could prove to be a severe handicap, at least until there were enough of them on the street to slow down the traffic stream.

Certain assumptions are made in our study in order to estimate market potential. The most important of these is that the electric car could take the place of the internal combustion engine car used as second, third, and more family cars. It could also replace 20 percent of the passenger cars owned by governments at all levels, by military personnel living on base, by individuals living in institutions, and by businesses—amounting to a fifth of all passenger cars. No long-distance electric cars are considered: only urban passenger cars, buses, and delivery vans. We also assume that air pollution regulations will raise the price of internal combustion engine cars somewhat, thus making electric vehicles slightly more competitive. Ten

TABLE 5.1 The Potential Market for Electric Vehicles (in $000,000)

1 Year	2 Passenger Cars	3 Other Than First Family Car	4 Business & Government Market[a]	Total Market		Sales of Electric Cars
				5[b]	6 Percentage of Total Passenger Cars	
1960	62	9	2	11	18	
1965	76	15	3	18	24	
1970	87	19	4	23	26	
1975	99	23	4	27	27	
1980	110	27	4	31	28	2
1985	120	30	5	35	29	4

[a] 20% of a fifth of column 2 (4%)   [b] Column 3 + column 4.

years will be required to develop, test, and tool up for mass production of electric vehicles.

Social and economic assumptions in our study are that there will be no significant improvement in the performance characteristics of electric vehicles. No compelling new need will develop for electric vehicles. Consumer tastes will not change, nor will any new markets develop.

On the basis of these assumptions and information from the Federal Power Commission, Table 5.1 shows a potential market for 35 million electric cars in 1985, close to a third of all passenger cars. If development had begun in 1975, the study shows a possible sale of 2 million electric cars in 1980 and 4 million in 1985. Annual sales of buses, small vans, and urban trucks could run from 100,000 to 200,000 per year during the period 1980–1985.

TABLE 5.2   Net Present Worth of the Electric Car Project (in $000,000)

1	2 Cost		3	4	5	6
Year	Research & Development	Plant		Net Profit on Sales	P/F, 15, N	Present Worth
1971	1				0.8696	−0.87
1972	1				0.7561	−0.76
1973	1				0.6575	−0.66
1974	1	100[a]			0.5718	−57.75
1975	2	200[a]			0.4972	−100.43
1976				60	0.4323	+25.94
1977				63	0.3759	+23.68
1978				67	0.3269	+21.90
1979		100[b]		71	0.2843	−8.25
1980				75	0.2472	+18.54
1981				83	0.2149	+17.84
1982				93	0.1869	+17.38
1983		100[b]		108	0.1625	+1.30
1984				126	0.1413	+17.80
1985				150	0.1229	+18.44
1986				150	0.1069	+16.04
1987				150	0.0929	+13.94
1988				150	0.0808	+12.12
1989				150	0.0703	+10.55
1990				150	0.0611	+9.17
						+55.92

[a] Initial   [b] Expansion

The Economic Analysis

Table 5.2 summarizes the economic analysis before taxes for our hypothetical automobile manufacturer at a discount rate of 15 percent. A present worth of approximately $56 million is the net return on the project, which means that it should be undertaken. Once again notice the powerful effect of a 15 percent discount rate. The $150 million 20 years in the future has a positive effect on the present worth of only $9 million. It is valued in the present at only 6 percent of its value in 1990.

The assumptions in this project are vital. Chief among them are the assumptions on which the estimate of sales is based. Will 2 million electric vehicles really be sold in 1980 and 4 million in 1985? Two million is less than 10 percent of the potential market assumed to exist in 1980 as shown on Table 5.1. No, they will not be, because the project has never been tried. No one of the Big Four automobile manufacturers came forth with an electric car project. Therefore, we cannot tell how close this study came to reality.

REFERENCES

Grant, Eugene L., W. Grant Ireson, and Richard S. Leavenworth, *Principles of Engineering Economy*, 6th ed. New York: Ronald, 1976, pp. 87–106.

U.S. Federal Power Commission, *Development of Electrically Powered Vehicles*. Washington, D.C.: Government Printing Office, 1967.

6

Comparing Benefits and Costs: Annual Worth

The annual worth method is similar to the present worth method. Each method can be used to evaluate alternatives incrementally or one by one. The correct solution may be achieved either way.

Present worth and annual worth are similar in another sense as well. Each can be used to form the benefit/cost ratio, as we see in the next chapter.

Annual worth can be considered in two ways. First, the difference between annual cost and annual benefit is either annual profit or annual loss, depending on whether or not annual benefit exceeds annual cost. Second, if only costs differ among alternatives, and benefits are the same, then annual worth becomes simply annual cost, and judgments are made by choosing the alternative with minimum annual cost after single-period costs are converted to annual costs. In some texts, this is known as the *equivalent uniform annual cost* (EUAC) method.

DEFINITIONS AND FORMULAS

Annual worth is defined as the amount left over when total annual costs are subtracted from total annual revenue. If one course of action shows a greater annual worth than another, it should be preferred.

$$B_A - C_A \geqslant 0 \tag{1}$$

is the equation that justifies an alternative where

$B_1 = B_2 = B_3 = \ldots B_N = B_A$, the annual benefit

and

$C_1 = C_2 = C_3 = \ldots C_N = C_A$, the annual cost.

Conversion of a single payment cost or benefit into a series of equal annual costs or benefits is the main problem. It is overcome by use of the capital recovery factor, $(A/P, i\%, N)$.

The annual worth method is most useful when benefits and costs are expressed in annual terms, as is normal in private projects and frequent in public ones.

The same concept of incremental costs and benefits that we have seen in the previous methods applies to this one as well. The following examples clarify the situation:

Example 6.1 ───────────────────────────────────

The situation is the same as in Example 5.1 on page 51.
For alternative 1:

$$B_A - C_A \geqslant 0$$
$$B_A - (C_0) (A/P, i, N) \geqslant 0$$
$$100,000 - (1,000,000) (0.07358)$$
$$= 100,000 - 73,600$$
$$= 26,400$$

Therefore, alternative 1 qualifies.
The incremental consequences flow between alternative 2 and alternative 1 is treated as follows:

$$B_A - C_A \geqslant 0$$
$$B_A - (C_0) (A/P, i, N) \geqslant 0$$
$$50,000 - (500,000) (0.07358)$$
$$= 50,000 - 36,800$$
$$= 13,200$$

Therefore, accept alternative 2 rather than 1.

Example 6.2 ───────────────────────────────────

The situation is the same as in Example 5.2, from Chapter 5, page 53.
To analyze alternative 1 using the method of annual worth, it is

best to net out each year's payments. For alternative 1, this results in the cash flow of Figure 6.1.

The next step is to convert each of the end-of-period payments into an equivalent series of payments for the three years by discounting each to its present worth, summing all benefits and costs at time zero and applying the appropriate capital recovery factor. The present value of the cash flow at time zero is:

$$
\begin{aligned}
-1000 &+ 200\ (P/F,10,1) + 500\ (P/F,10,2) + 900\ (P/F, 10, 3)\\
&= -1000 + 200\ (0.909) + 500\ (0.826) + 900\ (0.751)\\
&= -1000 + 182 + 413 + 676\\
&= +271
\end{aligned}
$$

This is equivalent to an annual profit of:

$$
\begin{aligned}
(B_A - C_A) &= P\ (A/P, i, N)\\
&= 271\ (A/P, 10, 3)\\
&= 271\ (0.402)\\
&= 109
\end{aligned}
$$

Therefore, alternative 1 should be accepted because a profit does exist.

Alternative 2 is tested by incremental analysis. The incremental consequences flow between alternative 2 and alternative 1 is as in Figure 5.2.

Because benefits are already in terms of a series of equal payments, we convert 200 into the annual cost necessary to recover it, including interest and principal, and subtract that annual cost from the annual benefit to obtain the annual worth or annual profit.

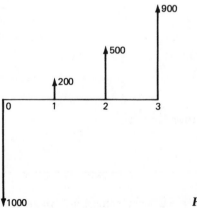

Figure 6.1 Netting out the cash flows.

$$\text{Annual profit} = 100 - 200 \ (A/P, \ 10, \ 3)$$
$$= 100 - 200 \ (0.402)$$
$$= 100 - 80$$
$$= 20$$

Choosing alternative 2 rather than alternative 1 results in an incremental worth of 20, and therefore alternative 2 should be chosen rather than alternative 1.

INCLUDING SALVAGE VALUE

The alternatives often include a salvage value. An easy way to handle this in annual profit or annual cost calculations is to observe that the salvage value enters the calculation only insofar as interest must be paid on its amount. We may subtract the salvage value from the original cost of the asset, therefore, and add to the annual cost the amount of the salvage value multiplied by the opportunity cost of capital as follows:

$$\text{Annual cost} = (P - L) \ (A/P, \ i, \ N) + Li$$

It is also possible to handle salvage value by the use of the sinking fund factor, which spreads payments backward over time much as the capital recovery factor spreads payment forward. If costs are considered positive, then salvage value must be given a negative sign as it is in the following formula for annual cost:

$$\text{Annual cost} = (P) \ (A/P, \ i, \ N) - (L) \ (A/F, \ i, \ N)$$

Individual preference will rule in the choice of formulas. Later examples show how these formulas are to be used.

If less than economic lives are employed in an analysis, assets must be assigned a residual value at the end of the time horizon being considered. This amount is usually positive; it is rarely the accountant's book value. It should represent the best estimate possible of the market value of the asset.

Sometimes salvage values are negative, representing the cost of removal or restoral. For example, strip mining operators are frequently required to restore the landscape to its original condition. This represents a large cost.

UNEQUAL LIVES IN ANNUAL WORTH

The annual worth method has a great advantage over the other three methods explained in this book: It avoids the necessity of equalizing the lives of alternatives by repeating cycles of investment and cost as is necessary in all other methods. As you will recall from the previous chapter, alternatives must be compared on the basis of equal periods of service. To do anything else is illogical. Sometimes this necessity involves the analyst in complicated cash flows. We discussed the example of lives of 10 and 11 years where the lives equalize at 110 years. At the discount rates normally used, any consequence more than 50 years away is usually negligible. (At 10 percent, the present worth factor at 50 years is 0.0085).

The annual worth method avoids such difficulties without violating the principle that lives must be equal. Consider how Example 5.3 of the last chapter would be handled in the annual worth method.

Example 6.3 ─────────────────────────────────────

The benefits of each alternative are the same. Therefore this example is solvable by the minimum annual cost criterion.

Let us treat the alternatives one by one, compare their equivalent uniform annual costs (EUAC), and choose the minimum.

For plan I (with costs as positive):

$$
\begin{aligned}
C_{1-10} &= 28,000\ (A/P,\ 15,\ 10) - 3000\ (A/F,\ 15,\ 10) + 5500 \\
&= 28,000\ (0.19925) - 3000\ (0.04925) + 5500 \\
&= 5579 - 148 + 5500 \\
&= 10,931
\end{aligned}
$$

This is the annual cost for 10 years. We know, however, that we must compare over a 20-year time horizon. The ensuing 10-year period will have an annual cost of:

$$
C_{10-20} = 28,000\ (A/P,\ 15,\ 10) - 3000\ (A/F,\ 15,\ 10) + 5500
$$

This is exactly the same as the previous equation. The annual cost of the second 10-year cycle is $10,931. We need not have performed the calculation for any repeated cycle.

For plan II:

$$
\begin{aligned}
C_{1-20} &= 50,000\ (A/P,\ 15,\ 20) + 2600 \\
&= 50,000\ (0.15976) + 2600 \\
&= 7988 + 2600 \\
&= 10,588
\end{aligned}
$$

We should choose plan II, which will save $10,931 less $10,588, or $343—say, $340 per year over plan II.

Could we have tackled the problem by incremental methods? Yes, although we would not have been any more correct. The incremental cash flow appears as the bottom sketch of Figure 5.3. It must be evaluated over 20 years. Notice that benefits have appeared in a problem where only costs were present. The benefits are the savings, both annual and in investment cost, of one plan over the other. We now have a problem in annual worth. If the result is positive, it means that the extra savings of plan II over plan I more than justified its extra cost. If the result is negative, it means that the extra savings of plan II did not make up for its extra costs. Costs will be negative and benefits positive.

$$
\begin{aligned}
\text{Annual worth} &= -22{,}000\ (A/P,\ 15,\ 20) + 2900 + (28{,}000 - 3{,}000) \\
&\quad (P/F,\ 15,\ 10)\ (A/P,\ 15,\ 20) - 3000\ (P/F,\ 15,\ 20) \\
&\quad (A/P,\ 15,\ 20) \\
&= -22{,}000\ (0.15976) + 2900 + 25{,}000\ (0.2472) \\
&\quad (0.15976) - 3000\ (0.0611)\ (0.15976) \\
&= -3515 + 2900 + 987 - 29 \\
&= +343
\end{aligned}
$$

The incremental cash flow has been reduced to an annual worth of +$343. This compares with the answer to Example 5.3 of a present worth of +$2148. That these are equivalent may be easily checked:

$$343(P/A,\ 15,\ 20) \overset{?}{=} 2148$$

$$343(6.259) \overset{?}{=} 2148$$

$$2147 \approx 2148$$

The difference results from rounding off.

The annual worth of the incremental cash flow of $343 confirms the difference between the annual costs of plan I and plan II.

Example 6.4 ——————————————————————————————

Two road graders are to be compared by a construction company analyst. The records of many years indicate that the Loomis machine has an expected life of six years whereas the Whitmore model lasts seven years. Other data are as follows:

	Loomis	Whitmore
First cost	35,000	40,000
Annual operating and maintenance	3,000	2,500
Salvage value	600	600

Figure 6.2 shows the cash flows.

Before-tax opportunity cost of capital for this firm is 20 percent. Which machine should be purchased assuming that their technical abilities are equal?

Because the revenues of the company will be the same no matter which machine is chosen, it is sufficient to compare them on the basis of annual cost only. The $600 salvage values are not to be disregarded because they are differential costs that, although equal in amount, occur at different times.

$$AC_{Loomis} = (35,000 - 600)\ (A/P,\ 20,\ 6) + 600(0.20) + 3000$$
$$= 34,400\ (0.30071) + 120 + 3000$$
$$= \$13,464$$

$$AC_{Whitmore} = (40,000 - 600)\ (A/P,\ 20,\ 7) + 600(0.20) + 2500$$
$$= 39,400\ (0.27742) + 120 + 2500$$
$$= \$13,550$$

The Loomis machine should be selected.

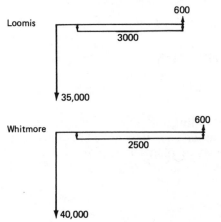

Figure 6.2   Road grader cash flows.

A FACTUAL STUDY: RURAL HIGHWAYS

Two proposals for the relocation of a rural highway are being considered. Facts about each location are presented below:

Location	I	II
Distance (miles)	15.5	13.3
First cost	$3,000,000	$3,500,000
Economic life	20	20
Annual maintenance	$5000/mi.	$6000/mi.
Opportunity cost of resources	10%	10%

Traffic Data

Vehicles	Av. Speed	Number Per day	Incremental Cost/mile
Autos	40 mph	1500	5¢
Light trucks	30 mph	200	10¢
Heavy trucks	30 mph	100	25¢

Time costs for all vehicles are estimated at 6 cents per vehicle per minute for autos and light trucks and 12 cents per vehicle per minute for heavy trucks.

These facts require some explanation. The first cost will be greater for location II, even though it covers a shorter distance by 2.2 miles, because its construction requires deeper cuts and higher fills. The economic life of the two highways is considered to be the same because at the end of 20 years it is thought that a totally new location will be required. In other words, the same circumstances that require a new location now because of higher vehicle speeds will be repeated in 20 years. Annual maintenance costs are higher for location II principally because of the deeper cuts and possible greater damage owing to erosion and slides. The opportunity cost of resources is that used as a standard by the U.S. Department of Transportation.

Traffic per day will not increase over the next 20 years. Speeds are thought to be the average which will prevail over the next 20 years. The incremental cost per mile is the extra cost of fuel, oil, maintenance, and tires for each mile of use. Fixed costs of the vehicles, such as first cost and insurance, are not included.

Time costs are the same for automobiles and light trucks on the theory that time saved by the driver of a passenger vehicle and his passengers is worth just as much as the wages of the driver of a light commercial vehicle. Operation and maintenance costs of these vehicles are equal. Heavy trucks have a cost per extra mile traveled of 25 cents. This extra cost covers fuel, oil, maintenance, tires, operators' wages, and the opportunity time cost of the truck—that is, the cost incurred because the truck is operating on this route and sacrificing the profits that might be made using the time on some other trip.

The analysis is best conducted by means of the extra costs associated with one location over the other. The main assumption is that the existing road will be relocated, so that we need not compare either alternative with the status quo. The location selected is that which has the least annual cost.

First cost of location II is $500,000 more than that of location I or

$$500,000 \ (A/P, \ 10, \ 20)$$
$$= 500,000 \ (0.11746)$$
$$= 58,700$$

Extra maintenance cost for location II is:

$$(13.3) \ (6000) - (15.5) \ (5000)$$
$$= 79,800 - 77,500$$
$$= \$2300 \text{ per year}$$

Vehicular operation costs are more for location I. Extra cost may be calculated using the 2.2 mile extra distance.

For autos:

2.2 extra miles times 365 days per year times 1500 autos/day times an extra cost per auto per mile of $0.05 equals $60.200 per year.

For light trucks:

$$(2.2) \ (365) \ (200) \ (0.10) = \$16,100$$

For heavy trucks:

$$(2.2) \ (365) \ (100) \ (0.25) = \$20,100$$

Time costs are also more for location I. Calculating the extra time and cost required by location I for each vehicle type:

$$\text{Auto: } 2.2 \text{ miles} \div 40 \text{ mph} = 0.055 \text{ hr.}$$

and

0.055 hrs. times 60 minutes per hour times $0.06 per vehicle minute times 1500 vehicles per day times 365 days per year equals $108,400.

Light trucks:

$$\left(\frac{2.2}{30}\right) (60) \ (0.06) \ (200) \ (365) = \$17,300$$

Heavy trucks:

$$\left(\frac{2.2}{30}\right) (60)\ (0.12)\ (100)\ (365) = \$19,300$$

All this may be summed in a cost table as follows:

Incremental Annual Cost

Location	I	II
First cost		$58,700
Maintenance		2,300
Vehicular operation		
Auto	$ 60,200	
Light truck	16,100	
Heavy truck	20,000	
Time		
Auto	108,400	
Light truck	19,300	
Heavy truck	19,300	
Totals	243,400	61,000

Thus location I costs $182,400 more per year than location II. Location II should be chosen.

7

Comparing Benefits and Costs: The Benefit/Cost Ratio

The benefit/cost ratio method of comparing benefits and costs and the internal rate of return method are related in one particularly significant way—neither can be used except in conjunction with incremental analysis. In this they contrast with the previous two methods in which either incremental analysis or a one-alternative-at-a-time valuation gave equally correct answers. In the two methods discussed in this chapter and in the following chapter, total analysis that treats each alternative separately is totally wrong. True, it may give correct answers some of the time, but this is also true of incorrect structural analysis or any other type of analysis in engineering or science.

BENEFIT/COST RATIO METHOD

The benefit/cost ratio method of deciding among alternatives uses the rule that the ratio of the present worth of the benefits of a course of action divided by the present worth of the costs is equal to or greater than 1:

$$\frac{B}{C} \geq 1$$

where B is equal to the discounted benefits and C the discounted costs. In the mathematical symbols used previously:

74

$$\frac{\overset{N}{\underset{}{\Sigma}} (B_N) (P/F,i,N)}{\overset{N}{\underset{}{\Sigma}} (C_N) (P/F,i,N)} \geq 1 \tag{1}$$

where B_N and C_N are the benefit and the cost at the end of any period N, and $(P/F, i, N)$ is the single payment present worth factor at discount rate of i percent for period N. When either the benefits or the costs or both are a series of equal payments, then $(P/A, i, N)$, the series present worth factor, may be substituted for $(P/F, i, N)$. This equation, as in the case of the benefit/cost method, serves to qualify an alternative when other alternatives are nonexistent except for the null alternative—that is, that nothing whatever will happen to the existing situation if the project is not undertaken. It also serves to test the advisability of undertaking an incremental investment in a mutually exclusive alternative. In other words, it may be used to try incremental consequence flows.

The procedure to be followed when two alternatives exist is to rank them starting with the lower of the two initial investments, then to subtract the consequences of the first investment from the second—exactly the procedure that was followed in the benefit minus cost or present worth method. The resulting consequence flow should then be tested by equation (1) above. If the resulting ratio is greater than 1, then the alternative requiring the larger investment should be selected. If it is equal to 1, then the decision maker will be indifferent between the two alternatives. (However, in this book we take a B/C equal to 1.0 as indicating acceptance.)

Finally, it is easy to derive the expression given as the benefit/cost ratio in equation (1) from the equation for the benefit minus cost equation:

$B - C \geq 0$

$B \geq C$ (moving C to the right-hand side of the equation)

$\dfrac{B}{C} \geq \dfrac{C}{C}$ (dividing both sides by C)

$\dfrac{B}{C} \geq 1$

Example 7.1 ───────────────────────────────

The situation is the same as Example 5.1 of Chapter 5. Using equation (1) on alternative 1:

$$\frac{\sum\limits_{N} (B_N)\,(P/A, i, N)}{\sum\limits_{N} (C_N)\,(P/A, i, N)}$$

$$= \frac{(100{,}000)\,(P/A, 4, 20)}{(1{,}000{,}000)\,(P/F, 4, 0)}$$

$$= \frac{(100{,}000)\,(13.590)}{(1{,}000{,}000)\,(1.000)}$$

$$= \frac{1{,}359{,}000}{1{,}000{,}000}$$

$$= 1.359$$

Therefore alternative 1 qualifies.

For alternative 2, the incremental consequences flow (alternative 2 − alternative 1):

$$\frac{\Delta B}{\Delta C} = \frac{(50{,}000)\,(P/A, 4, 20)}{(500{,}000)\,(P/F, 4, 0)}$$

$$= \frac{(50{,}000)\,(13.590)}{(500{,}000)\,(1.000)}$$

$$= 1.359$$

Therefore, according to the rules of incremental benefit/cost analysis, alternative 2 should be accepted rather than alternative 1.

It would not have changed this conclusion if the result of the incremental calculation had been 1.001 rather than 1.359. Even at a benefit/cost of 1.001, the investment returns 4 percent, and because no other opportunity for investment is available at better than 4 percent—by the definition of opportunity cost—alternative 2 should be chosen. Nor does it matter that the benefit/cost ratios for alternative 1 alone and for the incremental benefit/cost ratio (2 − 1) are equal. The only condition that need be met for qualifying alternative 2 has been met.

Example 7.2 ———————————————————————————

The situation is the same as in Example 5.2 of Chapter 5. Using equation (1) on alternative 1:

$$\frac{\sum\limits_{N} (B_{N_1})\,(P/F, i, N)}{\sum\limits_{N} (C_{N_1})\,(P/F, i, N)}$$

$$= \frac{\begin{array}{c}(300)(P/F, 10, 1) + (900)(P/F, 10, 2) \\ + (1500)(P/F, 10, 3)\end{array}}{\begin{array}{c}(1000)(P/F, 10, 0) + (100)(P/F, 10, 1) + (400)\,(P/F, 10, 2) \\ + (600)(P/F, 10, 3)\end{array}}$$

$$= \frac{(300)(0.909) + (900)(0.826) + (1500)(0.751)}{\begin{array}{c}(1000)(1.000) + (100)(0.909) + (400)(0.826) \\ + (600)(0.751)\end{array}}$$

$$= \frac{270 + 740 + 1130}{1000 + 90 + 330 + 450}$$

$$= \frac{2140}{1870}$$

$$= 1.14$$

Therefore, alternative 1 qualifies.

For alternative 2 the incremental consequence flow over alternative 1 must be found and equation (1) applied to it. This appears as:

$$\frac{\sum\limits^{N} (B_N)\,(P/F, i, N)}{\sum\limits^{N} (C_N)\,(P/F, i, N)}$$

$$= \frac{(100)\,(P/A, 10, 3)}{(200)\,(P/F, 10, 0)}$$

$$= \frac{(100)\,(2.487)}{(200)\,(1.000)}$$

$$= \frac{249}{200}$$

$$= 1.25$$

Thus alternative 2 should be chosen rather than alternative 1. The incremental benefit/cost ratio is greater than 1.0, and for this reason alone, completely independent of the magnitude of the ratio, alternative 2 should be chosen. It simply means that the discounted extra net benefits divided by the discounted extra net costs are greater than 1.0.

NETTING OUT AND THE RULE OF Δ

The rules inherent in the preceding discussion may seem definitive. They are not. The difficulty arises because benefits and costs are not always readily identifiable. This difficulty is not evident in Example

7.1 because only one cost is present in each alternative, and there is only one annual benefit for each alternative. In Example 7.2, however, a number of costs and benefits occur at different times. If equation (1) is used, the B/C ratio is 1.14 as determined previously. But what if the costs and benefits at each period N were netted out? The B/C ratio would be defined as:

$$B/C = \frac{\sum\limits^{N}(B - C)_N(P/F, i, N)}{C_0} \tag{2}$$

where C_0 is the cost of the project at time 0—that is, the construction or installation cost. This I call the Rule of Δ. The cash flow of alternative 1 becomes that of Figure 6.1, page 66. Its B/C ratio, using equation (2), is:

$$B/C = \frac{200(P/F, 10, 1) + 500(P/F, 10, 2) + 900(P/F, 10, 3)}{1000}$$

$$= \frac{200(0.909) + 500(0.826) + 900(0.751)}{1000}$$

$$= \frac{182 + 413 + 676}{1000}$$

$$= 1.27$$

This contradicts the previous B/C ratio of 1.14 for the same alternative.

By netting out benefits and costs at each period *before* performing any further operations, a different B/C ratio is obtained than if the benefits and costs are accepted as they appear.

BENEFITS, DISBENEFITS, AND COSTS

Yet another difficulty arises in B/C ratio calculation. It is possible to calculate benefit/cost ratios in other ways, depending on arbitrary distinctions between benefits and costs. For example, if a cost is labeled a disbenefit and subtracted from the numerator of the B/C ratio rather than added to the denominator, a different ratio is obtained.

As a disbenefit, $1000 affects the B/C ratio as in the example below:

$$\frac{B}{C} = \frac{10,000 - 1000}{5000} = 1.80$$

where all sums are already discounted.

As a cost the $1000 changes the B/C to:

$$\frac{B}{C} = \frac{10,000}{5000 + 1000} = 1.67$$

This difficulty is avoided by a rigorous use of incremental analysis and the Rule of Δ. Let us state that when two or more alternatives are being considered, netting out at each time period must take place before any other operation is performed on the cash flows. I defend this as follows: If it is true—and it certainly is—that the extras or marginal amounts are worth counting in a decision, then surely the extras or marginal amounts must be determined before any operation is performed on them. Netting out the first alternative considered is the same as comparing it incrementally to the null alternative. Thus, netting out before discounting is simply employing correctly the rule of incrementality. To do anything else would be to violate the definition of incrementality. Thus, it follows that whether costs are called costs or disbenefits does not affect the benefit/cost ratio.

The rule for determining the benefit/cost ratio is, therefore:

Step 1: Net out the benefits and costs at the end of each period.

Step 2: Apply equation (1).

You may wonder why equation (2) cannot be used in place of these two steps. The reason is that equation (2) does not cover the case when a cost occurs as a result of netting out at a period other than time zero.

Some federal agencies insist on using disbenefits. Thus, the origins of the ratios must be investigated by the sophisticated decision maker before drawing conclusions. No matter how costs are labeled and treated in the B/C ratio, a project cannot be made to fail if it passes the ratio test, however defined. It *can* be made to appear more or less beneficial.

ZEROES IN THE BENEFIT/COST RATIO

What shall we do if either costs or benefits become zero? If the cost is zero, the B/C ratio cannot be determined because division by zero is not permissible according to the rules of algebra. The benefit/cost ratio must be abandoned and another method used in its place.

If a zero occurs in the numerator, the B/C ratio is zero, which indicates unacceptability. This is not surprising because no one would invest in a project with real costs but without benefits.

A FACTUAL STUDY: THE STATE MARITIME ACADEMY

A study of the State Maritime Academy (SMA) was ordered by the State Educational Commission. The objective of the study was to define and compare the benefits and costs of producing graduates of the SMA. The purpose of the benefit/cost analysis was to provide the commission with a means of assessing the value of this educational institution in the development of the state's educational resources. Once all state educational programs had been analyzed, the commission could more rationally recommend an overall program to the governor.

Background

The State Maritime Academy was founded in 1962 and located in Seaview. It is a component of the state university system and offers a four-year program leading to the Bachelor of Science degree in Marine Transportation or Marine Engineering. This program is designed to produce qualified and licensed Third Mates or Third Assistant Engineers for the merchant marine. If qualified, a graduate may earn a commission in the U. S. Naval Reserve or the U. S. Coast Guard Reserve. As of the fall of 1970, the entire four years of instruction were provided at the school's campus in Seaview. (Previously, the first two years were given at the state university.) Enrollment in 1969—the year of the report—was 132, close to a 5 percent increase over the previous year, with 35 in the graduating class. The capacity of the school was 300.

SMA is one of six state maritime academies, others being located in California, Maine, Massachusetts, New York, and Texas. SMA is the youngest and the smallest of the academies. The federal government also has a maritime academy, the U. S. Merchant Marine Academy, located at King's Point, Long Island, operated under the Maritime Administration. The seven academies produce 600 to 650 graduates annually, up 174 percent from 1952.

Viewpoint

Kaufman et al. provide a model for the quantification of the benefits and costs of education. They maintain that three possible points of view may be taken—those of the individual, the community, and the society. In this study, the viewpoint of the society was taken. In this light, the resource costs are those for which the society loses an opportunity to benefit. These are the buildings and grounds in the sense of the loss that society suffers because they are being used to train merchant marine cadets and not for some other productive use.

The same may be said of the equipment, such as training ships, lifeboats, machine shop equipment, and so on. The opportunity cost of instructors and all other personnel used to operate the school must be included in the costs. Operating costs such as fuel must also be added.

What about tuition? Tuition should not be included as a cost under the viewpoint taken in the study. It does not represent any use of resources, being much more in the nature of tax. It is, therefore, a transfer payment. But insofar as the students are being withdrawn from other production in the society, their time represents a real opportunity cost. A young man who had been working as a machinist before entering the school costs the society the value of the production he would have put forth as a machinist. This opportunity cost was not quantified in the study, presumably because of lack of data.

As to benefits, the viewpoint taken requires that these be the benefits to the society provided by the graduates of the school throughout their career over and above those they would have provided had they not received their education as merchant marine officers. No attempt was made in the study to compare the salaries of the officers with the salaries they might be presumed to have made in another career. Difficulties of predicting what might have happened had they not gone to the school were thought to be insurmountable. The best that might have been done would have been to evaluate the career they did not follow on the basis of national average salaries over a lifetime for young men of their age and, therefore, life expectancy.

Costs and Benefits

Costs were considered to be properly represented by the state and federal appropriations for the SMA during the school years 1966 through 1970. These are shown in Table 7.1. They are accepted as representative of all opportunity costs to the society.

Notice that depreciation has probably been included in the item "Department and ship operation." Because depreciation represents a sunk cost spread over years and not an opportunity cost, this item has been overstated by some quantity. The construction cost of the Seaview school has been included as a lump sum for 1968–1969. This seems acceptable in a present worth benefit/cost ratio. The table shows a number of unexplained gaps and inconsistencies, but these we must accept for lack of further information.

These four years are chosen because the study fixes on the graduates of these years and no others to determine the benefits of the operation.

Benefits were the current annual base salaries, averaged over nine vessel classifications, likely to be earned by SMA graduates serving as deck officers over a 20-year career. In computing these salaries it was assumed that (1) the salary pattern of a deck officer was sufficiently

TABLE 7.1   State Maritime Academy Appropriations

Item	School Year			
	1966–1967	1967–1968	1968–1969	1969–1970
Administration	49,498	50,829	52,511	63,713
Resident instruction				
Teaching salaries	128,204	98,054	121,729	155,003
Department and				
ship operation	153,730	260,064	264,377	302,688
Instructional				
administration		11,874	12,430	14,042
Library				7,005
Seaview school				
construction			500,000	
Major repairs		10,000	10,000	
Total appropriation	331,432	430,821	961,047	542,451

like that of an engineering officer to represent both, (2) a deck officer will spend two years as a Third Mate, three years as a Second Mate, and the balance of his career as a First Mate, never reaching Master, (3) a 20-year career was a suitable horizon because merchant marine officers may retire after 20 years with full benefits, and most do so. Times in grade and nonpromotion to Master were believed to be representative. Table 7.2 illustrates how average annual salaries were calculated.

The discount rate used was 10 percent. The report assigns no other reason to the choice of this rate other than that it represents a value judgement.

The Benefit/Cost Ratio

Table 7.3 shows the annual cost calculations per student. Figure 7.1 shows the cash flow of four years' costs of education and 20 years of salary as benefits. Reducing these to time zero—June, 1970—is done in Table 7.4. The benefit/cost ratio is:

$$B/C = \frac{101,\,201}{20,712}$$

$$= 4.9$$

It appears that with this historically favorable benefit/cost ratio that the SMA should be continued.

TABLE 7.2 Average Annual Salary Calculation

Example: Average annual base salary for Third Mate as of June, 1968:

Vessel class	Monthly wage rate
A–4	$848
A–3	814
A–2	798
A–1	782
A	750
B	720
C	688
D	672
E	656
	$6728

Average over the nine vessel classifications and multiplying by 12; we get:

$$\frac{6728}{9} \times 12 = \$8,976$$

Annual salaries thus computed:

Master	$20,760	Chief Engineer	$21,168
First Mate	13,884	First Asst. Engineer	14,064
Second Mate	9,756	Second Asst. Engineer	9,744
Third Mate	8,976	Third Asst. Engineer	8,964

Intangibles

The school benefits the merchant marine of the United States and thus the nation by assuring a vital service in peace and an irreplaceable service in war. It would be unrealistic in the extreme to rely on the merchant marine of other nations at a time when the national economy or national survival depended on sea transport. No benefit can be assigned to the avoidance of national destruction. It is immense.

In addition, there are benefits present in all education: the satisfaction of a public need, increased efficiency of production, redistribution of income, and national stability because of politically mature voters.

TABLE 7.3 Annual Cost Calculations

Year	1966–1967	1967–1968	1968–1969	1969–1970
1 Appropriation (From Table 7.1)	$331,432	$430,821	$961,047	$542,451
2 Enrollment	114	120	126	132
3 Cost per student (Line 1 ÷ line 2)	$2,907	$3,590	$7,627	$4,109

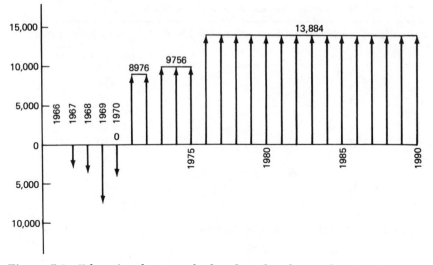

Figure 7.1 *Educational costs and salary benefits of a merchant marine officer.*

Critique of the Report

The report is weak in several areas. I have already pointed out that the benefit measure should really be the difference between the streams of salary benefits with and without the educational experience. But even if the difference were half the "with" stream of benefits, a benefit/cost ratio of over 2.0 would be achieved.

TABLE 7.4 **Costs and Benefits Discounted at 10%**

Year	Current Value	Factor	Present Value
	Costs	F/P, 10, N	
1967	$2,907	1.3310	3,869
1968	3,590	1.2100	4,344
1969	7,627	1.1000	8,390
1970	4,109	1.0000	4,109
		Costs Σ	20,712
	Benefits	(P/A, 10, N)(P/F, 10, N)	
1971–1972	8,976	(1.736)(1.0000)	15,582
1973–1975	9,756	(2.487)(0.8264)	20,051
1976–1990	13,884	(7.606)(0.6209)	65,568
		Benefits Σ	101,201

An assumption of the study is that even if graduates leave the sea, they will still provide benefits to the society at least equal to those they would have given if they had stayed on ships. The rate of attrition of graduates of the SMA was thought to be about 45 percent by the second year after graduation and 6 percent annually thereafter.

Behind all benefits based on salaries is the assumption that the benefits represent opportunity cost for the society—that is, that the salary is the benefit that the society forgoes by not having the officer work elsewhere.

A further seeming objection is the burdening of the year 1969 with the total cost of the installation at Seaview. Spreading the cost over the life of the installation would seem to be more correct procedure, especially if the life is longer than 20 years—the time horizon of the study. The effect of using the capital recovery factor would be to lower the cost in the annual benefit/cost ratio—all costs and benefits would have to be rendered in annual form if one were. This would cause the ratio to be even higher.

This is an example of a historical benefit/cost study. For this reason the study was conducted just as though it were planned and not yet executed. Thus sunk costs were included.

REFERENCES

Kaufman, Jacob J., Ernst W. Stromsdorfer, Teh-wei Hu, and Maw Lin Lee, *An Analysis of the Comparative Costs and Benefits of Vocational versus Academic Education in Secondary Schools* (University Park, Pa.: Institute for Research on Human Resources, The Pennsylvania State University, 1967).

8

Comparing Benefits and Costs: The Internal Rate of Return

The internal rate of return is the last of the methods I review. It is similar to the benefit/cost ratio method in one important respect—it can be used only in conjunction with incremental analysis. I make this point later in the chapter by means of an example. Keynes called the internal rate of return the "marginal efficiency of investment." It is a useful device, especially when dealing with bankers and businessmen who think in terms of rate of return.

DEFINITION

The *internal rate of return* (i^*) of a consequences flow is that rate of discount at which the discounted benefits just equal the discounted costs. In other words, it is the discount rate at which the present worth of the benefits of a course of action exactly equal the present worth of the costs. In formal terms the relation is:

$$\sum_{}^{N} (B_N)(P/F, i^*, N) = \sum_{}^{N} (C_N)(P/F, i^*, N) \tag{1}$$

where i^* is the internal rate of return. It may also be stated as:

$$\sum_{}^{N} (B_N)(P/F, i^*, N) - \sum_{}^{N} (C_N)(P/F, i^*, N) = 0 \tag{2}$$

The procedure for using this method is usually one of trial and error because in most examples more than one unknown exists in a single equation. In special cases, such as the example following this discussion, a definitive solution is possible where only one unknown exists.

When the internal rate of return exceeds the opportunity cost of resources, a course of action is accepted. When the internal rate of return is less than the opportunity cost of resources, an alternative is rejected. To be accepted, therefore:

$$i^* \geq i$$

where i^* is the internal rate of return (sometimes shortened to IROR).

As in the previous methods, alternatives should be ranked for testing from the lowest to the highest initial investment. The first alternative's consequence flow should be treated by trial and error to discover its internal rate of return, which should then be compared with the opportunity cost of capital. If the first alternative qualifies under this test, the incremental consequence flow between the first and second alternative should be solved for its internal rate of return. If the incremental internal rate of return is greater than the opportunity cost of capital, then alternative 2 should be accepted rather than alternative 1. If it should happen that the first alternative does not qualify, then the second alternative should be tested against the null alternative, and if its internal rate of return exceeds the opportunity cost of capital, then the second alternative should be accepted.

As in preceding methods, the internal rate of return of the incremental consequence flow need not exceed the internal rate of return of the first alternative. It need only exceed the opportunity cost of capital in order that the second alternative be accepted rather than the first.

Example 8.1

The situation is the same as in Example 5.1 of Chapter 5. Substitution in equation (1) is necessary. For alternative 1:

$$\sum_{}^{N} (B_N)(P/F, i^*, N) = \sum_{}^{N}(C_N)(P/F, i^*, N)$$
$$(100{,}000)(P/A, i^*, 20) = (1{,}000{,}000)(P/F, i^*, 0)$$
$$(100{,}000)(P/A, i^*, 20) = (1{,}000{,}000)(1.000)$$

$$(P/A, i^*, 20) = \frac{1{,}000{,}000}{100{,}000} = 10.000$$

Referring to the interest tables of the Appendix and moving along the rows for $N = 20$, we find the closest factor to 10.000 to be 9.818 in the table for $i = 8$ percent. The internal rate of return for this flow is between 6 and 8 percent and much closer to 8 than 6. (Interpolation between these two points is possible, of course, but is justified only when the input quantities are exact to some degree, which is not the case in this example.) Therefore, at least alternative 1 should be accepted.

For incremental consequences flow between alternatives 2 and 1:

$$(50,000)(P/A, i^*, 20) = (500,000)(1.000)$$
$$(P/A, i^*, 20) = 10.000$$

therefore $i^* = 8$ percent approximately. Since 8 percent exceeds the resource opportunity cost of 4 percent, the incremental benefits of alternative 2 are greater than its incremental costs. Alternative 2 should be accepted over alternative 1.

Example 8.2

Again the situation is the same as in Example 5.2 of Chapter 5. To find the internal rate of return of the consequences flow of alternative 1, it is necessary to substitute the net payments in equation (1) as follows:

$$\sum_{N}^{N} (B_N)(P/F, i^*, N) = \sum_{N}^{N} (C_N)(P/F, i^*, N)$$
$$(200)(P/F, i^*, 1) + (500)(P/F, i^*, 2) + 900(P/F, i^*, 3)$$
$$= 1000(P/F, i^*, 0)$$

The unknown in the above equation is i^*, and the only method of solving it is by trial and error. (See Table 8.1 for the trial calculations.)

At a 12 percent discount rate, benefits exceed costs by 220. A new trial should, therefore, be carried out, which will discount benefits at a greater rate than costs. A higher discount rate should be applied.

At i equal to 14 percent, the difference between discounted benefits and discounted costs still amounts to 170.

It is evident that Δ is reducing slowly. Therefore, I jump to 22 percent.

Since at an i of 22 percent, discounted benefits equal discounted costs and at an i of 24 percent discounted costs exceed discounted benefits by 40, the discount rate at which discounted benefits equal discounted costs is a little more than 22 percent. (A graph of discounted present value against discount rate for alternative 1 appears in Figure 8.1.)

Because the opportunity cost of resources is 10 percent, alternative 1 is justified. Following the procedure previously outlined, the incre-

TABLE 8.1 Finding the Internal Rate of Return for Alternative 1

N	B_N	C_N	$P/F, 12, N$	Discounted		$P/F, 14, N$	Discounted	
				B	C		B	C
0	—	1000	1.000	—	1000	1.000	—	1000
1	200	—	0.893	180	—	0.877	180	—
2	500	—	0.797	400	—	0.769	380	—
3	900	—	0.712	640	—	0.675	610	—
				$\Sigma = 1220$	1000		$\Sigma = 1170$	1000
					$\Delta = +220$			$\Delta = +170$

N	B_N	C_N	$P/F, 22, N$	Discounted		$P/F, 24, N$	Discounted	
				B	C		B	C
0	—	1000	1.000	—	1000	1.000	0	1000
1	200	—	0.820	160	—	0.806	160	—
2	500	—	0.672	340	—	0.650	330	—
3	900	—	0.551	500	—	0.524	470	—
				1000	1000		$\Sigma = 960$	1000
					$\Delta = 0$			$\Delta = -40$

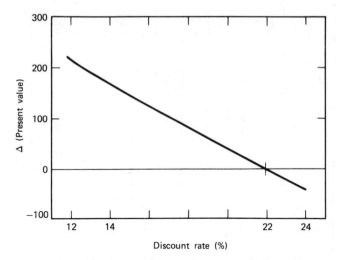

Figure 8.1 The internal rate of return of alternative 1.

mental consequence flow between alternative 2 and alternative 1 should now be tested for its internal rate of return, as follows:

$$\sum_{}^{N} (B_N)(P/A, i^*, 3) = \sum_{}^{N} (C_N)(P/F, i^*, 0)$$
$$(100)(P/A, i^*, 3) = (200)(1.000)$$

$$(P/A, i^*, 3) = \frac{200}{100} = 2.000$$

Referring to the interest tables of the Appendix and moving across the row for $N = 3$, a factor of 1.952 is encountered in the table headed 25% and 2.106 in the table headed 20%.

Interpolating:

25%	1.952
x	2.000
20%	2.106

x = 3.44 and i^* = 23.44 percent—say, 23 percent.

The incremental internal rate of return of alternative 2 over alternative 1 is 23 percent, well exceeding the 10 percent designated as the opportunity cost of resources. Therefore alternative 2 should be accepted over alternative 1.

The interpolation procedure hides an important supposition—that the relation between the two interest rates is a linear one with regard to the series present worth factor. This is not true. For short intervals between the interest rates, no great error enters, but when there are longer gaps the error can be large, especially with factors whose graph deviates markedly from a straight line.

THE INTERNAL RATE OF RETURN VERSUS PRESENT WORTH

For over 20 years analysts have recognized that the internal rate of return must be used with care. For the first few of the 20 years, many students in the field believed that a discrepancy existed between the internal rate of return, or marginal efficiency of capital method, and the net present value, or present worth method. In reality, no such discrepancy exists between the two methods if they are correctly used. The difficulty arises when the analyst determines the internal rate of return of each alternative in a mutually exclusive set of alternatives and then chooses the alternative with the highest IROR. In certain cases, the analyst will find that the alternative chosen by the IROR method is not the same as the alternative chosen by the present worth method. However, if incremental analysis is used and an incremental internal rate of return determined, no conflict will occur between the internal rate of return method and any other. Let us look at this matter in detail.

Table 8.2 shows the cash flows associated with two mutually exclusive alternatives, A and B, during two years. The column labeled $B - A$ shows the difference in the cash flows between the alternatives. The present worth of the cash flows was found at five different interest rates: 0, 10, 20, 30, and 40 percent. Figure 8.2 illustrates the profiles of the two alternatives and the present worth profile of the incremental cash flow between A and B. The internal rate of return of the cash flow of alternative A is approximately 27 percent and of B about 23 percent.

The controversy over the use of internal rate of return as a decision tool arose because students of the subject noted that in cash flows patterned like those in Figure 8.2 the following occurred at an opportunity cost of capital of, let us say, 10 percent. Because A has an IROR of 27 percent and B of only 23 percent, A is to be preferred to B. But at 10 percent, B has present worth of +397 and A of only +223. Therefore, B is to be preferred to A! Check Figure 8.2 to assure yourself of the truth of this analysis.

The error in the preceding sequence is that total analysis is being used rather than incremental. Following the decision rules outlined at the beginning of this chapter, the top portion of Table 8.3 develops. At 10 percent opportunity cost of capital or minimum attractive rate of return (MARR), at least alternative A will be chosen because 27 exceeds 10 percent. Will B be chosen over A? The incremental rate of return of B over A is 20 percent, which exceeds the opportunity cost of

TABLE 8.2 Present Worth of Two Mutually Exclusive Alternatives and Their Difference

					P.W. @ i = 10%				P.W. @ i = 20%		
Year	A	B	B − A	P/F, 10, N	A	B	B − A	P/F, 20, N	A	B	B − A
0	−1000	−2000	−1000	1.0000	−1000	−2000		1.0000	−1000	−2000	
1	+800	+1000	+200	0.9091	727	909		0.8333	667	833	
2	+600	+1800	+1200	0.8264	496	1488		0.6944	417	1251	
	Σ +400	+800	+400		Σ 223	397	+174		Σ 84	84	0

					P.W. @ i = 30%				P.W. @ i = 40%		
Year	A	B	B − A	P/F, 30, N	A	B	B − A	P/F, 40, N	A	B	B − A
0	−1000	−2000	−1000	1.0000	−1000	−2000		1.0000	−1000	−2000	
1	+800	+1000	+200	0.7692	615	769		0.7143	571	714	
2	+600	+1800	+1200	0.5917	355	1065		0.5102	306	918	
	Σ +400	+800	+400		Σ −30	−166	−136		Σ −123	−368	−245

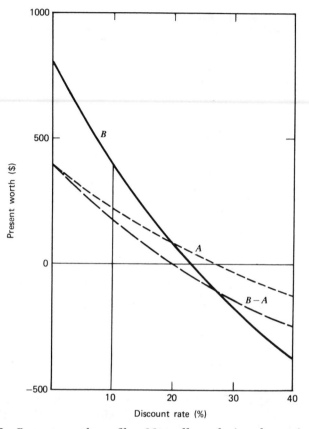

Figure 8.2 Present worth profiles. Mutually exclusive alternatives A and B.

capital. Therefore, the decision favors B, because the extra investment required by B is more than justified by its benefits. At 20 percent opportunity cost of capital, the analyst will at least accept A because 27 exceeds 20. He will accept B, according to the rule we have followed in this book, because the IROR of $B - A$ is exactly 20 percent. (The economist would say that the analyst would be indifferent between A and B.) At 22 percent the decision would favor A because A's IROR still exceeds the opportunity cost of capital. The extra investment in B fails to justify itself because 20 percent IROR is less than the opportunity cost of capital of 22 percent. At 24 percent A is still chosen over B for the same reasons as at 22 percent. At 26 percent the reasoning remains the same as at 22 and 24. At 27 percent opportunity cost of capital, the analyst will be content with A, although just barely. At 30 percent, A will be rejected because its IROR is 3 percent less than the threshold of 30 percent opportunity cost of

TABLE 8.3　Decisions Based on IROR versus PW: Case 1

i (MARR) (%)	IROR (%) A	IROR (%) B − A	Decision Favors
10	27	20	B
20	27	20	B
22	27	20	A
24	27	20	A
26	27	20	A
27	27	20	A
30	27	NA	Neither
40	27	NA	Neither

i (%)	P.W. @ i A	P.W. @ i B	Decision Favors
10	223	397	B
20	84	84	B
22	60	35	A
24	40	−15	A
26	20	−65	A
27	0	−100	A
30	−30	−166	Neither
40	−123	−368	Neither

capital. The IROR of $B − A$ is no longer applicable because we must never compare increments using an alternative that has failed. Therefore, both alternative A and B fail. Similar reasoning prevails at 40 percent.

Now compare the results we have just determined by using the internal rate of return criterion correctly with those we would arrive at by using the present worth criterion. At the same opportunity costs of capital, the decisions are precisely the same.

The subject is not fully covered yet. It is possible to encounter cash flows where incremental IROR analysis will coincide perfectly with present worth analysis in decisions on mutually exclusive alternatives, and so will total IROR analysis, thus proving once more that it is possible to arrive at the correct answer by using the wrong methods. Table 8.4 presents a cash flow pattern of this type. The time span is five years, and the cash flows of alternatives I, II, and II − I are as noted. The discount rates used to determine the present worth profile are 10, 20, 25, 30, and 40 percent. Figure 8.3 illustrates the present worth profiles of the two mutually exclusive alternatives and their incremental difference. Table 8.5 follows through on the decision process. The internal rate of return of alternative 1 is about 25 percent and of the increment II − I, 27 percent. At 10 percent opportunity cost

TABLE 8.4 Present Worths of Alternatives I, II, and Their Differences

Year	I	II	II − I	P/F, 10, N	P.W. @ i = 10% I	P.W. @ i = 10% II	II − I	P/F, 20, N	P.W. @ i = 20% I	P.W. @ i = 20% II	II − I
0	−1000	−1200	−200	1.0000	−1000	−1200	−200	1.0000	−1000	−1200	−200
1	600	300	−300	0.9091	546	273	−273	0.8333	500	250	
2	400	400	0	0.8264	331	331	0	0.6944	278	278	
3	300	500	200	0.7513	225	376	151	0.5787	174	289	
4	200	600	400	0.6830	137	410	273	0.4823	97	289	
5	100	700	600	0.6209	62	435	373	0.4019	40	281	
	Σ +600	+1300	+700		Σ 301	625	324		Σ 89	187	98

Year	P/F, 25, N	P.W. @ i = 25% I	P.W. @ i = 25% II	II − I	P/F, 30, N	P.W. @ i = 30% I	P.W. @ i = 30% II	II − I	P/F, 40, N	P.W. @ i = 40% I	P.W. @ i = 40% II	II − I
0	1.0000	−1000	−1200		1.0000	−1000	−1200		1.0000	−1000	−1200	
1	0.8000	480	240		0.7692	462	231		0.7143	429	214	
2	0.6400	256	256		0.5917	237	237		0.5102	204	204	
3	0.5120	154	256		0.4552	137	228		0.3644	109	182	
4	0.4096	82	246		0.3501	70	210		0.2603	52	156	
5	0.3277	33	229		0.2693	27	189		0.1859	19	130	
		Σ 5	27	22		Σ −67	−105	−38		Σ −187	−314	−127

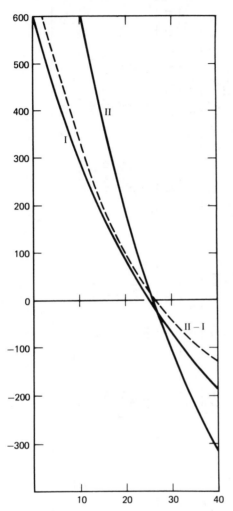

Figure 8.3 Present worth profiles; mutually exclusive alternatives I and II.

of capital, we would choose at least project I because 25 percent exceeds 10 percent. On investigating whether or not the extra investment in II is justified, we notice that is has an IROR of 27 percent, which also exceeds the opportunity cost of capital. The decision favors II. The same reasoning holds at 20 and 25 percent opportunity cost of capital, the latter according to the rule of this book. At 26 percent opportunity cost of capital, something interesting occurs. Project I fails, of course. The incremental IROR is therefore no longer applicable. Our criterion of choice is now the IROR of alternative II which is 26 percent. Alternative II just qualifies at this opportunity cost of capital. At 30 and 40 percent, neither alternative qualifies.

The bottom portion of Table 8.5 shows the decisions that would be made were the present worth criterion followed. They are exactly the same as those made by incremental IROR analysis.

TABLE 8.5 Decisions Based on IROR versus PW: Case 2

i (MARR) %	$IROR_I$ (%)	$IROR_{II - I}$ (%)	Decision Favors
10	25	27	II
20	25	27	II
25	25	27	II
26	25	N.A.	II
30	25	N.A.	Neither
40	25	N.A.	Neither
i (%)	$P.W._I$ @ i	PW_{II} @ i	Decision Favors
10	301	625	II
20	89	187	II
25	5	27	II
26	−18	0	II
30	−67	−105	Neither
40	−187	−314	Neither

Now let us do the analysis the wrong way. At all opportunity costs of capital up to and including 26 percent, alternative II will be chosen. A glance at the present worth profile of II in Figure 8.3 reveals this. The 26 percent IROR of alternative II exceeds the 25 percent IROR of alternative I. For this particular pattern of cash flows, all methods— even the wrong ones—work.

ENTER BENEFIT/COST RATIOS

The preceding section could have been titled "Benefit/Cost Ratios versus Present Worth" and the same kinds of examples and reasoning could have been presented to show that incremental analysis is as necessary in properly employing the benefit/cost ratio method of judging projects as it is in using the internal rate of return method in correct fashion. And with that remark we leave the fascinating subject of Keynes's marginal efficiency of capital.

A FACTUAL STUDY: ELECTROPLATING WITH SOLAR ENERGY

The study investigated the economic feasibility of using solar energy in conjunction with energy derived from natural gas to perform the heating duties in a small electroplating shop.

Within a few years, considering the amount of research now being conducted on solar energy systems, the efficiency and cost of solar heat collectors will cause them to enter the lists of alternatives for energy production along with gas, oil, electricity, and coal. Some estimates indicate that energy reserves in the United States will be greatly depleted within the next two decades. Users of natural gas along the East Coast have been threatened with interruption of service, and this has indeed occurred. Utility interruption that will force temporary shutdowns of manufacturing companies is already a reality. Shutdown, coupled with rising costs of energy, may make solar collectors an attractive alternative to other energy sources much sooner, notwithstanding the elementary state of their efficiency and their high cost.

A small electroplating shop was used as a simple, practical model to test the economic feasibility of solar collectors. The shop's energy requirements were analyzed. These requirements were then filled using commercially available solar collectors. The alternatives considered were continued use of gas versus a mix of gas and solar energy supplied by a solar collector. Solarvoltaic equipment, which converts solar energy directly to electricity, cost too much and was not considered.

A Small Plating Plant

The plant under consideration has a plating capacity of 100 square feet of $\frac{1}{16}$th-inch steel per hour. The process involves passage of the plate through 11 tanks, all of which measure 2 feet by 3 feet by 3 feet, contain 100 gallons, and weigh 833 pounds. Table 8.6 gives the contents of each tank and its temperature.

TABLE 8.6 Tanks and Temperatures

Tank	Temperature (F)
Anodic clean	140
Cold water rinse	70[a]
Copper strike	140
Copper plate	140
Cold water rinse	70
Nickel plate	140
Cold water rinse	70
Chromium plate	110
Recovery	70
Cold water rinse	70
Hot water rinse	140

[a] Room temperature

The energy requirements for the system are needed for:

1. Start up.

2. Heat restoration. Loss of heat occurs because of surface evaporation and radiation, and cool plates.

3. Heating during winter months of entering make-up air for tank ventilation.

4. Drying.

5. Plating current.

Of these energy requirements, the analysis considered only start-up and heat losses. Make-up, energy for drying, and plating current did not come from solar sources.

All the tanks above room temperature operated at 140° F. Assuming a room temperature of 70° F, the start-up requirements were based on a differential temperature of 70° F applied to 833 pounds of liquid. This meant 58,310 BTU were required because a BTU is the amount of energy needed to raise 1 pound of water 1° F. This applied to five tanks. The sixth tank required a rise in temperature of 40° F. Total requirements for start-up came to 324,870 BTUs.

Heat restoration was calculated in two steps—one for evaporation and radiation, the other for the cooling effect of the plates passing through the tanks. The losses due to evaporation and radiation summed to 133,248 BTUs per hour. A 1-inch wall insulation for all tanks was assumed. Plate heat restoration required 2160 BTUs per hour. Heat losses therefore required 135,408 BTUs per hour. For an 8-hour day this came to 1,083,264 BTUs.

System Costs

The gas system used a boiler and heat exchangers to heat the tanks. A solar collector was to be introduced before the boiler with a hot water storage tank to provide a more or less constant temperature source for boiler feed water. Gas heat would still be available on standby to raise the water temperature of the circulatory system to the point necessary to keep the tanks at their operating temperature. This would occur infrequently. Gas costs for standby would run to about $120 per year. Extra costs for pumps, accumulator, differential thermostat, and an insulated storage tank came to $2220.

The collector square footage on which the collector's cost was based was computed using assumptions of a 15-mile per hour wind, the month of January, latitude of 40 degrees north, and a tilt of latitude plus 15 degrees. New England cloud cover conditions were assumed.

The square footage necessary was calculated at 2430. At $11 per square foot cost, plus $1 per square foot installation, the total bill for the collector was $29,160. Thus, total system additions to adapt the gas to gas-plus-solar-supported came to about $31,000.

Gas system costs initially were $3500, with a $900 annual operating cost. Projected life was 10 years for full service, with no salvage value. If used for standby, its life would be extended to 20 years.

The solar collector system was assumed to have a life of 20 years and a salvage value of $5000 with a gas cost of $120 per year.

One week's shutdown would cause a $12,000 loss to the company. Minimum acceptable rate of return before taxes was 20 percent.

Economic Analysis

Figure 8.4 displays the cash flows of the gas system alone, the solar system plus gas, and the differential between the two. Because we are

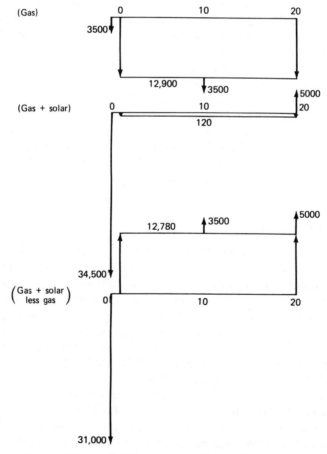

Figure 8.4   Cash flows for an electroplating plant.

TABLE 8.7 Solar Energy Addition with Shutdown

Year	Cash Flow	Discount factors i = 20%	Present Worth	Discount factors i = 40%	Present Worth	Discount factors i = 45%	Present Worth
0	−31,000	1.0000	−31,000	1.0000	−31,000	1.0000	−31,000
1–20	+12,780	4.870	62,239	2.497	31,912	2.221	28,384
10	+3,500	0.1615	565	0.0346	121	0.0243	85
20	+5,000	0.0261	131	0.0012	6	0.0006	3
	Σ +233,100		Σ +31,935		Σ +1,039		Σ −2,528

trying to decide if the solar addition can justify itself, the graph of interest is the last one. It shows the difference between the gas-alone system and the gas-plus-solar system.

The gas-alone system has a small initial cost and a large annual cost if one week's shutdown per year is considered a certainty. (If shutdown cost is not considered at all, the solar addition has a negative rate of return.) The gas-plus-solar system has a huge initial cost and a tiny annual cost. The incremental cash flow shows the $31,000 cost of the solar additions, the $12,000 per year saved by avoiding shutdowns plus the $780 saved annually in gas. It also shows the $3500 avoided because of the 10-year extension in the life of the gas installation and the $5000 salvage value of the solar system.

Table 8.7 displays the incremental cash flow. The present worth of the incremental cash flow at 20 percent is $31,935, which indicates acceptance under the present worth criterion. This is not, of course, the answer sought by the internal rate of return criterion. Trials at 40 and 45 percent show an internal rate of return of 41+ (41.46) percent. This more than meets the criterion of 20 percent cost of capital before taxes, and thus the project is acceptable.

Incommensurables

The main use of the solar addition is the avoidance of shutdowns. The report does not attempt to measure the inconvenience of such occurrences and the loss of customer confidence that is bound to occur if deliveries cannot be made on time. Shutdowns may also mean labor difficulties.

Fuel costs are likely to grow—a fact that does not appear in the cash flow of the gas-only system. The probability that shutdown periods may be extended or may occur more frequently also does not appear in the costs of the gas-only system.

The gas costs of the back-up to the solar system would increase at the same rate as the gas costs for the gas-alone system. A particularly cloudy year would cause them to become larger but would not affect their average over 20 years.

Space limitations have not been mentioned. The square footage of the solar collector is appreciable. It could be mounted on the roof of the plant or in a parking lot, but it must be recognized that its efficiency depends on its never being shadowed by surrounding buildings. Thus, a location in a small industrial park or in the suburbs is probably advisable.

Finally, if gas service can be guaranteed once again, solar collectors at present cost and efficiency will have difficulty in becoming economically feasible.

9

Multiple Alternatives

Multiple alternatives are encountered when a particular problem has more than one solution. In the pages that follow, I discuss the situation in which three or more alternative solutions exist but in which only one can be selected. The alternatives are mutually exclusive. If one is chosen, none of the others may be chosen. The problems of interdependency are avoided at this stage of discussion.

INTERNAL RATE OF RETURN

Imagine a situation in which five plans have been suggested to accomplish the same purpose. The minimum attractive rate of return in this situation is 10 percent. All plans have 100 percent resale value at the end of 20 years. Capital available is 130 monetary units. Only one of the plans will be selected as the solution. Table 9.1 summarizes the plans. Notice that the plans have been ordered according to increasing investment.

A solution of this example by means of the internal rate of return criterion requires that we use the notion of incrementality. The logic in incremental analysis goes something like this: We are interested in that plan which will return an incremental rate of return of 10 percent or more, because our minimum attractive rate of return has been cited as 10 percent. The status quo is the unwritten alternative that precedes Plan 1. What we will do, then, is to compare the first plan with the status quo to find out if the investment will return greater than 10 percent. If it does, we will then compare the next plan with it and observe whether the plan with the next higher investment is better than the first plan. We will do this by comparing the increased investment required by the next plan with the increased receipts—comparing the increase in benefits with the increase in costs—to find

TABLE 9.1   Five Plans

Plan	1	2	3	4	5
Total investment	80	100	110	115	130
Annual net receipts	20	21	23	24	25

out if it is worth our while to spend the extra money to receive the extra benefits. We will always compare the next increment of investment with the plan that has proved to be acceptable preceding it. We will never compare a loan requiring an investment with a plan that has failed our test. Our criterion of choice will be whether the incremental rate of return is equal to or greater than 10 percent. If we proceed, we will find that the incremental rate of return for Plan 1 over the status quo is 25 percent, as follows:

$$\overset{N}{\Sigma} B_N(P/F, i^*, N) = \overset{N}{\Sigma} C_N(P/F, i^*, N)$$
$$20(P/A, i^*, 20) + 80(P/F, i^*, 20) = 80$$

At 25%:

$$20(3.954) + 80(0.0115) = 80$$
$$79.08 + 0.92 = 80$$
$$80 = 80$$

Twenty-five percent exceeds our minimum attractive rate of return of 10 percent. Therefore, we will accept Plan 1 (see Table 9.2).

TABLE 9.2   Comparing the Plans

Comparison	Plan 1 over Status Quo	Plan 2 over Plan 1	Plan 3 over Plan 1	Plan 4 over Plan 3	Plan 5 over Plan 4
Incremental investment	80	20	30	5	15
Incremental receipts	20	1	3	1	1
Incremental internal rate of return (%)	25.0	5.0	10.0	20.0	6.6

Plan 2 requires an extra investment of 20, the difference between 100 and 80. It will return extra net receipts over Plan 1 of 1, the difference between 21 and 20. This is an incremental rate of return of but 5 percent. (Calculations are similar to those of the preceding problem in which 25 percent was determined. You are invited to perform them.) Therefore Plan 2 should be dropped from consideration.

When we consider Plan 3, we should relate it to the previous successful alternative, which is Plan 1. Plan 3 requires an extra investment over Plan 1 of 30, the difference between 110 and 80. It will return an annual net receipt of 23 and an incremental net receipt of 3. The internal rate of return of this differential cash flow is 10 percent. According to our criterion, we should accept Plan 3 because the rate of return on our extra investment meets the criterion we have set up— that the minimum attractive rate of return be 10 percent.

Plan 4 requires an extra investment of 5 and will return extra annual net receipts of 1 when we compare it to Plan 3. Our incremental internal rate of return on Plan 4 is 20 percent. Therefore, we should accept at least Plan 4.

It remains only to compare Plan 5 with Plan 4. Plan 5 requires an extra investment of 15 monetary units and will return extra annual net receipts of 1 percent. The internal rate of return of this differential cash flow is about 6.6 percent. Plan 5 does not meet our criteria of 10 percent minimum attractive rate of return, and therefore it should be rejected. Our decision is to accept Plan 4.

The observant reader may have noted a curious relation between the internal rate of return as determined by the usual calculations, performed on page 104 where the 25 percent rate of return was found, and the annual rate of return determined by dividing the incremental investment by the incremental receipts. They are the same—20 is 25 percent of 80—and the reason they are the same is that 100 percent of the first cost of the investment is recovered at the end of 20 years. The investor experiences all the annual benefit as applied to his original capital. No part of that annual benefit need be withheld, as it were, for making up the difference between first cost and salvage value.

It is also worth noting that the length of life is not in point in determining the internal rate of return in this highly specialized case. Whether the life be one or 20 or 50 years is irrelevant to the internal rate of return so long as all the investment is recovered at the end of the investment's life. (See the Appendix at the end of this chapter.)

Table 9.3 shows the internal rate of return on the total cash flow. The internal rate of return on the total cash flow is included to illustrate the fact that it may lead to incorrect solutions. If, for example, we were mistakenly to accept the internal rate of return on the total cash flow as a criterion, we would possibly choose Plan 1, as having the

TABLE 9.3   The Internal Rate of Return on Total Cash Flow

Plan	1	2	3	4	5
Internal rate of return on total cash flow (%)	25.0	21.0	20.9	20.8	19.2

highest internal rate of return. This would be incorrect, as we have seen. Or we might choose Plan 5 because it has a total investment greater than any of the others and an internal rate of return on the total cash flow greater than 10 percent. This criterion also would lead to an incorrect answer. There are a number of other criteria we could use in relation to an incorrect method. The only logical way to proceed, however, is according to the method of incremental analysis. Incremental analysis is analogous to the standard microeconomic problem of choosing the point at which the optimal production will occur when marginal costs are rising. The rule requires that as long as the marginal revenue exceeds the marginal costs, more units should be produced. (This will be explained in Chapter 18 entitled "How the Price System Allocates Resources Efficiently.") At exactly the point at which marginal revenue equals marginal cost, production should be stabilized.

Confusion as to the correct method of using the internal rate of return has resulted in incorrect advice in much of the literature concerned with investment decision. Readers should be careful to observe whether or not incremental analysis is being used.

It is possible to solve multiple alternative situations using methods other than the internal rate of return. The same incremental analysis should be applied in all methods and must be applied in the case of benefit/cost ratios, whether based on the present worth of the benefits divided by the present worth of the costs or annual benefits divided by annual costs.

BENEFIT/COST RATIO SOLUTION

An underwater tunnel can be constructed in three ways. Each way excludes the other two. Opportunity cost of resources is 10 percent, and the economic life of all alternatives is 20 years. All ways are equally risky. The costs are so set up that it is easier to find annual costs. Benefits appear annually. A benefit/cost ratio approach will be best understood by those deciding on the project. Table 9.4 shows the investment required by each way, and the annual net benefits.

Calculations are shown in Table 9.5. A final line, B/C, total benefit/cost ratio, is shown for discussion purposes.

TABLE 9.4 Three Plans for an
Underwater Tunnel

Alternative	1	2	3
Investment	130	152	184
Annual Net benefits	16	22	26

TABLE 9.5 Incremental Benefit/Cost Ratio Calculations

Alternative	1	2 over 1	3 over 2
Incremental annual benefit	16	6	4
Incremental annual investment cost	15.3	$17.9 - 15.3 = 2.6$	$21.6 - 17.9 = 3.7$
$\Delta B/\Delta C$	1.05	$\dfrac{6}{2.6} = 2.31$	$\dfrac{4}{3.7} = 1.08$
Benefit/cost ratio	1.05	1.23	1.20

Alternative 1 qualifies with an incremental benefit/cost ratio of
1.05. (The incremental benefit and incremental cost in this case is in
comparison with the "do nothing" alternative.) The figures for the
incremental annual investment cost were obtained by multiplying the
investment cost by the capital recovery factor (A/P, 10, 20). Alternative
2 also qualifies with an incremental benefit/cost ratio of 2.31, thus
excluding alternative 1 from consideration. Finally, alternative 3 wins
out over alternative 2 with an incremental benefit/cost ratio of 1.08.
Alternative 3 is therefore chosen.

Had the analysis been conducted incorrectly, using total benefit/
cost ratios for each alternative, alternative 2 would have been chosen
with the resultant waste of public resources.

A FACTUAL STUDY: THE CHARLESTON AVENUE BRIDGE

In January 1974, a routine inspection of the Charleston Avenue bridge
in a small southern city revealed evidence of structural deterioration.
The bridge was important because it connected the southern with the
northern section on one of the principal streets. It was one of only four
bridges across the Seminole river, which divided the city. In addition,
Charleston Avenue was the main street of the central business district.
Subsequently, more detailed examinations produced a finding that the
cantilever-supported curb lanes were unsafe for heavy trucks and

buses. As a consequence, a 3-ton load limit on the bridge was enforced.

The administration of the city was considering alternative ways to repair or rebuild the bridge. Average daily traffic volumes were at or above capacity levels in 1973. A major increase in traffic across the Charleston Avenue bridge was not anticipated in the decade 1974–1984 because of a new, fifth bridge expected to be completed in 1974, which would take care of increased traffic in the city. But the Charleston Avenue bridge was expected to carry its share of the traffic, which meant capacity operation. Therefore, at the least, minor repairs to the bridge were necessary to prevent further deterioration leading to volume as well as load restrictions.

A report was prepared to compare three renovation alternatives by means of incremental benefit/cost analysis. The remainder of this study summarizes the report and its conclusions.

The Charleston Avenue bridge was an open spandrel arch concrete bridge constructed in 1909 and widened in 1960. Widening was accomplished by the addition of 12-foot cantilever sections to both sides. The bridge consisted of four 12-foot traffic lanes and two 4-foot pedestrian walkways on a 60-foot deck built in a 120-foot right of way. The bridge was 945 feet long. Gas and water mains, major telephone cables, and ducts for primary electric distribution lines crossed the river on the bridge. Over the years, some 16 inches of paving materials were added in successive layers to the deck. This extra material greatly increased dead load without adding to structural strength.

Costs

Bridge user costs formed part of the analysis of the three alternatives reviewed in the report. These costs were as follows:

Cost per vehicle mile:	
Passenger cars and delivery vans	$0.05
Heavy trucks and buses	0.25
Cost per vehicle minute:	
Passenger cars and delivery vans	0.06
Heavy trucks and buses	0.12

Because the report was prepared in haste, repair and construction costs were preliminary estimates computed on the basis of square feet of bridge surface without regard to specific design or construction details. Nor were detailed studies of the effects of the several alternatives on traffic flow patterns, volumes, and average speeds developed.

The authors of the report—city engineers aided by the state highway department—had sufficient experience in similar cases that the numbers were thought to be reliable for the purposes of an economic analysis.

Three Alternatives

Alternative A

The first alternative was to make minor repairs sufficient to prevent further deterioration. Because this would not strengthen the bridge, load restrictions would have to remain in force. The economic life of the repaired bridge was estimated to be 10 years. The benefit of this alternative was ascribed to the continued use of the two outside lanes by traffic of three tons or less during the 10-year life of the bridge. The two outside lanes would have to be abandoned in 1977—three years hence—if the minor repairs of this alternative were not performed. The cost of closing the two outside lanes to passenger car traffic and small delivery vehicles was estimated by the cost of extra vehicle miles that would result from having to divert about 25 percent of current traffic to a nearby bridge. (See the "without" alternative of Figure 9.1.) Average speed of 20 miles per hour was assumed. Thus, the major benefit of the alternative was the continued use of these lanes after 1977.

Loss of the lanes in 1977 would have reduced average traffic by about 6000 crossings per day. By estimating certain centroids of traffic origin and destination derived from previous studies performed by the

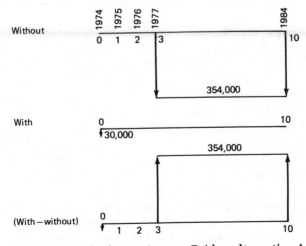

Figure 9.1   Charleston Avenue Bridge alternative A.

city, it was determined that the distance the traffic would have been forced to divert was 0.7 miles. Time per trip was:

$$(0.7 \text{ mi/trip}//20 \text{ mi/hr})(60 \text{ min/hr}) = 2.1 \text{ min/trip}$$

The cost of distance and time by passenger cars at 6000 crossings per day was:

$$0.7 \text{ mi/trip} \times \$0.05/\text{mi} \times 6000 \text{ trips/day} = \$210/\text{day}$$
$$2.1 \text{ min/trip} \times \$0.06/\text{min} \times 6000 \text{ trips/day} = \$760/\text{day}$$
$$\overline{ \$970/\text{day}}$$
$$\$970/\text{day} \times 365 \text{ days/year} = \$354,000/\text{year}$$

This was the annual benefit of the first alternative, delayed three years on a "with–without" basis. The cost of the first alternative was $30,000—the cost of the "with" alternative of Figure 9.1.

Alternative B

The second option considered was to strengthen the bridge to accommodate bus and heavy truck traffic. This approach involved removing excess material from the bridge deck, relocating the utility lines to other crossings, erecting girders under the cantilever sections, and installing a new roadway slab. As in the first alternative, the economic life of the strengthened bridge was estimated at 10 years. The cost of the "without" option was the denial of the bridge to all vehicles. Dollar costs were determined by estimating the costs of routing all heavy vehicles, as well as light ones, over another bridge (see Figure 9.2).

In addition to repair costs, extra vehicle operating costs resulting from closing the bridge for as long as six months had to be taken into account. From traffic counts taken subsequent to discovery of deterioration, it was estimated that heavy vehicles accounted for 6.7 percent of bridge traffic immediately prior to the imposition of load limits.

It was assumed further that as a result of greater use of mass transit, heavy truck and bus traffic would increase slightly to an average of 7.0 percent over the 10 years of economic life of the repaired bridge. The same assumptions as to traffic origin and destination were made as in the first alternative. The traffic speed of 20 miles per hour of the first alternative was also assumed for the second.

The major benefit of this alternative was to avoid load or volume restrictions of any kind on the Charleston Avenue bridge, either at time zero or three years hence. (See the "with–without" alternative of Figure 9.2.) This option would permit use of the bridge by all vehicles

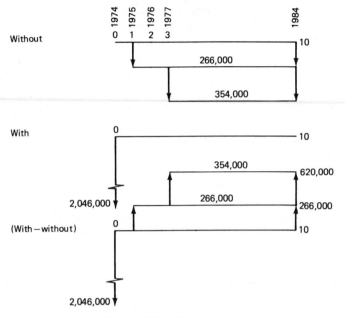

Figure 9.2   Alternative B.

as soon as reconstruction was completed. An average number of crossings over the 10-year life of the rebuilt bridge was estimated to be
24,600 per day. Distance and time saved under this option were the
same as those calculated for the light vehicles: 0.7 miles and 2.1
minutes per trip. Because 1700 heavy vehicles per day would be
affected (24,600 × 0.07), the savings produced by not having to reroute
all heavy vehicles were:

$$0.7 \text{ mi/trip} \times \$0.25/\text{mi} \times 1,700 \text{ trips/day} \quad = \$300/\text{day}$$
$$2.1 \text{ min/trip} \times 0.12/\text{min} \times 1,700 \text{ trips/day} \quad = \$430/\text{day}$$

$$\overline{}$$
$$\$730/\text{day}$$

$$\$730/\text{day} \times 365 \text{ days/yr} = \$266,000/\text{yr}$$

This savings would result as soon as construction was completed in
late 1974.

The savings produced by not having to reroute light vehicles that
would not have begun until 1977 were as those computed in the
previous alternative—$354,000 delayed three years.

Cost of this alternative appeared under two separate headings:
increased vehicle user costs incurred because of the necessity of using
alternate routes while the bridge was under repair and the costs of the
repairs themselves.

Increased vehicle user costs were calculated by distributing the traffic displaced (22,500 automobiles and 1600 heavy vehicles) by closing the bridge for repairs to the three older bridges and the new bridge that would be completed in 1974, the same year as construction would be started and completed—that is, time zero. Congestion was taken into account in these estimates. The weighted average distance was then computed as 0.9 mile per trip. Another effect of congestion was taken into account by assuming that average traffic speed would drop to 15 miles per hour. The extra time resulting from this distance and this speed were:

$$(0.9 \text{ mi/trip}//15 \text{ mi/hr}) \times 60 \text{ min/hr} = 3.6 \text{ min/trip}$$

The extra expenses resulting from automobiles using alternate routes were:

$$0.9 \text{ mi/trip} \times \$0.05/\text{mi} \times 22,500 \text{ trips/day} \quad = \$1,010/\text{day}$$
$$3.6 \text{ min/trip} \times \$0.06/\text{min} \times 22,500 \text{ trips/day} = \$4,860/\text{day}$$

and for heavy vehicles were:

$$0.9 \text{ mi/trip} \times \$0.25/\text{mi} \times 1600 \text{ trips/day} \quad = \$ \ 360/\text{day}$$
$$3.6 \text{ min/trip} \times \$0.12/\text{min} \times 1600 \text{ trips/day} \quad = \$ \ 690/\text{day}$$
$$\overline{\$6,920}$$
$$\$6920/\text{day} \times 180 \text{ days} = \$1,246,000$$

The costs of the repairs themselves were estimated at $800,000. The total cost of this alternative was therefore $2,046,000.

Alternative C

The third alternative was to rebuild the Charleston Avenue bridge, widening it to six lanes with provision for a hike–and–bike way. This option also included removal of excess material, relocation of utility lines, installation of a new bridge deck, and design features to maintain the appearance of the original arches. The economic life of the rebuilt bridge was estimated to be 20 years. The major benefit from this alternative resulted from the relief of traffic congestion on the Charleston Avenue bridge and the Mowbray Street bridge nearby. As with the previous alternative, increased vehicle user costs resulting from the closing of the bridge for a year had to be included in the costs. This fact required some adjustments to the cash flow worths, as we will see. No attempt was made to quantify the recreational value of the hike–and–bike way or the aesthetic value of the arches.

The benefits caused by relief of congestion were calculated for the two bridges affected: the Charleston Avenue bridge itself and the Mowbray Street bridge immediately west of it. Consistent with an assumed economic life of 20 years, calculations of dollar benefits were based on projected 1984 traffic volumes of 25,000 crossings per day for the Charleston Avenue bridge and 18,000 crossings per day for the Mowbray street bridge. It was estimated that the two new lanes on the former would reduce congestion on both bridges, increasing average speed by 5 miles per hour, from 20 to 25 miles per hour, for a distance of one mile on both routes. Thus:

$$(1.0 \text{ mi}//20 \text{ mi/hr}) \times 60 \text{ min/hr} = 3.0 \text{ min/trip}$$
less $\quad (1.0 \text{ mi}//25 \text{ mi/hr}) \times 60 \text{ min/hr} = 2.4 \text{ min/trip}$
$$\text{Time saved per trip} = 0.6 \text{ min/trip}$$

Total average daily crossings for the two bridges would be 43,000: 39,500 automobiles and 3,500 heavy vehicles. (These were 1984 estimates at half way through the life of the bridge.)

Savings in user costs by automobile operators were:

$$0.6 \text{ min/trip} \times \$0.06/\text{min} \times 39,500 \text{ trips/day} = \$1,420/\text{day}$$

and by operators of heavy vehicles:

$$0.6 \text{ min/trip} \times \$0.12/\text{min} \times 3,500 \text{ trips/day} = \underline{\$ \ 250/\text{day}}$$
$$\$1,670/\text{day}$$
$$\$1670/\text{day} \times 365 \text{ days/yr} = \$610,000/\text{yr}$$

This is shown as the benefit of the "with" alternative of Figure 9.3.

The cost of denying heavy vehicles the use of the new bridge, calculated for alternative B and adjusted for increased average daily traffic, was included in the "without" alternative. Daily crossings of heavy vehicles of the new bridge in 1985 were based on an increased percentage of heavy vehicles to 8 percent:

$$25,000/\text{day} \times 0.08 = 2,000/\text{day}$$

Adjusting the $730 per day of alternative B upward by the ratio of the heavy vehicle crossings:

$$\frac{2,000}{1,700} \times \$266,000 = \$314,000/\text{yr}$$

The dollar cost of $354,000, delayed three years, calculated for

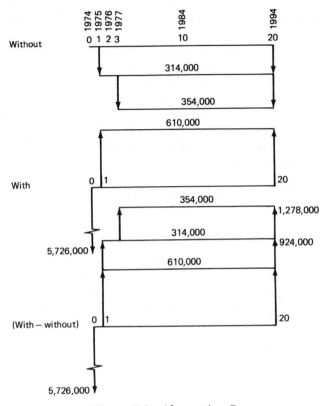

Figure 9.3   Alternative C.

alternative A was also included in the "without" alternative for the years 1977 to 1994. Figure 9.3 opposite the "without" cash flow for alternative C shows this.

Extra vehicle user costs as a result of closing the bridge for repairs were the $6920 per day calculated for alternative B. Costs for the one-year reconstruction and widening period were:

$$\$6920/\text{day} \times 365 \text{ days} = \$2,526,000$$

Reconstruction and widening costs were estimated at $3,200,000. These costs are shown as the cost of the "with" alternative.

Figure 9.3 illustrates the cash flow associated with the "with–without" situation. The $314,000 annually for 20 years shows as a benefit of not closing the bridge to heavy vehicles for that period. The $354,000 annually from 1977 to 1994 is the benefit of not closing the two curb lanes in 1977. The same figure shows that the $610,000, which accrues as a savings from the relief of congestion, is a benefit. It also shows the costs at time zero summing to $5,726,000.

The Incremental Benefit/Cost Ratio Analysis

The procedure followed was to compare alternative A with the status quo to discover whether or not A qualified. Reference to Figure 9.1 opposite the cash flow labeled "with–without" for alternative A reveals that we must compare a benefit of $354,000 from 1977 through 1984 with a first cost of $30,000. The study chose a 10 percent opportunity cost of capital and the benefit/cost as a measure of worth. It was also decided that the benefit/cost ratio should be formed by the annual benefits divided by the annual costs. The $354,000 benefit was brought back to time zero by multiplying by the series present worth factor and the present worth factor for single payments; this result was spread forward by the capital recovery factor. The cost was spread forward by the capital recovery factor:

$$B/C = \frac{354,000(P/A, 10, 7)(P/F, 10, 3)(A/P, 10, 10)}{30,000(A/P, 10, 10)}$$

$$= \frac{354,000(4.868)(0.7513)(0.16275)}{30,000(0.16275)}$$

$$= 43.2$$

In this calculation the incremental benefit/cost ratio is the same as the total benefit/cost ratio for the alternative. Obviously, it was possible to cancel out the capital recovery factor from both numerator and denominator, which would have been equivalent to using the present worth of the benefits and the present worth of the costs. For reasons of consistency, this was not done.

Because alternative A qualified, alternative B was compared with it incrementally. This amounted to comparing the "with–without" cash flow diagrams shown in Figure 9.4 for the two alternatives. The result is shown in Figure 9.4 as B–A. Comparing incremental benefits with incremental costs:

$$\Delta B/\Delta C = \frac{266,000}{2,016,000(A/P, 10, 10)}$$

$$= \frac{266,000}{2,016,000(0.16275)}$$

$$= \frac{266,000}{328,000}$$

$$= 0.8$$

Alternative B does not qualify and disappears from the analysis.

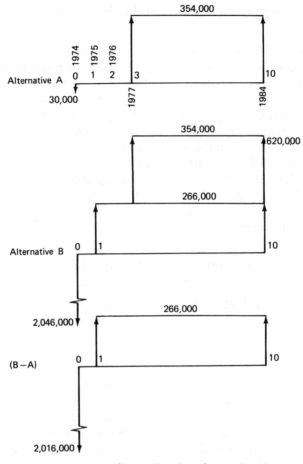

Figure 9.4   *Alternative B—alternative A.*

Alternative C was compared with alternative A as shown in Figure 9.5. The cash flow is the "with–without" cash flow for alternative A from Figure 9.1 but with the addition of another cycle of investment and benefit in order to equalize the lives. This made the graphic subtraction easy. (The annual cost and annual benefit figures from the alternative A calculation could have been graphed instead with the same final result.) The middle cash flow of Figure 9.5 is the "with–without" graph for alternative C from Figure 9.3. The bottom diagram is the incremental cash flow. Its ratio is:

$$\Delta B/\Delta C = \frac{314,000 + 610,000 + 30,000(P/F, 10, 10)(A/P, 10, 20)}{5,696,000(A/P, 10, 20)}$$

$$= \frac{314{,}000 + 610{,}000 + 30{,}000(0.3855)(0.11746)}{5{,}696{,}000(0.11746)}$$

$$= \frac{925{,}000}{669{,}000}$$

$$= 1.4$$

Alternative C was chosen.

Comments

The hike–and–bike way of alternative C was important to the analysis even though it was not quantified. It reinforced the decision in favor of C. The aesthetic value of the bridge arches also could not be

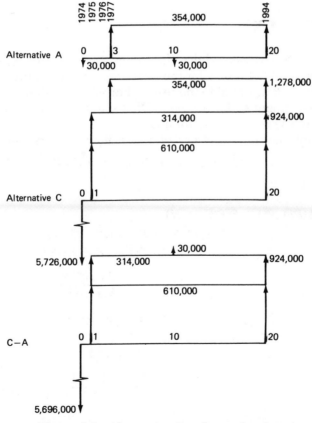

Figure 9.5 Alternative C—alternative A.

quantified—or was not. A comparison that would have quantified the cost of retaining the arches would have measured the difference in cost of a utilitarian new bridge with all the features of the reconstructed and widened old bridge except the arches. In a supply sense the decision makers would have known the aesthetic value of the arches. They would not have known their value in a demand sense, however. Perhaps the public would have valued the arches at 10 times the cost of keeping them. Keeping the arches also reinforced the decision in favor of C.

Average traffic values over 10 and 20 years were used in the analysis. A further refinement would have employed a gradient cost as the traffic increased. The authors of the report believed that this would not have materially changed the decision or the incremental benefit/cost ratios.

The study illustrates clearly the complexities of putting a name to costs and benefits and the immense usefulness of the "with–without" criterion in helping the analyst name the costs and benefits.

APPENDIX

On page 105 it was stated that the annual rate of return is the same as the internal rate of return for the total cash flow when the investment at time zero (P) is equal to the residual or salvage value (F) at the end of the investment's life. A proof of that statement, when a level payment only (A) is involved, follows.

The internal rate of return of a cash flow appears when:

$$A(P/A, i^*, N) + F(P/F, i^*, N) = P$$

Because $P = F$:

$$A(P/A, i^*) + P(P/F, i^*, N) = P$$
$$A(P/A, i^*, N) = P - P(P/F, i^*, N)$$
$$= P(1 - (P/F, i^*, N))$$

$$A/P = \frac{1 - (P/F, i^*, N)}{(P/A, i^*, N)}$$

$$= \frac{1 - \dfrac{1}{(1 + i^*)^N}}{\dfrac{(1 + i^*)^N - 1}{i^*(1 + i^*)^N}}$$

$$= \frac{(1 + i^*)^N - 1}{(1 + i^*)^N} \times \frac{i^*(1 + i^*)^N}{(1 + i^*)^N - 1}$$

$$A/P = i^*$$

which is what I have called the annual rate of return.

REFERENCES

Samuelson, Paul, *Economics*, 5th ed. New York: McGraw-Hill, 1961, pp. 523–532.

Grant, Eugene L., and W. Grant Ireson, *Principles of Engineering Economy*, 5th ed. New York: Ronald, 1970, pp. 213–250.

10

Special Problems

A few special situations present themselves—some frequently, some occasionally—that require explanation. They are treated in this chapter.

LARGE VERSUS SMALL INVESTMENTS

Some students of the subject—and some authors—seem to find difficulty in the handling of very large investments as compared to very small investments. Mutually exclusive investments are presumed. The difficulty seems to lie in the failure of the analyst to remember that funds on hand must amount to the large investment for it to be considered at all; if the small investment is chosen, the difference between the large and the small investment can be invested at the opportunity cost of resources. The opportunity cost of resources means that investments may be made freely at that interest rate or it means nothing at all.

Example 10.1 ──

Consider two mutually exclusive alternatives. Alternative 1 requires an investment of $1000, and alternative 2 requires an investment of $1,000,000. (The example is extreme in order to illustrate the point.) The opportunity cost of capital is 10 percent. The results of Table 10.1 appear after discounting. Evidently, the alternatives are equally attractive. If we choose alternative 1, we hold an investment whose present worth is $1000 and in addition $999,000, which we can invest at 10 percent (the opportunity cost of resources). The present worth of the $999,000 is, of course, $999,000, both on the benefit and the cost

TABLE 10.1 Large versus Small Investments

| Alternative | Present Worth | | Benefits–Costs |
	Costs	Benefits	
1	1,000	2,000	1,000
2	1,000,000	1,001,000	1,000

side. Our alternatives really appear as in Table 10.2. The investments are still equally attractive.

Let us try the benefit/cost ratio method on the same problem. The figures of Table 10.3 appear. The alternatives remain equally attractive.

When an analyst tries to use total benefit/cost ratios as a basis for comparison, his error causes confusion because, although the benefit/cost ratio of alternative 1 remains 2.0, the benefit/cost ratio of alternative 2 becomes 1,001,000/1,000,000 equal to 1.1001. He is thus incorrectly led to choose alternative 1 rather than recognizing that he should be indifferent between the two investments.

LARGE ANNUAL COST VERSUS SMALL ANNUAL COST

A variation on the theme of the previous section is to use large versus small annual *costs* in place of large versus small *investments*. Even to an experienced analyst it may seem that for projects of equal risk and equal annual profits the project requiring the smaller annual commitment of resources should be chosen. The line of reasoning seems to be that it is better not to have to tie up more resources than are necessary to produce the profit. The projects are, of course, mutually exclusive.

What is being forgotten is that if the agency has resources enough

TABLE 10.2 Large versus Small Investments: All Funds Invested

| Alternative | Present Worth | | Benefits–Costs |
	Costs	Benefits	
1	1,000	2,000	1,000
	999,000	999,000	0
	1,000,000	1,001,000	1,000
2	1,000,000	1,001,000	1,000

TABLE 10.3 Large versus Small
Investments: B/C Ratio Method

Alternative	Incremental B/C ratio
1	$\dfrac{2000}{1000} = 2.0$
2	$\dfrac{1,001,000 - 2000}{1,000,000 - 1000} = \dfrac{999,000}{999,000} = 1.0$

to meet the higher annual cost—and if it does not, it should not be considering the project at all—then it has enough to meet the other project's lower annual cost and have money left over equal to the difference between the annual cost of the costlier project and the annual cost of the less expensive project. This difference can be invested at the opportunity cost of resources, and both projects will be found to have exactly equal profits for exactly equal annual costs.

It should be emphasized that the projects should be of precisely equal risk. If for some reason they are not, then the foregoing discussion does not apply and the less risky project will be chosen.

EQUAL INITIAL INVESTMENTS: BENEFIT/COST RATIO ERROR

Project 1 has an initial cost of $500,000. It produces revenues of $110,000 annually for 10 years, from which annual operating costs of $10,000 may be deducted, giving net benefits of $100,000 per year. Project 2 also costs $500,000, but it produces annual benefits of $400,000 for 10 years. Operating costs are $300,000 per year, so net benefits are once again $100,000 per year. If the opportunity cost of resources is 10 percent, which project should be chosen? (The projects are mutally exclusive and have precisely the same amount of risk associated with them.)

The difference between the two alternatives is zero, shown by the horizontal line in Figure 10.1. And therefore, the analyst will be indifferent between the two projects.

It may seem that the total benefit/cost ratio of project 1 may be computed as 1.20.

$$B/C = \frac{110,000(P/A, 10, 10)}{500,000 + 10,000(P/A, 10, 10)}$$

$$= \frac{110,000(6.144)}{500,000 + 10,000(6.144)}$$

$$= \frac{675,840}{500,000 + 61,440}$$

$$= 1.20$$

The total benefit/cost ratio of the second project is 1.05.

$$B/C = \frac{400,000(6.144)}{500,000 + 300,000(6.144)}$$

$$= \frac{2,457,600}{500,000 + 1,843,200}$$

$$= \frac{2,457,600}{2,343,200}$$

$$= 1.05$$

Therefore, project 1 should be chosen. Project 1 may also look more desirable because of the lesser amount of annual resources necessary.

Three errors are present in this view. The first is the mistake of using total benefit/cost ratios rather than incremental benefit/cost

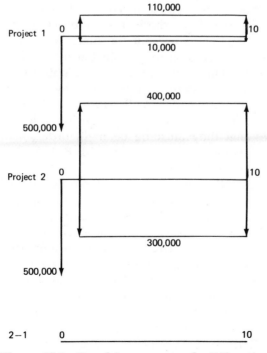

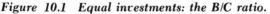

Figure 10.1 Equal investments: the B/C ratio.

ratios. The second is the failure to net out benefits and costs at each year. If this is done first, it becomes obvious that the *B/C* ratios of project 1 and project 2 are equal. The third is forgetting that $300,000 less $10,000, or $290,000, may be invested at the opportunity cost of capital. This latter move will not, of course, change the incremental analysis.

EQUAL INITIAL INVESTMENTS: INTERNAL RATE OF RETURN ERROR

Two mutually exclusive investments, each with a life of four years, present the cash flows as shown in Table 10.4. The incremental cash flow is also shown. Notice that the initial investments are the same at $10,000,000. When the present worths are plotted at 6, 10, 18, 25, and 35 percent, the present worth profile of Figure 10.2 appears. We have seen this pattern of present worth profiles with two mutually exclusive alternatives crossing in the positive present worth area before in Chapter 8 on the internal rate of return criterion. There we found that is was possible to use the internal rate of return criterion on such a pattern of cash flows, providing incremental analysis were used. We saw that incremental analysis was the only correct method. Let us try that same method on this equal initial investment problem. The top portion of Table 10.5 shows the favored alternative at each opportunity cost of capital. At 35 percent the incremental rate of return of alternative B over A is not applicable because A does not qualify above 27 percent. This seems perfectly straightforward.

Now we notice that there is no reason why we should not begin with alternative B rather than A. Because they both have the same initial investment and because the ordering rule for considering projects states that they must be taken in order of increasing initial investment, we may as well begin with B, as is done in the middle portion of Table 10.5.

The present worth profile of A − B is the reflection of the profile for B − A (B − A rotated 180 degrees). A − B has the same internal rate of return of 11 percent as B − A. See Figure 10.2.

Now we receive contradictory instructions relative to the top portion of Table 10.5, yet we have followed the correct procedure exactly. To resolve the dilemma we turn to the present worth method in the bottom portion of Table 10.5 and discover that it gives us the same indications as did the middle portion of the table.

Which oracle are we to believe? What is wrong? Any synthetic rules such as, "Choose the higher IROR of the two, check with the incremental IROR of that project over the other one, compare with

TABLE 10.4 Equal Initial Investments: The Internal Rate of Return (in $000,000)

	Alternative			Present Worth @ 6%				Present Worth @ 10%			
Year	A	B	B − A	(P/F, 6%, N)	A	B	B − A	(P/F, 10%, N)	A	B	B − A
0	−10	−10	0	1.000	−10	−10	0	1.000	−10	−10	0
1	2	7	5	0.943	1.87	6.60	4.72	0.909	1.82	6.35	4.55
2	4	5	1	0.890	3.56	4.45	0.89	0.826	3.30	4.12	0.83
3	6	4	−2	0.840	5.05	3.36	−1.68	0.751	4.51	3.00	−1.50
4	8	2	−6	0.792	6.34	1.58	−4.75	0.683	5.46	1.37	−4.10
					Σ 6.82	5.99	−0.82		Σ 5.09	4.84	−0.12

Present Worth @ 18%				Present Worth @ 25%				Present Worth @ 35%			
(P/F, 18%, N)	A	B	B − A	(P/F, 25%, N)	A	B	B − A	(P/F, 35%, N)	A	B	B − A
1.000	−10	−10	0	1.000	−10	−10	0	1.000	−10	−10	0
0.847	1.68	5.92	4.24	0.800	1.60	5.60	4.00	0.741	1.48	5.19	3.71
0.718	2.87	3.59	0.72	0.640	2.56	3.20	0.64	0.549	2.20	2.74	0.55
0.609	3.66	2.44	−1.22	0.512	3.07	2.04	−1.02	0.406	2.43	1.62	−0.81
0.516	4.12	1.03	−3.10	0.410	3.28	0.82	−2.46	0.301	2.40	0.60	−1.81
	Σ 2.33	2.98	+0.64		Σ 0.51	1.66	+1.16		Σ −1.49	0.16	+1.64

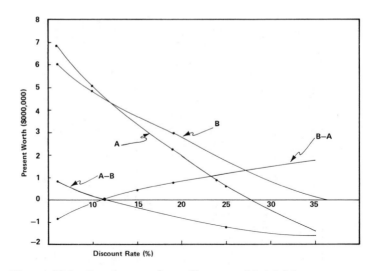

Figure 10.2   Present worth profiles: equal initial investments.

TABLE 10.5   Equal Initial Investments: Internal Rate of Return Criterion

i (%)	IROR$_A$ (%)	IROR$_{B-A}$ (%)	Decision Favors
6	27	11	B
10	27	11	B
18	27	11	A
25	27	11	A
35	27	N.A.	B

i (%)	IROR$_B$ (%)	IROR$_{A-B}$ (%)	Decision Favors
6	36	11	A
10	36	11	A
18	36	11	B
25	36	11	B
35	36	11	B

i (%)	P.W.$_A$ @ i ($000,000)	P.W.$_B$ @ i ($000,000)	Decision Favors
6	6.82	5.99	A
10	5.09	4.84	A
18	2.33	2.98	B
25	0.51	1.66	B
35	−1.49	0.16	B

opportunity cost of capital, and decide," do not work, as you may prove to yourself.

What is wrong is that the initial investments are not incremental, and therefore no incremental analysis can be based on them. But incremental differences do exist during the first period even though they are differences in benefits. Thus, we can order the projects and take the incremental difference between them such that the first cash flow encountered in the incremental cash flow diagram is an outflow. To do this it is necessary to order the projects with the algebraically larger cash flow shown first and the projects with the algebraically smaller cash flow shown second. The difference between the cash flows will then be found by following the usual rule of second cash flow minus first cash flow.[1]

In the example we have been considering in Table 10.4, alternative B with a +7 cash flow at the end of the second year will be shown first, and alternative A with a +2 cash flow at the end of the same year shown second. The increment, A − B, will show the opposite signs of the cash flow B − A of Table 10.4. The incremental cash flow will thus begin with a negative, −5, and the decision analysis will proceed as in the middle portion of Table 10.5. Thus, no contradiction in results is found when the internal rate of return criterion is compared with the present worth criterion. Each gives the same answer, as shown in the two bottom portions of Table 10.5.

---

[1] The rule enunciated here appears in Dietrich R. Bergmann, "Evaluating Mutually Exclusive Investment Alternatives: Rate of Return Methodology Reconciled with Net Present Worth," *Highway Research Record No. 437*, Washington, D.C.: Highway Research Board, 1973, pp. 75–82.

11

Income Tax Effects

In an economic analysis the effect of income tax is on after-tax consequences. As we have seen and will see again in this book, depreciation, book value, gain or loss on disposal of fixed assets, and similar considerations are not regarded as part of an economic analysis because they have no effect on cash flow. They arise because of the accountant's necessity to allocate costs and to be able to put forth a balance sheet and profit-and-loss statement at the end of the year. These matters come within the conventions universally agreed on and followed by the accounting profession. But as managers, that is to say, as economists concerned with practical decision making, we have avoided these notations in the books of the firm because they do not reflect yield, disbursements, or revenue.

However, when an after-tax economic analysis is performed, income tax disbursements immediately become relevant because they do represent real effects on our cash flow. The accountant's books and the conventions he uses to complete them become pertinent because they are used to calculate the tax payments to governmental agencies, or the tax effects, speaking more generally, on our cash flow. We do not see the accountant as an economist, which he is not, but we must know enough about his operations to determine the effects that his entries have on cash in or out.

VALUE

The value of an asset can have a number of meanings. It can be the undepreciated portion of its first cost, the so-called *book value.* (We see how book value is determined later in this chapter.) It can be the value to the owner. Or it can have a market value. This is not the place to carry out a discussion of valuation—a complete study in itself—but it is necessary to point out the association of concepts of value with the economic concept of opportunity cost.

Book value has no relation to opportunity cost, unless the opportunity cost coincidentally happens to be the book value. The market value of an asset has a direct relation to opportunity cost. *Market value* is that amount for which the asset could be sold in the existing market. It is the salvage value, not that determined by an accountant by guesswork, however sophisticated, but that amount of cash that would be received were we to sell the asset. (It is also possible to conceive of an asset as having a negative value. This situation arises when the removal cost of an asset exceeds its market value, such as in a large refinery unit that must be dismantled and converted into scrap.)

DEPRECIATION

Depreciation, according to the accountant's view, is that amount of original cost which must be periodically allocated such that the first cost of an asset is properly accounted for over the years of its life. Notice that this is an allocation and not an evaluation. The amount depreciated is subtracted from the original amount plus depreciation already taken so that at the end of each accounting period, usually a year, the book value may be stated. The *book value* is, therefore, first cost less accumulated depreciation.

The accountant defines depreciation as a cost and therefore as an amount deductible from taxable income. Because it is a deductible item, it affects the amount of income tax paid. It is important, therefore, to know how to calculate depreciation. Later, we observe its effect on cash flow.

We consider three types of depreciation: straight line, sum of the years digits (often abbreviated to years digits), and declining balance. In the straight-line method, the asset is assigned a depreciation charge for each year of its life. Having determined the asset life (that is, having estimated what the life would probably be), the accountant subtracts the estimated salvage value from the original cost of the asset and divides the result by the number of years of life. For example, an asset with a first cost of $1000, a salvage value of $100, and an estimated life of five years shows a depreciation charge computed as follows:

$$\frac{1000 - 100}{5} = 180$$

This may also be represented by the percentage rate that would be calculated by subtracting from 100 percent the estimated salvage value as a percentage of first cost and dividing the result by the estimated life of the asset. In the case just cited it would be:

$$\frac{100\% - 10\%}{5} = 18\%$$

Depreciation using a straight-line rate and the resulting book value are shown in Table 11.1.

The sum of the years digit method is handled in the following way. The sum of the years digits is formulated as follows:

$$\Sigma Y.D. = \frac{n^2 + n}{2}$$

where n is the estimated life of the asset. For example, for an asset with a five-year life, the sum of the years digits would be 15. The depreciation charge is calculated by multiplying the first cost of the asset minus its estimated salvage value by a fraction, the numerator of which is the remaining life of the asset and the denominator of which is the sum of the years digits. In our example the first year's depreciation charge for an asset costing $1000 and having a salvage value of $100, and therefore a depreciable value of $900, would be:

$$\$900(5/15) = \$300$$

That is, the first year's depreciation charge using the sum of the years digit method would be $300. Table 11.1 shows depreciation charges by this method, as well as the book value at the end of each year when this method is used.

In the double declining balance method, the first cost of the asset is considered, and the estimated salvage value is disregarded. In other words, the depreciation charges are computed on the basis of the first cost of an asset. The declining balance rate is computed by dividing 200 percent by the estimated life of the asset. In our example, for a life of five years, the declining balance rate is 40 percent. This 40 percent must be applied to the previous year's book value. For example, the first year's depreciation charge using a 200 percent declining balance method would be calculated by multiplying the $1000 by 40 percent, resulting in a first depreciation charge of $400, as shown in Table 11.1.

Notice that in the straight-line method and the years digit method the basis of the depreciation chart is the first cost less the salvage value. In the declining balance method, the basis is the asset's first cost, and salvage value is disregarded.

TABLE 11.1 Depreciation by Three Methods

Year	Annual Depreciation Charge by			Book Value at End of Year		
	Straight-Line	Years Digits	Double Declining Balance	S.L.	Y.D.	D.D.B.
0				1000	1000	1000
1	180	300	400	820	700	600
2	180	240	240	640	460	360
3	180	180	144	460	280	216
4	180	120	86	280	160	130
5	180	60	52	100	100	78
Depreciable Value	900	900	922			

Asset first cost = 1000

Salvage value = 100

Life = 5 years

$$\text{S.L. rate} = \frac{100\% - 10\%}{5} = 18\%$$

$$\text{Y.D.} = \frac{n^2 + n}{2} = \frac{30}{2} = 15$$

$$\text{D.B. rate} = \frac{200\%}{5} = 40\%$$

COMPUTING AFTER-TAX CASH FLOW USING STRAIGHT-LINE DEPRECIATION

In the following examples of the income tax effect of depreciation methods, the same conditions are assumed. The conditions are a five-year life of the asset, a first cost of $1000, a net benefit of $300 for each of five years, and no salvage value. An income tax rate of 48 percent is also assumed.

You will recall that the rule for computing the annual depreciation charge is that the first cost of the asset is divided by the asset life after first subtracting the salvage value. In this example, because the asset has no salvage value, the straight-line depreciation charge is $200 per year, as is shown in the second column of Table 11.2. The third column of Table 11.2 shows the taxable income, which is the sum of columns 1 and 2—in this case, $100 per year. The income tax payment at 48 percent is therefore $48, as is shown in column 4 of Table 11.2. The cash flow after taxes is the sum of columns 1 and 4, and this is shown in column 5. You should notice that the cash flow is concerned with just that, that is, with columns 1 and 4. Columns 2 and 3 are accounting items used to compute the real cash flow item, which is the income tax payment. Columns 2 and 3 do not represent true cash flows.

The before-tax rate of return, that is, the rate of return on the original cash flow, is 15 percent. The after-tax rate of return is 8 percent, as follows:

Before-tax:
PW @ 15% = $-1000 + 300 \, (P/A, i, 5)$

$$(P/A, i, 5) = \frac{1000}{300} = 3.333$$

IROR = 15%

After-tax:
PW = 0 = $-1000 + 252 \, (P/A, i, 5)$

$$(P/A, i, 5) = \frac{1000}{252} = 3.968$$

IROR = 8%

Notice that it is not possible to apply the income tax rate to the before-tax rate of return to compute the after-tax rate of return. If this were possible, the after-tax rate of return would be 7.2 percent rather than 8 percent.

TABLE 11.2 Income Tax Effect Using Straight-Line Depreciation

Year	Cash Flow (1)	Depreciation Charge (2)	Taxable Income (3) (1) + (2)	Income Tax Payment (4) − 0.48 (Col. 3)	Cash Flow After Taxes (5) (1) + (4)
0	− 1000				− 1000
1	+ 300	− 200	+ 100	− 48	+ 252
2	+ 300	− 200	+ 100	− 48	+ 252
3	+ 300	− 200	+ 100	− 48	+ 252
4	+ 300	− 200	+ 100	− 48	+ 252
5	+ 300	− 200	+ 100	− 48	+ 252
	+ 500	− 1000	+ 500	− 240	+ 260

$P = 1000$
$N = 5$
$A = 300$
$L = 0$
Income tax rate = 48%

Straight-line depreciation charge $= \dfrac{1000}{5} = 200$

COMPUTING AFTER-TAX CASH FLOW USING YEARS DIGIT DEPRECIATION

Using the same cash flow as in the previous example but now with a depreciation chart based on the sum of the years digit method, income tax effect is as shown in Table 11.3. The depreciation charge decreases for each of the five years. It totally depreciates the $1000 first cost of the asset. It results, however, in an after-tax cash flow in which considerably more money is received in the earlier years of the asset's life. The same amount of tax is paid as in the straight-line method.

The before-tax rate of return using years digit depreciation charges is 15 percent, the same as it was in straight-line depreciation because the depreciation charge does not affect the original cash flow. The after-tax rate of return, however, is more advantageous than in the straight-line method. It is 9 percent, computed as shown below:

After-tax IROR:
$$PW\ @i\% = 0 = -1000 + 316\ (P/F, i^*, 1)$$
$$+ 284\ (P/F, i^*, 2)$$
$$+ 252\ (P/F, i^*, 3)$$
$$+ 220\ (P/F, i^*, 4)$$
$$+ 188\ (P/F, i^*, 5)$$

or:

$$PW\ @\ i\% = 0 = -1000 + 316\ (P/A, i^*, 5)$$
$$-\ 32\ (P/G, i^*, 5)$$
$$PW\ @\ 9\% = -1000 + 1229 - 228$$
$$= +1$$
$$IROR = 9\%$$

In Table 11.3, columns 1, 2, 3, 4, and 5 have been added, and the sum of each is shown. It must be emphasized that these totals are included for an arithmetic check of the row operations. They do not in any way imply that sums associated with different years may be added. To do so would violate the concept of the time value of money.

COMPUTING AFTER-TAX CASH FLOW USING DECLINING BALANCE DEPRECIATION

Using the same conditions as in the previous two examples, the information contained in Table 11.4 can be calculated. The depreciation charge shown in column 2 is based on a double declining balance rate

TABLE 11.3 Income Tax Effect Using Years Digit Depreciation

Year	Cash Flow (1)	Depreciation Charge (2)	Taxable Income (3) (1) + (2)	Income Tax Payment (4) −0.48 (Col. 3)	Cash Flow After Taxes (5) (1) + (4)
0	− 1000				− 1000
1	+ 300	− 333	− 33	+ 16	+ 316
2	+ 300	− 267	+ 33	− 16	+ 284
3	+ 300	− 200	+ 100	− 48	+ 252
4	+ 300	− 133	+ 167	− 80	+ 220
5	+ 300	− 67	+ 233	− 112	+ 188
	+ 500	− 1000	+ 500	− 240	+ 260

$P = 1000$
$N = 5$
$A = 300$
$L = 0$
Income tax rate = 48%

$\Sigma \text{Y.D.} = \dfrac{n^2 + n}{2} = 15$

135

TABLE 11.4 Income Tax Effect Using Double Declining Balance Depreciation

Year	Cash Flow (1)	Depreciation Charge (2)	Taxable Income (3) (1) + (2)	Income Tax Payment (4) −0.48 (Col. 3)	Cash Flow After Taxes (5) (1) + (4)
0	− 1000				− 1000
1	+ 300	− 400	− 100	+ 48	+ 348
2	+ 300	− 240	+ 60	− 29	+ 271
3	+ 300	− 144	+ 156	− 75	+ 225
4	+ 300	− 86	+ 214	− 103	+ 197
5	+ 300	− 52	+ 248	− 119	+ 181
	+ 500	− 922	+ 578	− 278	+ 222

$P = 1000$
$N = 5$
$A = 300$
$L = 0$
Income tax rate = 48%

$$\text{D.B. rate} = \frac{200\%}{5} = 40\%$$

of 40 percent. It is a 200 percent declining balance. As noted previously in this chapter, the depreciation charge and the depreciation rate are based on first cost only. Salvage value is ignored. The cash flow after taxes results in after-tax rate of return of 8 percent. Calculations are shown below:

After-tax IROR:

$$PW @i*\% = 0 = -1000 + 348 \ (P/F, i*, 1)$$
$$+ 271 \ (P/F, i*, 2)$$
$$+ 225 \ (P/F, i*, 3)$$
$$+ 197 \ (P/F, i*, 4)$$
$$+ 181 \ (P/F, i*, 5)$$

$$PW @ 8\% = -1000 + 348 \ (0.9259)$$
$$+ 271 \ (0.8573)$$
$$+ 225 \ (0.7938)$$
$$+ 197 \ (0.7350)$$
$$+ 181 \ (0.6806)$$

$$= -1000 + 322$$
$$+ 232$$
$$+ 179$$
$$+ 145$$
$$+ 123$$

$$= +1$$

$$IROR = 8\%$$

It is evident that the depreciation method used can have considerable effect on the after-tax rate of return. In most cases it is the after-tax rate of return that will decide the quantitative portion of the analysis. In the example above, the after-tax rate of return was 8 percent using straight line depreciation, 9 percent using years digit depreciation, and 8 percent using double declining balance depreciation. At first glance, it may seem that some conclusion as to the optimum depreciation method is possible, based on the foregoing percentages. Such is not the case, however, because the choice of an asset depreciation method is made among mutually exclusive alternatives. Thus, incremental analysis must be used if the internal rate of return method is employed.

No general rule can be laid down on the economic advisability of a depreciation method. Each case must be analyzed separately.

INVESTMENT TAX CREDIT

The investment tax credit provision that is sometimes contained in the governmental rules of income tax means that the tax payer may subtract a certain percentage of the first cost of an asset from his tax payment. In the examples of this chapter in which the first cost of the asset was $1000, an investment tax credit of 5 percent would mean that $50 could be subtracted from total taxes owed. This is equivalent to saying that for analytical purposes the first cost of the asset was actually $1000 minus $50 or $950. The depreciable value of the asset has been at times based on the original first cost of $1000 and has during other tax years and under other tax regulations been based on the first cost less the investment tax credit. The reader should be clearly aware that the investment tax credit is a reduction in the tax itself, not in taxable income.

INTERNAL REVENUE SERVICE ASSET LIVES

The taxpayer is not allowed to set the taxable life of an asset capriciously. The Internal Revenue Service of the United States has indicated the allowable lives of assets that it recognizes for tax purposes. In 1962 the guideline lives were published. This was a list of assets with the allowable lives associated with them. The life of a warehouse building, for example, was 60 years. The only way that these guideline lives could be changed was by application to the Internal Revenue Service and by providing proof that the taxpayer had experience which showed that lives of an asset in his service had less a life than the required guideline life showed. More recently, in 1971, the so-called Asset Depreciation Range appeared. This allowed taxpayers to use lives as much as 20 percent longer or shorter than those specified in the guideline lives.

Notice that the shorter the life of an asset, the more the cash flow after taxes during the early life of the asset will be. Thus, the tendency of business to wish to depreciate assets as quickly as possible is understandable. For this reason such devices as guideline lives have been necessary.

DISPOSAL OF FIXED ASSETS

In Table 11.1 the book value at the end of the asset's life was $100 in the case of the straight-line method, $100 in the case of the years digit method, and $78 in the case of the double declining balance method. What if the asset is sold on the market for $100? In the case of the straight-line and years digit depreciation methods, no further notation is necessary because the salvage value and market value are equal. The estimated salvage value is not taxed because it is what is left of the owner's capital and is therefore not income. In the case of the declining balance method, however, the asset has been sold for a price more by $22 than its value as shown in the company's books. How is that $22 treated?

The answer to this question depends, once again, on the IRS rules in force at the time. In this book, such a gain on the sale of a fixed asset will be treated as though it were revenue received during the final year of the asset's life.

Notice that rules relating to the gain or loss on the disposal of fixed assets change. In some cases it is possible to treat assets held longer than six months as capital assets, and therefore to treat the gain or loss on their disposal as a capital gain or loss at a different tax rate.

Example 11.1 ───────────────────────────────

A piece of equipment costs $150,000. Its service life is 10 years with an estimated salvage value of 10 percent at the end of its life. Its adoption will result in a savings of $20,000 per year over the existing equipment, whose remaining life is also 10 years but whose salvage value at the end of that time is zero.

The firm interested in this equipment has an income tax rate of 48 percent. Straight-line depreciation will be used. (The firm's after-tax minimum acceptable rate of return is 8 percent.)

1. Management wishes to know what the rate of return after taxes will be if all the above predictions come true.
2. Management also wishes to know what the rate of return after taxes will be if the new equipment turns out to have a salvage value of 30 percent after 10 years, even though the equipment has been depreciated on a straight-line basis using the 10 percent estimated salvage value. Gain on disposal of fixed assets will be shown as income rather than capital gain.

Figure 11.1 shows the cash flow before taxes for the situation in which salvage value is 10 percent of original cost. Table 11.5 summarizes the data and calculations. Notice that the estimated salvage value is not taxable. The internal rate of return of the after-tax cash flow is:

$$
\begin{aligned}
0 &= -150,000 + 16,880 \, (P/A, \, 4, \, 10) \\
&\quad + 15,000 \, (P/F, \, 4, \, 10) \\
&= -150,000 + 16,880 \, (8.111) + 15,000 \, (0.6756) \\
&= -2,952
\end{aligned}
$$

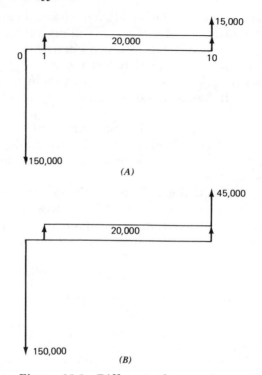

Figure 11.1 Different salvage values.

Therefore, the IROR is slightly less than 4 percent (3.6).

The cash flow after taxes is augmented by the 30 percent salvage value rather than a 10 percent salvage value in situation 2. Table 11.6 shows the cash flow.

$$
\begin{aligned}
0 &= -150{,}000 + 16{,}880 \ (P/A, \ i^*, \ 10) \\
&\quad +30{,}600 \ (P/F, \ i^*, \ 10) \\
&= -150{,}000 + 16{,}880 \ (7.722) \\
&\quad +30{,}600 \ (0.6139) \\
&= -868
\end{aligned}
$$

Therefore, the IROR is slightly less than 5 percent (4.9). The proposal again fails to qualify.

TABLE 11.5 Salvage Value at 10 Percent of Original Cost

Year	Cash Flow	Depreciation Charge	Taxable Income	Income Tax Payment	Cash Flow After Taxes
0	−150,000				−150,000
1–10	+20,000	−13,500	6,500	−3,120	+16,880
10	+15,000				+15,000

TABLE 11.6 Salvage Value at 30 Percent of Original Cost

Year	Cash Flow	Depreciation Charge	Taxable Income	Income Tax Payment	Cash Flow After Taxes
0	−150,000				−150,000
1–10	+20,000	−13,500	6,500	−3,120	+16,880
10	+45,000		30,000	−14,400	+30,600

Notice that the gain on the disposal of fixed assets of $30,000 has been treated as ordinary income for the tenth year and taxed as such, that is, at 48 percent.

A FACTUAL STUDY: COMPANIA LA FLECHA, S.A.

In November, 1975, the three partners of the Compania La Flecha, S. A. met to decide if they would continue with the project they had under way. It consisted of gathering together 93,000 pesos, buying a bus line that carried passengers and freight in the central portion of their Latin American country, operating the business for five years, and then selling it.

Background

The company would provide service along two routes:

1. Aldama–Burgos–Ocampo–Jimenez–Las Norias–Ebano.

2. Aldama–Burgos–Hidalgo–La Mesa.

Routes further to the east and west in the country had not been taken into consideration because they required greater investments and meant more competition; several well-organized companies with strong financial backing operated there. Some routes in the central part of the country were also rejected because of small passenger traffic.

The promoters of the new company had studied the feasibility of establishing it. Passenger traffic was expected to increase from 650,000 per year in 1973 to 850,000 in 1979, a straight-line rate of increase of 33,000 per year. Although airlines provided service to some of the towns along the routes contemplated, their passengers belonged to a higher economic level. A railroad also offered competition, but its passenger traffic had been falling off and was expected to continue to do so. The railroad was no longer interested in attracting passengers, having decided that they represented a losing portion of their operations. Thus, their service, in frequency and reliability, had greatly deteriorated. In addition, new government projects—a hydro-electric plant, a new highway, and new agricultural ventures—were expected to attract people to the area. General population increases and bettering economic conditions were strong indicators of steadily increasing demand for passenger transportation.

The firms operating in the area had two forms of organization. In one, the owners of the firm actually owned only the ticket agencies, handled the expense involved in operating them, and received 20 percent of the gross ticket revenue in exchange. The owners of the buses handled all the expenses related to the actual hauling of the passengers and received 80 percent of gross revenue for doing so. In the other form of organization, the owners of the firm owned the ticket agencies and the vehicles. This second form of organization carried with it many problems of a technical nature that the partners did not believe they had the experience to solve in an efficient way. Therefore, they adopted the first form.

One of the quickest and easiest ways of going into business was to buy the operating license of a firm already in being. It was thought the partners could buy the operating license of a firm that was the sole owner of seven agencies for which the asking price was 100,000 pesos, cash. But the partners were sure that the owner would accept payment at the rate of 40,000 pesos on signing the contract of sale and 20,000 pesos each year for the following three years. The last three payments would be made from profits.

Office furniture and equipment for all the agencies would be needed in the amount of about 27,000 pesos. About three times as much would be needed for Aldama, the capital of the country, as for any of the other six cities. About 12,000 pesos were thought necessary for advertising. All this was presented in an initial balance sheet for 1976 shown in Table 11.7.

Because the firm would own only the agencies, it would be necessary to sign contracts with the bus owners. Eleven vehicles were considered necessary, each with a capacity of 15 passengers. A most important part of the contract was that the owners of the buses would become proprietors of the agencies after five years. This provision in the contract balanced the rather high percentage of ticket revenue that the agencies were going to retain.

The number of passengers to be transported during 360 days per year was based on the buses being filled to capacity for the trips. The fares were established in accordance with the regulatory commission of the federal government.

Personnel requirements would be fulfilled by the three partners in

**TABLE 11.7 Initial Balance Sheet—1976
Compania La Flecha, S.A. (in pesos)**

Assets		*Liabilities*	
Current assets		Accounts payable	
Cash	14,000	Within one year	20,000
Deferred assets	12,000	Over one year	40,000
Total	26,000	*Equity*	
Fixed assets			93,000
Equipment	13,000		153,000
Furniture	14,000		
Depreciation	—		
Total	27,000		
Purchase of op- erating license	100,000		
	153,000		

the top administrative position as a triumvirate that would determine
the policies and make the major decisions for the company. A manager
for each of the seven agency offices would be needed. For each office
would by employed an accountant, a mechanic to check on the operation of the buses, and clerks whose number would depend on the size
of the office. The salaries of these personnel are shown in Table 11.8.

**TABLE 11.8 Estimated Agency Personnel
Requirements (in pesos)**

Aldama Office	*Yearly Salary*
1 manager	12,000
1 mechanic	7,200
1 accountant	4,800
3 ticket clerks	10,800
Total	34,800
Provincial Offices (each)	
1 chief inspector	3,600
2 ticket clerks	4,800
Total	8,400
Total personnel salaries	34,800
$6 \times 8,400 =$	50,400
	85,200

TABLE 11.9 Annual Agency Expenses
(in pesos)

	Aldama	Other Cities (each)
Personnel	34,800	8,400
Advertising	5,800	4,800
Lease	8,200	4,600
Supplies	2,400	600
Utilities	2,200	600
Social benefits	1,800	600
Others	2,800	800
	58,000	20,400

Other expenses are shown in Table 11.9. Office furniture and equipment would be depreciated over five years. The overhead for the Aldama and Burgos offices would be prorated among the agencies because these offices were jointly used by both routes. The profit and loss statements, the projected cash flows, and the balance sheets are shown for five years in Tables 11.10, 11.11, and 11.12.

The tax rate in the country depended on the profit level. A 2 percent welfare tax was included in the tax shown in Figure 11.2.

TABLE 11.10 Projected Profit and Loss Statements (in 000 pesos)

Year	1976	1977	1978	1979	1980
Total income from ticket sales	1,079	1,256	1,334	1,666	1,666
20% of ticket sales	215.8	251.2	266.8	333.2	333.2
Less Sales and Administrative expenses	180.4	180.4	180.4	180.4	180.4
Subtotal	35.4	70.8	86.4	152.8	152.8
Less depreciation on license, equipment, and deferred assets	27.8	27.8	27.8	27.8	27.8
Profits before taxes	7.6	43	58.6	125	125
Less taxes	0.8	8.6	13.0	32.6	32.6
Profit after taxes	6.8	34.4	45.6	92.4	92.4

TABLE 11.11 Projected Cash Flow (in 000 pesos)

Income	1976	1977	1978	1979	1980
Initial cash balance	14.0	28.6	70.8	124.2	244.4
Ticket sales	215.8	251.2	266.8	333.2	333.2
Total	229.8	279.8	337.6	457.4	577.6
Expenses					
Costs of sales and ad- ministrative expenses	180.4	180.4	180.4	180.4	180.4
Taxes	0.8	8.6	13.0	32.6	32.6
Debts	20	20	20	—	—
Total	201.2	209	213.4	213	213
Cash balance	28.6	70.8	124.2	244.4	364.6
Annual cash increase	14.6	42.2	53.4	120.2	120.2

TABLE 11.12 Projected Balance Sheets (in 000 pesos)

Assets	1976	1977	1978	1979	1980
Current Assets					
Cash	28.6	70.8	124.2	244.4	364.6
Prepaid items	12	12	12	12	12
(Depreciation)	(2.4)	(4.8)	(7.2)	(9.6)	(12)
Total	38.2	78	129	246.8	364.6
Fixed Assets					
Equipment	13	13	13	13	13
Furniture	14	14	14	14	14
(Depreciation)	(5.4)	(10.8)	(16.2)	(21.6)	(27)
Total	21.6	16.2	10.8	5.4	—
License ownership	100	100	100	100	100
(Depreciation)	(20)	(40)	(60)	(80)	(100)
Total	80	60	40	20	—
Asset total	139.8	154.2	179.8	272.2	364.6
Liabilities and Equity					
Accounts payable					
Within one year	20	20	—	—	—
Over one year	20	—	—	—	—
Equity	93	93	93	93	93
Surplus	6.8	41.2	86.8	179.2	271.6
	139.8	154.2	179.8	272.2	364.6

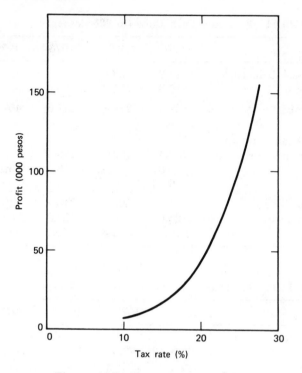

Figure 11.2   Tax rate on profits.

Deciding

The important line in the tables is the last line of Table 11.11, "Annual cash increase." It shows the cash flow after all expenses and taxes have been paid. It is to this line that the analyst must refer the 93,000 pesos that the partners must put up to finance the deal. The annual cash increase appears as follows:

Year	Cash flow
0	−93,000
1	+14,600
2	+42,200
3	+53,400
4	+120,200
5	+120,200
	+257,600

As far as the analysis goes, the tables could conclude with Table 11.11. Table 11.12 is included so that you may see the relationships among the profit and loss statement, the projected cash flow, and the balance sheet.

To evaluate the cash flow the partners decided on the internal rate of return. Because the decision was either to accept or to reject the project, no question of incrementality entered. The partners discovered the following relation between discount rate and net present value of the cash flow:

Discount rate	NPV
20%	+86,000
35%	+26,000
40%	+12,000
50%	−9,000

The internal rate of return was about 45 percent.

The partners' comparison with their personal opportunity cost of capital left them undecided. It was close enough to 45 percent to cause them to consider the factors that had not entered their analysis.

First, none of the cash flow had been withdrawn in their projections to compensate for the time that they as chief administrators must surely spend to direct the business. They could not simply act as a board of directors because the organization required that they act as operating officials as well.

Second, the projections had been set forth as though they were certain to occur. Yet large risks were present in the enterprise. The most important of these was the possibility of heavy inflation in the costs of all their expenses, with fares being held constant by the regulatory commission of the federal government.

Third, the business depended on another business that had to perform as expected for the cash flow to be realized. Yet the small, single-owner buses were in constant danger of being repossessed by the companies that had financed their purchase. The bus owners had little idea of business operations and thought of expenses in terms of immediate cash outlays for fuel, tires, and lubricants. They set nothing aside for minor disasters. Thus, they were in constant danger of losing their buses, which would mean loss of ticket sales.

Finally, a constant danger existed that the partners' competitors would manage to damage the business by any number of ways that the partners had not imagined.

All things considered, the project appeared to be too risky, and the partners decided not to continue.

12

Risk and Uncertainty

Up to this point, we have talked as though all outcomes, no matter how far in the future, were certain. We have accepted the forecasts knowing that they could not possibly come out exactly in the way predicted except in certain cases, such as the interest on a bond. Even in this case, there is always the possibility of bankruptcy of the company or the collapse of the government issuing the bonds. A risk has been involved in all our predictions that we have not attempted to quantify. Now we make that attempt, and the result is that in most cases our calculations cover a range of results rather than single results.

CERTAINTY, RISK, AND UNCERTAINTY

The definition of certainty is intuitively known to all. *Certainty* is the situation that obtains when future events admit of no variation. If the probability distribution of future events is known, the risk is correspondingly known, and this is the definition of *risk*. *Uncertainty* exists when the probability distribution of future events is completely unknown.

We have dealt with certainty. We now deal largely with risk and decisions made under risk. Decisions made under uncertainty are not considered.

Under risk conditions, because the probability distribution of input data is known, the results of any study we might make using the data will also be known in the form of a distribution. Even when the probability distributions of outcomes are unknown, they can often be simulated, and this brings into our range of possible solutions a number of problems that could not have been handled until a few years ago. Simulation is an acceptable procedure except when the participants in a market are few, or when the strategies of the participants are chosen to maximize their expected utilities. Game theory is used in such situations and is not treated here.

Specifically, risk is that possibility of variations in the outcomes with which we are concerned. As we have seen, these outcomes are either costs or benefits, that is, cash flow. Variation may also occur in the investment required in a project, especially when the investment occurs over a long period, as it often does in major projects such as multipurpose dams or in metropolitan heavy-rail construction. This aspect of variation is especially significant in times of inflation. An excellent example is the enormous increases in cost of the Bay Area Rapid Transit District metropolitan rail system, which was planned and built over a period of about 15 years and which eventually cost far more than the original planners ever imagined.

In this chapter, we consider risk as sufficiently taken into account by finding the expected values of the probability distributions of the factors that go into our equations—such as cost, benefits, investments, and salvage value. Using these values, we calculate a rate of return, or a benefit/cost ratio, or a net present value, or an annual cost. We ignore the fact that many firms in the private sector hedge against risk at a rate in excess of what our calculations indicate.

DEFINITIONS AND FORMULAS

Probability is defined as the ratio of the number of occurrences of a particular event to the number of trials in which it is possible for the event to occur as the number of trials is increased without limit. These trials and occurrences must be derived from past data. It may be that experiments were performed, or that historical data such as rainfall, have been kept, or that data have been developed by using Monte Carlo simulation methods.

The ratio mentioned in the definition is always less than one when more than one trial is taken. A zero means that the event will never occur; a 1.0 means that the event is certain. When more than one trial is taken in which the event occurs, the ratios must add to 1.0.

The following example describes the formulas involved in probabilistic analysis.

Example 12.1 ————————————————————————

A certain long-distance trucking company discovered by testing its trailers that the weight of the trailers varied in frequency such that the probability of a trailer's being loaded to its maximum weight of 40,000 pounds was 30 percent. The probabilities of other weights occurring are shown in Table 12.1.

TABLE 12.1 Expected Value of Trailer Weight

Trailer Weight	Occurrences	Probability	Expected Value of Trailer Weight
40,000	300	0.30	12,000
39,000	200	0.20	7,800
38,000	150	0.15	5,700
37,000	140	0.14	5,180
36,000	110	0.11	3,960
35,000	100	0.10	3,500
	1,000	1.00	38,140

The probabilities of the various weights occurring sum to 1.0. In other words, no weight above 40,000 or below 35,000 pounds will appear. The expected value of a frequency distribution is given as:

$$\mu = E(X) = \sum_{i=1}^{n} P_i X_i \tag{1}$$

where P is the probability of the ith value of the variable, which is X_i, falling into a certain range. Using this formula, the expected value is shown to be 38,140 in the last column of Table 12.1. If all the weights appeared with equal frequency, the average weight would be given by the expression:

$$\bar{x} = \frac{\sum_{i=1}^{n} X_i}{n} \tag{2}$$

This average weight is 37,500 pounds. The standard deviation is defined as:

$$\sigma = \left[\sum_{i=1}^{n} P_i (X_i - \mu)^2 \right]^{0.5} \tag{3}$$

In the case of Example 12.1, the standard deviation is 1691. Its calculation is shown in Table 12.2.

INCORPORATING EXPECTED VALUE INTO ECONOMIC ANALYSIS

The question of how to incorporate expected value into economic analysis is best explained through a series of examples. Examples 12.1 and 12.2 show how expected value may safely be used. The third illustrates the importance of including a measure of variance—the

TABLE 12.2 Trailer Weight Standard Deviation

Trailer Weight	Expected Value	$X_i - \mu$	Probability	$P_i (X_i - \mu)^2$
40,000	38,140	1860	0.30	1,037,880
39,000	38,140	860	0.20	147,920
38,000	38,140	−140	0.15	2,940
37,000	38,140	−1140	0.14	181,944
36,000	38,140	−2140	0.11	503,756
35,000	38,140	−3140	0.10	985,960
				$\Sigma = 2,860,400$
				$\sigma = 1,691$

standard deviation. The fourth shows pitfalls that can mislead the analyst under certain extreme conditions.

Example 12.2

A small earth dam is planned for a pond on a cattle ranch. The creek feeding the pond floods during some years but never more than once a year. Overtopping will destroy the dam. The results shown in Table 12.3 may be expected for each height of dam planned. (Benefits from increased irrigation augment as more water is stored.) Maintenance costs are negligible. The life of the dam is 15 years. Before-tax opportunity cost of capital is 15 percent. What dam height should be selected?

Clearly, the yearly benefits depend on the existence of the dam. If the dam is destroyed by overtopping during a flood, no benefits will be forthcoming from pastureland irrigation. Therefore, the probabilities of overtopping should be related to the benefits by multiplying the annual benefit by $1 - p$. When this is done, the expected

TABLE 12.3 Irrigation Dam Projections

Dam Height (Feet)	Number of Years Out of 50 During Which Dam Will Be Overtopped	Annual Benefits ($)	First Cost ($)
10	13	12,000	23,000
15	7	13,000	30,000
20	5	14,500	40,000
25	3	16,000	50,000
30	2	18,000	65,000

values of annual benefits are as shown in column 5 of Table 12.4. The rule is:

$$\text{Max} \ (1 - P_i) \, B_i - CR_i$$

The optimal height is 25 feet.

Should the annual costs also be multiplied by the associated probabilities to obtain the expected value of annual cost? If the dam is built at all, the first cost will be incurred and therefore the annual cost, which is a reflection of the first cost, also will be incurred. With each probability that a dam of a given height will be destroyed is a $1 - p$ probability that the dam will survive to live out its 15 years. Notice that in either case, destruction or survival, the cost will be incurred. Therefore, to apply the probability of overtopping to annual cost would be double counting.

The matter is clearer in a present worth analysis. The present worth of the benefits is the expected value of the discounted benefits for the 15 years multiplied by the probability of obtaining those benefits, which is $1 - p$, where p is the probability of the flood overtopping the dam and destroying it. But the cost must be incurred to obtain the benefits, whether or not the dam is destroyed during its life, and therefore it is incorrect to apply a probability to the dam's first cost to obtain its present worth. Its present worth is its full first cost.

If the flood cost were considered to be the loss of benefits as a result of the dam's destruction, then a minimum annual cost solution could be obtained by using the negative of the maximization function because:

$$\begin{aligned} \text{Max} \ (F) &= \text{Min} \ (-F) \\ &= \text{Min} - ((1 - p_i)B_i - CR_i) \\ &= \text{Min} - (1 - p_i)B_i + CR_i \end{aligned}$$

This means that we should choose the alternative i, which minimizes the expected value of the loss of benefits, $-(1 - p_i)B_i$, plus the annual cost, CR_i, resulting in the last column of Table 12.4 becoming negative. The least annual worth is then -6489 for dam 4.

Example 12.3 ─────────────────────────────────────

Proposals for two commercial office buildings show annual profits for any one year in column 1 of Table 12.5.

A profit analyst in the real estate developer's office estimates the probabilities of achieving the profits listed in column 1 due to differences in interior layouts of Building A and Building B. These probabilities appear in column 2. The expected annual profits from each building are shown in column 3.

The expected profit values of $45,000 are equal. The important

TABLE 12.4 Choosing the Dam Height

i	Dam Height 1	p (Overtopping) 2	$(1-p)$ 3	Annual Benefits ($) 4	E(Annual Benefits) ($) 5	P (First Cost) ($) 6	Capital Recovery Cost ($) 7	$E(B) - CR$ ($) 8
1	10	$\frac{13}{50} = 0.26$	0.74	12,000	8,880	23,000	3,934	4946
2	15	0.14	0.86	13,000	11,180	30,000	5,131	6049
3	20	0.10	0.90	14,500	13,050	40,000	6,841	6209
4	25	0.06	0.94	16,000	15,040	50,000	8,551	6489
5	30	0.04	0.96	18,000	17,280	65,000	11,116	6164

$CR = P(A/P, 15, 15)$
$\quad\ = P(0.17102)$

TABLE 12.5   The Returns on Two
Commercial Office Buildings

Profit	Probability	Expected Value (in $)
Building A		
$30,000	0.02	600
31,000	0.04	1,240
35,000	0.19	6,650
45,000	0.50	22,500
55,000	0.19	10,450
59,000	0.04	2,360
60,000	0.02	1,200
	Σ 1.00	Σ 45,000
Building B		
$10,000	0.02	200
24,000	0.09	2,160
30,000	0.12	3,600
40,000	0.17	6,800
45,000	0.20	9,000
50,000	0.17	8,500
60,000	0.12	7,200
66,000	0.09	5,940
80,000	0.02	1,600
	Σ 1.00	Σ 45,000

difference between the two estimates does not appear in the expected value. It appears in the measure of variance, that is, the standard deviation. It is not necessary to compute the standard deviation for each of these distributions to see that they will be significantly different (see Figure 12.1). The standard deviation of the distribution for Building A will be much smaller than the standard deviation for Building B.

Which of the two estimates would the real estate developer favor? The answer to this question depends on the financial resources of the real estate development firm—and here size may be important because financial resources, if large, would make the shock of very low profits in some years a negligible matter. However, if the capital available to the real estate developer were small, a low profit in a given year might have shattering effects on the company. In general, a company with a large capability for withstanding the shock of low profits would probably prefer the layout of Building B. The company with smaller financial resources cannot afford to gamble. Such a company would probably prefer the relative security of a reasonable re-

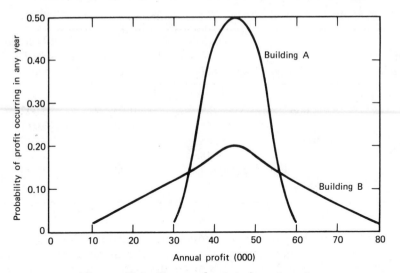

Figure 12.1 Two real estate investments.

turn annually that would deviate little from the average, as occurs with Building A. On the other hand, a company with substantial financial resources might well be willing to gamble on high returns even though at a higher risk of low returns, as will be present if Building B is chosen.

In Figure 12.1 the areas beneath the two curves are equal.

The preferred standard deviation depends on the situation: Are we dealing with a public or a private agency, what is the capital structure of the agency, and how liquid are its assets? Is there a possibility of disaster if lower profits are received in a number of consecutive years? The answer to questions such as these determines the preferred standard deviation.

Example 12.4

An oil company operating in Saudi Arabia regularly faced the problem of evaluating the exploration activity of the company. It decided to do this by benefit/cost ratios. Because the company was incorporated in California, it was required to pay United States income tax. However, any losses in the exploration operation could be credited to the tax burden incurred by its more successful operations. Its tax rate at the time was 48 percent. Table 12.6 shows the size of the field and its probability of occurrence. The net present value of the field is the discounted benefits less the discounted costs of developing the field. The benefit/cost ratio, whose calculation is not shown, includes the effect of income taxes.

The expected value of the benefit/cost ratio is approximately 1.7.

TABLE 12.6   Expected Value of Oil Exploration

Size of Field	Probability	Net Present Value ($000)	Benefit/Cost Ratio	B/C Ratio Expected Value Calculation
Dry Hole	0.968	0	0.48	0.4646
1	0.005	300	0.70	0.0035
2	0.010	2,000	1.70	0.0170
3	0.011	10,000	20.00	0.2200
4	0.005	200,000	100.00	0.5000
5	0.001	1,000,000	500.00	0.5000
	1.000			Σ 1.7051

This is far from the whole story, however. An examination of the table reveals that the major sources of the benefit/cost ratio greater than 1 are the possibility of a dry hole, a discovery with a net present value of $1 billion with only one chance in a thousand of encountering it, and a hole with net present value of $200 million with only five in a thousand chances of finding it. The high benefit/cost ratios tied to long odds result in an acceptable expected value of the benefit/cost ratio. The interpretation of the expected value calculation and its benefit/ cost ratio is open to some question as to its meaning and usefulness. It is necessary to view measures developed under extreme conditions with great care.

CONCLUSION

Economics can be introduced without much effort into many of the problems of other disciplines. I have decided against including examples in which economics forms so small a part of the problem that its inclusion strikes one as forced. For example, decision trees have traditionally formed a part of operations research. It is no great matter to include in the decision tree notions of the time value that some of the factors will possess, and thus drag in the necessity for a present worthing, for example, of some of those factors. Similarly, fixed investment frequently forms part of a business logistics problem, and thus is usually treated as part of the annual cost by the use of the capital recovery factor. An expected value of future investment may be necessary, and out of this will arise an expected value of annual cost. It is possible and necessary to include economic calculations in many other disciplines, but I do not consider it necessary, for that reason, to include a discussion and problems from every discipline in which economics is used.

REFERENCES

Miller, David W., and Martin K. Starr, *Executive Decisions and Operations Research*, 2nd ed., Englewood Cliffs, N. J.: Prentice-Hall, 1966, pp. 178–186.

Quirin, G. D., and A. D. Hunt, "A Method of Evaluating Investment Opportunities in Wildcat Acreage," *Proceedings of the 6th World Petroleum Congress*, Section VIII, Frankfurt, 1964, pp. 65–75.

13

Sensitivity Analysis

Sensitivity means the change in one of the variables in an analysis that results in a reversal of the decision of the analysis. This is the definition of sensitivity found in textbooks on engineering economy. It is the one we employ in the early examples in this chapter. Later, we use another, broader definition.

Example 13.1 ────────────────────────────────

Construction of a dam is being considered with the following characteristics:

$$P = 800$$
$$N = 100 \text{ years}$$
$$L = 0$$
$$A = 33$$

at $i = 5\%$

$$B/C = 33 \frac{(P/A, 5, 100)}{800}$$

$$= 33 \frac{(19.848)}{800}$$

$$= 0.82$$

The dam is therefore unacceptable. We may now ask: At what opportunity cost of capital will the dam become accepted? Or put another way: At what opportunity cost of capital is this analysis sensitive?

At $i = 4\%$

$$B/C = 33 \; \frac{(P/A, \, 4, \, 100)}{800}$$

$$= 33 \; \frac{(24.505)}{800}$$

$$= 1.01$$

At $i = 3\%$

$$B/C = 33 \; \frac{(P/A, \, 3, \, 100)}{800}$$

$$= 33 \; \frac{(31.599)}{800}$$

$$= 1.30$$

We can see that the analysis is sensitive at a little above a 4 percent opportunity cost of capital. The opportunity cost of capital selected can make or break the project.

This comes as no surprise to those interested in seeing dams constructed, such as the federal Corps of Engineers and the Bureau of Reclamation. Because dams have long lives and thus a long series of benefits, a high opportunity cost of capital effectively wipes out later benefits. At 4 percent, the single payment present worth factor for 100 years is 0.019800. That is, benefits 100 years in the future will be discounted to 2 percent, approximately, of their value when brought to time zero. At 10 percent opportunity cost of capital, the factor for 100 years is 0.000073, which means that benefits that far out are negligible. The fact is that even to reach the 2 percent figure in the 10 percent table, the life of the project would have to be reduced to 40 years! This is the reason why dam-building agencies are anxious to have their projects analyzed at an opportunity cost of capital as low as the oversight committees will accept because it means that more dams will be found to have an acceptable benefit/cost ratio and thus will be built.

Agencies whose product is generally shorter lived, such as the Department of Transportation, do not object to higher rates of opportunity cost of capital. In fact, they prefer them if such rates are uniformly applied in all governmental agencies, because it means that the DOT will receive a larger share of the budget in relation to the Corps of Engineers and the Bureau of Reclamation.

Example 13.2

Following the line of the remarks in the previous paragraph, let us see what sensitivity means in a highway example. We also use a shorter method to determine the point at which a project is sensitive.

A highway has the following characteristics:

$$P = 1000$$
$$N = 20$$
$$L = 0$$
$$A = 80$$

At $i = 10\%$

$$B/C = 80 \ \frac{(P/A, \ 10, \ 20)}{1000}$$

$$= \frac{(8.514)}{1000}$$

$$= 0.68$$

At this opportunity cost of capital, the highway is unacceptable. But at what opportunity cost of capital is the project sensitive? Set $B/C = 1.0$ to find this point.

$$B/C = 1.0 = 80 \ \frac{(P/A, \ i, \ 20)}{1000}$$

$$(P/A, \ i, \ 20) = \frac{1000}{80} = 12.5$$

$$i = 5\% \ \text{(approximately)}$$

At 5 percent the project would just achieve acceptability. At what annual net benefit is the project sensitive?

$$B/C = 1.0 = A \frac{(P/A, \ 10, \ 20)}{1000}$$

$$A = \frac{1000}{(P/A, \ 10, \ 20)}$$

$$= \frac{1000}{8.514}$$

$$= 118$$

The net benefit would need to be raised to 118 in order to make the project just acceptable.
At what economic life is the project sensitive?

$$B/C = 1.0 = 80 \frac{(P/A, \ 10, \ N)}{1000}$$

$$(P/A, \ 10, \ N) = 12.5$$

$$N > 100 \text{ years}$$

This is the answer that might be determined directly from the tables. Closer inspection of the tables reveals that there is *no* maximum life at which the project will be acceptable because the factor can never rise above 10.0. Thus, the project is completely insensitive to economic life.

THE BROADER DEFINITION

Sensitivity may also be defined as the change that results in some important variable as the result of a change in another variable. The change may or may not cause a change in the decision. In example 13.1 we observed the changes that took place in the benefit/cost ratio as a result of changes in the opportunity cost of capital:

5%—0.82

4%—1.01

3%—1.30

These changes follow the first definition, because the changes in the opportunity cost of capital caused a change in the decision. Had we observed from 4 percent downward or 5 percent upward, no change would have occurred in the decision, but we would have known how quickly the *B/C* ratio changed with respect to this variable. This fits the broader definition. Both definitions are illustrated in the following factual study.

A FACTUAL STUDY: ECONOMIC PENETRATION ROADS IN MEXICO[1]

The Bureau of Planning and Programming of the Ministry of Public Works, Government of Mexico, used a so-called "production index" to rank economic penetration roads in the hinterlands of Mexico. These roads stimulated agricultural production in their zone of influence by lowering the transport cost. The production index was defined as the value of the production induced in the fifth year divided by the first

---

[1] Adapted from Henry Malcolm Steiner, *Criteria for Planning Rural Roads in a Developing Country: The Case of Mexico*, doctoral dissertation, Palo Also, Stanford University, 1965, pp 210–218.

cost of the road. For example, on a project whose first cost was 500,000 pesos and whose value of fifth-year agricultural production was 1,000,000 pesos, the production index would be:

$$\frac{1,000,000}{500,000} = 2.0$$

If, instead of using the production index for comparisons among projects, it is decided to make comparisons by an economy study, the sensitivity of the results to various assumptions as to rate of growth becomes important. The assumptions considered are straight-line growth, diminishing growth, and approximate "S" (ogival) growth of agricultural production.

Straight-line Growth Assumption

The specifics of the straight-line growth assumption and road costs are as follows:

1. The growth curve is a straight line to a maximum production level of 1,500,000 pesos annually.

2. No induced agricultural production is achieved during the first year after the road is built to allow for acclimation to the new situation, selection of crops, and first plantings.

3. Agricultural production induced by the road adequately measures all favorable market consequences (benefits).

4. The road has a 20-year life with zero salvage value at the end of its life.

5. The first cost at year zero and maintenance cost incurred at the end of the second year, and every year thereafter, adequately measure the unfavorable market consequences of the project.

6. The social cost of resources is 12 percent. The benefit/cost ratio may be defined here as the net present worth of the benefits—we net benefits and maintenance cost at the end of each year—divided by the first cost of the road. For calculation of present worths we use the gradient series table of the Appendix.

The first cost of the road is 500,000 pesos. Maintenance cost is 50,000 pesos per year. Agricultural production increases as shown in Table 13.1. Figure 13.1 shows the net benefits on the straight-line assumption.

The present worth of the net yearly benefits is:

$$PW = G_{1-7} \, (P/G,\ 12,\ 7) + A_{8-20} \, (P/A,\ 12,\ 13)(P/F,\ 12,\ 7)$$

TABLE 13.1   Straight-Line Agricultural Production Increases (in 000 pesos)

Year	Production value	Maintenance costs	Net yearly benefit
1	0	0	0
2	300	50	250
3	550	50	500
4	800	50	750
5	1050	50	1000
6	1300	50	1250
7	1550	50	1500·
8–20	1550	50	1500

where

$G_{1-7} = 250{,}000$ and $A_{8-20} = 1{,}500{,}000$. In thousands,
$$PW = 250(11.6443) + 1{,}500(6.424)(0.4253)$$
$$= 2911 + 4358$$
$$= 7269$$

and,

$$B/C = \frac{7{,}269}{500}$$

$$= 15$$

Diminishing Growth Assumption

To test the sensitivity of the growth assumption we assume that the curve of growth is as portrayed in Figure 13.1, labeled "Diminishing

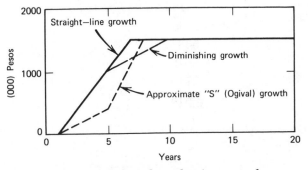

Figure 13.1   Agricultural production growth curves.

TABLE 13.2 Diminishing Growth Production Increases (in 000 pesos)

Year	Production value	Maintenance costs	Net yearly benefit
1	0	0	0
2	300	50	250
3	550	50	500
4	800	50	750
5	1050	50	1000
6	1150	50	1100
7	1250	50	1200
8	1350	50	1300
9	1450	50	1400
10	1550	50	1500
11–20	1550	50	1500

growth" and showing the agricultural production increases of Table 13.2.

The present worth of the net yearly benefits are:

$$PW = G_{1-5}(P/G, \ 12, \ 5)$$
$$+ \ G_{6-10}(P/G, \ 12, \ 6)(P/F, \ 12, \ 4)$$
$$+ \ A_{6-10}(P/A, \ 12, \ 3)(P/F, \ 12, \ 5)$$
$$+ \ A_{11-20}(P/A, \ 12, \ 10)(P/F, \ 12, \ 10)$$

where $G_{1-5} = 250,000, G_{6-10} = 100,000, A_{6-10} = 1,000,000,$ and $A_{11-20} = 1,500,000.$ In thousands of pesos,

$$PW = 250(6.3970)$$
$$+ \ 100(8.9302)(0.6355)$$
$$+ \ 1000(3.605)(0.5674)$$
$$+ \ 1500(5.650)(0.3220)$$
$$PW = 1599$$
$$+ \ 568$$
$$+ \ 2046$$
$$\underline{+ \ 2729}$$
$$6,942$$

Because no change occurs in the costs,

$$B/C = \frac{6942}{500}$$
$$= 14$$

Approximate "S" (Ogival) Growth Assumption

To approximate ogival growth, the curve so designated in Figure 13.1 is used. The curve is an approximation to the curve of normal growth. Both ogival and diminishing growth have been experienced in economic penetration roads. Table 13.3 presents the income stream.

The present worth of the yearly net benefits is:

$$
\begin{aligned}
PW = \ & G_{1-5}(P/G,\ 12,\ 5) \\
& + G_{6-8}(P/G,\ 12,\ 4)(P/F,\ 12,\ 4) \\
& + A_{6-8}(P/A,\ 12,\ 3)(P/F,\ 12,\ 5) \\
& + A_{9-20}(P/A,\ 12,\ 12)(P/F,\ 12,\ 8)
\end{aligned}
$$

Where $G_{1-5} = 100{,}000$, $G_{6-8} = 367{,}000$, $A_{6-8} = 400{,}000$, and $A_{9-20} = 1{,}500{,}000$. Therefore, in thousands of pesos,

$$
\begin{aligned}
PW = \ & 100(6.3970) \\
& + 367(4.1273)(0.6355) \\
& + 400(2.402)(0.5674) \\
& + 1500(6.194)(0.4039) \\
= \ & 640 \\
& + 963 \\
& + 545 \\
& + \underline{3753} \\
& \ \ 5901
\end{aligned}
$$

The first cost is the same. Therefore,

$$
B/C = \frac{5901}{500}
$$

$$
= 12
$$

TABLE 13.3 Ogival Growth Production Increases (in 000 pesos)

Year	Production value	Maintenance costs	Net yearly benefit
1	0	0	0
2	150	50	100
3	250	50	200
4	350	50	300
5	450	50	400
6	817	50	767
7	1184	50	1134
8	1550	50	1500
9–20	1550	50	1500

CONCLUSIONS

The three assumptions gave three different benefits and thus three different benefit/cost ratios:

Straight-line assumption—15
Diminishing growth assumption—14
Approximate "S" growth assumption—12

None of the assumptions reversed the decision in favor of this particular road project; therefore, the analysis is not sensitive to the assumption as to growth curve, using the strict definition of sensitivity of the early part of this chapter. But there is no doubt that benefits change according to the growth curve assumption employed, and thus the project is sensitive in the broader sense. In another project, the sensitivity could be much greater. For example, had the road's first cost been 6,000,000 pesos, and all else remained the same, the three benefit/cost ratios would have been:

$$B/C \text{ (straight-line)} = \frac{7269}{6000} = 1.21$$

$$B/C \text{ (diminishing)} = \frac{6942}{6000} = 1.16$$

$$B/C \text{ (approximate "S")} = \frac{5901}{6000} = 0.98$$

Clearly, the decision would have been sensitive to the assumption on the characteristic growth curve of the project.

A FACTUAL STUDY: RENTAL HOUSING INVESTMENT

During 1977, 1978, and 1979 more and more small investors, who would normally have kept their savings in banks or savings and loan companies, turned to real estate in an attempt to protect themselves against the increasing inflation. (The cost-of-living price index rose to 9 percent in 1978.) This study deals with an investment in a single-family house that is a one-story, two-bedroom, one-and-a-half bath dwelling on about 8000 square feet of land. The rental property is located in Bethesda, Maryland, about 8 miles from the Washington Monument in Washington, D. C.

Data

The market value of the house was $74,000 in 1977. Taxes on the sale, legal fees, and escrow fees, which are payable by the buyer when he closes the deal, amounted to $5000. For the basic analysis, before testing for sensitivity, the mortgage terms were: 9.5 percent interest rate, a 30-year mortgage term, and a 10 percent down payment. These were the acquisition data.

The operating data were as follows:

Rent	$475 per month
Taxes	$1200 per year
Fire insurance	$124 per year
Repairs	$600 per year
Rental agent's commission at 9 percent	$513 per year
Vacancy rate	5 percent

It was assumed that the property would appreciate by 10 percent per year. All operating costs given in the preceding paragraph were also assumed to appreciate by 5 percent per year. Rental income was also assumed to increase at 5 percent annually.

A tax bracket of 32.5 percent was assumed. This included 25 percent federal tax, 5 percent state tax, and 2.5 percent local tax.

Real estate commission on sale of property was considered to be 1 percent because the owner expected to sell the property himself without an agent.

The long-term capital gain deduction for income tax purposes was assumed at 50 percent.

The Analysis

Internal rate of return on total cash flow, including financing charges, after taxes was the method used in the investigation. Financing charges were included because they were inseparable from the investment. (In normal cases of investment, financing charges are not differential and thus are not included in investment comparisons.)

Eight years were considered to be an appropriate time horizon for the analysis because the internal rate of return had leveled off at or before the eighth year.

Finally, notice that appreciation of the value of the property and rental income takes place, whereas operating costs inflate.

Table 13.4 shows the basic case inputs. Table 13.5 displays the

TABLE 13.4 The Basic Case

Market value	$74,000
Gross income	$ 5,700 per year
Operating cost	$ 2,437 per year
Vacancy rate	5%
Appreciation rate	10%
Tax bracket	32.5%
Sales commission	1%
Other sales costs	0
Depreciation method	Straight line
Depreciation basis	$55,500
Depreciation period	30 years
Down payment at 10%	$ 7,400
Loan amount	$66,600
Interest rate	9.5%
Loan period	30 years
Payments per year	12
Other investment costs	$ 5,000

TABLE 13.5 Sensitivity Analysis

Analysis Number	Item Changed	Eight Year Internal Rate of Return (%)
1	None	25.00
2	Tax bracket = 27.5%	24.81
3	Tax bracket = 37.5%	25.23
4	Depreciation method = 125% declining balance	25.32
5	Interest rate = 12%	22.31
6	Interest rate = 7%	27.72
7	Loan period = 25 years	24.81
8	Down payment = 20%	22.39
9	Down payment = 30%	19.34
10	Appreciation rate = 12%	29.67
11	Appreciation rate = 8%	19.20
12	Appreciation rate = 5%	9.25
13	Appreciation rate = 0%	−6.61

sensitivity analysis by showing the item in the basic case changed and to what. It asks the "what if" question. Table 13.5 also shows the internal rate of return resulting from the change in the item.

Conclusions

Changing the tax bracket of the investor 5 percent down and up—a spread of 10 percent—resulted in a 0.42 percent spread in the internal rate of return.

Changing the depreciation method changed the IROR by only 0.32 percent. (You may continue the changes item by item, if you so desire.)

The grave changes came when the appreciation rate was changed. From 12 percent to 0 percent resulted in a 31.61 percent drop in the internal rate of return! Thus, it was the most significant factor of all those considered.

14

Capital Budgeting

Thus far, this book has dealt only with mutually exclusive projects—a set of projects such that, when one is chosen, all the rest are automatically excluded. This chapter deals with the choice among a group of projects, some of which may be mutually exclusive, such that their total cost fits within a given budget and that they are the best choice under a given definition of "best."

There are other views of capital budgeting than the foregoing one. Some analysts consider capital budgeting to be nothing more than a way of presenting investment proposals with appropriate printed forms to be filled in. Others equate the term with the whole gamut of the material seen thus far in this book—and more—with economic analysis, discounted cash flow methods, engineering economy, or incremental analysis. In fact, capital budgeting is the name regularly applied in business schools to the methods we have seen in this book.

We begin with some definitions. An *independent project* is one that can be performed without affecting other projects. It is the only one considered for a certain job, and its only alternative is not to do it.

Interdependent projects are those that are contingent upon each other. For example, a new machine is expected to need a new building to house it. The machine project and the building project are interdependent. Why not consider the building and the machine as a single project? The reason is that the building will have other uses and may therefore qualify by itself. The machine requires the building, but the building does not have to have the machine.

Another class of budget exists in which mutually nonexclusive projects and mutually exclusive projects are combined. This is more normal than interdependence, and I devote more space to it later.

CAPITAL RATIONING: INDEPENDENT PROJECTS

Capital rationing is the simplest case. If the budget is unlimited—that is, if no funding restriction is placed upon the analyst—then the budget is the first cost of those projects that qualify economically according to one of the methods we have seen. It is usual to list the projects from the one delivering the highest yield to the one delivering the lowest.

If the budget is fixed, then the problem is to choose the best projects of those proposed whose first costs fit into that budget. The method is to list the projects, ordered from best to worst according to some measure that allows us to compare independent projects, such as benefit/cost ratio or internal rate of return. We must:

$$\text{Max } Z = \sum_i^m b_i x_i$$

where b_i is the measure of worth of the project and x_i is the decision variable that indicates how much of project i should be undertaken or, in the case of an indivisible project, whether or not the project should be performed at all.

$$\text{Subject to: } \sum_i^m c_i x_i \leq M$$

where c_i is the cost of project i, x_i is the decision variable, and M is the budget. I assume for the moment that all funds not used in the budget are returned to their source, where they are employed in a way and at a rate of return unknown to the analyst. This occurs in budgets in which the total first cost of all the acceptable projects is less than M, because of indivisibilities—so-called "lumpiness." (This point is made clear in the first example below.) I also assume that the discount rate is fixed by higher authority (exogenous). Thus, it is independent of the final capital budget. In addition, it must be assumed that the present value profiles of all alternatives do not cross one another. The reason for this assumption is seen in the next section of this chapter.

The assumptions might fit a government agency—say, the Urban Mass Transit Administration (UMTA) of the federal government of the United States. All funds not used will be returned to the general funds of the government. The Department of Transportation, at the direction of the Office of Management and Budget, imposes a discount rate (opportunity cost of capital) on UMTA of 10 percent on all projects analyzed within UMTA. Let us ignore the fact that government agencies are loath to return funds and that UMTA would probably have enough economically attractive projects to more than use up its budget. In addition:

$$x_i \geq 0$$

because we cannot have a negative project and:

$$x_i \leq 1$$

because we cannot do a project more than once. Thus:

$$0 \leq x_i \leq 1$$

Example 14.1

Consider the example shown in Table 14.1. With an unlimited budget, all projects would be constructed according to the priority listed in the last column, because all projects qualify. (I have removed those projects with a benefit/cost ratio less than 1.0. The projects need not be ordered by increasing first cost.) Notice that the benefit/cost ratio furnishes priority ratings; the net present worth does not. Both measures include all projects in the budget.

Now let us restrict the budget to $50 million. The benefit/cost ratio informs us that the projects selected will be 7, 1, 3, and 6, with a total cost of $46 million and a total net present value of $82 million. But were we to restrict ourselves to the first cost and net present worths of the projects, ignoring the B/C ratio column, we would not have been able to select the projects to be built under our $50 million budget without a programming solution, described by the equations written previously. This is the reason why the B/C ratio and the internal rate of return criteria are so often lauded as measures of the efficiency of capital.

TABLE 14.1   Example 14.1 (in $000,000)

Project	Present Worth of Benefits	First Cost	Net Present Worth	B/C Ratio	Priority
1	90	30	60	3.00	2
2	60	30	30	2.00	3
3	20	10	10	2.00	3
4	40	20	20	2.00	3
5	35	20	15	1.75	4
6	10	5	5	2.00	3
7	8	1	7	8.00	1
	Σ 116				

The programming solution would have been more realistic had we included:

$$x_i = 0, 1 \text{ for } i = 1, 2, \ldots m$$

which means that a linear program with variables restricted to zero and one would need to be employed to accommodate the implicit assumption introduced by the B/C ratio—no partial projects allowed.[1]

The equations are:

$$\text{Max } Z = 60x_1 + 30x_2 + 10x_3 + 20x_4 + 15x_5 + 5x_6 + 7x_7$$

subject to:

$$30x_1 + 30x_2 + 10x_3 + 20x_4 + 20x_5 + 5x_6 + 1x_7 \leqslant 50$$
$$x_1 = 0, 1 \text{ for } i = 1, 2, \ldots 7$$

The calculations, done by hand or by computer, give the same project selections as those determined by the B/C ratio.[2]

Example 14.2

A river basin development in the northwestern region of the United States requires that a number of dams be built. The time horizon for all dams is 100 years. The discount rate imposed by the federal agency planning the project is 5 percent. If all dams are independent of one another, or assumed so, which dams would qualify for construction if the budget were set at no more than $800 million in construction costs, all adjusted to time zero? As in the previous example, all unused funds must be returned to the federal government.

Table 14.2 contains the 10 projects with the net present worth of each shown, where net present worth means the present worth of benefits less first cost. As the table stands, if the projects are indivisible, the answer to the question of the previous paragraph is impossible to determine without a linear programming solution with the value of the variables restricted to zero or one according to the equations of the earlier portion of this chapter. Performance of such a program elicits projects 1, 4, 5, 8, and 10 with net present worths totaling $203.1 million and construction costs totaling $750 million.

---

[1] A computer is a great help even for a simple problem, especially if one does not recognize that Example 14.1 is the so-called "knapsack" problem. (See H. Martin Weingartner and David N. Ness, "Methods for the Solution of the Multi-dimensional 0/1 Knapsack Problem," *Operations Research*, Vol. 15, No. 1, January-February, 1967.) A computer program that can be adapted for use is GINTLP, 36512, BASIC, Hewlett-Packard Co., 1976.

[2] See William J. Baumol, *Economic Theory and Operations Analysis*, 2nd ed. (Prentice-Hall, Englewood Cliffs, NJ: 1965), for a complete description of the integer programming problem and solution.

TABLE 14.2 Northwestern Dams (in $00000)

Project	First Cost	Annual Benefits	P/A, 5, 100	Present Worth	Net Present Worth
1	1500	84.7	19.847	1681	181
2	2500	131.5		2610	110
3	3000	160.2		3179	179
4	1000	69.3		1375	375
5	2000	132.0		2620	620
6	3000	169.3		3360	360
7	1500	77.3		1535	35
8	1000	67.5		1340	340
9	1500	84.4		1675	175
10	2000	126.7	19.847	2515	515
	Σ $19000				

The equations are:

$$\text{Max } Z = 181x_1 + 110x_2 + 179x_3 + 375x_4 + 620x_5 + 360x_6 \\ + 35x_7 + 340x_8 + 175x_9 + 515x_{10}$$

subject to:

$$1500x_1 + 2500x_2 + 3000x_3 + 1000x_4 + 2000x_5 + 3000x_6 \\ + 1500x_7 + 1000x_8 + 1500x_9 + 2000x_{10} \leq 8000 \\ x_i = 0, 1 \text{ for } i = 1, 2, \ldots 10$$

Fifty million dollars must be returned to the federal government as unusable for this program. No other group of dams will maximize net present worth within the $800 million constraint as much as these five projects.

An internal rate of return or benefit/cost ratio solution leads to the same project selection, as you should determine for yourself.

NET PRESENT VALUE AND INTERNAL RATE OF RETURN COMPARED

Under certain conditions, described in the following example, net present value results and internal rate of return (or benefit/cost ratio) solutions to the capital budgeting problem may differ, if the methods are not handled properly.

Table 14.3 shows five projects, each costing $1 million. Imagine

TABLE 14.3 Five Independent Projects

Project	Internal Rate of Return	Cost ($000)	Net Present Value[a] ($000)					
			(%) 25	20	18	15	10	0
A	25	1000	0	600	800	1300	2200	4000
B	20	1000	−600	0	400	1000	2200	5000
C	18	1000	−200	−200	0	200	800	2200
D	15	1000	−1200	−800	−600	0	1200	4600
E	10	1000	−1200	−1800	−1600	−1100	0	2700
		Σ 5000						

[a] To the nearest $100,000.

that the company considering these projects assigns an analyst to evaluate them and set up a capital budget. The company specifies an opportunity cost of capital of 10 percent, determined from calculations related to their dividends paid on common and preferred stock, and returns on equity capital. The analyst dutifully proceeds to find the internal rates of return of projects A through E, having been informed that he is to assume a budget of $5 million. All the projects qualify. Their order is A, B, C, D, and E from best to worst according to the internal rate of return criterion.

The analyst decides to check his selection by the present worth method, using the opportunity cost of capital he has been given of 10 percent. He records the present value of each of the projects in the 10 percent column of Table 14.3. On inspecting these values he discovers that the same projects are selected but that the order is slightly but significantly different. It is now A, B, D, C, and E. Projects A and B are equally attractive, and C and D have switched places. To clarify the matter he computes the remainder of Table 14.3 at 25, 20, 18, 15, and 0 percent and graphs the present worth profiles of the five projects as in Figure 14.1. It is now clear that the change in ranking took place because of the differing patterns of the present worth profiles. The different patterns occur because the projects differ—and not proportionately—in their net current value at the end of each year over the time horizon the analyst is considering.

Shortly after performing the preceding analysis, the analyst is informed that the budget has been reduced to $3 million. By the net present value criterion, at the 10 percent opportunity cost of capital he has been assigned, he selects from Table 14.3 projects A, B, and D, thus using up the budget. But on checking his selection against the internal rate of return criterion, he discovers that he must choose projects A, B, and C, at 25, 20, and 18 percent respectively. This is a severe contradiction that he finds irreconcilable.

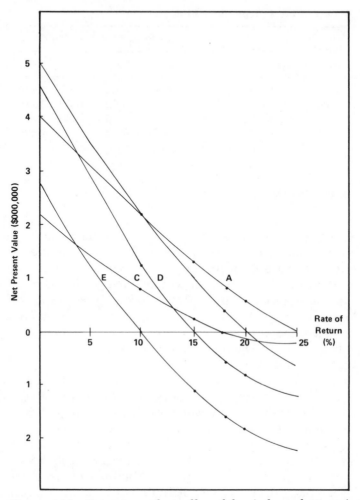

Figure 14.1   Present worth profiles of five independent projects.

The point is that the discount rate chosen for evaluating the projects must be the same as the *implicit* opportunity cost of capital, not the opportunity cost of capital determined from calculations unrelated to the capital budget. The implicit opportunity cost of capital is equal to the internal rate of return of the last project selected in the capital budget. This definition follows exactly the doctrine of opportunity cost, because to invest in any other project yielding less than 18 percent would be to forgo the benefit of the last project selected, project C at 18 percent.

The analyst presently notices the point. He has been selecting projects according to the net present value criterion at an opportunity cost of capital of 10 percent, a value totally unrelated to the capital budget. At 18 percent he finds no contradiction between the net present value criterion and the internal rate of return criterion, and the budget of $3 million is used completely.

He has not only determined the capital budget; he has also found the cut-off point that fixes the opportunity cost of capital for the firm until a new budget comes along.

THE FINANCIAL COST OF CAPITAL

Now it is worth asking, "Is there any use at all for a cost of capital that is independent of the capital budget?"

I will go through a weighted average financial cost of capital example to answer that question and then proceed to criticize the method.

A company has the capital structure shown in Table 14.4. The average financial cost of capital is 6.7 percent. The figure was obtained by dividing the total average payment for the use of company funds by the total of those funds and multiplying by 100. Imagine now that the capital budget for the current year has been set at $10 million. The bottom project that will fit into the budget has an internal rate of return of 5 percent. (All the projects are independent.) Should it be funded? Purely on the information set out here, the answer would have to be, "No." The financial cost of capital, which we will assume is valid in every way, is 6.7 percent; the opportunity cost of capital within this budget is 5.0 percent. To fund anything below 6.7 percent would be to suffer a loss under the assumptions of the example. The use of the financial cost of capital figure is to provide a floor to the opportunity cost of capital. No project should be funded below the level of the financial cost of capital. So goes the standard formulation of the matter.

TABLE 14.4 Capital Structure

Source of Funds	Amount ($000,000)	Average Dividend or Interest Rate (%)	Total ($000,000)
Common stock	100	6	6.0
Preferred stock	50	5	2.5
Bonds	20	7	1.4
Short term bank loans	5	10	0.5
Retained earnings	10	20	2.0
	185		12.4

$$\frac{12.4}{185} \times 100 = 6.7\%$$

As we look at Table 14.4 a little more closely, an interesting point appears. Should not the financial cost of capital be 10 percent? In other words, should it not be the marginal financial cost of capital that can be avoided? This is the avoidance of the $5 million in short-term bank loans. If that were considered a project, it would pay off at 10 percent. We would certainly fund nothing below 10 percent, because it would be ridiculous to borrow at 10 percent in order to profit at 5 percent.

The whole subject of the financial cost of capital is fraught with such pitfalls. It is probably beyond the scope of this book to go into it, but I bring it up so as to warn you against erroneous simplifications of the subject, such as the example presented here. The trouble with the example is that it oversimplifies by implicitly assuming away many a difficulty. Some of the difficulties follow.

Are we to value common and preferred stock at its par or market value? Remember that a possible "project" is to buy back the company's own stock and thus avoid paying dividends on it. Market price seems to be the proper way to value stock; par value for the purposes of economic analysis before income tax would seem to be a sunk benefit—since the company received the proceeds of the stock sale in the past—and therefore useless. But stock prices fluctuate continuously and for some stocks, wildly. How are we to set a period for valuing the stock, therefore? We could choose a period in which prices were high and get one answer, or we could choose one in which prices were low and get an entirely different result.

If we decided, in view of the opportunity of buying back our own stock, to project its future value over some sort of project time horizon average, we would be faced with extreme values for some companies, depending on the probabilities of our stock prices reaching certain figures. The matter could be carried on and on into deeper and more winding pathways—and has been in many studies.

Another grave difficulty of determining the cost of capital in relation to stock prices is that the projects we choose affects the price of our stock, which in turn affects the floor of our capital budget, which contains the projects we choose. The interdependence of stock prices and choice of project has been the subject in financial circles of articles whose complications we will not dwell on here.

The item marked "Retained earnings" in Table 14.4 was assigned a 20 percent cost. Determining that cost is far from an agreed-upon procedure among writers on the subject.

Finally, when one considers the many accounting conventions used to compute company profit, which itself is used in determining the values of Table 14.4, the difficulties become monumental. Such matters as the depreciation method for any number of assets and asset classes, book value for income tax purposes, and book value for internal accounting purposes, and the choice of how to recognize prepaid items, or such intangibles as good will, make the financial cost of capital computation an arbitrary procedure.

CAPITAL RATIONING: INDEPENDENT AND MUTUALLY EXCLUSIVE PROJECTS COMBINED

This book has treated mutually exclusive projects at length. In an earlier section of this chapter I discussed independent projects. Another class of projects exists in which independent and mutually exclusive projects are combined in the same list proposed for approval. The same conditions are present as for the previous class of projects except that now both row and column subscripts must be included, where all i's of the same number represent mutually exclusive projects and all j's represent independent projects.

$$\text{Max } Z = \sum_i^m \sum_j^n b_{ij} x_{ij}$$

subject to:

$$\sum_i^m \sum_j^n c_{ij} x_{ij} \leqslant M$$

$$x_{ij} = 0, 1 \text{ for } i = 1, 2 \ldots m$$
$$\text{and } j = 1, 2 \ldots n$$

We must include a constraint that will prevent the program from selecting more than one mutually exclusive project. That is, it must select only one project from any row i. Therefore,

$$\sum_j^n x_{ij} \leqslant 1$$

For example, if there are three mutually exclusive projects in row i, we will have:

$$x_{11} + x_{12} + x_{13} \leqslant 1$$

Since x_{ij} must be either zero or one, only one number of the row can be chosen.

The measure of worth, b_{ij}, must be present worth because I will solve the examples using that measure. Thus b_{ij} equals $B_{ij} - C_{ij}$ where B is the present worth of net benefits and C the cost at time zero of any alternative.

Example 14.3 ───────────────────────────────

The table of Example 14.1 is modified so that projects 1, 2, and 3 are now mutually exclusive, as are projects 4 and 5, and 6 and 7. The situation is shown in Table 14.5, all projects in the same row are mutually exclusive, indicated by the word "or" between the column numbers. Projects in any column are independent, as indicated by the word "and" between the row numbers. That is, no more than one project from any row may be chosen, but any columnar project may be chosen.

The assumptions are the same as in Examples 14.1 and 14.2. That is, we are dealing with a fixed budget; any leftover funds must be returned to their source; and the discount rate is given to us.

The equations are:

$$\text{Max } Z = 60x_{11} + 30x_{12} + 10x_{13} + 20x_{21} + 15x_{22} + 5x_{31} + 7x_{32}$$

Subject to:

$$30x_{11} + 30x_{12} + 10x_{13} + 20x_{21} + 20x_{22} + 5x_{31} + 1x_{32} \leq 50$$
$$x_{11} + x_{12} + x_{13} \leq 1$$
$$x_{21} + x_{22} \leq 1$$
$$x_{31} + x_{32} \leq 1$$
$$x_{ij} = 0, 1 \text{ for } i, j = 1, 2, 3$$

TABLE 14.5 **Mutually Exclusive and Independent Projects (in $000,000)**

Net present value matrix				
1	or	2	or	3
1				
60		30		10
and				
2				
20		15		—
and				
3				
5		7		—

Initial cost matrix				
1	or	2	or	3
1				
30		30		10
and				
2				
20		20		—
and				
3				
5		1		—

The solution is x_{11} and x_{21} with net present value maximized at $80 million and first cost exactly at $50 million.

An unlimited budget would have included project x_{32}. Such budgets require only that the best project be chosen from each row by methods we have seen before the present chapter, thus making a programming solution unnecessary.

Example 14.4

Example 14.2 is modified such that the tableau of Table 14.6 appears, with all row projects mutually exclusive and all column projects independent.

Imagine that the river basin development is now restricted to four rivers, each of which will be dammed. River 1 has three mutually exclusive possibilities that differ in location, design, benefits, and costs. River 2 has three mutually exclusive alternative projects. River 3 has only one alternative, and river 4 has three alternatives, each of which excludes the others.

The budget is once again $800 million. With it we must maximize the value of the net present value matrix subject to the initial cost

TABLE 14.6 Northwestern Dams
(in $000,000)

Net present value matrix					
	1	or	2	or	3
1	181		110		179
and					
2	375		620		360
and					
3	35		—		—
and					
4	340		175		515

Initial cost matrix					
	1	or	2	or	3
1	1500		2500		3000
and					
2	1000		2000		3000
and					
3	1500		—		—
and					
4	1000		1500		2000

matrix and to the other constraints described earlier in this section. The solution is x_{11}, x_{22}, x_{31}, and x_{33}, with a net present value of $135.1 million and a total initial cost of $700 million. One hundred million dollars must be returned to the government.

CAPITAL RATIONING: INDEPENDENT, MUTUALLY EXCLUSIVE, AND DEPENDENT PROJECTS WITH EXCESS FUNDS INVESTED

All the remarks of the previous sections on capital budgeting in this chapter apply, with the important addition that we now remove the assumption that all budget not used must be returned to its source. Now all unused budget may be invested at the opportunity cost of capital. This is much more akin to the situation encountered in private industry. We assume that the opportunity cost of capital is determined by the internal rate of return of the last project selected, thus avoiding the difficulties inherent in the dependency of net present value and internal rate of return brought out in the second section of this chapter.

The present worth of the unused dollars in a budget is the exact amount of those dollars. Let us call W_M the optimal worth under any budget M. If the measure of worth is benefit present worth, then:

$$W_M = \text{Max } Z + (M - \sum_i^m \sum_j^n c_{ij}x_{ij})$$

where all symbols are as explained previously in this chapter.

Now dependence (contingency): Let one project depend on another's selection. Let us use the example from the beginning of the chapter of a machine that requires a building to house it. Let us say that project x_{31} is the machine and x_{42} the building. The constraint that prevents x_{31} from being chosen unless x_{42} is also chosen is:

$$x_{31} \leq x_{42}$$

But x_{42} must be either zero or one. If x_{42} is zero, x_{31} must also be zero. If x_{42} is one, then x_{31} may be one, that is, may also be selected, or zero, that is, rejected by the programming process of maximization. Implied here is that project x_{42}, the building, has other uses than simply to house the machine, x_{31}, and may therefore qualify completely on its own merits.

Before attempting to apply the model, since we have called the measure of worth present worth, notice that b_{ij} has become B_{ij} where B

is the present worth of net benefits, and c is that first cost of any alternative. The complete equation is:

$$W_M = \sum_i^m \sum_j^n B_{ij}\, x_{ij} + M - \sum_i^m \sum_j^n c_{ij} x_{ij} \tag{1}$$

Example 14.5 ───────────────────────────────

A simple example, susceptible to a solution without using an electronic computer, follows. It is composed of the seven alternatives of Example 14.3, some of which are mutually exclusive, but none of which is dependent. The projects are presented in Table 14.5. The present worth of the optimal combination of projects is, from equation (1):

$$W_M = 90x_{11} + 60x_{12} + 20x_{13} + 40x_{21} + 35x_{22} + 10x_{31}$$

$$+ 8x_{32} + M - \sum_i^m \sum_j^n c_{ij} x_{ij}$$

subject to:

$$M \geqslant \sum_i^m \sum_j^n c_{ij} x_{ij} = 30x_{11} + 30x_{12} + 10x_{13} + 20x_{21} + 20x_{22}$$
$$+ 5x_{31} + 1x_{32}$$
$$\sum_j^n x_{ij} \leqslant 1$$
$$x_{ij} = 0, 1 \text{ for } i, j = 1, 2, 3$$

With an unlimited budget, we are free to choose the best project from each row without concern for its cost, thus:

$$W_M = 90(1) + 60(0) + 20(0) + 40(1) + 35(0) + 10(0) + 8(1)$$
$$= 90 + 40 + 8$$
$$= 138$$

The first cost is:

$$M = C = 30 + 20 + 1$$
$$= 51$$

Reducing the budget to 50 and choosing projects x_{11} and x_{21}:

$$W_M = 90(1) + 60(0) + 20(0) + 40(1) + 35(0)$$
$$+ 10(0) + 8(0) + 50 - 50$$
$$= 130$$

$$C = 30(1) + 30(0) + 10(0) + 20(1)$$
$$+ 20(0) + 5(0) + 1(0)$$
$$= 50$$

but if we choose projects x_{11} and x_{32}, for example:

$$W_M = 90(1) + 60(0) + 20(0) + 40(0) + 35(0)$$
$$+ 10(0) + 8(1) + 50 - 31$$
$$= 117$$
$$C = 30(1) + 30(0) + 10(0) + 20(0)$$
$$+ 20(0) + 5(0) + 1(1)$$
$$= 31$$

Our previous solution of Example 14.3 is optimal at $M = 50$, including the effect of the presence of leftover funds, whose worth must be added into the present worth equation. At $M = 50$, the projects chosen are still x_{11} and x_{21} with the remaining budget invested at the opportunity cost of capital.

CONCLUSION

You must by now have realized that capital budgeting under constraints is no simple matter. Although the examples presented have been simple ones, some solvable by inspection, it must be evident that these are the exception rather than the rule. The least complication requires that the analyst resort to programming techniques, either with pencil in hand or with computer and canned program available. Additionally, the dependence among internal rate of return, net present value, and the opportunity cost of capital must be well understood if costly mistakes are to be avoided.

REFERENCES

Bierman, Harold, Jr., and Seymour Smidt, *The Capital Budgeting Decision*. New York: Macmillan, 1966.

Grant, Eugene L., W. Grant Ireson, and Richard S. Leavenworth, *Principles of Engineering Economy*, 6th ed. New York: Ronald, 1976, pp. 510–527.

Quirin, G. David, *The Capital Expenditure Decision*. Homewood, Ill.: Irwin, 1967. pp. 175–197.

Weingartner, H. Martin, "Capital Budgeting of Interrelated Projects: Survey and Synthesis," *Management Science*, 12(7) 485–516 (March 1966).

15

Cash Flow with Multiple Rates of Return

The multiple rate of return question has been thought to be largely a theoretical one, and if at all practical, related only to the extractive industries. However, new trends in our society more and more require that industry, whether public or private, clean up after itself, so that an investment is required not only at the beginning of an enterprise's life but also at its end. The cash flow of such an enterprise shows a down arrow—or several—at time N. Sometimes incremental cash flows display reversals in direction during their middle or later periods. These are not the usual cash flow we have seen with its down arrow at the beginning of the time horizon and up arrows after that. The special significance of this is that the cash flow with more than one reversal of sign has more than one internal rate of return. The question then arises: "Which of these rates of return is correct, or are any of them correct?"

Worse yet, in certain patterns of cash flow, a contradiction arises between the decision as determined by an internal rate of return and as indicated by the maximum present worth or net value criterion. Figure 15.1 illustrates the difficulty. The cash flow from which this present worth profile is drawn has two solving rates of return, i_1^* and i_2^*. If i is the opportunity cost of capital for this enterprise, the analyst will reject the project this cash flow describes on encountering i greater than i_1^*. Yet if he checks the present worth of the project at the opportunity cost of capital i, he will find the project acceptable!

Leaving aside for the moment the option of avoiding the difficulty by turning to another method, let us look into the question in detail.

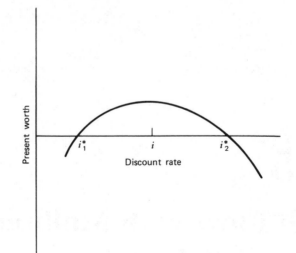

Figure 15.1   The multiple internal rate of return dilemma.

DESCARTES' RULE OF SIGNS

We learn in elementary algebra that a single-variable equation has the same number of roots as the highest power to which its variable is raised. Thus, the equation:

$$-P + A_1 x + A_2 x^2 + A_3 x^3 \ldots + A_{N-1} x^{N-1} + A_N x^N = 0 \qquad (1)$$

has N roots. These roots may be positive, negative, or imaginary.

Descartes' rule of signs points out that equations with only one sign change have only one real positive root. This is the case in the preceding equation, because its terms change from a $-P$ to $+A_1 x$ and thereafter remain positive. Notice that this is the situation we have dealt with in our usual pattern of cash flows—an outflow of cash $(-P)$ followed by a series of inflows $(+A_1 \ldots +A_N)$. Now if we imagine that x represents $\dfrac{1}{1+i}$, it is evident that $\dfrac{1}{1+i}$ is equal to a single, positive, real number:

$$\frac{1}{1+i} = x$$

and

$$i = \frac{1-x}{x}$$

A little experimentation with this last equation reveals that i may be either positive or negative depending on whether x is between zero and one or greater than one, meaning merely that the usual cash flow may have a positive or negative rate of return. It has but one, however.

Now take the case in which equation (1), which is now seen as the present worth equation with x equal to $\frac{1}{1+i}$, changes sign more than once:

$$+P - A_1 x + A_2 x^2 = 0$$

or

$$-P + A_1 x - A_2 x^2 = 0$$

In fact, it changes sign twice. Descarte's rule of signs requires that each of the preceding equations have two positive real roots or none, because each has two sign changes. The two solving rates of return must be real and may be positive or negative, if they exist, or there may be no real roots. Substituting for x:

$$+P - A_1 \left(\frac{1}{1+i}\right) + A_2 \left(\frac{1}{1+i}\right)^2 = 0$$

and

$$-P + A_1 \left(\frac{1}{1+i}\right) - A_2 \left(\frac{1}{1+i}\right)^2 = 0$$

I will deal with the two-root case only. Three and more roots are possible but not nearly so usual.

Example 15.1 ───────────────────────────────────

A petroleum engineer who specializes in secondary recovery discovers the following possibility for quick profit. He believes that a certain well that has been producing for many years offers high returns if it can be recharged by water injection. The preparations after the arrangements are made will take one year. The well will be sold off again in two years. The cash flow appears in Table 15.1.

The present owner agrees to sign the deal immediately so that the engineer receives $100,000 at signing, with the understanding that the present owner will receive $400,000 at the end of one year, after the engineer has had time to raise money that may be used for only

TABLE 15.1 Oil Well Cash Flow

Year	Cash Flow ($)
0	+100,000
1	−800,000
2	+1,200,000

this project. The $800,000 outflow at the end of year 1 is made up of the $400,000 payment to the owner, $500,000 cost of recharging, and $100,000 net profits from the well's operation during year 1. The $1,200,000 at the end of year 2 is the net proceeds from the year's operations and the sale.

What is the internal rate of return, also known as the marginal efficiency of capital, from this operation?

Figure 15.2 shows the present worth profile of this cash flow, and Table 15.2 shows the present worths at 0, 20, 50, 100, 300, and 500 percent. Two solving rates of return are evident—at 100 and 500 percent, for here the present worths of the cash flow are zero. The existence of two internal rates of return should not come as a surprise because the cash flow has two reversals of sign. According to Descartes' rule, this means two positive, real roots of the equation or none, which in terms of rates of return—the i's—means two rates of return, either positive or negative, or none.

Before proceeding, I should emphasize that this engineer does not belong to a company, the funds are to be borrowed for this project only, and that thus his next best opportunity for investment of these

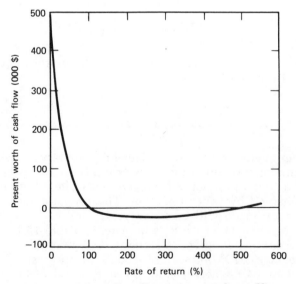

Figure 15.2 Oil well present worth profile.

TABLE 15.2 Present Worths of Oil Well Cash Flows
(in $000)

Year	Cash Flow ($000)	$P/F, 0, N$	@0%	$P/F, 20, N$	@20%	$P/F, 50, N$	@50%
0	+100	1.000	+100	1.0000	+100	1.0000	+100
1	−800	1.000	−800	0.8333	−667	0.6667	−533
2	+1200	1.000	+1200	0.6944	+833	0.4444	+533
			+500		+266		+100

$P/F, 100, N$	@100%	$P/F, 300, N$	@300%	$P/F, 500, N$	@500%
1.0000	−100	1.0000	+100	1.0000	+100
0.5000	−400	0.2500	−200	0.1667	−133
0.2500	−300	0.0625	+75	0.0278	+33
	0		−25		0

funds at equal risk does not exist. His opportunity cost of capital for his own money is about 8 percent, which he can receive on certificates of deposit, but this fact is not relevant to his decision on the project. If there is no other opportunity for the investment of the funds for this project, then no opportunity cost of capital *for these funds* exists. Thus "the opportunity cost of capital" is a meaningless term for this investment. (We must also assume that borrowing capital for this project will not affect his credit.)

The $100,000 he receives at the deal's signing he regards as money he does not have to borrow elsewhere. Thus, he makes two computations. At 0 percent borrowing rate, the $100,000 can be imagined to be balancing part of the $800,000 cost at the end of year 1, leaving $700,000 as a cost. With that $700,000 invested in the project, he will receive $1,200,000 at the end of year 2. This gives him a rate of return of 71 percent. Figure 15.3 shows the original cash flow and the two phases of the project—the borrowing–lending phase of the first year and the investment phase of the second.

The 71 percent return is calculated by the engineer as follows:

$$-700 + 1,200(P/F, i^*, 1) = 0$$

$$(P/F, i^*, 1) = \frac{700}{1,200} = 0.5833$$

$$\left(\frac{1}{1 + i^*}\right)^1 = 0.5833$$

$$i^* = \frac{1 - 0.5833}{0.5833}$$

$$i^* = 0.71$$

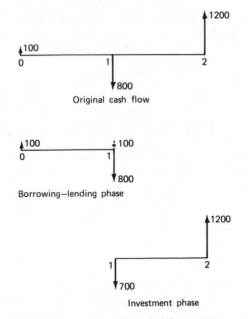

Figure 15.3   Cash flows separated at 0% borrowing rate (in $1000s).

He makes another calculation, assuming that the borrowing rate for the $100,000 he received at time zero is 20 percent—the rate at which he is raising money for this project. At the end of the first year it is equivalent to $120,000. This is shown as the dashed arrow in Figure 15.4. In the investment phase, the project then matches $680,000 against a $1,200,000 return one year later. By a calculation similar to the preceding one, the rate of return is computed at 77 percent for the entire project.

Thus, looked at in a practical way, the rate of return of the project is neither 100 percent nor 500 percent but 71 or 77 percent, depending on the borrowing rate the analyst selects as realistic.

Notice that the only way 100 percent could be accepted as a rate of return would be if it were also accepted as a reasonable borrowing rate. The same statement may be made for the 500 percent rate of return.

Does not opportunity cost enter here? It enters only as the engineer compares his 77 percent with the rate he can get elsewhere—8 percent on certificates of deposit, although the risks are nowhere near comparable. The engineer would probably compare the time he spends on this project and the return he stands to make on it with alternative uses of his time and energies. He might say, "I can do this or go to work for XYZ Petroleum at $40,000 per year. Or I can try to hunt up another such deal." For the expenditure of two years of his

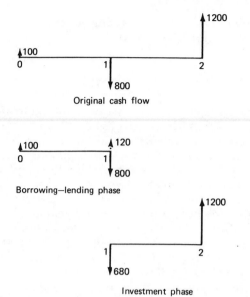

Figure 15.4 Cash flows separated at 20% borrowing rate (in $1000s).

time—provided he works full time on his own project—and $800,000 of borrowed money, he has made at the end of two years:

	$1,200,000	(revenue)
less:	800,000	(borrowed)
less:	160,000	(interest due on $800,000 at 20%)
	$240,000	

This is the profit on the operation on which he would base his decision.

You may argue that this calculation is no more than an appoach to our engineer's own opportunity cost of the capital that he possesses in terms of the use of his professional abilities. His decision is really a certain $40,000 per year indefinitely versus an uncertain $240,000 at the end of two years. His decision is sure to be highly subjective, although it will undoubtedly be partially based on his estimate of the probability of obtaining the $240,000.

Notice that we have strayed far away from the 77 percent rate of return as a basis for decision. It now also seems irrelevant. The decision in the last analysis must be based on personal estimates of personal opportunities perhaps fortified with some probabalistic analysis involving expected values. The 100 and 500 percent appear not at all.

Opportunity cost does not enter into any calculation related to the original $100,000 because this is being used to advance the project and is not available for investment.

Example 15.2 ───────────────────────────────────────

The Giant Slide amusement concession is offered to an entrepreneur and investor in a small midwestern city. It will cost only $4000 to erect because it is merely a framework of scaffolding that supports the Giant Slide—an undulating surface down which people slide on sacks. The stairs to the top of the slide and a ticket booth complete the installation. The contract must run for two years. The investor foresees a $25,000 net return at the end of the first year. He wishes to calculate his rate of return if he holds on for a second year and business falls off, since such attractions often have a short life. In the worst of cases he foresees a $25,000 loss, which would include the $2000 it would cost to remove the Giant Slide. Table 15.3 shows the Giant Slide cash flows. Notice that the cash flow sums to a negative $4000, yet as we will see, it has positive rates of return.

Table 15.4 shows the present worths of the cash flow at 0, 25, 200, and 400 percent with solving rates of return at 25 and 400 percent. Figure 15.5 shows the present worth profile. Two solving rates were to be expected because two sign reversals occur in the cash flow. But does the project earn 25 percent, or 400 percent, or neither? The investor finds it hard to believe that it earns 400 percent. To bring the matter down to earth, he sees the cash flow divided into two phases—an investment phase and a borrowing phase. These are shown in Figure 15.6.

Let us now see the effect of the source of funds in the following four situations.

First, the entrepreneur is offered at 10 percent exactly enough funds ($4000) but with the provision that they be used only for this project. Thus, because no other opportunity exists in which to use the funds, opportunity cost of capital does not exist for these monies, the same situation as in the previous example.

Because the investor's borrowing rate is 10 percent, $4400 at the end of the first year is the capital cost of investing in the project. This leaves an excess of $20,600. The question now becomes, "If $20,600 is

TABLE 15.3 Giant Slide Cash Flows
(in dollars)

Year	Cash Flow
0	− 4,000
1	+25,000
2	−25,000
	Σ −$4,000

TABLE 15.4 Present Worths of Giant Slide Cash Flows
(in dollars)

Year	Cash Flow	P/F, 0, N	@0%	P/F, 25, N	@25%	P/F, 200, N	@200%	P/F, 400, N	@400%
						Discount Rates and Single Payment Present Worth Factors			
0	−4,000	1.0000	−4,000	1.0000	−4,000	1.0000	−4,000	1.0000	−4,000
1	+25,000	1.0000	+25,000	0.8000	+20,000	0.3333	+8,333	0.2000	+5,000
2	−25,000	1.0000	−25,000	0.6400	−16,000	0.1111	−2,778	0.0400	−1,000
			−4,000		0		+1,555		0

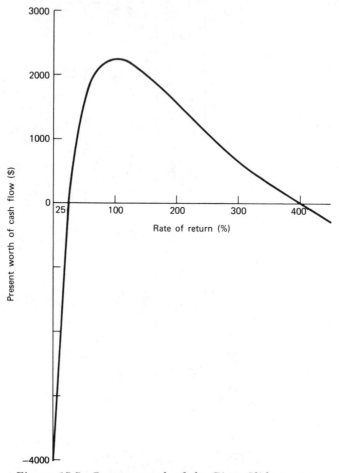

Figure 15.5 Present worth of the Giant Slide venture.

borrowed now, at what borrowing rate will I be repaying the loan if I pay back $25,000 in principal and interest at the end of one year?

$$25,000 = 20,600 \ (F/P, i^*, 1)$$
$$= 20,600 \ (1 + i^*)^1$$
$$i^* = \frac{25,000 - 20,600}{20,600}$$
$$= 0.21$$

The borrowing rate is 21 percent. This rate is higher than the rate at which our investor can borrow the money for the projects. He will reject the project under this "worst" view.

Why would we not consider having the entrepreneur invest the $25,000 at the end of the first year at his opportunity cost of capital?

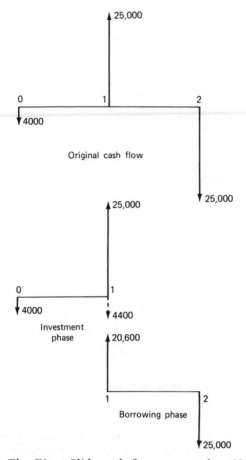

Figure 15.6 The Giant Slide cash flow separated at 10% borrowing cost of capital.

The answer is straightforward. The money is needed to finance the present project. There is no opportunity cost, therefore. In this sense the investor is lending it to his project as though he were a bank.

Second, imagine that the entrepreneur has an enthusiastic backer who will finance any project under the entrepreneur's direction at 15 percent borrowing cost of funds. Imagine, too, that the entrepreneur estimates his opportunity cost for a project of equal risk at 30 percent.

Figure 15.7 illustrates the situation. The borrowing rate is:

$$i* = \frac{25,000 - 19,800}{19,800}$$

$$= \frac{5,200}{19,800}$$

$$= 0.26$$

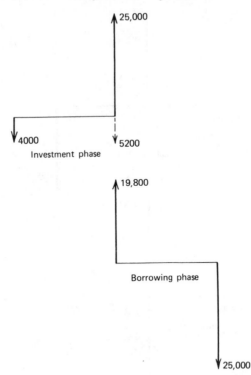

Figure 15.7 The Giant Slide cash flow at 15% borrowing cost of capital.

Twenty-six percent is higher than the entrepreneur need pay to his backer. He will reject the project. This is in direct contradiction to the decision mandated by the net present worth criterion using Figure 15.5. At 30 percent this criterion would indicate acceptance of the project. Therefore, the net present worth criterion is useless and misleading for the conditions of this example.

These three examples show that in no case are the two rates of return internal to the cash flow relevant, although they are mathematically correct. They also show that the concept of the opportunity cost of capital must be used with care. In addition, the last example demonstrates a situation in which the net present value criterion leads to an incorrect conclusion. The borrowing–lending rate emerges as a standard of choice for the first time.

THE EFFECT OF SOURCES OF FUNDS

In the previous examples we have considered investors whose financing came from sources other than themselves. Now let us consider the question of multiple rate of return projects within a firm. Here the opportunity cost of capital and the rate at which money may be allocated among competing projects—the internal borrowing rate—is the same. It is the same because money diverted from one project to another must be costed at the cut-off point in the capital budget, which is the marginal cost of capital in the sense of benefit forgone.

Example 15.2 (continued) ────────────────────────────

Let us now suppose that in Example 15.2—its third use—the question of whether or not to invest is being considered by a large amusement park company. Fifty or sixty other projects are also being analyzed so that the Giant Slide is being forced to compete with many other investments. This company, Luna Park Amusements, posts a 25 percent cut-off rate for capital project qualification. Under this situation, how would our Giant Slide worst-case condition fare?

The present worth profile remains the same. Two internal rates of return are present—25 and 400 percent.

The analyst attacks the problem in the same way that it was approached by the private investor. The investment phase of the first year presumes that from the company's point of view, the $4000 at time zero would be drawn from other uses where it would have made money at the opportunity cost of capital. Since that cost is 25 percent, the company would have to charge the project $1000 for the use of that money during year 1. At the end of year 1, the $4000 would have accumulated to $5000, obtained by adding the $4000 investment and the $1000 charge. At the end of year 1, the matter might be looked at in this way: The investment has cost up to this point $5000, but also at this same time it pays back $25,000. If the analyst nets the up and the down arrows of Figure 15.8 at the end of year 1—that is, the income against the opportunity cost of capital—the effective inflow is $20,000, the difference between $25,000 and $5000. This inflow must now be balanced against the outflow at the end of year 2 of $25,000. The internal borrowing rate is:

$$25,000 = 20,000(F/P, i^*, 1)$$
$$= 20,000(1 + i^*)^1$$
$$i^* = \frac{25,000 - 20,000}{20,000}$$
$$= 0.25$$

What does this situation mean? We have received $20,000 and must pay back $25,000 in one year, indicating a borrowing rate of 25 percent. In other words, this investment would require a payment for the money involved of exactly the opportunity cost of capital for this firm. And this would be just barely acceptable. The company would

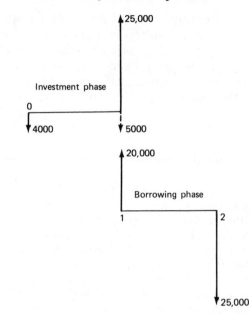

Figure 15.8 The Giant Slide as part of Luna Park Amusements—25%.

neither loose nor gain. (In this book I have laid down the rule that, in situations in which the indications are pointed toward indifference, the project is accepted.) The project would be accepted, because it is exactly level with the threshold of opportunity cost and internal borrowing.

As our fourth use of Example 15.2, let us now move the company to a developing country where the cost of capital is very high. The cut-off rate is set at 200 percent. Following the same method, the analyst calculates that a net of $13,000 was received at the end of the first year (see Figure 15.9). The rate of internal interest for the borrowing phase is:

$$25,000 = 13,000(F/P, i^*, 1)$$
$$= 13,000(1 + i^*)^1$$

$$i^* = \frac{25,000 - 13,000}{13,000}$$

$$= 0.92$$

This is far less than the rate at which the project can borrow funds within the firm—200 percent. And therefore the project would be accepted even in its worst case.

Notice that as far as Luna Park Amusements is concerned, when

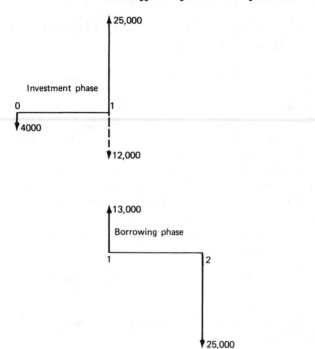

Figure 15.9 The Giant Slide as part of Luna Park Amusements—200%.

the opportunity cost of capital and the borrowing rate within the firm are the same—as they must be—the present worth profile of Figure 15.5 gives proper answers. If the opportunity cost of capital of the firm is less than 25 percent, the project will be rejected, if between 25 and 400 percent, accepted, and greater than 400 percent, rejected. This is no more or less than the present value criterion.

In summary, we must differentiate between two situations.

The first is the single investor case, in particular the case in which all the funds needed are available at a particular borrowing rate. In this case, the technique of Example 1 and the first two situations of Example 2 of this chapter is applicable.

The second is the capital budgeting situation in which funds are limited. In this case the cut-off point of the capital budget—cut off because no more funds are available—is the opportunity cost of capital. It is the same as the internal-to-the-company lending–borrowing rate used to judge the trade-off of projects undertaken by the company.

THE APPLICABILITY OF THE PRESENT WORTH CRITERION

In view of the foregoing examples, I must conclude that in the case of projects with more than one solving, positive, real rate of return the present worth criterion is applicable in the case of capital budgeted projects only—in other words, when the opportunity cost of capital and the within-the-company borrowing rate are the same.

The present worth criterion is not always valid in those multiple rate of return situations when funds are available to handle the project under consideration only from a source external to the organization considering the project and at an externally determined borrowing rate.

When no other opportunity for the use of the funds is allowed, or exists, the opportunity cost of capital is meaningless as it applies to such funds.

THE PUBLIC SECTOR

None of the examples of this chapter have considered the public sector. What about multiple rates of return on public sector projects?

As we have seen, the major question to be asked is: "What is the effect of source of funds, in particular as to the opportunity cost of capital?"

In Chapter 22, I deal with the issue of the opportunity cost of capital and how it is determined in the public sector. It is certainly not determined at the budget cut-off rate of return for all projects, both private and public, in the economy. This would be the ideal situation. If it were determined in this fashion, both borrowing and opportunity cost of capital would be the same, the net present value criterion would be valid as a measure of worth, and the internal rates of return would be useful when they were the same as the borrowing–opportunity cost of capital. That is, it would be possible to say, if one rate were 18 percent, for example, and this were the borrowing–opportunity cost of capital, that 18 percent was the project rate of return. In general, when project internal rate x is the same as borrowing–opportunity rate y, rate x is the rate of return of the project.

The solving rates of return would not be useful, by themselves, at borrowing–opportunity costs of capital other than themselves because we would need the net present value profile in order to determine whether it were positive or negative at the cost of capital in question. For example, if the internal rates of return of a cash flow were 25 and 400 percent and the endogenous opportunity cost of capital were 15 percent, we would have to know the shape of the present worth profile to determine the net present value of the cash flow at the opportunity cost of capital. Thus, the internal rate of return in multiple-root cases has meaning only for discussions relative to the net present value profile.

Because the opportunity cost of capital is not determined by the budget, we are faced with the techniques of the borrowing rate. But what is that, in a national sense? It may be that the only way out of the difficulty is to assume that the discount rate as it is mandated by the appropriate government agency does represent the opportunity cost of capital as implicitly determined by the internal rate of return of the last project in the budget. (When it does not, we find ourselves in the difficulties described on page 175, of the chapter entitled "Capital Budgeting.")

COMPUTER USE: A WARNING

Most computer programs for internal rate of return determination do not detect multiple rates of return, although it is completely possible to write a program that does. They will put forth a single answer. They must be used with care, therefore.

A good way of discovering whether or not a computer program provides for the possibility of multiple rates of return is to try a simple example, such as those contained in this chapter, for which the solutions are known. If the computer detects the correct multiple roots, it can be used with confidence.

A FACTUAL STUDY

A few years ago the Department of Transportation of the United States contracted with a consulting firm to investigate the "cost effectiveness" of railroad electrification in the United States. The purpose of the study was to put together many other studies, reports, papers, and the like that had been done over the years in the country, add to them the experience of foreign nations in the field, and finally emerge with a study and a recommendation for a decision on the matter of diesel-electric locomotives (the public knows these as diesel locomotives) versus electric locomotives.

By *cost effectiveness*, the consulting company meant what we have called in this book *minimum cost analysis*. In other words, the benefits of choosing either alternative were assumed to be the same—electric locomotives could manage to get the same amount of freight per year to the same destinations as well as diesel locomotives and vice versa; the difference would be in the cost.

It is possible to use a number of methods, given the costs of two alternatives, to compare them. Among the methods are minimum annual cost and minimum net present worth of each alternative. We may also use the incremental benefit/cost ratio. Finally, we may use—with care—the incremental internal rate of return. It was this last that the consulting company decided to use, in response to the request of the Department of Transportation. What occurred is relevant to the previous material in this chapter.

The period studied was 1975–2005 because the economic life of the principal actor in the play, the electric locomotive, was thought, on the basis of a number of studies, to be 30 years.

The consulting company chose to make the assessment from two points of view, those of the public sector and the private sector. The public sector portion was to be based on costs in terms of total national resources. The private sector costs were those that would appear on the books of the railroads.

Cost comparisons were not to be based on the total trackage existing in the United States but on a skeleton network made up of high-traffic-density routes. This network carried about half the tonnage and was 14,290 miles long.

The study was to answer four specific questions:

1. Is electrification in the period 1975–2005 attractive from a national cost point of view?

2. Where and under what conditions is electrification appropriate?

3. How much electrification is needed?

4. What will the traffic growth be?

The study was also to comment on the practical problems of putting the whole scheme into practice. What would be the effect on the railroads? Could they do this by themselves? What would be the effect on the electric power industry? What about labor problems, railroad supplier problems, and so on?

Data were difficult to obtain. The federal government was prepared to give as much data as it was able, but it was constrained in this by the proprietary nature of much of the data from the railroads. Many costs and revenues differ among individual railroads. Knowledge of another company's operating costs could prove advantageous. Hence, many data were considered secret. Another limitation was the total absence of fundamental data on how much of what was being carried where and at what date on United States railroads. A 1 percent waybill survey supposedly existed, but it was thought to be faulty. No overall origin and destination survey was in existence. Average data had to be used on equipment, way, operations, and management. In spite of information shortcomings, the study was carried on because of its importance in illuminating a question of grave national importance.

Nondifferential costs were not included. That is, costs that were the same no matter which type of propulsion system was selected were excluded. The cost savings of one system over another were all that the study would supply, not the total cost of either.

The Federal Railway Administration's (FRA) Basic Rail Network was used, as were the FRA traffic projections for 1980. There were about 120,000 miles of mainline links in the United States. These were divided into four regions: the East Coast, South, Mid-West, and Far West.

Locomotives were the same weight and had the same number of axles for both diesel and electric. The latter had almost twice as much power, however. Freight cars were current designs. No passenger service was considered. Fixed installations were the catenary (that is, the overhead electrical lines that supplied the locomotives with power), substations, distribution lines, signals, and communications. Other fixed installations were new tunnel and subway clearances because these had to be heightened to accommodate the catenary, bridge, trestle, and culvert clearance, shops and engine houses, and shop equipment.

Existing equipment was given a value. New equipment was priced as of the year 1975 with no attempt being made to raise prices in the future to account for inflation. All equipment was given a salvage value and an economic life. I have already mentioned the electric locomotive's assigned economic life of 30 years. The diesel locomotive was given an economic life of 15 years. The catenary received an estimated economic life of 45 years. All necessary costs associated with a growing system were estimated.

A discount rate of 13 percent was used, upping the rate 3 percent from the usual 10 percent used in government studies. This was supposed to take care of inflation. The correctness of this procedure is open to doubt, as is seen in a later chapter on inflation.

Figure 15.10 shows the cash flows for both systems, as well as the incremental cash flow of the electric minus the diesel. The amounts shown are no more than the general order of numbers encountered in the study. The D section of Figure 15.10 shows a relatively small investment at time zero followed by heavy yearly operation and maintenance expenses of $600 million, and in the thirtieth year a salvage value of $750 million, the same as the value at time zero.

The middle cash flow shows a heavy investment at year zero of $2750 million, which reflects the much higher cost of electric locomotives in comparison to diesel—$575,000 versus $391,000, and the

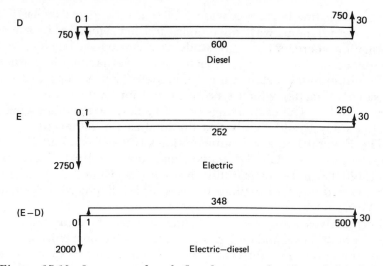

Figure 15.10 Incremental cash flow between electric and diesel systems.

existence in 1975 of a large number of diesels in service with few electrics on the rails. For simplicity's sake, the purchases of both types of locomotive are shown as occurring at time zero. In the consulting company's study, diesel purchases were spread over the years 1975 to 2005, with the purchase of electrics occurring close to time zero.

The middle cash flow shows a $252 million annual operating and maintenance cost for electrics. At the end of 30 years, the salvage value of the electrics is shown as $250 million. This is less than the diesel salvage value because the diesels started the 30 years with a large pool of locomotives with an average value per locomotive that did not vary much over the time horizon of the study. Thus, unlike the electrics, the value of the pool at the end of 30 years was the same as the value at the beginning.

The bottom part of Figure 15.10 shows the incremental cash flow occurring when the diesel cash flow is subtracted from the electric cash flow. The differences are $2,000 million in first cost, $348 million in operating and maintenance costs in favor of the electric locomotives, and $500 million in favor of the diesel system. And here the difficulty becomes apparent. The $500 million must appear as a down arrow. The incremental cash flow has two reversals of sign.

The consulting company had made use of a computer program furnished by a consultant on operations research from a large university. The program made no provision for detecting multiple rates of return. Another consultant detected the reversal of the cash flow brought about by the salvage values and alerted the consulting company to the difficulty. Immediately he was questioned as to which of

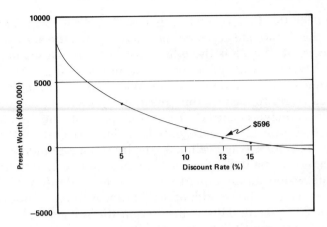

Figure 15.11 Present worth profile of the electric-diesel incremental cash flow.

the two rates of return was correct. He advised the consulting company to avoid the whole difficulty by using some other method, such as present worth. After some objections, because the Department of Transportation had insisted on a rate of return measure, the consulting company followed his advice.

The final report showed a present worth, at 13 percent, of the incremental costs between the two systems of $596 million. (Figure 15.11 presents the present worth profile for the incremental cash flow I have been discussing. Table 15.5 demonstrates the incremental cash flow present worths.) Therefore, the report concluded that a switch from diesel to electric rail systems over the 30 years between 1975 and 2005 was desirable.

But Figure 15.11 reveals more than a present worth of $596 at the selected discount rate of 13 percent. It shows also that the solving rate

TABLE 15.5 Incremental Cash Flow Present Worths

$$PW = -2{,}000 + 348(P/F, i, 30) - 500(P/F, i, 30)$$

Discount Rate	P term	A term	L term	Present Worth
0	−2000	+10,440	−500	+7940
5	−2000	+5,350	−116	+3234
10	−2000	+3,281	−29	+1252
13	−2000	+2,609	−13	+596
16	−2000	+2,150	−6	+144
18	−2000	+1,920	−4	−84
20	−2000	+1,733	−2	−269

of return for the incremental cash flow is a little over 17 percent because that is the rate at which the curve crosses the axis. But this is only one point. Where is the other? We know by Descarte's rule of signs that two reversals of sign must mean two real positive roots of the present worth equation or none. Where, then, is the second?

Let us begin to answer this question by assuring ourselves that the curve as drawn is correct. Table 15.5 presents the equation suitably marked with the usual symbols: P for first cost, A for annual amount, and L for salvage value. As the discount rate increases, the P term remains constant, the A term decreases, and the L term decreases in absolute value. From a quarter of the P term, the L term drops in absolute value to a thousandth of the P term, as the discount rate goes from 0 to 20 percent. This is the reason the salvage value and the whole matter of multiple roots may often be neglected in cash flow patterns such as the one we are dealing with. With terminal cash flows considerably less than the zero year cash flow in the minus-plus-minus pattern of sign changes, ignoring salvage value is often possible. It is increasingly possible at higher discount rates.

Even more interesting is the shape of the curve, for it is the same as the usual single-solving internal rate of return curve that we are accustomed to. It avoids the inconsistency between the present worth solution and the internal rate of return solution explained at the beginning of this chapter, being concave upward rather than downward. But perhaps it will rise again, as in Example 15.1, until it intersects the horizontal axis. A little thought on the behavior of the terms of Table 15.5 as discount rates increase causes us to reject this notion. This, then, must be the project rate of return. The consulting company could have used it and saved itself some arguments with the Department of Transportation. No harm was done by the change to another method, however, because the recommendations are the same and just as solidly supported.

In this case the 17 percent does not contradict the net present value criterion. If the direction of the cash flow were reversed—that is, all the up arrows became down arrows and vice versa—a contradiction would exist. The 17 percent under this latter situation would still be a solving rate of return for the net present value profile because a 180-degree rotation would have occurred around the horizontal axis. It would not be a project rate of return relative to the opportunity cost of capital of 13 percent.

But our question about the other solving rate of return remains. To answer it, let us consider a simplified form of the rail system cash flows. Figure 15.12 illustrates the pattern. Now

$$PW = -P + Ax - Lx^2$$

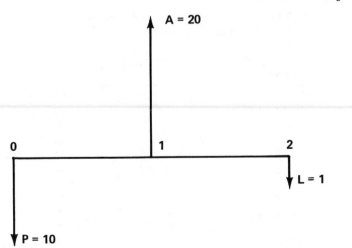

Figure 15.12 A simple cash flow pattern with two solving rates of return.

and two real, positive roots for x must exist or none, according to Descartes' rule of signs. Let $P = 10, A = 20$, and $L = 1$. The equation then becomes, if we let $PW = 0$:

$$0 = -10 + 20x - x^2$$

Using the quadratic formula to solve the equation:

$$x = \frac{-b \pm (b^2 - 4\,ac)^{\frac{1}{2}}}{2a}$$

$$x = +19.5 \text{ or } +0.5 \text{ (approximately)}$$

These are the two, positive, real roots predicted.

Now let $x = \left(\frac{1}{1+i}\right).$

When $+19.5 = \frac{1}{1+i}, i = -0.95 = -95\%$

When $+0.5 = \frac{1}{1+i}, i = +1.0 = +100\%$

We now have as solving rates of return -95 percent and $+100$ percent. Table 15.6 presents the present worth of the cash flow equation at various discount rates. Figure 15.13 shows the resulting curve.

TABLE 15.6 Present Worth Versus
Discount Rate for a Simple Cash Flow
Pattern

Discount Rate (%)	Present Worth
−95	−10
−94	+45
−91	+89
−90	+90
−80	+65
−50	+26
−10	+11
0	+9
+10	+7
+50	+3
+100	0

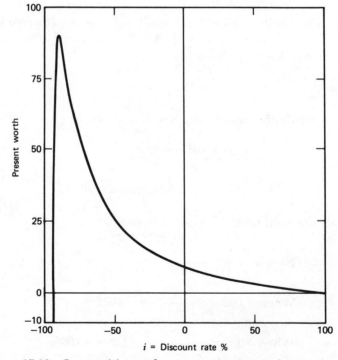

Figure 15.13   One positive and one negative internal rate of return.

It reveals solving rates of return at $+100$ percent and just a little short of -95 percent. Its maximum is found as follows:

$$PW = -10 + 20x - x^2$$

$$\frac{d(PW)}{dx} = 20 - 2x$$

Setting the first derivative equal to zero, $x = 10$. Since $x = \dfrac{1}{1 + i}$:

$$10 = \frac{1}{1 + i}$$

and

$$i = -0.9 = -90\%$$

which Figure 15.13 confirms.

It is now clear what has happened to the curve of the present worth profile of the electric–diesel incremental cash flow. It has curved up and over in the negative area of the discount rate and crossed the axis at a negative rate, which has no meaning in this discussion.

Cash flows of this pattern will normally have one positive and one negative internal rate of return as solutions. The positive rate may be accepted with confidence as the single, relevant solving rate of return.[1] In the railroad electrification case, it was a little over 17 percent.

The electrification study concluded with the recommendation that the heavily traveled 50 percent of the nation's railroads be electrified.

Sensitivity tests of locomotive characteristics, ruling grades, investment and operating costs, operations, and discount rates were undertaken to determine at which of their values the decision would reverse itself and indicate continued use of diesel locomotives rather than electrification.

On the basis of the private sector analysis, electrification was also recommended. As traffic increased, the desirability of electrification also increased.

Electrification, as recommended in this factual study, has not been implemented as of the date of this writing (1979). Since the study was made, we have witnessed the heavy increase in petroleum prices over those of 1973, and our increased vulnerability to foreign oil price decisions. It is more than probable that were the study done today, the

---

[1] Norstrom has shown that cash flow coefficients $(P, A_1, A_2, A_3 \ldots A_N)$ with accumulated cash flows $(P, P + A_1, P + A_1 + A_2, \ldots P + \overset{N}{\underset{1}{\Sigma}} A_N)$ have a unique, nonnegative internal rate of return if the accumulated cash flow changes sign once and $P + \overset{N}{\underset{1}{\Sigma}} A_N \neq 0$.

recommendation would be even more overwhelmingly in favor of electrification of the nation's main rail routes.

REFERENCES

Baumol, William J., *Economic Theory and Operations Analysis*, 3rd ed. Englewood Cliffs, New Jersey: Prentice-Hall, 1972, pp. 464–469.

Grant, Eugene L., W. Grant Ireson, and Richard S. Leavenworth, *Principles of Engineering Economy*, 6th ed. New York: Ronald, 1976, pp. 543–562.

Hirschleifer, J., "On the Theory of Optimal Investment Decision," *Journal of Political Economy*, **66** (August 1958). Reprinted in Ezra Solomon, Ed., *The Management of Corporate Capital*. New York: The Free Press 1959.

Hirshleifer, J., "On Multiple Rates of Return: Comment," *Journal of Finance*, **24**(1) p. 98 (March 1969).

Jean, William H., "On Multiple Rates of Return," *Journal of Finance*. **23**(1) pp. 187–191 (March 1968).

Jean, William H., "On Multiple Rates of Return: Reply," *Journal of Finance*, **24**(1) pp. 99–100 (March 1969).

Lorie, J. H. and L. J. Savage, "Three Problems in Rationing Capital," *Journal of Business*, **28**(4) pp. 229–239 (October 1955).

McLean, John G., "How to Evaluate New Capital Investments," *Harvard Business Review*, **36**(6) pp. 59–69 (November-December 1958).

Norstrom, Carl J., "A Sufficient Condition for a Unique Nonnegative Internal Rate of Return," *Journal of Financial and Quantitative Analysis*, **7**(3) pp. 1835–1839 (June 1972).

16

Equivalence and the Reinvestment Fallacy

Perhaps more confusion exists as to the meaning of reinvestment and its application in economic analysis than any other single subject. Many analysts believe that the internal rate of return of a cash flow implies that the positive cash flows must be possible of investment at the internal rate of return in order that the internal rate of return be a valid measure of the worth of an investment alternative. Let us investigate at once the implications of this idea.

Referring to Table 16.1, it is evident that the cash flow shown has an internal rate of return of 50 percent if it is treated as has been described earlier in this book. Does this mean that to qualify as an investment returning 50 percent the investors must search about for another investment that will return 50 percent on the $7500 received at the end of the first year as well as on the $11,250 received at the end of the second year? The answer is evident. If, for every investment returning high rates, it were necessary to ensure reinvestment of the proceeds at the same high rate, few high-return projects would be undertaken. In developing countries, where high rates of return are often possible but not necessarily the rule because risk is often high also, much investment would be forgone, because the IROR determined without reinvestment would be meaningless. No one would be able to guarantee reinvestment of the proceeds at an equally high rate of return. As one considers this interpretation of the meaning of the internal rate of return criterion, so widely heard, its lack of foundation becomes apparent. The cash flow of Table 16.1 is so desirable that to forgo it because of the lack of further investment opportunities would be tantamount to saying that the mink coat that the $7500 would buy or the trip for two to the Orient that the $11,250 would finance are not realizable.

TABLE 16.1   A 50 Percent Investment

Year	Cash Flow	P/F, 50, N	Present Worth
0	−10,000	1.0000	−10,000
1	+7,500	0.6667	+5,000
2	+11,250	0.4444	+5,000
			Σ 0

In other words, the cash flow of an investment stands up to analysis totally on its own merits, whether or not its proceeds are invested or wasted—not that trips to the Orient are a waste.

The preceding example and its discussion illustrates an important economic fact: Investment returns may be invested or consumed. Thus, a definition of internal rate of return, which is the same as rate of return, that requires reinvestment of the returns violates a fundamental economic concept that is universally recognized by writers on the subject.[1] A moment's thought brings to mind many instances in which reinvestment of total product would be disastrous for society— agricultural production, for example. If all the returns of agriculture were invested as seed, following the usual economic example of consumption and investment, nothing would be left for food.

Other analysts believe that the positive cash flows need only be possible of reinvestment at the internal rate of return of the cash flow for the IROR to have meaning. To refute this assertion, let us review the derivation and implications of the original single payment compound amount formula and the single payment present worth formula. (See page 31.)

One thousand dollars was invested at time zero for three years at 10 percent. This sum accumulated to $1331 at the end of three years. The accumulation was more than the original $1000 because of the effect of compound interest. That is, principal was not withdrawn, nor was interest. In other words, both principal and interest were reinvested year after year. Does this fact prove that the internal rate of return criterion requires reinvestment of its positive cash flows, since its definition is based on equating the present worths of benefits and costs? Additionally, recall that the formula for present worth was obtained directly from the compound amount formula, which was a result of our deliberations on this very example.

I believe that it does not. Notice that it was not necessary to invest the sum, $1331, at the end of the third year in order to induce our formula $F_N = P(1 + i)^N$. We merely had to reinvest the original investment itself and its interest. But this is the very meaning of investment.

[1] See the Keynes and Samuelson references.

By extension, any cash flow of benefits resulting from investment may be considered single B_Ns thrown off because of each one's part of the original investment.

To drive the point home, consider a perpetual investment, P, from which an amount, A, will be thrown off each year at interest rate i. The present worth of such an investment is P, because:

$$A = iP \tag{1}$$

$$\text{or } P = \frac{A}{i} \tag{2}$$

The internal rate of return of such an investment is i, because P is the discounted present worth of the costs, $A\left(\frac{1}{i}\right)$ the discounted present worth of the benefits, and equation (2) shows them as equal.

Is it necessary to invest A at i for equation (2) to hold? The answer is no. Yet the belief that such is necessary forms the basis of the contention that reinvestment of the benefits of an investment must be made or be capable of being made for IROR analysis to be valid.

Finally, you may ponder for yourself the implication of the reinvestment fallacy that, since benefits must be reinvested, so must costs.

Examples of the reconciliation of supposed contradictions between the IROR method and the net present value appear on page 91 for mutually exclusive alternatives whose first costs are unequal, and on page 124 for mutually exclusive alternatives whose first costs are equal. Supposed contradictions between the benefit/cost ratio method and the net present value method can be reconciled in a similar manner.

To understand more fully how compound interest operates, we must consider in detail what is meant by equivalence.

EQUIVALENCE

Effects experienced at different times may be equivalent to each other. To be equivalent, the time span of all the consequence flows must be equal for the investment plans or projects under consideration, and the present worths of the cash flows for each plan must also be equal—and therefore their internal rates of return, benefit/cost ratio, and annual worths.

Of what use is the concept of equivalence? It illustrates that different series of cash flows are possible at the same interest rate. For example, it is possible, when applying for a loan, to select a schedule of repayment to suit one's needs. Table 16.2 shows Projects 1 through

TABLE 16.2 Three Plans at Zero Percent Interest

Year	Cash Flow	$P/F, 0\%, N$	Present Worth
Project 1			
0	−10,000	1.000	−10,000
1	+2,500	1.000	+2,500
2	+2,500	1.000	+2,500
3	+2,500	1.000	+2,500
4	+2,500	1.000	+2,500
			$\Sigma\,0$
Project 2			
0	−10,000	1.000	−10,000
1	+4,000	1.000	+4,000
2	+3,000	1.000	+3,000
3	+2,000	1.000	+2,000
4	+1,000	1.000	+1,000
			$\Sigma\,0$
Project 3			
0	−10,000	1.000	−10,000
1	0	1.000	0
2	0	1.000	0
3	0	1.000	0
4	+10,000	1.000	+10,000
			$\Sigma\,0$

3, which all have an internal rate of return of zero percent. Their cash flows are equivalent, by definition, because they have the same rate of return over the same period of time, although they involve different magnitudes at the same dates. They repay the investment fully, with interest at zero percent in this case.

If these projects were, in reality, financial plans that an organization of a special category—a charitable one, say—were considering, the 0 percent interest rate would not be surprising. All the plans would be equivalent for this home for the ill and aged, and there would be no question, financial or legal, that 0 percent was being charged at interest, and that the lender would receive all his money back, although at different amounts each year under the three plans.

Table 16.3 illustrates the principle of equivalence at an interest or discount rate—in this case 10 percent.

Plan 1 shows, from the lender's point of view, the repayment of $10,000 by a series of equal payments of $3,155 per year for four years. The payment includes principal and interest on the declining balance. As the present worth calculation shows, the internal rate of return is 10 percent, equal to the interest or discount rate.

TABLE 16.3 Three Plans at 10 Percent Interest

Year	Cash Flow	P/F, 10, N	Present Worth
Plan 1			
0	−10,000		−10,000
1	+3,155	0.9091	+2,868
2		0.8264	+2,607
3		0.7513	+2,370
4		0.6830	+2,155
			Σ 0
Plan 2			
0	−10,000		−10,000
1	+1,000	0.9091	+909
2	+1,000	0.8264	+826
3	+1,000	0.7513	+751
4	+11,000	0.6830	+7,513
			Σ −1
Plan 3			
0	−10,000		−10,000
1	0	0.9091	0
2	0	0.8264	0
3	0	0.7513	0
4	+14,641	0.6830	+10,000
			Σ 0

Note: $(A/P, 10, 4) = 0.31547$ $(F/P, 10, 4) = 0.14641$

Plan 2 illustrates a so-called "interest only" repayment schedule in which the $10,000 is repaid by four payments of $1,000 each, and the principal of $10,000 is paid at the end of the fourth year. The internal rate of return is again 10 percent.

Plan 3 is a "balloon payment" plan. All interest and principal are deferred until the final year, being in the single payment of $14,641. Once again, as the table shows, the internal rate of return is 10 percent.

Notice that the plans are all equivalent because they all have the same time span, internal rate of return, interest rate, or discount rate, although they all involve different end-of-the-year payments. Notice, too, that they could just as easily have been called projects rather than repayment plans. Had they been, there would have been no question that the analyst would have determined that the internal rate of return for each project was 10 percent and would therefore have been indifferent among them, given the standard assumption that the opportunity cost of capital is the same for all projects and remains constant over the life of the projects.

EQUIVALENCE VIOLATED

Imagine that Projects 1, 2, and 3 of Table 16.2 are evaluated using the fallacious principle that the rate at which the proceeds of a project may be reinvested governs its rate of return. (This is slightly different from the principle of the previous example, although both are equally wrong. Notice that we are not now assuming that the cash flow at zero percent must be invested at zero percent in order to affirm that the internal rate of return of the cash flow is zero.) Say that any net proceeds may be invested at 10 percent. The result will be the cash flow shown in Table 16.4. Each year's positive cash flow is reinvested at 10 percent, and the result is added to the cash flow for the current year. Thus, the column labeled "Year End Balance" is obtained. If the

TABLE 16.4   The Reinvestment Fallacy

Year	Cash Flow	Reinvestment at 10% of Previous Year's Balance	Year End Balance
Project 1			
0	−10,000		
1	+ 2,500		+ 2,500
2	+ 2,500	(2500)(0.10) = 250	+ 5,250
3	+ 2,500	(5250)(0.10) = 525	+ 8,275
4	+ 2,500	(8275)(0.10) = 828	+11.603

$$(P/F, i, 4) = \frac{10,000}{11,603} = 0.8619$$
$$i = 3.8\%$$

Year	Cash Flow	Reinvestment at 10% of Previous Year's Balance	Year End Balance
Project 2			
0	−10,000		
1	+ 4,000		+ 4,000
2	+ 3,000	(4000)(0.10) = 400	+ 7,400
3	+ 2,000	(7400)(0.10) = 740	+10,140
4	+ 1,000	(10140)(0.10) = 1014	+12,154

$$(P/F, i, 4) = \frac{10,000}{12,154} = 0.8228$$
$$i = 5.0\%$$

Year	Cash Flow	Reinvestment at 10% of Previous Year's Balance	Year End Balance
Project 3			
0	−10,000		
1	0		0
2	0	0	0
3	0	0	0
4	+10,000	0	+10,000

ending balance for the fourth year is discounted at the rate that causes it to equal $10,000, that rate is the internal rate of return. In the case of Project 1, it is 4 percent. For Project 2, it is 5 percent. For Project 3, it is zero percent. In the case of Projects 1 and 2, cash flows that were obviously returning at the rate of zero percent have now developed a positive rate of return. Project 3 remained at zero percent because there were no returns that could be reinvested in the period under consideration.

What has happened? It is clear that the analyst has mixed together two separate projects, one that paid off at zero percent and another—in which he invested the proceeds of the first—that paid off at 10 percent. Thus, he has violated the standard rule that separate projects must be evaluated separately. Combining good projects with mediocre ones can cause the latter to be accepted when they should not be. In this case, were the minimum attractive rate of return 4½ percent, Project 2 would have been accepted in spite of the fact that its true rate of return is zero percent.

It is sufficient, therefore, to judge projects by discounting them at the opportunity cost of capital, which is the same as comparing the consequences of choosing a project to the consequences of choosing to invest at the opportunity cost of capital. To observe the further effect of reinvesting at the opportunity cost of capital, which is the reinvestment rate by another name, is to violate the whole economic concept of opportunity cost.

Indeed, we could have taken the original $10,000 and invested it at 10 percent from the beginning of the period of time under consideration. Is there any doubt that it would have been a better investment than investing in projects paying zero percent and reinvesting their proceeds at 10 percent?

The projects of Table 16.4 show different rates of return because they have different cash flow patterns. More money sooner, as in Project 2, results in a higher reinvestment rate of return than proceeds at a constant amount per year.

Finally, it is clear that if reinvestment is made at rate x and the project considered without reinvestment returned at rate y the reinvestment rate of return will lie between x and y.

FURTHER NOTES ON EQUIVALENCE

Figure 16.1 shows the cash flow diagrams of each of three possible arrangements for repaying a loan of $1 billion. Loans of such magnitude are made for major infrastructure additions to developing countries or by the governments of industrially developed nations to private-sector enterprises that they wish to support. Repayment ar-

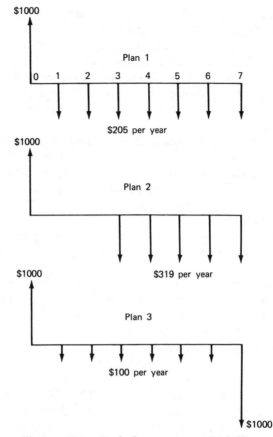

Figure 16.1   Cash flow to repay $1 billion.

rangements differ because, for example, a project may not begin to pay off for several years after its inception, particularly if colonization of an area is required to realize its benefits. Plan 2 might appear more attractive in such a situation than either of the other plans. The only difference among the three plans is the amount of the payments at the ends of the seven years because all have the same present worth at 10 percent. They are all equivalent at that rate.

The first plan shows seven equal yearly repayments of $205 million. Table 16.5 shows the year, total payment, interest payment, principal payment, and balance owed. The total payments have been separated into their interest and principal components in Table 16.5.

Two important points can be seen by inspecting the top portion of the table. First, the interest payment is based on the balance owed at the end of the previous period, and the balance steadily declines. Interest, therefore, is said to be based on declining balance. It need

TABLE 16.5 Repaying $1 Billion in Three Ways
(in $000,000)

Year	Total Payment	Interest Payment at 10%	Principal Payment	Balance Owed
Plan 1				
0				1000
1	205	100	105	895
2	205	90	115	780
3	205	78	127	653
4	205	65	140	513
5	205	51	154	359
6	205	36	169	190
7	205	19	186	0
	1435	439	996	
Plan 2				
0				1000
1	0	100[a]	0	1100
2	0	110[a]	0	1210
3	319	121	198	1012
4	319	101	218	794
5	319	79	240	554
6	319	55	264	290
7	319	29	290	0
	1595	595	1210	
Plan 3				
0				1000
1	100	100	0	1000
2	100	100	0	1000
3	100	100	0	1000
4	100	100	0	1000
5	100	100	0	1000
6	100	100	0	1000
7	1100	100	1000	0
	1700	700	1000	

[a] Interest owed but not paid.

not be done this way, however, and often is not. Interest can be based on the original sum borrowed, which results in much higher interest payments than the situation in which the interest is based on the declining balance. Second, the separation of the interest payment and the principal payment allows the total interest paid to be calculated. This is useful because borrowers often wish to know the total interest that will be paid over the life of a loan. In the United States, in some

TABLE 16.6   Equivalence at Ten Percent
(in $000,000)

Interest Rate	Net Present Value of Interest Payments Plan		
	1	2	3
0%	1435	1595	1700
5%	1186	1253	1290
10%	1000	1000	1000
15%	853	809	792
20%	739	663	640

situations such as those involving home mortgages, the law requires that the total amount of interest to be paid be made known to the borrower. Interest payments are deductible from taxable income in the United States.

In Plan 2 the repayment of the loan is made in five equal payments starting at the end of the third year (see Table 16.5). The payments are also equal, and as in Plan 1, each payment is composed of interest, based on the balance outstanding on the loan at the end of the previous year, and some portion of the principal. In the first two years of this plan, the interest owed, but not paid, is added to the balance at the end of the year. Thus, at the end of the second year $1,210 million is owed, and the third year's interest is computed against it.

Plan 3 is a so-called "interest only" repayment plan with principal being paid off in one stroke at the end of the loan period—in the case shown, at the end of the seventh year. The interest payment in Plan 3 is based on the principal owed at the time zero. The balance does not decline during the period of the loan because no principal is being paid off.

All these plans are equivalent to one another at 10 percent. They pay off the principal sum with interest compounded at 10 percent. The present worths of the three plans are equal at 10 percent, as well. They are not equal at any other rate of interest, and the plans are not equivalent at any other interest rate.

The present worths of these repayments at other rates of interest are shown in Table 16.6. You will notice immediately that as the interest rate rises, the present worths of each plan falls, and conversely. Another way of saying this is to say that the more the future payments are discounted, the less the present worths are. The plans have equal present worths of $1,000 million at 10 percent. Below 10 percent a government would choose Plan 1 if its objective were to

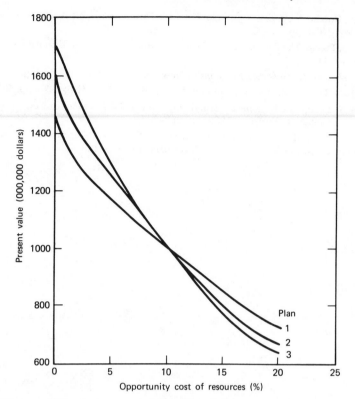

Figure 16.2   Present worth profile of three repayment plans.

minimize the present value of the loan cost. Above 10 percent a government would choose Plan 3. At 10 percent opportunity cost of resources, a government would be indifferent among the plans, all other things being equal.

Figure 16.2 illustrated the present value of each plan's repayment schedules plotted against opportunity cost of resources in percentages.

REFERENCES

Bussey, Lynn E., *The Economic Analysis of Industrial Projects.* Englewood Cliffs, New Jersey: Prentice-Hall, 1978, pp. 252–266.

Baumol, William J., *Economic Theory and Operations Analysis,* 2nd ed. Englewood Cliffs, New Jersey: Prentice-Hall, 1965, pp. 439–448.

Grant, Eugene L., W. Grant Ireson, and Richard S. Leavenworth, *Principles of Engineering Economy,* 6th ed. New York: Ronald, 1976, pp. 563–571.

Keynes, John Maynard, *The General Theory of Employment Interest and Money.* New York: Harcourt Brace, 1936, pp. 135–146.

McKean, Roland N., *Efficiency in Government Through Systems Analysis*. New York: Wiley, 1958, pp. 82–93.

Quirin, G. David, *The Capital Expenditure Decision*. Homewood, Illinois: Irwin, 1967, pp. 40–44.

Riggs, James L., *Engineering Economics*. New York: McGraw-Hill, 1977, pp. 261–262.

Samuelson, Paul A., *Economics*, 10th ed. New York: McGraw-Hill, 1976, pp. 599–601.

Weston, J. Fred, and Eugene F. Bringham, *Managerial Finance*, 3rd ed. New York: Holt, Rinehart & Winston, 1969, pp. 202–207.

White, John A., Marvin H. Agee, and Kenneth E. Case, *Principles of Engineering Economic Analysis*. New York: Wiley, 1977, pp. 148–149.

II

THE PRICE SYSTEM
AND ITS
ADJUSTMENTS

17

The Price System

The first part of this book has been concerned with the proper decision rules to apply in choices among alternative courses of action in
investment. The underlying assumption of the entire first part was that
the prices and costs in money terms reflected the value of the
resources—people, money, materials—that were to be used in the
projects. This is not always so. When the price system is working
perfectly as an allocator of resources among competing uses, prices
and cost do reflect what we will loosely call *value to society* of the
resources used. But when the price system is not operating properly,
wide misallocation—misuse—of resources may occur. Whenever he
attempts to defend his evaluation, an unsophisticated analyst is at the
mercy of those who understand the occasions when prices and costs
can be trusted to reflect value and the occasions when they cannot.

Therefore, the purpose of Part II is first to investigate the way the
price system is supposed to work. How does it properly allocate
resources? Then, in the section on welfare economics, we see the
conditions under which the price system can be only partially trusted.
Next we investigate the certain special aspects of the price system and
its efficiency under the headings "Social Benefit/Cost Analysis,"
"Inflation," and "The Cost of Capital in the Public Sector."

To whom is this knowledge of background economics in economic
decision making of use? Certainly to all those analysts who study
projects in the public sector, either in the United States or other
countries. Those analysts who deal with developing countries will
find the matters touched on here of first importance. These two groups
include analysts in the government itself at all levels, federal, state,
and local; those who act as consultants to any of these governmental
bodies; and those who staff or advise government overseas.

Of what use is all this to those analysts who remain in the private
sector? More and more during recent years the question of the impact

of private sector projects on society has been discussed. In such matters as air and water pollution, water supply, sewage disposal, automobile design and manufacturing, and so many other areas that a complete list would require many pages of this book, an understanding of the foundations of the price system is necessary. To continue to believe that private costs and benefits are all there is to decision making in the kinds of investments that have been discussed in the first part of this book is to take a narrow view. Decisions taken on this basis may easily be in error.

We now ask ourselves, "What is the price system? How does it work? More important, what are the assumptions on which it is based?" The answers are surprising.

To understand the price system as an allocator of resources in an efficient manner, it is necessary to grasp some fundamental ideas in economics. This discussion is selective and only those portions of the theory that have use in a direct way are explained. Any of the standard beginning texts in economics may be relied upon to furnish a complete view of the subject. Emphasized here are the assumptions that lie behind the price system as an efficient allocator, and so heroic are these that they appear as nothing short of shocking. The price system itself is a startling concept, little understood except by those who have taken a good deal of time and trouble to study it. If it is working perfectly, all incomes, wages, rents, and all that persons and firms buy with them are priced automatically at the exact number of dollars and cents such that the satisfaction of the society will be greater than if it had been arranged any other way. In light of this fact, the marvellous mechanism deserves to be investigated at length.

SUPPLY AND DEMAND

We begin with that portion of the subject that almost everyone has heard repeated time after time: the law of supply and demand.

Begin with supply. Let us fix upon a single good, say, soybeans, and a whole society, say, the United States. How can a meaningful and convenient relationship be decided on? Economists have selected from among the many variables possible in speaking of soybeans and society two variables—price, or cost per unit, and number of units produced. We select the units of cost in dollars per bushel and the unit of quantity in bushels. If we plot cost per bushel on the vertical axis and number of bushels on the horizontal axis, we arrive at the curve of Figure 17.1. Cost increases upward, and output increases to the right. The curve is in the short run; that is, it pictures the relationship when the existing situation is projected with no time allowed for increasing

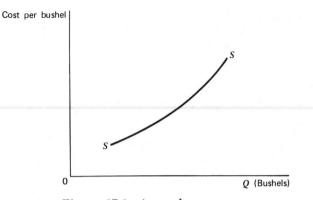

Figure 17.1 A supply curve.

the number of acres sowed to soybeans or increasing investment in any significant way, as contrasted with the long run when all costs of production may vary.

The supply curve normally slopes upward to the right, indicating that as output is increased, the cost per bushel increases. We are assuming here that more and more resources such as labor and land are being drawn away from competing uses, thus forcing the unit cost of soybeans higher and higher. A supply curve shows how much the producers will be willing to supply to the market at each and every price or cost.

A demand curve is a picture of how much a person, in the case of an individual demand curve, will pay for increasing amounts of a good. It characteristically slopes downward and to the right—and for an important reason. It obeys the law of diminishing marginal utility, which means that as we consume more of a good, such as automobiles, we derive less utility or satisfaction or pleasure from each succeeding unit, or car, than we did from the first. The first car was a necessity, the second was nice to have, the third we had to have or we would not have bought it, and the fourth was forced on us by circumstance. If we assume that the utility we derive from each extra—or marginal—unit of consumption lessens, we arrive at a figure like Figure 17.2. This is the downward-sloping demand curve, D–D.

To arrive at total demand for a good such as hamburgers, the individual demands of all hamburgers lovers—$D_1, D_2 \ldots D_n$ in Figure 17.2—are summed up horizontally at each price to arrive at the demand of a society.

Similarly, the supply of a good such as soybeans is arrived at by summing up horizontally all the supply curves of all producers of the good.

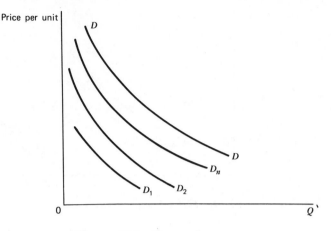

Figure 17.2   Demand curves.

CURVE SHIFTS

We must distinguish between movements along the supply or demand curve that are occasioned by changes in price and the movements of the curve itself that happen because the underlying assumptions when we draw a supply or demand curve are violated. In the case of the demand curve, some of the assumptions are that individual preferences will not change, the number of consumers will not change, substitutable goods will not change in price, and, most important, consumers' incomes will remain constant. Should any of these change, the demand curve will shift. For example, if incomes increase, it will shift to the right.

Supply curves will shift, for example, if prices of the resources used in the manufacture of the product change, or if a new invention occurs that reduces the costs of production. The lessening of costs of production causes the curve to shift to the right. Increasing costs of production cause the curve to shift to the left.

TOTAL REVENUE AND PRICE ELASTICITY

Total revenue is defined, using the curves of demand, as price multiplied by quantity (Q). In Figure 17.3, total revenue at Q_1 is $p_1 Q_1$. As price is reduced from p_1 to p_2, the total revenue from the sale of the good increases. The increase is measured by the difference between the rectangle $O\ p_2\ B\ Q_2$ and the rectangle $O\ p_1\ A\ Q_1$. As price is lowered even further to p_3, revenue decreases to that measured by the rectangle $O\ p_3\ C\ Q_3$. Thus, lowering the price does not necessarily

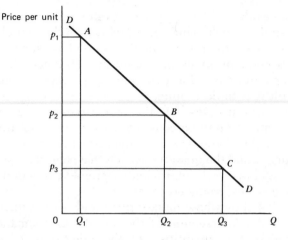

Figure 17.3 Total revenue.

mean either increasing or decreasing the total revenue from the sale of the product. Total revenue depends on where on the demand curve the producer sets his price. Involved is a principle called *price elasticity of demand.*

Price elasticity of demand is the degree of responsiveness of the quantity demanded to changes in the market price. It is defined as:

$$E = - \frac{\Delta Q/Q}{\Delta p/p}$$

The negative sign sometimes associated with this number indicates the negative slope. Quite often, however, the negative sign is neglected.

When a drop in p increases total revenue, as it did when we reduced p_1 to p_2, the elasticity of demand as measured by the previous equation is greater than one. When a drop in p results in no change in total revenue, the curve is said to be perfectly elastic, and the price elasticity of demand as measured by the previous equation is equal to unity. When price is reduced, as from p_2 to p_3 above, and total revenue decreases, the price elasticity of demand given by the previous equation will be less than unity but greater than zero.

Economists sometimes use this concept loosely and speak of a curve that is almost vertical as being highly inelastic. A curve that is close to horizontal is called an elastic curve because small changes in p result in large changes in Q.

Thus, it is important for a producer to recognize where he stands on the demand curve. Because it is often difficult to determine the demand curve a producer faces—for example, in fare fixing in mass transit—the result of changing prices is often unknown. Experimentation to determine the demand curve facing a producer is almost always difficult; thus, the producer is usually aware of his demand curve over only a short range of prices and quantities. One need but ask for the complete demand curve for a common good such as eggs to realize how difficult it is to determine.

We may ask ourselves how the two curves can serve a purpose. The answer must surely be connected with the determination of the proper price to be charged for a bushel of soybeans, or an automobile, or a hamburger, and the quantity of each that should be produced, and both of these at just that point where societal satisfaction with all the goods and services produced by an economy will be greatest.

Figure 17.4 shows how market price and market quantity are determined by the intersection of the supply and demand curves. If price is at p and thus quantity at Q, the quantity demanded and the quantity produced will be exactly balanced. No surplus of goods, in this case natural gas, will occur as would happen at price p_1. At that price the quantity demanded will be smaller than the quantity produced, and a surplus will exist. On noting the surplus, producers will reduce production and come down the supply curve to the point p where the quantity supplied and the quantity demanded are equal. At price p_2 a shortage will exist because the quantity supplied will be less than the quantity demanded at that price. In this case, producers will increase production up the curve of supply until reaching equilibrium price p and the equilibrium quantity Q.

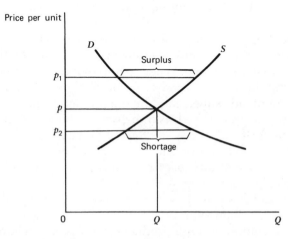

Figure 17.4 Natural gas equilibrium.

THE ECONOMIC PROBLEM

And thus we have hit upon the economic problem, which is to answer the question: "How much of each good and service of the many millions of goods and services available to a society such as the United States should be produced? And at what price should each of these be sold?" Connected with this question are other matters that enter into the answer, such as the allocation of labor to various tasks throughout the society. Who and how many will be doctors, lawyers, truck drivers, cooks, and bottle washers? How will agricultural land be used? How much of a transportation system does a society need? In particular, how many trucks, trains, rail lines, subways, airports, and airplanes will be required? This is an infinitesimally tiny number of the questions that must be asked and answered to solve the economic problem I have presented so blithely in my examples of soybeans and hamburgers.

Economics is a social science that has accompanied man's civilizing path forward. So to answer the central question of the preceding paragraph, we can investigate how societies in the past have answered it, and how societies in the present attempt to answer it.

The oldest answer is that of *tradition*. This field has always been planted to corn, and I will always plant it to corn. My father was a carpenter, and therefore I will be a carpenter. The women have always been wives, mothers, and cooks, and therefore they will continue to be those things. The traditional answer to the question is a strong one—far stronger in ancient societies than today's. A good example of how society was arranged by using tradition was the society of Peru headed by the Inca before the Spanish conquest. All was arranged, and all was traditionally arranged. No one aspired to be anything more than he actually was or to do anything greater than his destiny—the same one his father had also pursued—marked him out for. In many of the traditional societies it was a horrifying crime to attempt to step out of one's social position, and it was horrifyingly punished. Agricultural patterns of production were fixed as well. In the mountains of Peru those same patterns are being followed today, and the traditional society that fell victim to Pizzaro has, in many important ways, changed little from those times.

Another way of managing to answer all the almost innumerable questions that can be posed in relation to an economy is the *command alternative*. Soybeans will be priced at $7 a bushel, and we will produce 10 million bushels per year. A Buick will be priced at $6250, and we will produce 500,000 per year. Hamburgers will be limited to the MacDonald chain, and after 10 billion have been produced they will be removed from the market. We will need a railroad system of

70,000 miles, we will reduce the number of automobiles to 50 million within the next 10 years, and we will fly nothing but Boeing 747s. Many societies are run in exactly this way but not at all as capriciously as the remarks I have made would indicate. In a command economy, a great deal of study must go forward in order to estimate goals and the resources that will be needed to fulfill them. However, the questions cannot go unanswered and thus are answered within the limits of the technical abilities available. The command economies are exemplified by the USSR and China.

A third possible answer to our questions is the *competitive allocative system*, the price system. Theoretically, all the economic questions are answered perfectly if the price system is working. The United States and a number of other economies attempt to a greater or lesser degree to take advantage of the automatic features of the price system so that the decisions necessary are made in the freest way possible. (As a matter of fact, the United States has a mixed system of command and competition.) If the conditions set forth later in this book are fulfilled, the price system will allocate resources, which include the doctors, lawyers, cooks, seamstresses, and housewives, yet without ordering each person to assume a certain occupation. The price system will allocate land to various agricultural uses without a central authority ever ordering to what use each parcel shall be put. The price system will answer the question of how many Buicks should be produced without any government official's ever entering into the matter. The price system will manage all these things and thus will contribute to the society of free men. In this way, economics and politics are intertwined. And those who warn us that our personal freedom and our economic system are connected are referring to this aspect of the competitive system.

THE COMPETITIVE SYSTEM

The competitive system answers the questions posed in the previous section with a minimum of government intrusion into the process. It does this under certain assumptions that we investigate more thoroughly in the chapter entitled "Welfare Economics." The free enterprise system, as this competitive system is sometimes called, is pictured graphically in Figure 17.5. The great questions that every economic system must answer—what to produce, how much of each good to produce, how to produce, that is, what methods and resources shall go into the production of goods and services—are answered here.

For whom shall these things be produced? In this question is the further question of income. How shall incomes be distributed among the producers, given a starting distribution? The most prominent

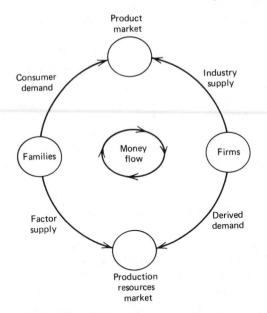

Figure 17.5 The economic system.

features of Figure 17.5 are the two markets, the product and the production resources or factors market. It is in these that the freedom of goods to reach an equilibrium price between supply cost and demand price is reached. These markets are considered to be the kinds of places that existed in the early days of the industrial revolution in England. For example, an agricultural laborer might have appeared at a market square in a small English town early in the morning and there offer his services by the day to those agricultural owners, the farmers, who also appeared at the market. Between the farmer and the laborer a price was reached that was agreeable to both. The farmer and the laborer are an example of the situation in the factor market, and the grain being bought and sold on the Chicago commodity market is an example of the product market still functioning today.

In Figure 17.5 families and firms appear, and these two entities generate the forces in the product and the factors market. Both families and firms come from the same group—society—and thus a member of a family may also be a worker in a firm. From families, the consumer demand is directed into the product market where it meets the industrial production from the firms. Families also supply the land, labor, and capital to the production resources market where they meet the *derived* demand from the firms. The demand is derived from the consumer demand that appears in the product market because to produce what consumers want, the firm needs resources. In the center of Figure 17.5 the flow of money in one clockwise direction may be seen.

This simplified graph of a society excludes one great force—government. We include it later in the discussions that follow the explanation of the economy under perfect competition.

It can be shown that a market under pure competition, which is synonymous with perfect competition, will maximize the satisfaction of all members of a society, while producing at the lowest possible cost, given the existing technology, and it will do this under a certain set of assumptions, which I now list.

ASSUMPTIONS OF PURE COMPETITION

The assumptions of pure competition are related to the figure I have just discussed. On the family side, the assumption is that these consumers know what they want. This means that they are aware of just how much utility they will receive from any amount consumed of all particular goods. No family ever makes a mistake and buys something that it does not really like, or even that it does not appreciate to the fullest.

In addition, the existing income distribution, meaning the amount of money that each family receives from the sale of its services in land, labor, and capital, must be taken as equitable. This assumption means that no measure of income distribution as a goal to be achieved may enter the analysis of any part of the competitive economy. This assumption is a difficult one to swallow, but it must be swallowed if the purely competitive analysis is accepted. From this assumption, it follows that the dollar votes of each participant in the economy are weighted equally. This is not nearly as difficult to accept as the further assumption that an extra dollar to a rich man, who has $10 million preceding the one he just received, means just as much in satisfaction as an extra dollar to a poor man who has only $10.

On the firm's side it must be assumed that producers are pursuing profit and no other goal, which means they are not pressuring expansion, or prestige, or any of the other goals that firms in reality do pursue.

In the product market no buyer or seller can purchase or sell enough of any one product so that he can affect the market price. This is important enough to deserve an example. Take the small wheat farmer. Even though he throws all of his product on the market at one time, his production is so small in relation to the total market that he cannot affect the price of the good being sold. On the other hand, no buyer can purchase so much wheat that he will drive up the price.

In the production resources market, it must be assumed that all resources are completely and instantaneously mobile. In other words, a laborer who cannot find work in Seattle can be transferred to Mobile, where his services can be used with no time lapse. The same is true for a pair of shoes that cannot find a buyer in New York and can find one in Los Angeles. In addition, firms are completely free to enter any industry they choose. There are no barriers because of lack of funds. The economic system supplies any amount of funds providing that the price for those funds can be paid.

There are some conditions that apply to both the product market and the production resources market: All buyers and sellers are aware of all prices throughout the economy so that they may choose the lowest. Their information on these matters is perfect. It is also assumed that commodities and resources are infinitely small. They are like atoms so that any quantity may be bought or sold.

The above assumptions may appear to be so far-reaching that they in fact assume the whole problem away. But it must be remembered that the ideal situation, even though it does not exist nor ever could exist, can serve as a standard measurement against which actual economic matters may be compared. This comparison is the subject of welfare economics, which is treated in a later chapter.

The assumptions are those we must make before an analysis of pure competition and the rules that force it to allocate resources in an economically efficient manner may be investigated.

18

How the Price System Allocates Resources Efficiently

We must make clear the difference between the assumptions of pure competition and the statements about pure competition that may be derived from them. The assumptions about the firms, families, the product market, and the production resources market that ended the previous chapter are to be taken as given in the discussion that follows. From these I will derive the basic rules.

THE PRODUCTION FUNCTION

One wishing to bake a cake will need a recipe. The recipe is the production function for making one cake. It is stated, in general terms, as follows:

$$Q = f(X_1, X_2, X_3 \ldots X_N)$$

where Q is the quantity of the good or service produced—one cake—and X_is are the inputs—flour, sugar, milk—that go into the production process. The production of steel, or automobiles, or energy is analogous to cakes. The reader may imagine Q as ingots and X_is as scrap, coke, energy, and so on.

If the production operation is a bakery, a number of questions arise:

1. What is the least cost combination of the inputs?

2. If I have more than one output—cakes, cookies, bread, and so on—what is the best combination of the outputs?

3. How much of each product should I produce to maximize profit?

These questions can be answered rigourously under the perfectly competitive market system. Economic efficiency can be achieved by application of the rules to be developed in this chapter—always remembering the assumptions that lie behind the perfectly competitive economic model.

OPTIMIZING THE INPUTS

In any production process it is desirable to optimize the inputs by choosing them such that the least cost combination is encountered. For example, in a production process involving a number of inputs such as labor, three or four kinds of material, and capital, the amount of each one required to arrive at a certain level of production must be found. But rather than speak of many dimensions, let us restrict the discussion to only two inputs that the reader may imagine to be as many as needed. The theory is not changed by adding inputs.

We use two kinds of lines in this discussion. The first is called an *isoquant,* which means a line that indicates at any point on its length the two quantities of inputs necessary to achieve a constant output. Budget lines, also called *isocost* lines, indicate the amount of inputs that may be purchased with each given production budget.

Figure 18.1 shows the isoquant or constant output lines. In this illustration Q_a, Q_b, and Q_c represent increasing quantities of product that may be produced by using various combinations of capital and labor, where Q_c is greater than Q_b, which is greater than Q_a. Their characteristic shape is explained as follows: First, the curves slope downward and to the right. Why? Start at point M. Moving to the right off the curve means increasing output. But by definition, an isoquant indicates points of constant output. Therefore, to maintain constant output while at the same time moving to the right we must also move downward to some such point as N.

Second, they must be convex to the origin, because as the inputs are substituted one for the other, say, labor for capital in Figure 18.1, the ability of labor to substitute for capital decreases. In other words, as we move to the right along the horizontal axis the amount of capital substituted for by each unit of labor is large. As we move further to the right, however, the ability of labor to substitute for capital decreases; it takes more and more labor to substitute for a unit of capital.

Last, notice that these isoquants, or equal product curves, never

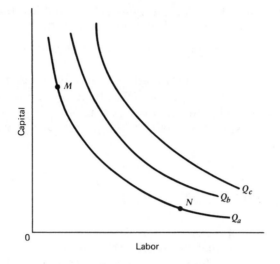

Figure 18.1   Isoquants.

cross, for this would mean that two different outputs could be produced with the same inputs.

Watson uses the example of two inputs: one, power saws, and two,
the hand labor to operate them, as well as to clear brush and pile
wood. The output is cords of cut wood. In Figure 18.1, therefore,
capital is the number of power saws and labor is the number of men;
Q_a, Q_b, Q_c, are increasing numbers of cords of wood per day.

James and Lee give the example of channel improvements and
reservoir storage as the two inputs being used to produce a given level
of flood control. Each substitutes for the other; more channel improvement requires less reservoir storage to produce a given level of
flood control. If both channel improvement and reservoir storage are
increased, a higher level of flood control results. In the case of James
and Lee's example, the isoquants intersect both the vertical and the
horizontal axis, thus showing that either input by itself could produce
a given level of output without any other input.

It is now possible to see why the curves are convex to the origin in a
clear light. In the wood-cutting example, if only two power saws are
used with eight men, the effect of increasing the number of power
saws will be to reduce the number of men needed. The number of
men needed will be smaller and smaller as more and more machines
are added to the work crew. The output will remain constant while
these changes in the inputs are made. The law illustrated here is *the
principle of diminishing marginal rate of substitution.* The marginal
rate of substitution is sometimes called the *marginal rate of technical
substitution,* and thus it may be shortened to MRS or MRTS.

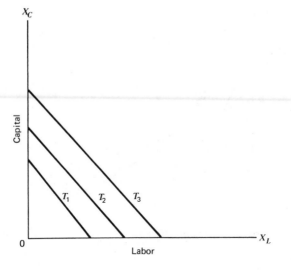

Figure 18.2   Isocosts.

Let us turn to the equal cost lines of Figure 18.2, which show the total cost associated with each amount of inputs used. The equation is:

$$T = p_L X_L + p_c X_c$$

where T equals the total cost, p_L is the price of labor, p_c is the price of capital, X_L is the amount of labor, and X_c is the amount of capital.

Later in the chapter I show how the intersection points of each total cost line with the axes may be calculated by reducing first labor, then capital, to zero and solving for the result.

As you look at Figures 18.1 and 18.2, you should recognize that any point within the axes represents a certain combination of capital and labor, and thus, because these are the only two inputs, a certain quantity of output. All that the isoquant, or equal product, lines represent are the trace of the points within the axes where the production outputs are equal. This could be represented by a surface on which the lines Q_a, Q_b, and Q_c are like contour lines on a surveyor's map. As we vary the combinations of capital and labor, we achieve different outputs.

Price is not represented in either Figure 18.1 or Figure 18.2, both of which represent only varying amounts of capital and labor. But price does appear in the sense that T_1, T_2, and T_3 contain the prices of both capital and labor within them.

It is also true that for every combination of capital and labor, that is, for every point in the area between the axes (providing prices remain constant), there is a certain total production cost. If we calculate the

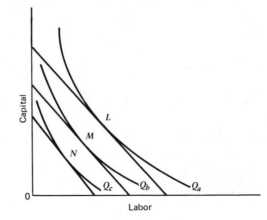

Figure 18.3 Isoquants and isocosts superimposed.

total cost for every possible combination of capital and labor, we find that we can join equal points of total cost and that they are straight parallel lines as shown in Figure 18.2.

If we now superimpose Figure 18.1 upon Figure 18.2, we obtain Figure 18.3. (The reader must imagine that both Figure 18.1 and Figure 18.2 are covered with an infinite number of isocost and isoquant lines.) I have chosen three isoquant lines and then have picked the three isocost lines that will be just tangent to the isoquant lines. These three total cost lines indicate the cheapest budget that will produce each of the three quantities indicated. The three tangent points L, M, and N also indicate the three combinations of capital and labor that will result in the amounts of product, using each of the three production functions in the optimal way.

The end points of the total cost curves, that is, the points at which they intersect the two axes, may be calculated. Hold the price of labor and the price of capital constant for each total cost. Then drop the amount of capital to zero. This will fix the point of intersection with the labor axis. Drop the amount of labor to zero and calculate the point of intersection of the total cost curve with the capital axis. Each total cost line is calculated at constant prices. In fact, each total cost line might also be called a constant input price line:

$$T = p_L X_L + p_c X_c$$

If $X_c = 0$, then

$$T = p_L X_L$$

and

$$X_L = \frac{T}{p_L}$$

or if $X_L = 0$, then

$$T = p_c X_c$$

and

$$X_c = \frac{T}{p_c}$$

The slope of the isocost line is therefore:

$$\frac{X_c}{X_L} = \frac{T}{p_c} \div \frac{T}{p_L}$$

$$= \frac{p_L}{p_c}$$

MULTIPLE INPUTS

Up to this point in our discussion we have confined ourselves to two inputs. What is the rule for multiple inputs? To answer this question we must define the concept of marginal physical product.

Go back to Figure 18.1 and draw a horizontal line that intersects the three curves shown there. It is evident as one proceeds along the line from left to right that the amount of product increases and that the increase in purely owing to additional units of labor, because the amount of capital is being held constant. If we measure the increases in product resulting from a unit increase in labor input, we determine the marginal physical product of labor. To define this concept: Hold all inputs constant but one and increase that input. The marginal physical product of that input is the resultant increase in product that we achieve by the addition of each unit of that input.

We can do the same thing with capital. If you draw a vertical line in Figure 18.1 that intersects all three curves, and if you measure the increase in product that results from each additional unit of input as you proceed up the line, you find that you have discovered the marginal physical product of capital.

The slope of the isoquant measures the ratio between the marginal

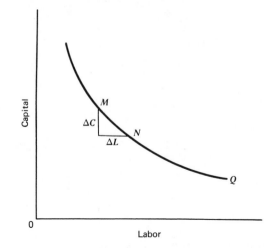

Figure 18.4   The marginal rate of technical substitution.

physical product of one input and the marginal physical product of the other. At first glance, it might seem that the slope of the isoquant is the marginal physical product of the capital over the marginal physical product of labor, but this is not so. In Figure 18.4, if we go down the curve of the isoquant an amount ΔC, we will have moved outward along the labor units axis a distance ΔL. The slope of the isoquant is ΔC over ΔL, the marginal rate of technical substitution (MRTS). The amount of output as we move from point M on the figure to point N remains the same by the definition of an isoquant. Therefore, as we come down the isoquant substituting labor for capital, the loss of product occasioned by reducing capital must be made up by gain in product from the increase in the labor input. In other words:

$$\Delta C \ (MPP_C) = \Delta L \ (MPP_L)$$

therefore,

$$\frac{\Delta C}{\Delta L} = \frac{MPP_L}{MPP_C}$$

and this is the marginal rate of technical substitution of labor for capital.

The marginal rate of technical substitution diminishes as we move down the isoquant from upper left to lower right. That is, as we move down the curve, it takes more and more labor to substitute for a unit of capital.

Now recall that the point at which the isocost and the isoquant lines are tangent is the optimum choice of inputs, that the slope of the isocost line is $\frac{p_L}{p_C}$, and that at this point the two slopes must be the same. It follows that:

$$\frac{p_L}{p_C} = \frac{MPP_L}{MPP_C}$$

We can now say,

$$\frac{MPP_C}{p_C} = \frac{MPP_L}{p_L}$$

We may now generalize that and say,

$$\frac{MPP_A}{p_A} = \frac{MPP_B}{p_B} = \ldots = \frac{MPP_N}{p_N}$$

This means that each input, no matter how many there are, should be used up to the point at which the marginal physical products per dollar cost of inputs are equal.

OPTIMIZING THE OUTPUT COMBINATION

This section deals with the combination of outputs that maximize revenue, not profit. It answers the questions: "What combination of outputs will maximize revenue? How much of $X, Y \ldots N$ should we produce so that our revenue will be maximized, given a fixed amount of production resources?" This is not the same as asking: "At what quantity should we produce a good, or goods, such that our profit will be maximized?" The word *combination* should be emphasized in the first question and the word *profit* should be emphasized in the second. We are dealing with combinations of output given a fixed amount of resources in the first question. In the second question, given cost and revenue figures for any amount of output, we are dealing with how we should produce to maximize the difference between revenue and cost.

Figure 18.5 shows the production possibility curves as concave to the origin. These are also isocost curves because each of them is the result of using a fixed amount of resources, each of which has an attendant cost. The combination of these inputs has already been optimized in accordance with the previous discussions in this chapter. Each curve shows the amount of X and Y that can be produced at a fixed cost; each curve shows the combinations of X and Y that can be

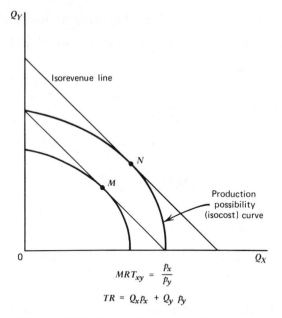

Figure 18.5 Production possibility curves.

produced while holding the total cost of production constant. The slope of this curve at any point is equal to the so-called marginal rate of transformation of X for Y or MRT_{XY}. I now develop the slope of this curve by reference to its point of tangency with the isorevenue curve, not from an analysis of the production possibility curve itself. The straight lines are lines of equal revenue—isorevenue lines. They are straight because the total revenue to be derived from fixed prices is a linear function. The price of X and the price of Y are fixed. Because the two curves shown are parallel lines, the prices have not varied. Moving outward from the origin indicates increased amounts of output being produced. Their equation is:

$$TR = Q_X P_X + Q_Y P_Y$$

The slope of the isorevenue line is P_X/P_Y, for reasons similar to those of the discussion of optimum input combinations where isocost slopes were determined.

The points of optimum combination of outputs are shown in the figure as M and N, which are the points of tangency between the production possibility curve and the isorevenue curve. At these points the marginal rate of transformation (MRT) between X and Y is equal to the slope of the isorevenue curve. In other words, the slopes of the two curves are equal at their point of tangency:

$$MRT_{XY} = \frac{P_X}{P_Y}$$

Points M and N also indicate the combination of outputs while the enterprise follows an expansion path.

The production possibility curve is concave to the origin. This means that increasing the output of either X and Y signifies increasingly larger sacrifices in the output Y or X. Evidently, the production possibility curve must be concave, for if it were convex or a straight line, the firm would produce only one product, not two. You should test this by drawing a convex production possibility curve and assuring yourself of the truth of the one-product statement.

HOW MUCH Q?

Table 18.1 shows an example of costs and price. Quantity is shown from zero to seven units. These points on the abcissa of Figure 18.6 may be considered as representative of hundreds or thousands in order that smooth curves may be drawn.

The fixed cost does not change with the quantity produced. Examples are building rent, insurance, and office overhead. Variable cost is a rising function of quantity. A good example is cost of materials. These costs are shown in Figure 18.5. All are *total* costs.

Unit costs are shown in Figure 18.7, as is unit price. Marginal cost (MC) is the difference in total cost as production increases by each extra unit. (Notice that marginal cost is not the same as variable cost.) Average cost (AC) is the total cost divided by the amount being produced. It is related to the marginal cost because each drop in marginal cost pulls down the average whereas each rise in marginal cost pulls up the average. Thus, the MC must pass through the lowest point of the AC.

Price is shown as a horizontal line in accordance with the assumptions of pure competition. It is also the demand curve facing the seller, at 68 per unit.

As production is increased, notice that marginal cost falls and then rises. The logical rule that each unit of production must carry its own weight means in this case that marginal revenue—the price—must exceed or equal marginal cost when the marginal cost curve is rising. Thus, the production optimum occurs at six units. The enterprise would not produce less, because to do so would subtract from its total

TABLE 18.1 Quantity, Costs, and Price

Quantity Q	Fixed Cost FC	Variable Cost VC	Total Cost TC = FC + VC	Marginal Cost Per Unit MC	Average Cost Per Unit $AC = \frac{TC}{Q}$	Price Per Unit p
0	120	0	120			68
1	120	48	168	48	168	68
2	120	73	193	25	97	68
3	120	90	210	17	70	68
4	120	107	227	17	57	68
5	120	136	256	29	51	68
6	120	187	307	51	51	68
7	120	278	398	91	57	68

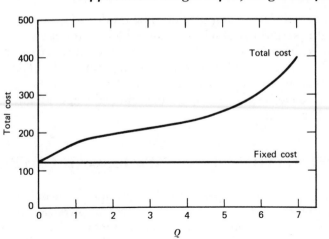

Figure 18.6   Total costs.

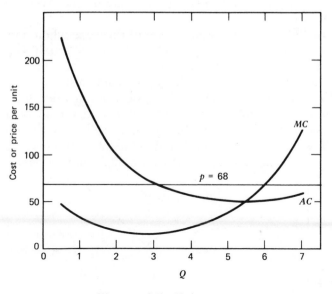

Figure 18.7   Unit costs.

profits. Neither would it produce more, for to do so would cause it to produce at a loss on the units after six.

APPLICATION: SINGLE INPUT, SINGLE OUTPUT

The simplest case of the principles that I have outlined in this chapter is the single input producing a single output. The method of deciding the point at which the output should be produced is that of equalizing marginal cost and marginal revenue, which in the case of pure competition is the price of the output. Therefore, in this case the output should be determined by marginal cost equaling price. (The assumption is that all production processes and resources that go into the input cost have been made optimal, technically speaking.) This is the case of Figure 18.7.

APPLICATION: TWO INPUTS, ONE OUTPUT

In a case of two inputs producing one output, the input combination may be determined by equating the marginal physical product/price ratios such that the marginal physical product per dollar of each input is equal, as in Figure 18.3. Output should be increased up until the point at which the marginal cost is equal to the marginal benefit, as in Figure 18.7. It is not necessary in a single output case to consider combinations.

Figure 18.8 shows the application of this case when benefits and cost are discounted to their present worth. Total benefit is a straight line passing through the origin, because in the case of pure competition, price does not change with output. Total costs have been minimized by equating their marginal physical product per dollar and by using the best technical methods available so that technological efficiency has been achieved. Output is increased up to the point X_1 at which the slope of the total benefit and the total cost curves are equal, and thus the maximum discounted benefits minus discounted costs

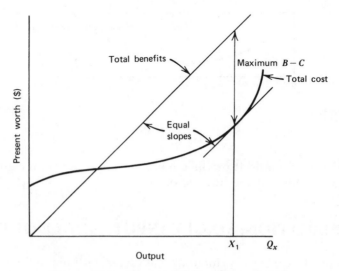

Figure 18.8   Discounted benefits and costs.

point achieved. This is the same point at which the marginal benefits, discounted, and the marginal costs, discounted, are equal in the unit curves. In economic analysis this is equivalent to equating incremental cost and incremental benefits.

MULTIPLE INPUTS AND OUTPUTS

To explain the optimization of production in the case of many inputs being used to produce many outputs, it is necessary to introduce the concept of the value of the marginal product (*VMP*). You will recall that the marginal physical product (*MPP*) of any input is the increase in product that results from an addition of one unit of that input. The *VMP* of, say, one input *A* producing one output is:

$$VMP_{AX} = (MPP_A)\,(p_X) = p_A$$

where p_A is the price of input *A* and p_X is the price of output *X*. The equation points out that, optimally, no more of input *A* should be used than can be justified by multiplying the amount of product attributable to that input by the price of the product and comparing it to the price—the cost—of that input. This is equivalent to saying that the value of the marginal product of *A* in the production of *X* should be no greater—or less—than the price of the input *A*. If VMP_{AX} is greater than p_A, then more *A* should be used until diminishing returns brings VMP_{AX} down to p_A. Conversely, if VMP_{AX} is less than p_A, less *A* should be used until the equality between VMP_{AX} and p_A is once again established.

One input producing one output is an extraordinary situation that serves to outline the theory of the value of the marginal product. More usual—and more useful—is the application of the value of the marginal product concept to multiple inputs and outputs.

Imagine a farm in an agricultural country on which two crops are grown—corn and wheat. The acreage devoted to each crop is the same. Besides the land, production also requires 40 laborers and certain amounts of fertilizer. The landowner decides to find out exactly what the effect of the fertilizer is on production. He therefore holds constant the amount of land and labor he has been using and varies the amount of fertilizer. The price of wheat is 8 pesos per hectoliter, of corn 6 pesos per hectoliter, and of fertilizer 30 pesos per ton.

The farmer discovers that one extra ton of fertilizer on the wheat field produces 20 extra hectoliters—the marginal physical product—and therefore that the value of the marginal product of fertilizer in the production of wheat is 20 hectoliters times 8 pesos (the price of wheat), or 160 pesos. This is more than the 30 pesos he spent for fertilizer.

$$VMP_{FW} = (MPP_{FW}) (p_W) \overset{?}{=} p_F$$

$$(20) (8) > 30$$

$$160 > 30$$

Therefore he will continue to add fertilizer to the wheat field. However, during the same experiment he also discovers that one extra ton of fertilizer on the corn field produces 30 extra hectoliters of corn. Thus:

$$VMP_{FC} = (MPP_{FC}) (p_C) \overset{?}{=} p_F$$

$$(30) (6) > 30$$

$$180 > 30$$

It now appears that the farmer should add fertilizer to the corn field also and to it first until the value of the marginal product per ton of fertilizer drops to that of wheat, or 160 pesos. Why will the *VMP* eventually drop? Because of the law of diminishing returns, which says that if all inputs to production are held constant except one—in this case, fertilizer—and that one increased, the beneficial effects of each further unit of increase will eventually start to fall. The land-owner will add fertilizer to both corn and wheat land until the *VMP* of the fertilizer reaches 30 pesos. And then he will stop adding fertilizer. Notice that at this point:

$$VMP_{FC} = VMP_{FW}$$

The example is simple: the lesson to be drawn from it, not so. The rule is that the value of marginal product of each input should be equalized in terms of each output. But this requires—note well—that these values are known. And this information is not always easy to come by. Take a complicated production process such as building automobiles. Would it be possible for the manufacturer to determine the effect on sales of increasing leg room in the rear seats of the four-door model versus a more fuel-saving engine versus better rest facilities for the employees?

In general:

$$VMP_{ij} = \text{Constant}$$

where *i*s are inputs and *j*s are outputs.

In words, the value of the marginal product of all inputs must be equalized. Because there is almost always an interdependence among inputs relative to their effect on outputs, the optimization process is an exercise in mathematical programming.

MARGINAL EFFICIENCY MEASURES IN SUMMARY

The purpose of the explanation of price theory given here is to establish the fundamental rules by which resources are allocated under the conditions of pure competition. You will have gained a sufficient idea, in my opinion, to judge effectively the ability of the pure competition model to allocate resources efficiently in practical situations.

I have shown that the marginal physical product of each input to the price of that input must be equalized for all inputs in order that technological efficiency be achieved. Additionally, the marginal rate of transformation between two outputs should be in the ratio of their prices. Production should be divided between outputs such that the marginal benefit of any input in the production of an output equals the marginal benefit of that input in the production of any other output. I have also shown that the price of any output should be equal to its marginal cost.

I have not mentioned any of the long-run versus short-run conditions. It can be shown that the long-run marginal cost must be equal to the long-run average cost, that supply must equal demand, that average revenue must be equal to average cost, and that with these conditions profit is maximized in the long run. Treatment of these conditions is standard in texts on price theory.

In addition, the reader can intuitively see that the consumer will equate the marginal utility per dollar of each of his purchases, that is, the marginal utility of each good will be equalized per dollar spent on that good.

It remains now to make some brief statement about the imperfections of the perfectly competitive system. I restrict myself to just one—monopoly—and leave to the interested reader discussions of imperfections such as oligopoly and monopolistic competition.

MONOPOLY: AN IMPERFECTION OF THE PRICE SYSTEM

Among the imperfections of the purely competitive model in economic theory, the most important is the existence of monopoly. Monopoly violates the condition that no producer is large enough to change the price at which he sells his product no matter how much he may put upon or withhold from the market. This means that the demand curve, which we have assumed as being horizontal in our discussion up to now, becomes sloping from upper left to lower right on the usual economic graph.

But what is really wrong with monopoly from the point of view of the consumer? Why is it a social evil when it is uncontrolled? Is there any technical, provable reason why monopoly should be avoided from the point of view of economic efficiency? The answer hidden in Figure 18.9 is that the monopolist produces too little of the goods that society wants. Society wishes the price of a unit of a good to be equal to the cost of producing the last unit at the social point in Figure 18.9—and remember that this means the full cost including a reasonable return on the firm's investment. The monopolist, however, is required not only by his stockholders but by logic to produce where his marginal cost is equal to his marginal revenue, that is, where the cost of the last unit he produces is exactly equal to how much he will be able to receive in revenue for it. Thus, in Figure 18.9 he produces where the marginal cost curve crosses the marginal revenue curve at Q_e. (*Marginal revenue* is the extra revenue achieved as each extra unit is produced and sold.) Where will he price the product? He will price his product for as much as he can get for it, and at Q_e he can sell at p_e.

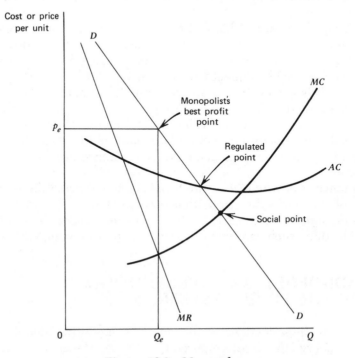

Figure 18.9 Monopoly.

(A vertical line erected at point Q_e intersects the demand curve at the height of p_e.) Another look at the figure should convince you that there is considerable profit over and above the normal profit contained under the average cost curve.

What is true of monopoly is true for any of the cases of downward sloping demand curves. It is true under oligopoly and monopolistic competition.

If government regulates monopoly, it will do so when average cost and average revenue—the demand curve—are equal. This is the regulated point of Figure 18.9.

APPENDIX 1

In the following discussion, the relationships between the usual terms of microeconomic analysis and benefit/cost analysis are cited. In addition, the fundamental optimal rule of microeconomics—that marginal cost must be equal to marginal revenue at the point of optimal production—is stated in benefit/cost analysis language and the rules of benefit/cost analysis derived from it. It is also shown that total benefit/cost ratios have no meaning in terms of microeconomics and thus represent a fallible guide for decision making.

Consider the case of the optimal number of berths in a projected port. All benefits and costs have been discounted, and all advantages and disadvantages of each possible number of berths have been included before discounting. Table 18.2 presents the necessary data to arrive at a decision as to the optimal number of berths, all of which are, of course, mutually exclusive alternatives. Some of the columns are headed by two titles: the first is standard to benefit/cost analysis and the one below it in parentheses is standard to microeconomic analysis.

We can now draw the standard microeconomic shapes of the total revenue and total cost curves, as is done in Figure 18.10a. The curves are smooth, again by microeconomic convention. In reality, the curves would be broken, because it is impossible to produce half a unit, either of a good or of a berth. In Figure 18.10b, drawn by plotting the data of Table 18.2, the upper curve is total discounted benefit (total revenue). The lower curve is total discounted cost (total cost). The maximum vertical distance between the curves is the point of greatest difference between benefits and costs (best profit). It appears at 5 berths (units). The greatest benefit minus cost is, according to the table, 4.5. The method of total benefit minus total cost thus gives the correct solution.

Incremental benefit (marginal revenue) is the difference between total benefits (total revenue) as each extra unit is produced. Incre-

TABLE 18.2   Deciding on the Number of Berths in a Port

Berths	Total Benefits (Total Revenue)	Total Cost (Total Cost)	Benefit Minus Cost (Profit)	Incremental Benefit (Marginal Revenue)	Incremental Cost (Marginal Cost)	Incremental Benefit Minus Incremental Cost (Marginal Profit)	Incremental Benefit/ Cost Ratio	Total Benefit/ Cost Ratio
0								
1	2.5	1.0	1.5	2.5	1.0	1.5	2.5	2.5
2	4.5	1.5	3.0	2.0	0.5	1.5	4.0	3.0
3	6.0	2.0	4.0	1.5	0.5	1.0	3.0	3.0
4	6.9	2.5	4.4	0.9	0.5	0.4	1.8	2.8
5	7.5	3.0	4.5	0.6	0.5	0.1	1.2	2.5
6	7.8	3.5	4.3	·0.3	0.5	−0.2	0.6	2.2
7	8.0	4.0	4.0	0.2	0.5	−0.3	0.4	2.0

mental cost (marginal cost) is the difference between the total cost of one unit and the next.

Incremental benefit minus incremental cost (marginal profit) reaches zero at five units in Table 18.2, indicating that units should be produced or berths constructed up until the point that the benefit resulting from each unit is exactly balanced by the cost of producing it. In other words, each extra berth must balance its extra cost to the general project by the extra benefit it will bring about. The number of berths the port will be designed for will be limited by the rule that when the next extra berth does not bring about benefits that will balance its cost, it should not be built. (Marginal profit must be greater than or equal to zero.)

The rule that marginal revenue must equal marginal cost is seen graphically in Figure 18.11b. The equality occurs at 5 berths. (Figure 18.11a shows the traditional microeconomic curves.)
In symbolic terms used in microeconomics:

$$MR = MC \tag{1}$$

In terms used in benefit/cost analysis:

$$\text{Incremental benefit} = \text{Incremental cost} \tag{2}$$

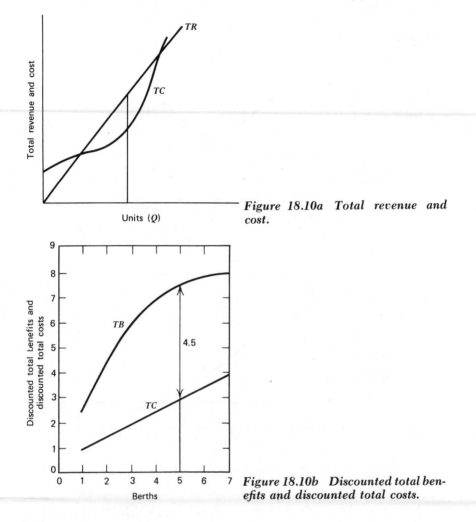

Figure 18.10a Total revenue and cost.

Figure 18.10b Discounted total benefits and discounted total costs.

or, transposing terms:

$$\text{Incremental benefit} - \text{Incremental cost} \geq 0 \qquad (3)$$

This is the rule used in the benefit minus cost method of benefit/cost analysis.

If equation (2) is divided through by the incremental cost, the fundamental rule of the incremental benefit/cost ratio is seen:

$$\frac{\text{Incremental benefit}}{\text{Incremental cost}} \geq 1.0 \qquad (4)$$

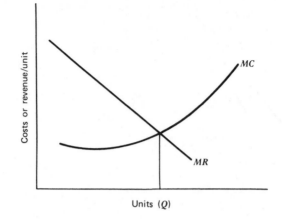

Figure 18.11a Cost or revenue/unit.

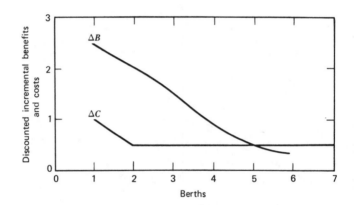

Figure 18.11b Discounted incremental benefits and costs.

Incremental benefit minus incremental cost selects, correctly, 5 berths, as does the incremental benefit/cost ratio. Were all costs and benefits expressed in annual terms, the preceding reasoning would be exactly the same and the incremental annual benefit divided by the incremental annual cost would always give the correct solution. Similarly, the reasoning would be no different for incremental benefit minus incremental cost if both were expressed in annual terms.

Although total benefit minus total cost gives the correct solution and is a correct method as explained earlier, total benefit divided by total cost—the traditional benefit/cost ratio—gives the incorrect solution in this particular example, of 3 berths at $B/C = 3.0$, and therefore, it is an incorrect method. In some other cases, total benefit/cost ratios indicate the correct solution, but this is accidental. Total benefit divided by total cost for each quantity (Q) has no useful meaning in microeconomics. As a matter of fact, its wide use can have come about only through custom and legislative requirements rather than economic analysis. Its use has caused a great deal of unnecessary controversy. It goes without saying that it should be discontinued.

REFERENCES

Baumol, William J., *Economic Theory and Operations Analysis*, 2nd ed. Englewood Cliffs, New Jersey: Prentice-Hall, 1965, pp. 297–298.

James, L. Douglas, and Robert R. Lee, *Economics of Water Resources Planning*. New York: McGraw Hill, 1971, pp. 67–69.

Leftwich, Richard H., *The Price System and Resource Allocation*, 3rd ed. New York: Holt, Rinehart & Winston, 1966, pp. 186–189.

Samuelson, Paul A., *Economics*, 5th ed. New York: McGraw-Hill, 1961, pp. 523–532.

Watson, Donald Stevenson, *Price Theory and its Uses*, Boston: Houghton Mifflin, 1963, pp. 143–144.

19

Welfare Economics

In Chapter 17 I introduced you to the assumptions of the price system, as well as to the fundamental concepts in classical economics. In Chapter 18 I demonstrated how the price system allocates resources, given the assumptions. Following the important assumption of pure competition, it was possible to make statements about allocation of resources that result in economic efficiency by analysis of the situation set up by the assumptions. For example, an assumption was made that we are dealing with many small producers. A statement was derived that in order to maximize profits, the single-product firm must produce at the point where marginal cost is equal to price. When assumptions are made and the statements derived, it is now possible to elaborate on the kind of economic relationships existing among the four points of the price system—families, firms, production and production re-source markets—shown earlier.

At the very end of the analysis an example of an imperfection was displayed—monopoly.

Now it is time to ask ourselves how closely the world conforms to the assumptions and to the statements that can be based on the as-sumptions. And this is the question of welfare economics. How efficiently is the economy performing?

Competition leads to economic efficiency, and this is why compe-tition is acclaimed as a social good. What most people mean by eco-nomic efficiency, however, and what economists understand by effi-ciency are often different. The ordinary citizen defines efficiency as production at lowest cost. The economist would stress the word *tech-nological* in front of a layman's definition. The economist might say something like this: "Technological efficiency is indeed production at lowest cost, but this is only a part of my definition. Economic effi-ciency must take in not only what things cost but what people want. Economic efficiency is the use of the resources owned by a society such that the society will receive the maximum satisfaction possible out of the products made with those resources."

Competition is a means to this end. In the ideal economy, competition will force prices down to the lowest level consistent with the producer's making a normal return on his investment. Technologically inefficient producers will be forced to leave the industry, and the resources that they would have used in production will be more efficiently used by others.

The economist's definition of economic efficiency implies conditions in areas of the economy other than that of the producer. The whole matter can be summarized by Figure 19.1, an extension of Figure 17.5. It shows an idealized economic society—what would happen if men had computers for minds and barometers for emotions.

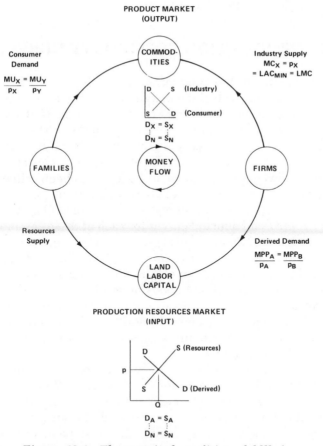

Figure 19.1 The marginal conditions fulfilled.

Figure 19.1 shows the so-called marginal conditions fulfilled. In the product market, which is the output, supply and demand curves are in equilibrium at a price and a quantity for all commodities. This product is supplied by firms operating where the marginal cost of each output is equal to its price, which is equal to its long-run average cost and long-run marginal costs. The firms are shown as demanding resources from the production resources market, the input, and so fixing their demands that the marginal physical product of each input is in proportion to its price, that is, that the marginal physical product of each input is the same per dollar. The production resources market is also in balance at a P and a Q for each one of the goods and services used in production. Resources are being supplied in terms of land, labor, and capital from families, and these families are optimizing their satisfaction by equating the marginal utility per dollar of each of the commodities they are buying. Money flow travels in a clockwise direction, operating with all the marginal conditions and the assumptions of perfect competition fulfilled.

THE PRODUCTION POSSIBILITY CURVES

Figure 19.2a shows the production possibility curve for an entire nation. It is an outgrowth of the marginal conditions and illustrates the economy on a national scale when all production is at a position at which no resource unemployment exists. I have shown it in terms of two outputs, the classical ones of guns and butter. The assumption is that all output of an economy can be classified in terms of either guns or butter. In the condition shown, full output has been achieved under conditions of full employment of all available resources—land, labor, and capital. Suppose the economy is producing at Q_{BE} and Q_{GE}. The auxiliary supply and demand curves for each of these commodities are shown in Figure 19.2b as having reached equilibrium at the same Q_{BE} and Q_{GE} where prices are p_{BE} and p_{GE}. There are no surpluses or shortages of guns or butter and thus, following our assumption, no surpluses or shortages of any goods or services within the economy. All goods and services are being produced at minimum cost, which constitutes technical efficiency. In addition, all resources are being used at a maximum. Maximum satisfaction, and thus economic efficiency, has been achieved.

Suppose that, because of failures of the price system to allocate resources properly, the conditions of Figure 19.2c occur. Now the price of butter is so low that more is being demanded than will be supplied at that price. A shortage exists. But, because the economy is operating at capacity, the resources that had been devoted to the production of butter are now being used for guns. Thus, gun produc-

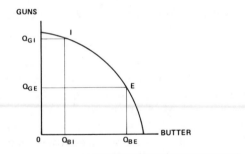

(a) THE PRODUCTION POSSIBILITY CURVE

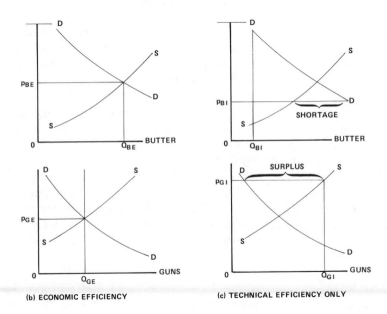

(b) ECONOMIC EFFICIENCY   (c) TECHNICAL EFFICIENCY ONLY

tion is up and a surplus exists; butter production is down and a shortage exists. All resources are being used to capacity, and technological efficiency is being achieved in both cases E and I in Figure 19.2a. But economic efficiency has been lost in the move from E to I.

The idea of opportunity cost is also present in Figure 19.2a. To obtain more butter it is necessary to give up some production of guns. Butter is achieved at a sacrifice of guns. This is the definition of opportunity cost. It is the sacrifice of the benefits of one good in order to achieve the benefits of another good. The curve is concave to the origin because the marginal rate of substitution for guns and butter requires that the substitution of one for the other occurs at an increasing rate.

Figures 19.1 and 19.2a and 19.2b are closely linked. All of them describe a situation in which economic efficiency is being achieved in all sectors of the economy. A condition of equilibrium exists. All the assumptions of pure competition and all the statements that may be derived from them are in perfect operation.

We have already seen what can happen to price system allocation capability when monopolies exist. We will investigate what happens to the price system when other realities impinge on it.

EXCEPTIONS TO EFFICIENCY

If any of the assumptions listed at the end of Chapter 17 are violated, the allocative mechanism of the price system fails. Needless to say, the failures in sum may be self-correcting and lead us back to efficiency again. Other exceptions worth listing are discussed in the following paragraphs. They are not all-inclusive.

The continued existence of noncompetitive firms—oligopolistic ones such as exist in the automobile industry and steel industry, monopolistically competitive systems such as occur in the marketing of oil products—these work to produce less or more than society wishes. Some of these firms, such as those in the transport sector, are subject to regulations, and some are not. The steel companies, for example, are totally unregulated except for some safety regulations related to the production process. A gasoline station's location and operation are also almost totally unregulated except for local zoning regulations.

Within the firms themselves, especially the smaller and more lightly financed ones, internal cost reductions that are completely known to the manager cannot take place because not enough financing exists for them. This is an outgrowth of the lack of mobility of financial resources. Theoretically, all possible cost reductions can be introduced immediately.

Another area of inefficiency in the national economy is the fact that much production occurs completely outside the market system. One need only think of the Department of Defense's enormous demands on the productive resources and facilities of the country to realize that this is an area in which a great deal of inefficiency in the economic sense can occur. The amount of defense in the United States is not determinable in a market. The defense contractors cannot present their wares in an open market where the citizen individually can purchase as much as he thinks he needs. It is possible to imagine that this was once true, say in a country like the Switzerland of 400 years ago, where each man owned his own sword and where each provided his own equipment. Now the amount of defense material demanded is a political decision made by a coalition of Department of Defense analysts with the agreement of the representatives of the people in Congress. The whole process is surrounded by secrecy. It is a long way from the open operation of a free market system.

Another area—the existence of externalities—is covered fully in the succeeding chapter. For the moment, all we need to say is that externalities are those consequences of production that are not valued in the costs or the benefits of the process. A typical external cost is air pollution caused by factory smoke. A typical benefit is that received by a farmer downstream on a river when another farmer builds flood control works upstream.

No savings are kept in the pure competition model. Everything is consumed, and thus consumption equals production. The introduction of savings causes complications undreamt of in our model.

No government is present in the picture of Figure 19.1. Yet government with its regulations and its enterprises can cause great effects on economic efficiency. The traditional imposition of taxes, setting a minimum wage, and social help programs—all are excluded from our model.

Price regulation by government can cause enormous dislocations in the perfectly competitive model. During World War II, the federal government regulated the price and quantity sold of many commodities—gasoline, sugar, meat, butter, and many others—in order to avoid the price rises and speculation that had occurred in World War I. Price setting by regulation such as occurs in railroads in the United States can also cause changes in the perfectly competitive model. Labor prices, set by labor unions, are exceptions to the model.

Government is also in conflict with another major assumption already mentioned in the assumptions of pure competition—fixed income distributions. This means that ownership of resources is considered to be constant in pure competition. Thus, everyone receives the income from the resources he owns. Those who have much retain much, if they invest properly, and those who have little except their labor benefit from the sale of only that pittance. In other words, no redistribution of income is considered possible or desirable in this model. Yet just this area is a major concern of government and an area it will enter strongly, usually in the attempt to equalize incomes so that society will be more stable. (Stability is, after all, a major interest of government.) In back of this desire for stability is the recognition that stability comes about if citizens believe they are being treated justly. Thus, government must be concerned not only with economic efficiency but also with economic justice. A wage earner who is single may be paid the same as a worker who is married with children when both do the same job, but government reduces the income taxes of the child-encumbered man in recognition of equity, thus effectively changing the rates of take-home pay of the two men.

Government must step in where private industry cannot or will not in large and risky projects. The Columbia River system of dams was beyond the financing possibilities of private companies. At the time Grand Coulee dam was built in the late 1930s, no industry was present to use the electric power it would furnish. The system was a typical economic development project that only governments are willing to undertake. Risky projects in which national vanity is involved, such as the United States space program, are not covered in the perfectly competitive model.

A decreasing cost industry is an exception. A railroad is a decreasing cost industry because, in its normal production range, its costs, both marginal and average, are falling, not rising. The more freight carried, the less the unit cost of carrying each additional unit of freight.

No unemployment of resources may exist in the perfectly competitive model; there is no capital or labor or land not fully employed in its best use when all automatic adjustments have been made.

Now that we have seen the "invisible hand" in action and its relation to economic efficiency, it is time to ask the central question: "If the purely competitive model is so ringed about with exceptions, how can we adjust the prices used in our analyses, when we know the price mechanism is badly out of kilter, to achieve economic efficiency?" To understand the answer to that question, we must enter more fully the area of welfare economics.

DEFINITIONS

Websters' New Collegiate Dictionary defines welfare as "the state of doing well especially in respect to good fortune, happiness, well-being, or prosperity." *Welfare* is a word that derives from the two words that put together mean "to fare well." The meaning of welfare is stressed here because it is associated in the minds of English speakers with government intervention in the economic affairs of society with a view to providing some sort of minimum standard for all citizens. *Welfare state* is defined in the same dictionary as "a social system based upon the assumption by a political state of primary responsibility for the individual and social welfares of its citizens." It is probably necessary to distinguish carefully between welfare and welfare state, recalling that welfare is associated with happiness and well-being, and therefore welfare economics must be the economics that has to do with the well-being of the citizens of a state. It says nothing about the agencies that may affect the happiness of these citizens, either by increasing it or by decreasing it. In welfare economics a business firm, a federal government agency, a county bureau all are viewed with an unprejudiced eye. It is not one of the tenets of welfare economics that the best agency to increase happiness in a citizenry is the state.

Welfare economics is prescriptive, not descriptive. It seeks to provide the norm by which a society's actions can be judged in the sense of how those actions affect the happiness of the citizenry. It is a rule provider. Its goal is to answer such questions as: "If we should build this dam, will the overall happiness of the citizenry be increased or decreased? And, indeed, which will be better, to build this dam or that one?" Descriptive economics attempts to examine and illuminate economic phenomena. It views the economic side of life dispassionately and attempts to tell us what is happening, or what would be likely to happen if we should take certain actions. It does not tell us whether such action is advisable or not. It certainly does not tell us whether such action will increase or decrease human happiness. Welfare economics is therefore much more philosophical in its background and goals than is descriptive economics. That is to say, it partakes much more of philosophy than of science. This means that although the subjects it treats are more fundamental than those of descriptive economics, it is much less manageable. It is much more open to controversy and disagreement among individuals—even individual scholars. This does not make it a subject of any less importance for study. The more unmanageable and difficult a study is, the more necessary it is, sometimes, to pay it close attention.

THE SOCIAL WELFARE FUNCTION

If it were possible to determine the goals of an entire society and to properly weight them, the result would be a social welfare function. This social welfare function could then be used to judge courses of action within the society. It would set the norms referred to in the previous section of this chapter as being the subject of welfare economics. In a sense, the attack on the problem of providing a social welfare function is the subject of welfare economics. In equation form it might be written as follows:

$$W = a_1 x_1 + a_2 x_2 + \cdots + a_n x_n$$

where: $\sum\limits_{i}^{n} a_i = 1.0$

$i = 1, 2 \ldots n$

Notice that x_i represents objectives or goals and a_i the weighting factors. Each a_i indicates the importance of that goal in achieving happiness or welfare in a society. Increasing W must mean increasing welfare. The units in which x_i is expressed must be commensurable.

It is possible to imagine such a function for an entire society in which improving W improves the happiness of everyone in it, but a moment's further thought shows the utopian quality of the idea. It would mean that every individual in the society would have to agree to the weights attached to each x_i. How would this vary by region, class, age group, education level, and so on? Clearly, this must be a political decision. Insofar as the people's representatives know and vote for the society's well-being, the social welfare will be optimized. Insofar as the representatives are ignorant of how to maximize their constituents' happiness or as they are indifferent to it for one reason or another, the happiness of all the people will not reach the levels it could have.

WELFARE ECONOMISTS

Some attempts have been made by economists specializing in welfare economics to lay the basis for decision making on the project level in order to make up for the deficiencies of the price system on the one hand and the lack of a social welfare function on the other.

Vilfredo Pareto's criterion was:

Any change which harms no one and which makes some people better off (in their own estimation) must be considered to be an improvement.

Although this is crystal clear and totally acceptable, it is applicable on few occasions. Almost no project fails to hurt someone. An effort of imagination brings to mind a dam in an uninhabited desert whose construction and operation in producing electricity from water trailing down unused to the sea has no side effects whatever. But, even in this example, would it not be true that money for the construction of the project would have to be removed from other projects? Would not those who would have benefited because of these neglected projects be considered to have been hurt by the construction of such a dam? The Pareto criterion seems to violate the principle of opportunity cost.

Kaldor gave us a refinement of the Pareto doctrine that makes it much more applicable: A change is an improvement if those who gain evaluate their gains at a higher figure than the value which the losers set upon their losses. If a mechanism is set up so that the gainers compensate the losers for their losses, a net gain will be experienced by the gainers. And thus the Kaldor criterion would meet the requirements of the Pareto optimum.

Paul Samuelson has put forth the following criteria:

1. There is no mutually exclusive better option available.

2. The wealth distribution is made no worse off than without the project.

3. The externalities have effects, both good and bad, which algebraically sum to zero.

It is difficult to argue with these principles. The efficiency of the criteria certainly lies in attempting to quantify the effects, both internal and external, of the project.

Henri Bergson came out for a formulation of value judgments so that the analyst would have criteria and criteria weighting sufficient to evaluate a project. Equity, justice, and virtue are all included in Bergson's doctrine. Society, either directly or through its representatives, would dictate what constitutes equity, justice, and virtue in project effects. This comes close to the social welfare function we have already discussed.

CONCLUSION

It is now necessary to see if we can detect when the price system is not operating properly. If it is not, we must apply corrections. In the following chapters we attempt to compensate for the deficiencies of the price system by a number of methods.

20

Social Benefit/Cost Analysis

Benefit/cost analysis usually means a comparison of the benefits of a course of action to its costs with a view to determining whether or not the course of action is justified. To be justified the benefits of an action should be equal to or exceed the costs; benefits and costs should have some allowance for risk and for the fact that they will be received over time.

The assumption behind this definition is that the price system is working close to perfection as an allocator of resources among competing uses in such a manner that the satisfaction of society is maximized. Although this is not the place to discuss in general the deficiencies of the price system in its usual role, it is necessary to describe the differences between social benefit/cost analysis and the benefit/cost analysis that can occur, but only theoretically, when the price system is working perfectly. Social benefit/cost analysis attempts to modify benefits and costs when market prices are not measuring all effects. Sometimes not all producers pay their full costs of production and not all those receiving benefits pay the full costs of those benefits. It is the purpose of social benefit/cost analysis to include all costs and benefits considered relevant to the project. This normally means all the costs and the benefits to society as a whole, with allowances for the point of view taken. The process involves an investigation of what economists call *externalities*.

Paul Samuelson defines an external economy "as a favorable effect on one or more persons that emanates from the action of a different person or firm . . . an *external diseconomy* is defined in the same way, except that it refers to external *harm* that is done to others" (Samuelson, 1961). An external diseconomy is found in the expansion of fishing in a certain area that tends to increase the cost of each boat's operation. The cost per fish caught rises. Samuelson also quotes the example of oil drilling in a single pool by a number of producers, which lowers the level of oil in the pool and thus increases each firm's unit cost per barrel produced. An external diseconomy moves the unit cost curves of the affected entity upward.

External economies are less easy to cite, but a traditional example is that of a farmer on the upper reaches of a river who, at his own expense, terraces his land to inhibit erosion. In some degree he reduces flood control costs for every other farmer downstream, as well as protecting his own land. But the other farmers downstream may not reimburse the farmer upstream for the reduction in costs that they have received. Another example: A beekeeper keeps his hives next to a neighbor's apple orchard. The bees produce honey by visiting the neighboring apple orchard when the blossoms are in bloom and returning to their hives. The beekeeper thus receives an external economy—an external benefit—from the fact that his hives are located near a neighbor who owns apple trees. He does not pay for this benefit, however.

Both social costs and social benefits—the externalities—are explained in the traditional economist's version in the next section. Later in this chapter an example of such social costs and benefits in economic analysis is undertaken.

SOCIAL COSTS AND BENEFITS

It is easier to understand the concepts involved in social costs and social benefits by means of an example. A traditional example—or one that has come to be almost traditional—is the example of pollution control. Consider a manufacturing plant whose production process emits smoke. The plant pays for all its other costs—electricity, labor, materials, management, taxes—but it does not pay for the adverse effects of the smoke pouring out of its chimney. Such effects are the damage to health of the persons breathing the air contaminated by the smoke, the dirt from the smoke that accumulates on buildings, on washing hung out to dry, and on windows, the haze that obscures vistas that might be enjoyed, and the general depression of spirit suffered by those living and working near the plant. The costs and benefits of the company are shown in Figure 20.1 where S_1 is the company's private cost curves and includes the normal private cost items. Suppose that the company is forced by some agency of the society, such as a pollution control board, to pay the pollution costs. The company cannot do this by going to all the citizens and paying them individually for the loss that they have suffered, but all the costs can be internalized. Internalization, that is, the inclusion of externalities in a private cost curve, can be accomplished by the installation of a pollution control device in the company smokestacks. Imagine

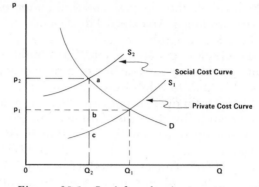

Figure 20.1 Social and private costs.

that this successfully controls all pollution. The company's costs will rise because of the installation and maintenance of the pollution control device. Imagine that they rise to the cost curve labeled S_2 in Figure 20.1. The curve S_2 is a representation of the social cost of the company's operations, providing it incurs no other external cost.

Notice some of the consequences of moving the company's cost curve from its private position to its social position. Price increases from p_1 to p_2. Production decreases from Q_1 to Q_2. Production cost increases from c to a at Q_2. The decrease in production means that resources may be allocated from this particular company's operations to others. If the price system's allocative capability is working efficiently, this means that a better use will be made of these resources and that general satisfaction will be increased. This is an important point, because it is often argued that pollution control devices and their use raise the price of the goods produced. As we have seen this is true, but this does not mean that satisfaction realized by the whole society is reduced. It merely means that production is shifted from one good to another, and that both these goods, if all social costs and benefits are being recognized, are produced at exactly the point at which the satisfaction to all people in the society is at maximum.

Regulation, taxation, and subsidy all attempt to internalize externalities. (Just how this is done is outside the scope of this book, but you are referred to standard microeconomic texts.)

Individual benefit curves must be summed vertically, not horizontally as in the case of demand curves. ("Demand" and "marginal benefit" are synonomous in social benefit/cost analysis.) This is because each person benefiting from the goods enjoys satisfaction from whatever is being produced, but his consumption does not imply depletion. A beach is enjoyed by all. In Figure 20.2, person 1's enjoyment of Q_1 miles of beach must be added vertically to person 2's

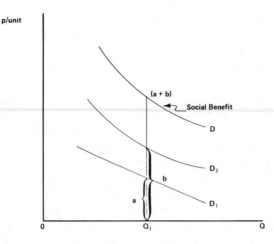

Figure 20.2   Social benefit curves.

enjoyment of Q_1 miles of beach. Notice that they are consuming collectively, not individually, as they would be if Q were hamburgers and not scenery and swimming.

Figure 20.3 shows the important point that marginal social cost increases from zero, unlike private marginal cost, which drops off as production increases and then ascends as plant capacity is approached. It increases because each extra unit provided of, say, clean environment costs more, if we think of Q as being a measure of quality or intensity from 0 to 100 percent. Take the cleaning of filthy streets. Minimal cleanliness, say the first 10 percent (picking up only cans and bottles and larger debris) will cost less per unit than the higher degree

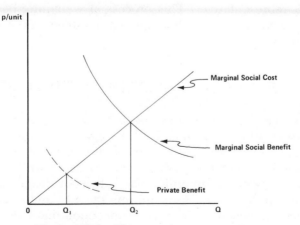

Figure 20.3   Clean environment curve.

of cleanliness of the second 10 percent, when all papers are collected as well as cans, bottles, and larger debris. The last 10 percent of the 100 would cost outrageously.

Marginal social benefit decreases as the cleanliness intensity increases from 0 to 100 percent. For example, satisfaction at seeing bottles and cans taken away is higher than the extra satisfaction of seeing papers also removed, and it is much higher than the extra satisfaction of seeing all debris, paper, and in addition dust and dirt washed away, as once was done daily in Paris.

Marginal private benefit is certain to be much less because each consumer will be willing to contribute much less, knowing that his neighbor next door may contribute nothing at all.

The point is clearer in the case of education. A consumer of education—a student—will spend up to the point at which his marginal *private* benefits equal his marginal private cost—Q_1 in Figure 20.3. A student of accounting, for example, might well calculate exactly how much he should spend by balancing it against how much he stands to make. (All private benefits summed up would be represented by the dashed curve of Figure 20.3.) But he might well be encouraged to take a broad humanistic program—thus becoming a better citizen, presumably—if education were subsidized and he did not have to pay for all its costs to educate him. He then would consume quantity Q_2 of education.

As may be imagined after this discussion, great difficulties attend any effort to determine a benefit curve. How can we measure benefit when the good being enjoyed is as difficult to quantify as a commuter's relief when mass transit saves him from sitting in his car for 20 minutes in a long freeway full of idling, smoke-producing engines and irritable drivers? We have no recourse except to the political process where preferences can be expressed, either by the people themselves or by their representatives. This process of weighting benefits and costs so as to obtain a utility function is the subject of the remainder of this chapter.

BENEFIT/COST ANALYSIS CRITICIZED

Much of the criticism directed at benefit/cost analysis arises from a mistaken conception. It is thought that such analysis measures only those benefits and costs that can be determined by prices in the market place. In other words, a direct application of private enterprise decision making—and a simplified one at that—is imagined. Benefits are revenues in this view. Costs are investments, and operation and maintenance are expenses. This is a conception that becomes unusable when more sophisticated approaches are taken in either the public or private sector. In the private sector, such consequences as labor problems arising out of a decision may be difficult to cost, yet they may be a vital part of the decision—even more important than the portion of the decision that can be measured in money. In the public sector much or most of the decision may be concerned with other than money costs and benefits or with consequences that, even though reducible to money measure, may not be priced in the market place.

The problem, therefore, of social benefit/cost analysis is to discover a logical method of adapting traditional discounted cash flow analysis to consequences that are not amenable to costing in the market place.

PARTIAL ANALYSIS

It is most important to understand that partial analysis is just that—a glance at, or a minute observation of, or a detailed analysis of, a part of the problem. And when pages and chapters and books are written on a part of a problem, the great temptation is to forget that only a part has been studied and to accept the conclusions on a part of the problem as being the solution of whole of it. This is especially true when numerical analysis has been used. Solutions based on numbers have a hypnotic quality about them. It becomes easy to fall under their spell and to consider a problem solved merely because a mathematical solution to a part of it has been carried out, and to say, "This number is greater than those, and therefore alternative A is preferable to alternatives B, C, and D." The fact that the numbers reflect consideration of only one aspect of the problem is forgotten.

And how does this come about? The thought process is something like this: "Here we have a problem to which a number of alternative solutions exist. The consequences of the alternative chosen splash over into many areas of life. We may expect economic consequences, both direct and indirect, in many areas. There are the direct benefits and costs of the project itself over a long time. There are costs and benefits that are much more indirect and subtle—for example, the effects on employment or the balance of payments. We may also expect social consequences, perhaps changes in the health of certain groups of citizens, or in their educational level, or even something as vague as increased political integration of a region or nation. No doubt all these consequences are important, but we can deal only with those that can be quantified in money terms. We have evolved certain techniques that will take care of the effect of costs and benefits at various times. We have also been concerned with other techniques, purely economic, that will tell us something about the effect of price changes, inflation, and such matters. But we cannot evaluate the broader social and economic results of this project. Therefore, we will confine ourselves to what we can do. In other words, we will do a partial analysis and analyze only those consequences of the decision about to be made that are amenable to methods presently known. At least, then, we will be acting upon solid considerations. The rest of these consequences we will analyze in the best way we know how, perhaps simply by listing them."

It is a rare analyst who goes even this far. For decades, important projects have been analyzed—if at all—purely on the basis of direct economic consequences, usually on the cost side only. The result has been that widespread effects of the most important order, whose seriousness far outweighed the portion of the analysis that could be handled in monetary terms, were neglected. These important effects were simply eliminated from the analysis because they could not be handled monetarily. (The increased air pollution resulting from a new urban freeway has become almost the standard example of this kind of error.) And all this was based on the argument that it would be a great mistake to ruin a quantitative analysis by the inclusion of nonquantitative factors.

Thus, for example, in the economies of highway construction and operation, only the investment cost, operation and maintenance cost, time-savings benefits, life of the highway, and discount rates were considered. Other effects, such as those on the safety of the users or the impact of the highway on local business, were not considered. (Impact studies were done but after the fact.) The more indirect effects of an urban highway on the growth of a city, or on its form, its esthetic appeal, on the social results of splitting the city into distinct economic areas and decreasing the accessibility of one portion of the city to another—these matters were not taken into account.

DECIDING ABOUT DECISIONS

To take indirect effects into account, it is first necessary to lay out a method for handling all the consequences of a decision on public investment. A consideration of objectives, alternatives, and consequences associated with a decision on investment in the public sector are all relevant to such a method. These three categories are discussed individually below.

Objectives

What are the objectives of the proposed project? What is the investment supposed to do? In the private sector, an investment is supposed to make a profit. Given this objective, the usual benefit/cost analysis may be used with perfect consistency. The benefits, which are revenues, can be expressed in monetary terms. Investment, operation, and maintenance costs can be expressed in the same terms. The methods for reducing these sums to a figure compatible with the concept of time value of money are well known. They are the benefit/cost ratio, present worth, internal rate of return, benefit minus costs, and some others.

In the public sector, the objectives are usually much more broad. Sometimes profit is not involved at all. Objectives are related to social good. They may be expressed in such terms as increasing safety on the highway, or providing more green space for urban areas, or providing an alternative for persons who are not able to use the automobile but must confine themselves to public transit. And these broad objectives tend to spread the thrust of the investment. No longer is it the desire for profit, as in most private investments. It is now a series of hoped-for effects. To bring these latter objectives into a workable framework, they must be weighted (Steiner, 1969). Someone or some body of persons must decide how important each objective is in relation to all the other objectives. But determining the preference of the public for public goods—in other words, determining the demand curve for public goods—is no easy matter. It has been proposed that this be done by the elected representatives of the people—a city council, a state legislature, the Congress of the United States. It has also been suggested that a new kind of voting for specific projects take place. In other words, a poll of the citizenry affected is taken and their preferences are determined. The state of this particular art is rudimentary at the moment. Sometimes the weighting of the objectives in public investment is conditioned by what consultants have suggested in the first place. In other words, the objectives are a function of the alternatives that the consultants propose as a solution to a problem. There is an interdependence in the process of choosing objectives, selecting alternatives, and determining consequences that makes the matter complicated indeed.

How can objectives be weighted? Let us imagine that a public project has objectives 1, 2, and 3. The first problem is to assign measurement units to each objective. The units may be, for example, dollars per time period, or hours per time period, or acres of land per time period, or similar units. Let us say that the units assigned to each objective are respectively U_1, U_2, and U_3. We must assign some constant to each unit. Let these constants be K_1, K_2, and K_3. We can now say:

$$W = K_1U_1 + K_2U_2 + K_3U_3 \cdots + K_nU_n \tag{1}$$

This is the social welfare function we have seen previously. The difficulty is that the units are not commensurable. To get around this, values of K will be assigned such that the following equation becomes true:

$$K_1 U_1 = K_2 U_2 = K_3 U_3 \cdots = K_n U_n \qquad (2)$$

The choice of K is determined by the weights that the citizenry wish to attach to each objective.

Example 20.1

Suppose that a city is considering a transport proposal that is designed to replace urban sprawl with satellite communities. To accomplish this, a rapid transit bus system has been suggested. This means that the whole paraphernalia of such a system must be designed, including one-way streets, with some lanes limited to buses only, a downtown station in the central district, and stations in the satellite communities themselves, exclusive bus lanes in the freeways connecting the downtown area with the satellite communities, and no doubt other equipment such as metering devices for restricting freeway use in order to encourage the use of rapid transit bus systems, special fare collecting devices, special buses with loading and exit doors on both sides, and so on (Meyer, Kain, & Wohl, 1965). Now let us say that the objectives of this proposal are consciously limited to three: a direct economic one—the making of a profit; an external benefit—relief of congestion on existing freeways; and a social benefit—the provision of green space between the city and the satellite communities. Although it is recognized that other consequences will occur, the city council has decided that these three alone will be considered. It has in effect decided that the weights of all other consequences but these shall be zero.

The city council meets, is requested to determine their weights of these objectives, and is given a lecture on how this might be done. After a number of argumentative sessions, a few public meetings, and a final executive session, the city council determines that $K_1 U_1$ shall be $2000 per year, that $K_2 U_2$ shall be 1000 hours per year, and that $K_3 U_3$ shall be 1 acre per year. U_1, U_2, and U_3 are, respectively, $1 per year in profit or loss, one hour saved per year, and one acre of green space per year. Equation (2) becomes:

2000 dollars per year = 1000 hours per year = 1 acre per year.

This is equivalent to saying that one hour saved per year is equal to $2 per year, and one acre of green space retained per year is equal to $2000 per year.[1]

---

[1] This example is based on Steiner, 1973.

DEFENDING WEIGHTING

An often-heard objection to the weighting procedure is that accurate estimates of cash flow are going to be algebraically added to relatively inaccurate estimates, thus causing the accuracy of the final results to be equivalent to that of the weakest estimates. ("A chain is only as strong as its weakest link.") And this criticism is, of course, true. The criticism implies, however, that the relative accuracy of measurement of an effect is the criterion for its inclusion in an analysis, not the effect itself. Thus, if profit can be predicted more accurately than the effect of the alternatives on green space, these critics would say that profit alone should be the criterion for a decision between two alternatives, and green space should be included only in a list of intangible items. It may well be that, so far as the citizens of the city are concerned, the green space effects far outweigh the profit aspects of a transport proposal, and to exclude green space considerations implies that the quality of life in the city has no importance—or a minimal one.

It is as though a pilot of an airliner far at sea in an emergency situation were trying to decide on which of two airports to head for. He has a relatively accurate estimate of fuel remaining in his tanks, fuel consumption, and therefore range of flight in dead air. His navigator's estimate of his position is relatively inaccurate owing to the difficulties of star sights because of overcast. The pilot's knowledge of wind direction and velocity on both of his possible routes are also inaccurate. Should the pilot then make his decision on fuel consumption alone because it is known with relative accuracy? Should he then tell himself, "I will ignore these relatively inaccurate estimates of my position and winds on the two routes and decide solely on the basis of fuel consumption?"

Another objection to this weighting procedure is that it is impossible to relate consequences in monetary terms when dealing with such diverse effects as time savings and green space. Yet when a decision is made in which both consequences will be felt, there exists a weighting, however unconscious, of the two consequences in the decision maker's mind—providing only that he is aware of both consequences. If this is admitted, it must be clear that the nonmonetary effect can be reduced to monetary terms, because so long as an equation exists among diverse units of measurement, any unit of measurement can be expressed in terms of any other. For example, to develop the relationship expressed in equation (2) in terms of U_1, it is necessary only to divide the equation by K_1:

$$U_1 = \frac{K_2}{K_1} U_2 \text{ and } U_2 = \frac{K_3}{K_1} U_3 \tag{3}$$

This means that $1 is equivalent to a half hour saved and one two-thousandth of an acre.

The conclusion must be that if one makes a decision in which one is aware of monetary and nonmonetary effects, the decision is made considering all effects, whether they are quantified or not. If, then, all the effects are considered, they must be in some way weighted, consciously or not. But any combination of effects that includes monetary effects must be therefore expressable in monetary terms. Therefore, all consequences must be expressible in monetary terms, if one of the consequences is monetary and all are considered.

Alternatives

The next portion of this chapter deals with the selection of alternatives. The alternatives used in the analysis are considered to be mutually exclusive, that is, the selection of any one excludes all the others. Implied is that there is no interdependence among the alternatives. Each is separate and definable, without reference to the other alternatives.

One alternative is always the status quo, if it is not decided to reject the status quo from the beginning. One can always continue to do what has been done before. Put another way, one can follow the policies that have been followed in the past.

What are the criteria for these alternatives? They must be independent—mutually exclusive. They must be technically possible. They must lie within the budget of the project. They must fulfill some of the objectives. They may not fulfill all the objectives. They may even have a negative effect on some of the objectives.

It is important to consider all possible alternatives that meet the foregoing criteria. It is unlikely that optimization will be achieved if the best alternative has never been considered at all.

Alternatives may be multiple. If they are, then incremental analysis must be used if the measure of optimality is the benefit/cost ratio, or incremental rate of return, or less well-known measures such as index of profitability. If the measure is benefit minus cost or least annual cost, then incremental analysis need not be used.

Example 20.1 (Continued) ———————————————————

In Example 20.1, two alternatives exist. One is to maintain the status quo in the city transportation system, which consists very largely of automobiles and some interurban buses running on streets, highways, and freeways. The other alternative is the rapid transit bus system as described previously.

Consequences

The consequences of following alternatives are either benefits or costs occurring in the future. But consequences to whom? The point of view of the analysis answers this question. Consequences are different according to the point of view taken.

Consequences must be measured in terms of objectives. Consequences expected but not included in the objectives are irrelevant to a decision in the matter.

Example 20.1 (Continued) —————————————————————

In the example of the rapid transit bus system, the consequences may be measured only in terms of the objectives, which were profit, relief of congestion (and therefore time saved), and the effect on green space where additions to green space or slowing down the loss of green space were considered to be benefits. The graph of the consequences as benefits and costs by alternative and objective is shown in Figure 20.4.

Figure 20.4 is arranged in two columns, one of which represents the status quo and the other the introduction of a rapid transit bus system. The objectives are shown along the left-hand edge as profit, time saved, and green space. The individual cash flow diagrams use the convention that down arrows mean cash out, or costs, and up arrows mean cash in, or benefits. Years are represented by the horizontal line increasing to the right. The time horizon chosen is five years.

Under the first objective—profit—revenues under the status quo are shown to be decreasing through years 1 to 5. Costs, on the other hand, are increasing as shown by the increasing size of the down arrows through years 1 to 5. The rapid transit bus system option opposite the same objective shows a large down arrow at time zero to indicate an investment. Revenues under this alternative are shown to be increasing. Costs are increasing as well but not quite as rapidly as under the status quo.

Opposite the second objective—time saved because of the reduction of congestion—the status quo alternative indicates that time lost will increase over the five-year projection. Under the rapid transit bus alternative, congestion will decrease and time lost to it will also decrease because the rapid transit bus will tend to remove cars from the highways and streets of the city. People who formerly drove their cars to the city will now be taking the bus.

The third objective—green space—shows the status quo as increasing the loss of green space and thus increasing cost under this alternative. Under the rapid transit bus system alternative, the cost of loss of green space exists but is lessened.

On the bottom graph of the Figure 20.4 the sum of all effects is shown. The sum is algebraic. At the very bottom the differences

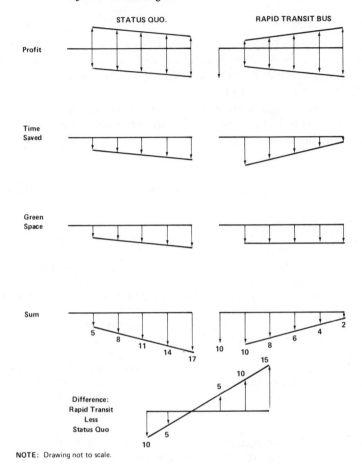

Figure 20.4   Consequences of two transport alternatives

between the alternatives are shown as rapid transit consequences less the consequence attributable to the status quo. This final diagram is drawn to illustrate the logical decision rule that it is only the difference between alternatives that is relevant to a comparison between them.

Let us now attribute dollar figures to these effects and proceed to show how the time dimension might be removed from the problem. (Of course, these figures must be supposed to have come from many months of study and research by teams of experts—engineers, economists, city planners, architects, sociologists, and others—from consulting companies and from the city itself.) Let us say, for example, that $P = \$10,000,000$, $C_1 = \$5,000,000$, $C_2 = 0$, $B_3 = \$5,000,000$, $B_4 = \$10,000,000$, and $B_5 = \$15,000,000$. These sums associated with years in which they occur are shown in Table 20.1. The middle column

TABLE 20.1   The Rapid Transit Bus System Incremental
Cash Flow

Year	Benefit (+) or Cost (−)	Single Payment Present Worth Factor $(P/F, i, N)$	Discounted Cost or Benefit
0	−10,000,000	1.000	−10,000,000
1	− 5,000,000	0.909	− 4,550,000
2	0	0.826	0
3	+ 5,000,000	0.751	+ 3,760,000
4	+10,000,000	0.683	+ 6,830,000
5	+15,000,000	0.621	+ 9,320,000
			B − C = + 5,360,000

shows the single payment present worth factor, if the discount rate is
assumed to be 10 percent. (Ten percent is chosen as the discount rate
because it is in general use by the U. S. Department of Transportation.)

The discounted benefits minus the discounted costs of the difference between the alternatives comes to $5,360,000 in benefits,
which illustrates that the rapid transit bus alternative has a present
value of that amount in comparison to the status quo alternative. In
other words, the rapid transit bus alternative is equivalent to over
$5,000,000 in the hand of the city at time zero.

A FACTUAL STUDY

The problem of weighting consequences is sometimes solved by
looking to the major goals of a country. These objectives are often
expressed quantitatively in national plans. Such plans were formerly
associated in people's minds with the more lurid aspects of planning
in the USSR. After World War II, however, national plans became
instruments of development in many of the countries that had been
colonies of the Western powers—India, for example. Such plans set
forth what improvements in the economy and in the society of a
country were to be attained over some period—five years was the
usual period. Some examples of goals in national plans are annual
percentage increases in gross national product (GNP), increase in
economically active population, increase in exports, decrease in im-
ports, decrease in illiteracy, increase in some health index, and so on.
From such plans a social welfare function can be made up.

In the middle 1960s in a certain Latin American country the national plan called for an annual increment of 5.9 percent in GNP and
3.3 percent in the economically active population. During these same

years, a major highway construction project was being evaluated that would have effects in both these areas. It was suggested that the scheduling of the sections of the highway to be built and indeed, whether or not to build certain sections of the highway at all, could be decided by using a social welfare function made up of the elements of the national plan that would be affected by the highway construction, maintenance, and operation. It should be explained here that sections of the highway could have been built separately from other sections simply because each section was self-sufficient. To be sure, not all goals of the national plan would be affected by this particular highway construction, and even some of the goals that were affected could not be treated because even approximate effects could not be guessed. However, the analysts believed that a much more realistic system of evaluation could be set up by basing the analysis on such goals as had been expressed rather than on some such partial measure as operating cost reduction of vehicles or increase in GNP alone.

Establishing the Social Welfare Function

Under the terms of the national plan, and considering that all goals set out therein were equally desirable, which hardly need be assumed at all, the social welfare function was based on a 1964 GNP of $3495 million and an economically active population of 3,398,000 persons. (Naturally, GNP and population were both going to increase. The question then arose, "On what do we base the percentage increases called for by the national plan?" It was decided for simplicity's sake to base them on a single year—1964.)

$$\Delta GNP = 5.9\% \text{ of } \$3495 \text{ million}$$
$$= \$206.2 \text{ million}$$
$$\Delta P = 3.3\% \text{ of } 3,398,000 \text{ persons} = 112,000 \text{ persons}$$

Thus from equation (2):

$$\Delta GNP = \Delta P$$
or, $206.2 million = 112,000 persons
or, 1 person = $18,410

It was determined that the GNP and population data shown in Table 20.2 would be reached in 10 years and would then remain stable. Thus, the result of building each section would be a single rise in both GNP and population that would remain in perpetuity.

A difficulty now arises. Are we to assume that the ΔGNP is an annual event and the ΔP a single nonrecurring event? It seems we should, because the ΔGNP will occur because the ΔP is there to produce it. Thus, one person is worth \$18,410 once, at the end of 10 years. What, however, is \$1 yearly worth? If the public rate of return is 10 percent and the ΔGNP occurs in perpetuity, as we will assume, then its present worth at full development 10 years hence is:

$$\frac{\$1.00}{0.10} = \$10$$

The social welfare function is, to repeat equation (1):

$$W = K_1 U_1 + K_2 U_2$$

Substituting the Ks and Us in the preceding equation with $U_1 =$ dollars of ΔGNP, $U_2 =$ dollars per person, $K_1 = 10$, and $K_2 = \$18,410$:

$$W = \$10 \text{ per dollar of } \Delta GNP + \$18,410 \text{ per person}$$

We are now prepared to evaluate each section of the road, assuming that we ignore the growth period of 10 years. Notice that the terms of the social welfare function are now commensurable. For section 1 of Table 20.2:

$$\begin{aligned} W_1 &= \$2,700,000 \,(\$10) + 22,700 \,(\$18,410) \\ &= 27,000,000 + 417,900,000 \\ &= \$444.9 \text{ million} \end{aligned}$$

The other sections are similarly calculated. The results, along with the original cost, and a $W - C$ amount are shown in Table 20.3.

TABLE 20.2 Two Consequences of Highway Building

Highway Section	Increase in GNP (\$000)	Increase in Economically Active Population (persons)
1	2700	22,700
2	1730	18,200
3	4330	43,700
4	2080	25,300
5	1140	9,600
6	1142	22,800
7	1480	26,600

TABLE 20.3 Highway Section Priorities

Highway Section	W ($000)	Cost ($000)	W – C ($000)	Priority
1	449,000	20,400	428,600	4
2	352,400	27,500	324,900	6
3	847,800	46,800	801,000	1
4	486,600	34,400	452,200	3
5	188,100	33,100	155,000	7
6	434,000	33,300	400,700	5
7	504,500	32,300	472,200	2

Evidently the priority list should be as shown in the last column of Table 20.3. Cost has proved to be a relatively minor factor because it does not alter the priority list based on W alone. The priority list is almost insensitive to ΔGNP; establishing the priority list on the basis of the increase in economically active population alone results in exchanging the position of sections four and five only, as you may discover for yourself.

Did the decision makers in this country intend to make the increase in economically active population so dominant? Probably not. The implications of the national goals' effect on project selection simply was not understood.

CONCLUSION

In this chapter we have seen a simple method of determining priorities in situations in which social costs and benefits—are important. For "social" you may substitute "environmental," "political," or similar words. It is hard to imagine a situation in which this would not be true whenever public projects are under scrutiny. The method comes down to deciding on objectives, determining alternatives, estimating and predicting consequences, assigning values to and weighting these consequences, discounting the consequences, and finally making the decision.

The logic of a social benefit/cost analysis has been developed in which the quantifiable in monetary terms and the nonquantifiable are united. I have shown that monetary and nonmonetary consequences cannot help being united and that further development in the political economy of public investment cannot proceed except along the lines of weighting consequences as a method of deciding among alternatives.

REFERENCES

Heilbroner, Robert L., and Lester C. Thurow, *The Economic Problem*, 4th ed. Englewood Cliffs, N. J.: Prentice-Hall, 1975, pp. 212–226.

Meyer, J. R., J. F. Kain, and M. Wohl, *The Urban Transportation Problem*. Cambridge, Mass.: Harvard University Press, 1965, pp. 379–389.

Samuelson, Paul A., *Economics*, 5th ed. New York: McGraw-Hill, 1961, p. 474.

Steiner, Henry M., "Social Benefit Cost Analysis of Transport Proposals," *Proceedings, Fourteenth Annual Meeting, Transportation Research Forum*. Oxford, Indiana: Richard B. Cross, 1973, pp. 673–682.

Steiner, Peter O., "The Public Sector and the Public Interest," *The Analysis and Evaluation of Public Expenditures: The PPB System*, Joint Economic Committee Compendium, 91st Congress, 1st Session, 1, 1969, p. 30.

21

Inflation

Since World War II, changes in the price level, which have been steadily upward in almost all indexes, have caused a new element to be included in economic analysis. What inflation is, its history in the United States and in other countries, some discussion of price indexes and what they mean, and finally some examples of how inflation can be combined with the time value of money so as to produce an analysis suitable for decision making is the subject of this chapter.

DEFINITION

By inflation is meant upward changes in the price level. Goods, services, and taxes become more expensive. A dollar will not buy as much this year as it did last year. To explain what is meant by this phenomenon I resort to the traditional analysis of macroeconomics. Figure 21.1 shows the inflationary gap on a traditional macroeconomic graph. On the abscissa is the net national product and on the ordinate, the total spending. Both are shown in billions of dollars. The diagonal line shows equality between total spending and net national product; this is the equilibrium line. Any point on this 45° diagonal is a point at which total spending and net national product are equal. Point E is such a point. In the diagram the vertical dashed line at 600 is the full employment line. This means that at $600 billion of net national product all the resources of the country—in this case, the United States—are being used. The dashed line shown as $C + I + G$ (consumption + investment + government expenditures) indicates the total spending that occurs at every net national product. The inflationary gap, therefore, is the distance RS. It is the amount by which spending exceeds net national product. In a situation when consumers, investors, and government are all together spending more than

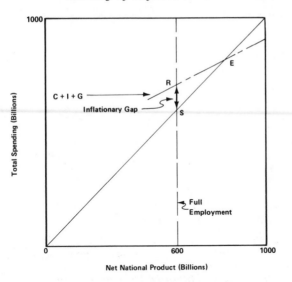

Figure 21.1 The inflationary gap.

the net national product, inevitably a price rise occurs because money is available to pay for more goods and services than can be supplied. Because it is impossible, at the growth point at which the society finds itself, to produce more, the slack must be taken up by a rise in the price level of purchases. I will not attempt to explain any other implications of Figure 21.1. Those who are interested are advised to consult any of the standard texts in economics (Samuelson, 1976).

HISTORY OF INFLATION IN THE UNITED STATES

Figure 21.2 shows the history of the consumer price index (CPI) in the United States since 1900. If consumer prices in 1900 are indexed at 100, the growth of inflation can be mapped. The sudden increase shown at 1917 and into 1920 is due to World War I. After World War I there was an abrupt deflation—the depression of 1920—a steady price level until 1926, and then a decending level of prices, or deflation, which reached a low point in 1932, the worst year of the Great Depression. During the Roosevelt era, there was a slow rise until 1937, then a gradual decline to 1940, and then the effect of World War II, which started in Europe in 1939, began to be felt in the United States. Since then, the index has risen steadily and more steeply in recent years. With its steady increase has come the necessity to deal with it. In planning, particularly of investments in fixed assets of the type that

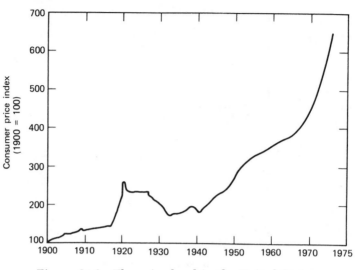

Figure 21.2   The price level in the United States.

we have been dealing with in this book, analyzing the effects of inflation is vital.

The consumer price index is measured by a market basket of goods and services standardized by federal authorities. The goods and services in this market basket are weighted in proportion to their use, so that a rise in the price of a little-used product, such as radishes, does not have the same effect on the index as a rise in the price of a heavily used product, such as meat. Each year, the cost of this market basket of goods and services is recomputed, and the percentage increase over the previous year is recorded. For example, if 1900 is indexed at 100 and a 5 percent price increase in the market basket is noted in 1901, then the consumer price index is listed at 105. An increase in the price index of another 5 percent above 1901, measured in 1902, causes the price index in 1902 to be listed at 110.3. If the price index continues to rise at 5 percent annually, the index for 1903 will be 115.8. Notice that this calculation is nothing more than computing the compound amount factor for a single payment. A glance at the first column of the 5 percent table in the Appendix reveals the truth of this observation.

Of course, the price index in the United States has not risen at a steady rate, but projections of the inflation rate for the purposes of economic analysis normally presuppose a fixed inflation rate. For a more detailed description of a price index, the standard economic texts are recommended.

Changes in the wholesale price index are shown from 1800 almost to the present in Figure 21.3. The variation has been more abrupt than

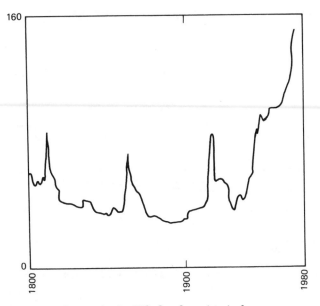

Figure 21.3 Wholesale price index.

in the consumer price index, but the general trend after 1940 is certainly the same—upward.

Figure 21.4 shows the index of selected timber products from 1957 almost to 1975. Such indexes are a useful guide to what has been happening and therefore to what may happen to individual costs in specific industries.

The United States has not been the only sufferer from inflation. In fact, in many other countries the phenomenon has been more marked. Table 21.1 shows price levels for 1966 and 1976 in a number of countries. Notice the Brazilian experience, where 20 percent was the average yearly inflation during these years. The Brazilians have evolved methods of dealing with such changes so that it still remains possible to make contracts for the future and thus to continue to conduct the economy. The main method used has been to tie payments on contracts to a government price index of inflation. Thus, all future payments may vary in *cruzeiros,* but their value in relation to the zero year with an index of 100 remains the same. By this method a constant contract *cruzeiro* is maintained.

The other countries in the table were chosen because of their location, except for the USSR and the United States, which were included to illustrate the situation in the two most powerful countries in the world. Notice, too, that except for the USSR and the United States, the other countries in the table are selected from a group

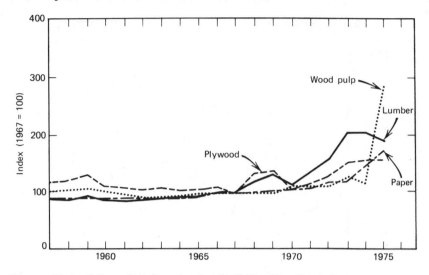

Figure 21.4   Selected timber products wholesale price indexes. 1957–1975.

considered by economists not to have yet reached full economic development.

HANDLING INFLATION

To describe how inflation can be included in an economic analysis, I will use an example. In Table 21.2 the first column shows current dollars, that is, the number of dollars actually paid in the year in question, or the number of dollars projected to be paid for the year in question. Column 2 is the price index, which in this case shows a constant increase of 5 percent. It is equal to 100 times the single payment compound amount factor at 5 percent. Column 3 reduces the current dollars in Column 1 to constant dollars at year zero, where the price index is 100. It does this by dividing Column 1 by Column 2 and multiplying the result by 100. In other words, current dollars are deflated to constant dollars in terms of the zero year. At this point it is possible to discount the cash flow in constant dollars of column 3. At a discount factor of 20 percent, shown in Column 4, the present worth of the deflated cash flow shown in Column 3 is obtained. This present worth of the deflated cash flow is seen to be −9,700. In other words, the internal rate of return of the cash flow in constant dollars is less than 20 percent.

TABLE 21.1 Consumer Price Index Numbers 1966–1976
(1970 = 100)

	1966	1976	Annual compound rate of change (%)
Brazil	42	254	20
Ghana	89	352	15
Greece	93	202	8
Indonesia	12	292	38
Israel	89	388	16
Mexico	88	204	9
Spain	83	208	10
Yugoslavia	74	271	14
USSR	100	100	0
United States	84	147	6

Source. United Nations, *Statistical Yearbook, 1977* (New York: United Nations, 1978), pp. 684–690.

THE COMPOSITE RATE

Is it possible to combine inflation rates and discount rates in a single composite rate that can be used in the same way that a discount rate has been used in this book up to now? If so, the result would be a cash flow such as appears in Table 21.2, Column 5, which shows the effect of both inflation and discounting. To derive a formula for the combined effects the following symbols are used:

F_N = future payment or current dollars in year N
N = year
C_{0_N} = constant dollars in terms of base year in year N
i = discount rate
f = constant inflation rate
$i{:}f$ = composite rate

To deflate current dollars in year N to constant dollars in year N, we divide current dollars in that year by the price index of that year, and multiply by 100, which is equivalent to multiplying by the single payment present worth factor for that year for the fixed inflation rate f:

$$C_{0_N} = F_N \left(\frac{1}{1+f} \right)^N \qquad (1)$$

TABLE 21.2 Handling Inflation

Year	Current $[a] 1	Price Index[b] 2	Constant $[c] (1 ÷ 2) 100 3	Discount Factors @ 20% 4	PW 3 × 4 5	Factors @ 26% 6	PW 1 × 6 7
0	-100,000	100.0	-100,000	1.000	-100,000	1.000	-100,000
1	+30,000	105.0	+28,571	0.833	+23,800	0.794	23,800
2	+50,000	110.3	+45,352	0.694	+31,500	0.630	31,500
3	+70,000	115.8	+60,469	0.579	+35,000	0.500	35,000
					-9,700		-9,700

[a] Actual year payments. [b] At 5 percent yearly inflation; equal to 100 $(F/P, 5, N)$. [c] In terms of year zero.

The present worth of constant dollars in year N is:

$$PW = C_{0_N} \left(\frac{1}{1+i} \right)^N \qquad (2)$$

Substituting for C_{0_N} in equation 2 from equation 1:

$$PW = F_N \left(\frac{1}{1+f} \right)^N \left(\frac{1}{1+i} \right)^N$$

$$= F_N \left[\frac{1}{(1+f)(1+i)} \right]^N \qquad (3)$$

It will now be recognized that $\left[\dfrac{1}{(1+f)(1+i)} \right]^N$ is simply the

present worth factor with $(1+f)(1+i)$ instead of $(1+i)$. Subtracting 1 reveals what I have called the composite rate:

$$i:f = (1+f)(1+i) - 1 \qquad (4)$$

In an example that uses the inflation rate and the discount rate of Table 21.2, the composite rate is determined to be 26 percent as follows:

$f = 5\%$
$i = 20\%$
$(1 + f)(1 + i) - 1 = (1 + 0.05)(1 + 0.20) - 1$
$= 1.26 - 1 = 0.26 \text{ or } 26\%$

If we now use the factors for 26 percent as shown in Column 6 of Table 21.2 and apply them to the cash flow in current dollars of Column 1, the result is shown in Column 7, which is exactly equal to the results of Column 5, as was to be expected. Notice that the inflation rate must be assumed or known to be a constant in order to apply this method.

THE DISCOUNT RATE

The general rule for determining the discount rate to be used in calculations when inflation must be considered is that the opportunity cost of capital appropriate to constant dollars should be used for the discount rate when a constant dollar cash flow is being scrutinized. An opportunity cost of capital associated with current cash flows should be used for the discount rate when current cash flows are being manipulated.

For example, in Table 21.2 "Handling Inflation," page 292, the cash flow appropriate to the constant dollar stream of Column 3 was 20 percent. The discount rate applicable to the current dollar cash flow of Column 1 was 26 percent—the composite rate.

A further example may clarify the procedure. If you have a next best alternative for investment available from a savings and loan account yielding 6 percent, then 6 percent is the opportunity cost of capital that should be applied to current cash flows because the money received at 6 percent will be in current dollars. In other words, the cash flow that will be received from the savings and loan association includes the effect of inflation, as well as the effect of compound interest. It is the composite rate. If it were desired to calculate the opportunity cost of capital of a constant dollar cash flow, that is, a cash flow in terms of a base year, it would be necessary to compute a new cash flow in terms of constant dollars and then to compute the rate of return of that cash flow. This rate of return would be the opportunity cost of capital that should be applied to any constant dollar cash flow.

Example 21.1 ────────────────────────────────────

Given a constant inflation rate of 5.2 percent and an opportunity cost of capital of 14 percent, find the present worth in constant dollars in terms of year zero of the cash flows of Table 21.3. Show also the price index for each year.

(a) Using equation (4):
$$i : f = (1 + i)(1 + f) - 1$$
$$= (1.14)(1.052) - 1$$
$$= 0.19928$$
$$= 20\% \text{ (approximately)}$$

The cash flows may now be solved using ordinary present worth methods at 20 percent.

$$PW = 100,000 + 20,000 \ (P/A, 20, 10)$$
$$= -100,000 + 20,000 \ (4.192)$$
$$= -16,160$$

(b)
$$PW = -2,000,000 + 1,000,000 \ (P/A, 20, 5)$$
$$+200,000 \ (P/G, 20, 5)$$
$$= -2,000,000 + 1,000,000 \ (2.991)$$
$$+200,000 \ (4.9061)$$
$$= +1,972,220$$

TABLE 21.3   Example 21.1 Cash Flows
(in dollars)

	Year	Cash Flow
(a)	0	−100,000
	1–10	+20,000
(b)	0	−2,000,000
	1	+1,000,000
	2	+1,200,000
	3	+1,400,000
	4	+1,600,000
	5	+1,800,000
(c)	0	−100,000
	1	+ 60,000
	2	+120,000
	3	+140,000

(c)

$$PW = -100,000 + 60,000\,(P/F, 20, 1)$$
$$+ 120,000\,(P/F, 20, 2) + 140,000\,(P/F, 20, 3)$$
$$= -100,000 + 60,000\,(0.8333) + 120,000\,(0.6944)$$
$$+ 140,000\,(0.5787)$$
$$= + 114,340$$

The price index by year is shown in Table 21.4. It is obtained by multiplying the previous year's index by 1.052.

Example 21.2 ──────────────────────────────

The price indexes and cash flows by year in a now-concluded investment in real property appear in Table 21.5. What rate of return existed in terms of constant dollars at year zero?

TABLE 21.4   Price Index by Year

Year	Price index
0	100
1	105.2
2	110.7
3	116.5
4	122.6
5	129.0
6	135.7
7	142.8
8	150.2
9	158.0
10	166.2

TABLE 21.5   Rate of Return Including Inflation

Year 1	Cash Flow ($000,000) 2	Price Index 3	Constant $ 4	P/F, 9, N 5	Present Worth at 9% 6
0	−3.0	100	−3.0	1.0000	−3.0
1	+0.4	106	+0.38	0.9174	+0.35
2	+1.0	116	+0.86	0.8417	+0.73
3	+1.3	126	+1.03	0.7722	+0.80
4	+1.2	136	+0.88	0.7084	+0.63
5	+1.1	142	+0.78	0.6499	+0.50
					+0.01

IROR = 9%

The problem data are given in the first three columns of Table 21.5. Column 4 is the result of dividing Column 2 by the price index for the year concerned and multiplying by 100. Column 5 is the single payment present worth factor for 9 percent. Because Column 6, the result of multiplying Column 4 by Column 5, sums to close to zero, the internal rate of return for this investment, which includes the effect of inflation, is 9 percent.

REFERENCE

Samuelson, Paul, *Economics,* 10th ed, New York: McGraw-Hill, 1976, p. 241.

22

The Cost of Capital

In this text I have often used *capital, investment, opportunity cost of capital in the public sector, discount rate,* and associated terms. It is time to define these accurately and to say as much as can be said at this writing about the controversial subject of the discount rate in the public sector.

DEFINITIONS

Capital is usually thought of as a certain amount of money available for investment, or an amount of money tied up in a business. "My capital in the bakery is so-and-so." We have a more-or-less clear idea of what the speaker means. But capital, to an economist, is not a sum of money; instead, it is real goods or assets. A building is a capital asset—or simply "capital." So are inventories of finished goods or half-finished goods. So is a bulldozer, or a yard full of tubing. So were Robinson Crusoe's fish hooks because he had to take time off from fishing to produce the hooks. He invested some of his time, which had to be subtracted from production time for fishing, to produce the hooks in order to increase his catch. He produced capital goods.

Capital is any asset used in the production of other goods and services.

Investment is the production of such a capital asset. For example, the building of a bridge by the Ministry of Public Works of Mexico is an investment in a capital asset. It takes time to build the bridge, and this taking of time is characteristic of investment in the production of a capital good. Resources are taken away from production and put to investment in capital goods. Robinson Crusoe stops fishing and turns to hook production.

297

Another example: Wine is laid down to improve its quality by aging. The stored wine is a capital good because time is being used to improve it. If it were sold immediately, then the wine would be a production item.

The *opportunity cost of capital* means the benefit forgone for a time by choosing to invest rather than to consume. This investment may be in either the public or the private sector.

INTEREST THEORY

Under perfect competition, the opportunity cost of capital is simply the equilibrium price, just as though capital were any other good or service, like hamburgers or house cleaning. Figure 22.1 reveals the situation. Under perfect competition, in equilibrium the opportunity cost and the market price do not differ.

The cost of capital is measured by the interest rate, in this case, i_E. The quantity of capital is a measure of the resources available for capital goods production. As in other supply–demand figures, Q measures capital available per time period, say, per year.

Equilibrium is achieved in the usual way: If the interest rate is higher than the equilibrium rate, then more resources for capital goods production will be available, but the demand at the interest rate will be smaller than the supply. The interest rate will fall in the capital market until the supply matches the demand. Opposite effects occur for an interest rate lower than i_E.

In Figure 22.1 I have not distinguished between private and public sector interest rates because in perfect competition no such divi-

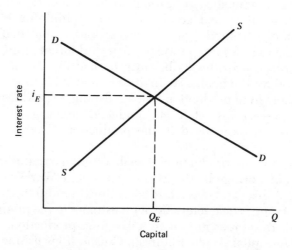

Figure 22.1 Equilibrium price of capital.

sion exists. Only the society exists. Thus, i_E is the social opportunity cost of capital.

It is also the marginal rate of time preference for all individuals in the society. *Marginal rate of time preference* means the amount an individual would have to be paid in order to restrict his consumption for a given period, usually a year. It is his opportunity cost of capital. For example, if an individual demands at least $10 as payment for investing (i.e., forgoing the pleasure of spending) $100, then his marginal rate of time preference is 10 percent. (You may now wish to review the "Time Value of Money" section of Chapter 4, "Consequences over Time.") If an individual is indifferent between spending $1 now or $(1 + i)^N$ dollars at some period N in the future, then i is his marginal rate of time preference, or opportunity cost of capital.

You are aware from previous chapters, however, that perfect competition and thus a perfect capital market is a rare bird indeed. Thus, adjustments must be made. How rare a bird may be imagined if one realizes that every individual will have exactly the same opportunity cost of capital under the perfectly competitive model. No one will have 12 percent while another has 8 percent for the last dollar he wishes to invest. In this strange and robot world, all will agree on exactly 10 percent.

In the real world, the capital market is imperfect, and individuals' opportunity cost of capital will differ. It is imperfect because of lack of knowledge of investment opportunities, because of the "lumpiness" of some investments—it is not possible to invest in dollar increments in many cases. To invest in a two-story rather than a one-story building requires a new lump or bundle of funds. Even with knowledge, opportunity is sometimes lacking. It may not be practical to invest in real estate at the other end of the country, even though the gains look attractive, because of the difficulties of long-range management. Taxes must be considered because the real world contains government on a number of levels. A higher rate of return must be sought by private companies, especially corporations, to compensate for this levy. Externalities exist. Rates of return, and therefore opportunity costs of capital, are distorted because not all costs are paid nor benefits accrued by the enterprise. Finally, risk is involved in interest rate determination. Riskier business projects must give promise of higher rates of return or they will not be financed. Taxes, externalities, and risk are treated more extensively later in this chapter.

COST OF CAPITAL: PRIVATE SECTOR

As we have seen, the private sector uses an opportunity cost of capital, which is also called the minimum attractive rate of return, or discount rate, or marginal cost of capital, or marginal interest rate, before and after taxes. If taxes are a nondifferential cost among alternatives, they can be excluded, and the opportunity cost of capital before taxes used. We have seen what an important part income tax effects play in an analysis.

The private sector analyst determines the after-tax opportunity cost of capital by observing the overall rate of return after taxes of his company. He may ask himself, "What rate of return after taxes did my company make last year on its investment?" He turns to the consolidated income statement (profit and loss statement) and finds the profit after taxes. Then he goes to the balance sheet and selects a figure for capital investment in the company—perhaps stock outstanding plus retained earnings for the year previous to the one in which the profit was reported. Profit divided by capital investment multiplied by 100 gives him an opportunity cost of capital after taxes that he uses as a discount rate or cutoff rate in his analysis of the revenues and costs of proposed projects. He does not concern himself with the financial cost of capital, for reasons we have already seen. This will be his procedure for all projects of equal risk.

As noted in Chapter 14, "Capital Budgeting," this procedure is fraught with all sorts of hidden assumptions, which make it dubious at best. But for the purposes of this discussion, let us assume that the matter is being handled correctly.

What does the analyst mean by "risk"? He means that the standard deviation of the net benefits distribution is the same for projects of equal risk and different for projects of unequal risk even when the expected values are the same, that is, that the risk is directly proportional to the standard deviation. (Figure 12.1 of Chapter 12, "Risk and Uncertainty," shows two projects of unequal risk with the same expected value.) The riskier project has more chance of smaller net benefits than the less risky one. Because expected values are the same, the riskier project has equally more chance of larger net benefits than the less risky project. Nevertheless, the private sector analyst normally accounts for higher risk by evaluating riskier projects at a higher discount rate than not so risky ones. For example, an oil company uses higher discount rates for exploration and drilling projects than for evaluating marketing projects, such as a delivery pipeline or a distribution storage plant. Whether or not this is a reasonable procedure, it is one generally followed.

For small companies, unable to stand the prospect of heavy losses, the projects with low standard deviations are preferred over those with higher standard deviations of net benefits, even if the expected values are the same. This preference is expressed by evaluating the riskier projects at a higher discount rate based on judgment and experience.

What about externalities in the private sector? First of all, they are considered. We have called them the *incommensurables*. An example frequently used is that of the effect on labor relations of a project that will cause workers to lose their jobs or to be displaced to others. This sort of consequence is difficult to quantify, yet it may be more important for the general welfare of the company than any of the quantifiable ones. The existence of such externalities is not reflected in a change in the discount rate as it is in the case of risk. It is taken into account as a "note well" item for consideration by the management authority that will make the decision.

COST OF CAPITAL: PUBLIC SECTOR

Imagine an analyst whose viewpoint is that of the entire society. Imagine, too, that he is concerned with all projects in the society, both public and private. The question facing him is what discount rate to use for all projects—from something as mammoth as the water resources development of the Columbia River basin to something as tiny as the replacement of one production line machine with another.

He may entertain for a while the possibility of using the growth rate of the Gross National Product (GNP) for the society over the past five years. But the GNP comes from two sources, capital and labor:

$$GNP = Lp_L + Cp_C$$

where: L = quantity of labor
C = quantity of capital
p_L = price of labor
p_C = price of capital

It is not possible to assign all the GNP to investment effects without also saying that the opportunity cost of labor, p_L, is zero. This may be close to the truth for many labor-intensive projects in developing countries such as India, but it certainly is not so in the United States (Harberger, 1962). Reluctantly, the analyst scraps the idea. He is then forced to look to the opportunity cost of capital resources in the society. Somehow he must adjust for the imperfections of the capital market, for risk, and for externalities.

If all funds for public sector investment come from the private sector through taxes and government borrowing, then he looks to the opportunities lost to the private sector because of taxes paid or money lent to the government and the rate of return on the marginal projects undertaken in the private sector. It does not matter whether the funds come from taxes or borrowing. In other words, the "sources of funds" approach, with its associated sacrificed rates of return is not to be used.

But whether or not one is prepared to go along with this functional finance criticism of the sources of funds approach to the estimation of opportunity cost one can surely argue that the method is unnecessarily complex. If it is true that, in real terms, what the government takes from the private sector is input resources, then to determine the relevant rate of discount one need not inquire beyond the rate of return currently being earned by the users of such inputs. One can ignore in this calculation the subjective time preferences of consumers, the difference between the disutility of paying taxes and of lending and a host of other issues. (Baumol, 1968, p. 792)

It may be that the government is heavily engaged in state-owned enterprises, as in the socialist countries and some developing countries. If this is the case, the analyst looks to the same area—the rate of return on marginal projects undertaken. I do not deal with socialist phenomena here, however, but confine myself to the more usual case of the mixed economy as it exists in the United States.

Income taxes paid from the private to the public sector are a transfer payment. Thus, the analyst considers only the marginal rate of return on projects before income taxes. (It is assumed that corporate income taxes are actually paid and not avoided, so that the rate of corporate income tax may be taken at 50 percent, for example. I also assume for the moment that neither risk differences nor externalities need be considered.) In a riskless world, it seems that the proper social discount rate to be used by society's analyst should be the marginal rate in use by the private sector. If this rate is i_p and the social discount rate i_s, then:

$$i_p = i_s$$

RISK

Now let us return to a consideration of risk. How should it enter the social discount rate? Should there be a so-called "risk premium" as in the private sector?

The answer is, "No." Society undertakes a great number of projects. So many, in fact, in the public sector alone, that the dispersion of the outcomes is irrelevant. Only the expected value of the consequences of a project is therefore relevant. Two projects each having two possible net benefits of $500 and $1500 and $100 and $1900, each with equal probability, will be judged as having equal net benefits because both have an expected value of $1000.

Look at it another way: By choosing to finance a large number of projects, as it must, the public sector ensures itself against loss on the projects whose payoffs occur in the lower range. Add all the net benefit frequency distributions of all projects undertaken, regardless of expected values. The result spreads the risk.

It may now appear that the social discount rate ought to be the rate for marginal riskless investment in the private sector—General Motors Corporation bonds, for example. Not so.

First, remember that the social analyst is reviewing all projects, both in the public and the private sector. He observes that private sector projects have a marginal rate of return of i_p. He also notices that all funds for public projects cost what they would return if left in the private sector.

He knows that part of i_p is a risk premium. Say i_p equals 20 percent and the risk premium is 5 percent. Should i_s, the social discount rate, then be 15 percent? Somewhat surprisingly, the answer is again, "No".

The fact is that the marginal private discount rate under which projects are being rejected is 20 percent. Does it matter that part of this 20 percent is thought to be a risk premium by private sector analysts? Should we therefore accept a project in the public sector that pays off at 18 percent? The truth is that no matter what the elements that go into the private sector cut-off rate are—risk premium, externalities, inflation, racial prejudice, or any factor you can think of, the end result is that projects making less than i_p are being rejected. Therefore:

$$i_p = i_s$$

in a risky world as well as a riskless one.

Another way of looking at the matter is that if all of society's projects, both public and private, were assembled in one grand list, and all the frequency distributions of all net benefits were summed, the result would be an even greater spreading of the risk over all projects than occurred with public projects alone. Moreover, if the cut-off rate for private sector projects is, say, 20 percent, all other things being equal, there is no reason, since the sources of funds is the private sector, to cut off public projects at a lower rate than 20 percent.

EXTERNALITIES

Externalities have been discussed in Chapter 20. The way in which they enter the social discount rate is by being used as an excuse for lowering it in public projects.

The argument is that because public projects have so many good side effects that cannot be quantitatively evaluated, they should be judged at a lower discount rate than private projects. Often overlooked, however, is that private projects also have many beneficial side effects. There seems to be a feeling among many planners that public project externalities are more good than bad and that the opposite is true of private project externalities. One need remember only the urban freeways of the 1950s and 1960s and the air pollution, congestion, and the destruction of efficient and pleasant city life that the exclusive reliance on the automobile caused, to question the statement. As to private sector projects, consider the stand-by benefits of private transport companies. The railroad, trucking, and air freight service all provide stand-by service for one another in case of bad weather, strikes, or other interference with ordinary service. Yet this benefit is not market-compensated. It is an externality.

Externalities should be taken into account in both private and public projects but not by adjusting the social discount rate. Quantification, listing, the use of a social welfare function—all are better methods of accounting for externalities than lowering the discount rate.

FUTURE GENERATIONS

One of the reasons often given for lowering the discount rate is the need to provide for future generations. When one considers that the real per capita income in the United States now is several times greater than that of a generation or two ago, the welfare of future generations might well be left aside while we attempt to solve the ills—poverty, ignorance, disease—of our own generation.

Few would deny the necessity of saving our irreplaceable Grand Canyon, or the whale, or historic buildings, for the enjoyment of our descendants. Often, however, the public project justified by a low discount rate does just the opposite. The dam destroys the canyon, the urban freeway the neighborhood, the interstate highway the joy of driving.

In some countries, if provision is not made for future generations by the government, the generations may come into a heritage of such misery that they will remember their forefathers with a curse. Programs of population control, for example, may be given special treatment but again, not by lowering the discount rate. A cost-effectiveness approach might be used where costs are the same as in the benefit cost analysis, but the benefit side is measured in terms of achieving a certain goal—in this case, reduced population growth.

POLITICS AND THE DISCOUNT RATE

The discount rate used in public projects has strong political consequences. A large dam is proposed for a western state: It has a life of
100 years, which is to say that its benefit stream—and the future
stream is overwhelmingly benefits—will stretch out that far. For long
future streams to have any effect on the benefit/cost ratio in the sense
of increasing it, the discount rate will have to be low. Figure 22.2
shows that at a discount rate of 5 percent, benefits 95 years out will be
included at only 1 percent of their value in the present value computation of benefits. Small wonder that agencies concerned with large
dam construction plump for low discount rates. The Corps of Engineers and the Bureau of Reclamation have never been advocates of
high discount rates, nor, by and large, have senators from western
states.

The Department of Transportation for years has used a 10 percent
discount rate. Figure 22.2 shows that at that rate the single payment
present worth factor reaches 0.01 at 50 years. One percent is surely
well within the accuracy of predictions of benefits and costs 50 years
out. If the Corps of Engineers used this rate, the benefits of half of the
dam life of 100 years would have no effect on the *B/C* ratio.

Now suppose that a private sector discount rate equal to 20 percent
were to be used. No effect more than 25 years in the future would be
considered at more than 1 percent of its undiscounted value! It should
be evident now why higher discount rates exclude effects on future
generations. No doubt it is presumptuous of us to imagine we can
decide anything beyond 25 years in the future. Developments—
scientific, engineering, political—seem to come faster and faster, and
the world changes its aspect more and more rapidly. Some modesty in
regard to our predictive power seems to be in order.

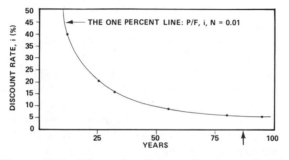

Figure 22.2   Where the discount factor equals 1%.

SUBJECTIVE TIME PREFERENCE

How does the consumer value the postponement of comsumption? When he buys government bonds, he appears to be indicating that it is around 5 percent, but is this a true signal?

First, the consumer is concerned with risk. Therefore, he buys government bonds, which are risk free. The social discount rate is riskless, however, because of the large number of projects concerned. We must therefore adjust the subjective time preference rate to account for this, to imagine what the consumer would do if he were able to invest in the same risk-free manner that the society does. No doubt his subjective time preference would rise but by how much is impossible to say.

Second, the individual investor is frequently not cognizant of all the opportunities for investment. Private sector bond issues may be outside his purview. When he invests, he thinks of the government bond offerings, conditioned as he is by patriotism or long exposure to government propaganda.

Third, the consumer is concerned with inflation, which the society as investor is not. This effect would cause him to seek a higher rate than, say, 5 percent, which does not keep pace with recent inflation rates. The recent moves to invest in real estate support this view.

Not enough is known about subjective time preference to allow any definitive statement about it. What would the consumer do if he had complete risk protection, knew all opportunities available for investment, and was not concerned about inflation? No one knows.

CONCLUSIONS

No definitive answer is possible to the question: "What should be the social discount rate?" The discussion so far seems to show that discount rates well below those used by the private sector before taxes result in misallocation of resources. Concern for future generations as an argument for lowering the social discount rate seems to me to be presumptuous, if not hypocritical. Raising the social discount rate to levels at which it will not encourage long-range government projects appears advisable, although this certainly should not mean a reduction in shorter-range areas but, rather, an increase in them.

Finally, the social discount rate should be the same for all government agencies. It makes no sense at all for the Corps of Engineers to be using a rate half that used by the Department of Transportation.

APPENDIX

To give the reader some flavor of the disarray in the federal government regarding the social discount rate, the following information is offered.

In 1962 the President's Water Resources Council, composed of the Secretaries of the Army, Interior, Agriculture, and Health, Education, and Welfare, stated:

> *Discount Rate.* The interest rate to be used in plan formulation and evaluation for discounting future benefits and computing costs, or otherwise converting benefits and costs to a common time basis shall be based upon the average rate of interest payable by the treasury on interest-bearing marketable securities of the United States outstanding at the end of the fiscal year preceding such computation which, upon the original issue, had terms of maturity of 15 years or more. Where the average rate so calculated is not a multiple of one-eighth of one percent, the rate of interest shall be the multiple of one-eighth of one percent next lower than such average rate. (Water Resources Council, 1962, p. 286).

As a result, the discount rates were 2.875 percent for 1963, 3.000 percent for 1964, 3.125 percent for 1968. Because of a change in policy in 1969 suggested by the Federal Water Resources Council, the rates were 4.625 percent in 1969 and 4.875 percent in 1970 (Chaykowski, 1975, p. 11).

According to a 1972 circular from the Office of Management and Budget directed to all agencies of the executive branch except the U.S. Postal Service, and specifically exempting discussions concerning water resource projects, the government of the District of Columbia, and non-federal recipients of federal loans or grants, a discount rate of 10 percent was ordered. This rate supposedly represented the average rate of return on private investment before taxes and after inflation (U.S. Office of Management and Budget, 1972, p. 4).

The Department of Transportation has used 10 percent since the "Dear Alan" letter of 1968 from Charles Zwick, then Director of the Bureau of the Budget to Alan S. Boyd, then Secretary of Transportation. So far as I know, nothing larger than 10 percent has been used by the United States government.

The discussion still goes on. The *Washington Post* on March 31, 1978 reported that a coalition of almost all the major environmental groups denounced the Carter administration on water policy. In one paragraph of the piece, it was stated that Congress had authorized 828 projects over the years, projects whose justification used discount rates as low as 3.25 percent.

REFERENCES

Baldwin, George B., "A Layman's Guide to Little/Mirrlees," *Finance and Development Quarterly*, (1) pp. 16–21 (1972).

Baumol, William J., "On the Social Rate of Discount." *American Economic Review*, **58**(4) pp. 788–802 (September 1968).

Chaykowski, Jon E., and J. Morley English, "What Discount Rate Should Be Used for Evaluating Development Projects?" World Congress on Educating Engineers for World Development, American Society for Engineering Education, Washington, D.C., 1975.

Grant, Eugene L., W. Grant Ireson, and Richard S. Leavenworth, *Principles of Engineering Economy*, 6th ed. New York: Ronald, 1976, p. 190.

Harberger, Arnold C., "Cost-Benefit Analysis and Economic Growth," *The Economic Weekly*, India, pp. 207–222 (February 1962).

Marglin, Stephen A., "The Opportunity Costs of Public Investment," *The Quarterly Journal of Economics*, **77** pp. 274–286 (1963).

Musgrave, Richard A., "Cost-Benefit Analysis and the Theory of Public Finance," *The Journal of Economic Literature*, **7**(3) (September 1969).

U.S., Office of Management and Budget, "Discount Rates to be Used in Evaluating Time-Distributed Costs and Benefits," Circular No. A-94, Revised, Washington, D.C., March 27, 1972.

U.S., The President's Water Resources Council, *Policies, Standards, and Procedure in the Formulation, Evaluation and Review of Plans for Use and Development of Water and Related Land Resources*, Senate Document No. 97, 87th Congress, 2nd Session, Washington, D. C., May 29, 1962, p. 12 as quoted in Robert L. Banks and Arnold Kotz, "The Program Budget and the Interest Rate for Public Investment," *Public Administration Review*, **27**(4) pp. 283–292 (December 1966).

III

SOCIOECONOMIC ANALYSIS IN THE DEVELOPMENT OF NATIONS

23

National Development

Parts I and II of this book have described the basis of economic analysis of investment projects. Part I was particularly concerned with the mechanisms of project selection when the price system was assumed to be working. That is, prices were assumed to represent social cost correctly. Part II explained the price system's allocative machinery. In particular, it emphasized the assumptions on which the whole allocation system was founded. This emphasis was necessary in order to convince the reader of the fragility of the price system in our economic world. Violate the assumptions, and the allocative mechanism fails. Prices no longer measure social costs, and waste of resources follows.

Waste is terrible when it occurs in any country, but when that country is also in deep poverty, avoidable waste becomes deeply disturbing to the populace. When one is starving, the sight of food being thrown away is maddening, yet this literally happens in many countries. When one sees littered streets and yet also observes men out of work and doing nothing, one's confidence in the existing socioeconomic system is shaken. When one in addition sees streets being swept by costly motorized sweepers while men who could easily do the job with brooms and shovels—and who are anxious to do the work—stand by and watch, one questions the wisdom of policies that idle men so that machines can work. The effect of such indignations and doubts is a drop in national morale. Something is obviously wrong, one thinks, and it does not take an economist to see the evil. The result is social unrest and a deep sense that all is not well. Corrective measures are not being taken. Perhaps no one knows how to make the corrections.

Waste of resources can occur for many reasons. The venality of public officials is one reason that will occur to many of us. Here, however, we are concerned with economic reasons for waste and how

311

waste can be avoided. Economic reasons for waste may also appear under a number of heads—inaccurate predictions of economic consequences is one of them. Only two particular economic reasons for waste are relevant for us. These are, first, the failure to evaluate the consequences of courses of action correctly because of incorrect methods, and second, the failure of the price system as an allocative mechanism. The most sophisticated use of the best methods of analysis will give improper signals if the price system is not working and will cause the prices used in the analysis to be more or less meaningless. Similarly, if the price system is working perfectly and the methods used to evaluate a project are naive, the results may be equally diastrous. The price system must be working well and the evaluation of projects must be correctly done if waste is to be avoided. This is the meaning of Part I and II of this book.

WHAT IS NATIONAL DEVELOPMENT?

In broadest terms, *national development* means an increase in the well-being, in the happiness, of the members of a society. Then one can say that any project that contributes to such an increase is worth considering and any one that does not is not. Well-being must be defined, of course, to be of any practical use in judging whether or not a project should be built and the order in which acceptable projects should be undertaken. But to define well-being, or welfare, one must know a good deal about the populace. What are its goals, for example? To know anything about this, one must know the history and institutions of the society, and something more—a vision of the direction the best future imaginable for that society should take.

Here a difficulty arises, for the last sentence smacks of authoritarianism, of "We know what's best for you better than you do yourselves." The difficulty can be avoided by an immersion in the society on the part of its planners. They must know who the people are and what they want, not only for themselves but for their children and grandchildren. Although Abraham Lincolns are not found behind every bush, nothing short of his kind of understanding of a nation should be sought in those who set up the criteria as to what national development shall mean. Is it necessary to add that only the best side of the populace should be accepted in defining welfare—the bravery and self-sacrifice of Don Quixote, but not his insane idealism and hallucinations, the practicality and toughness of Sancho Panza, but not his brutality and ignorant lust for power.

No reservations on my part exist in relation to development. Development may be defined as a rise in the gross national product for one society, as a rise in literacy for another, as an approach to equality in income distribution for yet another. Development may even be maintenance of existing ways of living, of existing institutions—down with the automobile, let's keep the oxcart! What E. F. Schumacher has called "Buddhist economics" implies standards of the way national development may be defined.

It is not only necessary to know the people; one must also understand their institutions. The interpretation of that word must be broad. People can express their collectivity—their group identity—in many ways. Compare the institution that is agriculture in the United States to that same institution in Mexico for an intimation of how far apart institutions embodying the same production goals can be. Compare the combines marching in echelon across the immense fields of wheat, the fine house, the broad technical education of the American farmer to the tiny field of corn, the adobe hut, the horse-drawn plow of his Mexican counterpart. This is not to say that one institutional arrangement is better than the other in terms of national development criteria. What I am saying is that the society as expressed in its collectivities must be understood—and its future direction understood—just as the John Does of the populace must be understood. To put it in a nutshell: The criteria for national development must be based on broad understanding of a society—the beliefs of its populace and the principles of its institutions.

For example, people in the United States believe that no one should be allowed to starve. This is expressed in all sorts of private and public agencies that, taken together, form the institution by which this expression of American belief appears. The tenet has important implications for United States planning. If no one is to be allowed to starve, then those out of work must.be fed. They are contributing nothing to the well-being of American society, yet they cannot be allowed to drop quietly into their graves as they would have been permitted to do in times gone by or in other, poorer countries in the world today. The social cost of their maintenance must be borne. Thus, the social calculus of private industry programs that will throw men out of work for any appreciable time must include the cost to the society of their upkeep and that of their families. Yet where is this done in the private sector? The failure to include social cost in private—or public—industry decisions causes misallocation of resources and therefore waste. However, American society demands that that social cost be borne.

Compare the situation in India where those out of work are not supported by anyone and die by the millions every year. In India the social cost and the private industry cost of throwing men out of work are the same. And whatever it is in terms of indirect costs such as the necessity for increased police protection, it is zero for the maintenance of the jobless worker and his or her family.

Many more examples of the influence of social mores on how national development is defined and how it is to be implemented could be cited. Not enough attention has been paid to this relationship.

THE DEVELOPED AND
THE DEVELOPING WORLD

The methods and ideas developed in Part I and Part II of this book can be related to problems of national socioeconomic development in a direct way. Their application has been particularly fruitful in the developing world, that is, in those countries that have become known as the Third World. As we have seen—the railroad electrification study in Chapter 15, for example—the methodology has been used in the United States. Yet one has the impression that a good deal more attention is paid to correct methods of economic analysis and planning in the Third World than in the First.

I would like to speculate for a little while on the reasons for this impression and then discuss the relevance of the factual studies that follow in Part III to the developed nations even though these studies deal with the developing nations. One of the chief reasons developing nations have had to use defensible and practical economic methods and planning is that they have been forced to apply for capital investment loans from international lending institutions. This has come to mean that their loan application must be accompanied by a project justification. An application from Indonesia to the International Bank for Reconstruction and Development (the World Bank) for a loan to finance a hydroelectic project had to be justified by a detailed study that included a system design that would stand up to the scrutiny of engineers of international reputation in the field; an economic analysis solidly based on a reasonable discount rate, economic life, benefits, and costs that would be criticized by economists who had spent their lives in just such analysis; and a financial plan for repayment that was well within reach and whose feasibility would be studied with utmost care by financial experts who knew the financial climate of the applying country—Indonesia—as well as the natives did. Contrast this situation with the planning and financing practices in a developed country—say the United States. A federal agency that planned and built a hydroelectric project was able to put forth a system design that was criticized by the agency itself. No outside corps of international experts sat in judgment on whether the geological structure was suitable for a dam on a river at that point, or whether the spillways were adequate. Congressmen, senators, and governors did comment and were listened to—possibly for better, possibly for worse. The economic analysis was performed by the same agency, usually at ridiculously low discount rates. Benefits were inflated. Costs were understated. No one criticized until recently. And so far the environmentalists have had little effect in this area of public spending. The financial plan? There was none because the government was using its own money. Is it any wonder that benefit/cost analysis is meaningless in many areas of public spending in the United States?

The United States is not the whole of the developed world. Perhaps these matters are managed better in Great Britain or France or West Germany. I do not know. Perhaps they are managed better in the Second World, the socialist countries. Again, I do not know. It seems certain, however, that as long as governments can spend for projects with no oversight on their planning and design, then that planning and design will not be as well done as it would were expert opinion to be delivered upon them and the money for the project given or withheld because of that opinion.

A word used in the preceding sentence is the key to another of the reasons why, in my opinion, developmental theory and practice are still in a rudimentary state in the United States—for I cannot include most of Europe in what I am about to say. "Planning" is the word. There exists in this country a revulsion against the word. It smacks of governmental bungling, the pork barrel, and waste in its more innocent sense. More darkly, it calls up visions of the excesses of the totalitarian states—the expulsion of the Kulaks and their exile and death in Siberia, the genocidal planning of the Nazis with their death machines. It seems to strike at the main principle of an economist Americans love to think they believe in, Adam Smith, who postulated that private greed can result in public good. It is pleasant for most of us to believe that letting out the worst of our materialistic impulses can and should receive public blessing. What, then, is this interference with "the invisible hand"? Was not the essence of what Smith said an injunction to leave things alone? And is there not a fundamental connection between economic and political freedom? For example, because labor is an input to the production process and because labor means the labor of citizens, economic planning must mean planning free men's lives. At very least, the planner must have a strong temptation to make sure of the labor for his project by force. (Of course, I am putting the best of the arguments against planning forward. Many of the objections to planning are based on nothing more than the fear that the government will somehow slow down the realization of those greedy impulses.) For all these expressed and hidden reactions to the word, planning has been anathematized in the United States, and its proper application has been left in a rudimentary state.

A third reason is the usual practical politician's rejection of any incursion into his domain. Anything that makes public decision making more logical and easy to understand, yet leaves out the politician, is naturally resented because it tends to reduce the area in which he can exercise his power. I am speaking of the man who can vote without hesitation for subsidy to tobacco growing while at the same time supporting a ban on cigarette advertising. Two powerful separate interests must be placated—and few will notice the contradictory votes. Even the best of congressmen can support low discount rates for water projects if the water project being voted on is in his western state. And thus it is that discount rates that would be considered laughable in international lending institutions are supported with a straight face in Congress.

That is why the studies that follow in this Part III deserve attention. Although they relate to developing countries, the ideas and methods used in them are worthy of discussion and for suggestions for improvement at times. They represent studies that will be needed in the United States and the developed world in coming years. None of the planning involved in them threatens individual freedom, I believe. This is not to deny that there is a connection between economic and political freedom. We must avoid the pitfalls of totalitarianism on the one hand and the excesses of complete private-sector domination of the economy on the other.

Three studies are discussed in the subsequent chapters. Each of them is related to the proper—and improper—use of the methods and ideas of the first two parts of this book. All are drawn from my personal experience in the broadest sense, that is, not only the experience of professional practice in design, construction, and operation of engineering projects, in teaching, and in consulting, but also in reading and conversation. Thus, the studies are based on the experience of many persons.

The countries, companies, and persons referred to in them are all mythical. No real nation, company, or person is represented, but the studies are based on factual data in the sense that the proportionality to real situations is preserved.

The material that precedes each of the factual studies discusses matters brought up by the study and is not meant to be an exhaustive treatment of a general subject.

24

New Developmental Projects

The factual study about which these preliminary comments are made concerns the socioeconomic justification for a new developmental project. It could have been the development of a river system, of a telephone network, of linked national medical facilities. It happens to be a new highway project. Nevertheless, some of the comments I make here refer to all new developmental projects. The general comments come first, and the particular follow.

THE QUESTION OF INDEXES

Projects are frequently evaluated by indexes because, although both benefits and costs are involved, the costs are not those of the total project but only of one of the inputs. It is clear that all the benefits cannot be credited to the costs of only one of the inputs; thus an index is proposed. The difficulty with such an index is that it can rate and order only those projects that use its particular form, whether these be mutually exclusive alternative solutions or a series of projects that can be built separately. One such index is illustrated in the factual study appearing later in this chapter. It is defined as the average annual increase in gross national product net of maintenance costs, divided by the cost of the road section that will bring about, or induce, the benefits in the numerator of the index.

Suppose that the project had been studied as a whole as an agricultural project. That is, all benefits from the agricultural project were included in the numerator of the ratio and all costs of the project in the denominator. The benefits would still remain as the increase in gross national project. The costs would include the original cost of the road, the annual maintenance cost, the labor of the agricultural workers, the seed to plant the crops, the capital cost of the farm equipment, and so on. The ratio of benefits to costs, annualized or present worthed, would then be the standard benefit/cost ratio for the total agricultural project and would be fully comparable to any other ratio in the economy for purposes of rank ordering. This would be eminently desirable.

The benefit/cost ratio states that the project will generate a certain number of dollars worth of benefits per dollar of costs. That last dollar of cost may represent the cost of seed, or farm equipment, or road. This is true because we are speaking of the marginal, or last, dollar invested in the project. It is immaterial whether that last dollar goes for seed or road. It must follow, then, that investment in any of the resource inputs will have the same benefit/cost ratio—farm equipment, farm labor, or roads. Thus, to set a benefit/cost ratio on any resource input, we need to evaluate the entire project. This is often not so difficult as it seems, and the result is far more useful because of its comparability with any other project in the economy.

Indexes can be avoided by total project analysis. When the cost of other inputs are trivial or zero, as in the case of zero opportunity cost, the avoidance of indexes may be an easy matter.

SHADOW PRICING

In the factual study that follows this short discussion, certain prices are assigned zero values. These are the price of farm labor, the price of land, and the price of seed. If there is heavy unemployment of labor in the country and if the colonizers are expected to be drawn from this pool of unemployed persons, then the zero opportunity cost of labor is justifiable because the economy is not forgoing any production—that is, any benefit—by transferring this labor from its unproductive state to a remote farm. The same can be said of land not previously in production. In this case, the land is so inaccessible that it has no market value. The seed is another matter, but its value may perhaps be considered negligible.

These prices, or costs, which are values assigned to inputs for the purpose of evaluating a project, are called shadow prices. Thus, the labor price of zero is a shadow price. Is the land price of zero a shadow price? No, it is not, because the market price and the cost used in the study are the same. Both are zero. The seed cost is definitely a shadow price because seed has a market value above zero, the cost assigned in the study. Here, the reasons for assigning a zero cost are somewhat shaky, but the cost itself is a shadow price.

I seem to be using the words "price" and "cost" synonymously in this discussion. Because I am speaking of national accounts, this is permissible. Costs are associated with supply, price with demand. Cost to the seller is price to the buyer. The number in dollars and cents is the same.

In the theoretical economy that we have seen in earlier chapters, an economy of pure competition, shadow prices are unnecessary because market prices represent the opportunity cost to the society for all goods and services. Indeed, market prices reflect social cost because in such an economy there are no externalities present.

In the real world, proper economic analysis from the national point of view requires that opportunity costs be used, which at times may differ markedly from market price. Labor, foreign exchange that represents the costs of imported goods and services, and fuel are examples of inputs to a project that may have differing opportunity costs and market prices. Prices within a country may also be controlled—the case of foreign exchange is a good example—and thus cannot represent free market price. Subsidies may exist.

Proper economic analysis on a national scale also requires that externalities be priced. Externalities often never appear in the market except in the most indirect way and often only far in the future. Recall the case of air pollution brought about by a cement plant. The cost of that air pollution is not reflected in the market price of the cement the plant produces. It is reflected, for example, in the abnormal quantity of soap that householders living near the plant buy. It shows up again years later in the medical cost of those who suffer from lung disease brought on by living near the plant.

Given that economies are never perfectly competitive, that opportunity costs are often not market costs, and that social costs are sometimes impossible to determine, is there any way that shadow prices can be assigned without an exhaustive study, price by price, of each input? (In a major project, with tens of thousands of inputs, this may be an impossible task.) The answer to this question is an unsatisfactory one, it must be admitted from the start. Social costs and opportunity costs may not be related at all. How can we possibly assign a true opportunity cost to the labor of the skilled machinist in charge of all machinery maintenance in the cement plant mentioned above whose wife is using abnormal quantities of soap and who, himself, will come down with severe emphysema 15 years from now? Oh, let's admit that theoretically it could be done. Studies of extra soap usage around cement plants could be undertaken by researchers and the incidence of emphysema in cement plant workers could be determined. But in any realistic sense, the task of assigning social costs by means of shadow prices to large projects is difficult, if not impossible.

The situation surrounding the relationship between market prices and opportunity costs is somewhat more encouraging. Let us assume that shadow prices representing opportunity costs are all that we are seeking. (We have given up on social costs.) Is there not some way that these may be determined without investigating them one by one? Perhaps the undoubted interdependence in the economy of all prices makes individual determination of shadow prices an uncertain procedure. There is a way, which I will discuss only briefly here because our factual study does not make use of the methods of input-output analysis.

An entire economy can be visualized as consisting of goods and service industries, each of which supplies the others. In addition, labor and consumer areas exist. In more complicated input-output tables, a financial section appears. It is possible, if the production function of each industry is known in terms of all the other industries, to set up a linear programming solution such that the amounts of production of each industry plus the labor necessary to produce them can be found for a particular set of consumer outputs. To do this, coefficients of production must be known. These are the proportions of each output used by each input industry, and they normally are considered to be fixed. If variable input proportions were used, the analyst would have to work out the relationship between each level of output of each industry and the quantities of each input required to produce that level of output.

The dual of this primal production linear programming problem is composed of the so-called "accounting prices" of each of the resource inputs. These accounting prices are what we have called opportunity costs.

The difficulties surrounding this process are enormous. First of all, the economy has to be studied in detail so that the interindustry relationships become known in the sense that interindustry coefficients of production can be determined. (A table involving 450 industries has been calculated. In one small Latin American country in which I have worked, 19 industries have been handled.) To obtain a linear programming problem, the production function of each industry must be linear. In other words, coefficients of production must be chosen such that they do not deviate far from the average of the production coefficients in the real nonlinear situation. Much engineering and statistical data must be digested in order to manage this. But if all this is done, the dual represents opportunity costs.

Interpretation of the dual is a study in itself. For example, if an input is not used up to capacity, an accounting price of zero is assigned to that input in some integer program solutions. Such matters must be checked carefully before the prices of the dual are labeled as opportunity costs.

Additionally, difficulties in assigning shadow price by means of input-output analysis present themselves when one is dealing with the prices of a small subgroup of a whole sector such as agriculture. The seed price of the following factual study is a good example. No known (to me) input-output program contains the price of agricultural seed as an accounting price because none contains the seed industry as a separate industry.

On the other hand, fuel prices may usually be obtained by use of input-output analysis because petroleum is often one of the industries handled in the input-output table. Fuel can be important in a study such as the one that follows these remarks, although they do not appear there.

No doubt I have emphasized this whole area of price determination sufficiently elsewhere in this book so that I need not do so any further.

SOCIOECONOMIC HIGHWAY CLASSIFICATIONS

Highways may be classified in a number of ways. The most usual is by jurisdiction. In the United States, highways are labeled interstate and U.S. (federal jurisdiction for construction), state, county, and certain special classifications such as farm-to-market roads in Texas that are under a special item in that state's budget. We are not concerned with this type of classification.

A second classification scheme is by type: paved (concrete or asphalt), surfaced (sometimes called all-weather surface or simply gravel), and embankment (earth roads). There can be many variations on this simple scheme with divisions and subdivisions.

A third classification is by terrain: flat, hilly, or rolling, and mountainous. The percentage of road, by type, that is present in each terrain class is the normal way of using this classification.

A fourth type is by socioeconomic function, and this is the type that interests us here. Under this classification are main routes or arterials, economic penetration roads, and social roads.

In many countries, different regions are in distinct stages of economic development. In a country like Peru, for example, the social and economic differences between the coastal region—*la costa*— and the mountains— *la sierra*—are so marked that the two areas resemble two different countries. The coast is an area in full economic development. It has agricultural areas that have been cultivated for thousands of years. Most of these are large landholdings and are worked by machine methods. The industry of the country is located in the coastal region. So is the central administration in Lima. On the other hand, the mountains are difficult to live in. There is little or no industry. Small farms exist, as well as very large ones, but neither are as productive as the coastal ones.

Social differences are equally as great as economic ones. The coast is populated and controlled largely by *mestizos*, the descendants of Europeans. The mountains are the domain of the *indios*, the descendants of the Indians who have lived there since thousands of years before the conquest of the Inca empire by Pizarro.

Arterial roads are located mostly in the coastal areas, although there is connection with almost all the main cities of the country by arterial roads. These roads tend to be paved on the coast but are not always so in the mountains. They are characterized by relatively heavy traffic, over 50 vehicles per day. These roads are analyzed on the basis of savings to the road user whenever some project is proposed for them. A familiar proposal for such roads is to raise the surface standard—from gravel to asphalt, for example. Whether or not this should be done is judged by analyzing the vehicle operating costs for projected traffic with the new surface on the road versus the vehicle operating costs for the existing traffic. The difference between the two costs form part of the benefits of the project. The costs are the new construction cost plus the increased cost of maintenance. The other part of the benefits is the saving in time by the users of the new surface at the projected traffic level over the time used at the old traffic level.

Economic penetration roads mean just what they say. They are roads constructed to open up new areas to some economic activity. Agriculture is the most common of these activities, although a road to an iron mine is also an economic penetration road. Economic penetration roads are built in less developed regions. The analysis method is based on increases in gross national product, with the whole project being evaluated and the road costs appearing as one of the inputs. The road project then shares the same benefit/cost measurement as the rest of the project. This kind of road is dealt with in the factual study following.

Sometimes it is necessary to evaluate rural roads already in existence but with a low volume of traffic with a view to upgrading one or more of their features—to go from an earth to an all-weather (gravel) surface, for example. In such cases user costs are not considered to be a sufficient indication of economic activity. So-called producer's surplus enters the analysis. Producer's surplus is measured by the savings in costs occasioned by the improvement, both in inputs to whatever the activity is and in outputs from the activity. Again, the road cost shares the same benefit/cost measurement as any other input to the project, such as seed or fertilizer. All costs are measured with the project, and all costs are measured without the project—the "with–without" criterion. The economics are a bit more complicated than the case in which no road previously existed.

There is another possible socioeconomic classification—the social road. The example of Mexico serves us here. Many villages in Mexico are isolated from all but minimal contact with the rest of the republic because of communication difficulties. There are no roads and no telephones. There is no electricity. The village exists as it has for many thousands of years. The problem is not to build roads so that people will settle an area but to bring an already settled area into contact with the rest of the country. No economic justification can be found for building a road, otherwise the road would be under the economic penetration road classification. However, some method is required to rank such roads. If a hundred are needed and there is money to build only a fraction of that number, which should be built?

The answer lies in a cost effectiveness index. The one that the Mexicans use is the cost per inhabitant served. An area of influence of the road is laid out. The number of inhabitants within that area of influence is determined, and the cost of the road is estimated. The ratio is determined. (It would probably be more in line with our practice of placing benefit in the numerator to invert the ratio—number of inhabitants to dollar spent.) The ranking runs from the project with the lowest cost per inhabitant served to the one with the highest cost per inhabitant served.

REPORT CONTENTS

Before beginning the factual study, a brief note on the contents of a real report is in order. A real report would contain a description of the country as an introduction—its geography, ecology, population, communication system—and then a section devoted to the history of the economic sector to which the project belongs.

Next would be the engineering design of the project with all the necessary drawings and maps, along with calculations.

After that, the economic justification section appears with its cost and benefit estimates and all supporting data.

You may wonder why all this is necessary. Why not include only the engineering design and the economic analysis? The reason is that the supporting portion containing a description of the country gives the reader of the report a background in facts about the country that will allow him to make comparisons from his own experience in other countries. It may also give him an idea of how the populace will respond to the project and warn him of any difficulties in this regard.

Human response is sometimes difficult to gauge, especially in countries other than one's own. A hint on what may be expected, socially speaking, is necessary, sometimes vital.

A FACTUAL STUDY

Some years ago in a certain Latin American country a road was proposed to link up several of a chain of countries in a way not hitherto contemplated. In its course, the highway was to connect an area that was suitable for agriculture, cattle raising, and wood production. This area, although its existence had been known for centuries, was so remote from previously settled regions that it had never been developed.

The American reader will wonder how it was, given good land, that no one ever went out to it and settled it. After all, this was what happened in the United States in the nineteenth century. Some significant differences between the situations did exist, however.

First, the American colonization of the Far West was not a penetration into wilderness without end. The Pacific coast of the United States had been settled since the beginning of the century. For many pioneers, crossing the plains meant traveling from a heavily settled area to a sparsely settled one.

Second, the transcontinental railroad's completion in 1869 meant that the pioneer could settle near a link to markets and civilization. As the railroads established more transcontinental crossings to the north and south of the first crossing and then branched out and interconnected them, the possibility of settling near a railroad was greatly increased. Railroads were the key to settlement.

Third, the Americans, who were immigrants or near descendants of immigrants, were questing spirits—after all, the more timid had stayed at home in Europe. They were people who had not suffered defeat by Europeans, as had the Mexicans and Peruvians; they were themselves Europeans. This meant a heritage of religion and culture that was adaptable to the search for freedom and economic independence.

The matter was quite different in Latin America. The new land in the case we are considering had to be reached by penetration, not passed through on the way to a settled coast. No railroads or transport of any kind had come closer than flying over it at widely separated points. Although rivers cut through it, they were not navigable, being close to their source and swift-flowing.

The prospective pioneers were humble peasants of almost pure Indian stock who had been mistreated for centuries after being divested of their land. Their culture had been ruined and much of their spirit with it. Centuries of exploitation did not breed the kind of trust in the exploiters by the exploited that allowed the latter to set off with family into an unknown land.

Many more differences might be cited between the case of the American Far West and modern colonization—education, health, age, financing, technology—but the foregoing brief explanation is enough, it is hoped, to lay the ghost of the fabled American pioneer who, with his Australian cousin, haunts colonization schemes proposed or influenced by planners from the industrialized world.

Ministers of public works from the countries whose territory would be crossed met and agreed to recommend a feasibility study. The contract for the study was granted to a prominent engineering company with offices in 20 cities in the world, a company of impeccable reputation and technical credentials of the highest order. The study was to suggest route locations, to demonstrate the project's regional and national significance, and to establish priorities for planning and construction.

The first part of the report as it was delivered to the governments of the contracting countries described the geography of the countries, including topography and climate, demography, communications and transport, ecology, and international links. In one of these countries—the country we will concentrate on—the connection between the settled portion on the coast and the interior was rudimentary: beast of burden, truck, and airplane. The trucks ran on gravel roads that were often closed by landslides. The airplanes served a few isolated prospecting, mining, and missionary communities. The beasts of burden could carry little weight. The planners recognized from the beginning that any development of the region depended on transport, both within the colonization area itself and that joining the area with the settled portion of the country.

The truck was chosen as the principal transport vehicle, along with its passenger counterpart, the bus. Railroads were rejected out of hand primarily because of the terrain. The steep grades meant that the railroad's length of track had to be about three times the highway's length in order to connect the same two termini. This meant that a train's travel time would be more than three times that of a truck.

In addition, no heavy, low-value products such as iron ore were going to be carried, so far as the planners knew, and therefore the economies of scale working in favor of a train for this type of good would be lost.

Furthermore, the colonists were likely to be small landholders, most of them illiterate. A railroad's operation, with its schedules, its rates, its waybills, was far less suited to the use of such people than the relatively informal truck where transport deals were made by the side of the road whenever the truck happened by between persons often known to each other.

Everyone was pleased to see the beast of burden not even considered. Donkeys and llamas are not the most pleasant of animals.

The second part of the report covered the social and economic aspects of the highway in its preliminary location. Detailed plans of the route with an exact line and grade, profiles, bridge and culvert locations, and plans were left until the project had been accepted in principle. However, some general plan of road location was necessary. The report suggested that existing roads be extended from the settled area into the proposed development area. Once there, more or less perpendicular sections could branch out from the new area terminal point until they hit some large natural barrier, such as a river. This arrangement would allow development around the "T" at the end of the penetration road. When such development had proceeded to a point where joining the "T's" was justified, this would be done.

Integration of this new area into the rest of the country would be accomplished by means of these roads, as well as the development of new agriculture, cattle raising, and wood production. As always, land value depended on its ability to produce and on its accessibility. The road project would serve both the social integration and the economic production.

Benefits

To evaluate the benefits of the highway, an estimate of the production it would induce was necessary. For this, a land classification scheme was established, an estimate of the new lands to be brought into production under each land type and the kind of production it would support was made according to the highway's zone of influence, and the rate of production growth and the value of production in the future were predicted. Prices also had to be estimated.

The land classification scheme went as follows:

Type A: Soils formed by alluvial deposits along rivers. Less than 5 percent of the project lands were of this type. They were fertile, well drained, and underwent periodic flooding. Average slope was less than 2 percent. Many crops were possible, as was fertilization.

Type B: Plains above river levels. Shallow, acidic soil was present. Its best use was for permanent crops and pasture. Slopes were between 0 and 10 percent.

Type C: Soils of high acid and low fertilizer content. Slopes varied between 10 and 50 percent. Possible crops were tea and coffee.

Type D: Land of low agricultural value. Some had slopes of more than 50 percent. Some marshland existed with valuable hard woods.

The number of hectares of new land to be brought into production depended on the zone of influence of the road. The zone of influence was determined by terrain. That is, steep terrain meant a small zone of influence; flat terrain would have a larger zone. How much land brought into production also depended on the type of soil, so that pasture land had a much greater zone of influence than land that could be devoted to corn or potatoes. Zone of influence was related to how far people were willing to walk or ride horses to cultivate their land. The matter of estimating zone of influence came down to educated guessing.

Predictions of land use were assumed to be inaccurate because 30 to 40 years is a long way to look into the future. Some estimate was possible, however, based on the use of similar land in the past in the same country—that is, the same agricultural skills, financial system, cropping patterns, and irrigation schemes were a guide. The introduction of new crops was also considered, based on the soils in existence, topography, climate, and market distance.

The rate of production growth was assumed to be straight-line, with full production of the new area to be reached in 20 years. Other patterns of growth were possible, of course. A Gompertz curve, which begins slowly, accelerates rapidly in the midyears of the growth cycle, then reverts to a slower rate of growth again as full production is approached, is perhaps more reasonable but more difficult to use computationally. In any case, the straight-line assumption was in line with similar broad assumptions—prices 20 years hence, for example.

The estimates of average returns per hectare were based on a study of yields and prices then current for each crop in the locality or the nearest market. They were "farm gate" prices. That is, the prices at the nearest market had the transport cost from the farm gate to the market subtracted from them. The transport costs were assumed to be the truck freight costs that would exist when the highway project and its feeder roads were completed. Four United States cents per metric ton–kilometer were thought to be a good average truck transport price for farm products at that time.

Tables 24.1 through 24.7 show the benefits for each section of road. The project within the Latin American country we are dealing with was divided into seven Ts with the crossbar of each T being a section. Four types of use are shown: crops, pasture, forests, and wasteland. The first two columns show the areas in hectares presently within the zone of influence of the section. The area that would be brought into production in the zone of influence of the projected highway is also listed. In the next three columns are displayed the annual benefits, that is, the proceeds in gross terms, from each type of land use. The present-production total income, the future total income, and the difference between these two quantities is listed. Each column is

TABLE 24.1 Land Production: Section 1

| Use | Area (hectares) | | Benefit (000 pesos) | | |
	Present	Future	Present	Future	Difference
Crops	3,920	13,400	907	3046	2139
Pasture	12,000	16,000	48	64	16
Forests	8,000	10,000	4	5	1
Wasteland	22,080	6,600	—	—	—
Total	46,000	31,600	959	3115	2156

TABLE 24.2 Land Production: Section 2

| Use | Area (hectares) | | Benefit (000 pesos) | | |
	Present	Future	Present	Future	Difference
Crops	316	4,200	41	636	595
Pasture	520	4,400	8	48	40
Forests	3,000	18,200	2	59	57
Wasteland	36,164	13,200	—	—	—
Total	40,000	40,000	51	743	692

TABLE 24.3 Land Production: Section 3

| Use | Area (hectares) | | Benefit (000 pesos) | | |
	Present	Future	Present	Future	Difference
Crops	160	9,000	25	1460	1435
Pasture	600	9,000	8	100	92
Forests	1,640	50,400	21	225	204
Wasteland	97,600	31,600	—	—	—
Total	100,000	100,000	54	1785	1731

TABLE 24.4 Land Production: Section 4

| Use | Area (hectares) | | Benefit (000 pesos) | | |
	Present	Future	Present	Future	Difference
Crops	1,900	6,000	299	960	661
Pasture	20	3,000	—	32	32
Forests	8,000	24,400	4	112	108
Wasteland	50,000	26,600	—	—	—
Total	59,920	60,000	303	1104	801

TABLE 24.5 Land Production: Section 5

	Area (hectares)		Benefit (000 pesos)		
Use	Present	Future	Present	Future	Difference
Crops	16	1,800	2	235	234
Pasture	—	2,200	—	18	18
Forests	100	7,400	—	207	207
Wasteland	17,884	6,600	—	—	—
Total	18,000	18,000	2	460	459

TABLE 24.6 Land Production: Section 6

	Area (hectares)		Benefit (000 pesos)		
Use	Present	Future	Present	Future	Difference
Crops	8	5,000	1	496	495
Pasture	—	2,000	—	16	16
Forests	40	30,000	—	15	15
Wasteland	65,952	30,800	—	—	—
Total	66,000	67,800	—	527	527

TABLE 24.7 Land Production: Section 7

	Area (hectares)		Benefit (000 pesos)		
Use	Present	Future	Present	Future	Difference
Crops	8	5,600	1	512	511
Pasture	—	6,000	—	60	60
Forests	52	40,000	—	20	20
Wasteland	79,940	28,400	—	—	—
Total	80,000	80,000	1	592	591

totaled. The total annual benefit, or value of the output, without subtracting any cost of input incurred to achieve it, is shown as the total of the last column. For section 1, this is 2,156,000 pesos.

The authors of the report believed that no deductions needed to be made from total agricultural income because inputs, such as labor, were not being employed anywhere else in the economy and therefore that their opportunity cost was zero. Thus, gross annual benefit or income and net annual benefit or income were equal, and the only input needed to achieve the output was the cost of the highway itself plus some other inputs, which are discussed in the next section.

Costs

The costs considered for the highway were construction or first cost, annual maintenance, feeder roads, and the costs of settlement of new families.

The construction cost included all the usual items of planning, design, and construction. No difference was made between inputs from sources within the country, such as fuel for a petroleum-producing country, and inputs from foreign sources, such as construction equipment, bridge steel, and the foreign report itself that recommended the project. Thus, such matters as balance of payments effects were ignored. No shadow prices were used.

The maintenance cost was an annual cost based on mileage and terrain. Terrain may be divided into three types: flat, rolling, and mountainous. Roads may be divided into three types: paved, gravel, and earth. (Many more subclassifications are possible.) Data were available from world sources on the costs of maintenance of each type of road by terrain classification, using modern heavy machinery, principally the patrol or motor grader. No labor-intensive methods were contemplated.

The costs of feeder roads were included to allow for the capillary system necessary to feed the main arteries of the project. (Each of the seven sections was designed to be a broad two-lane highway.) Provision had to be made for the earth roads on which most of the farms would abut.

The costs of settlement of families were estimated at a figure considerably lower than would appear now on the basis of later experience. If both public and private costs are included, as they must be for a proper national evaluation, the cost items are many. They include:

1. Family moving expense
   a) Persons
   b) Goods

2. Financing expense to provide loans until the settler begins to receive income

3. Financing expense for tools, seed, and fertilizer

4. Public education costs

5. Police and security provisions

6. Public health services

7. Community and religious establishments

8. Public administration offices such as birth and death registries

9. Judicial establishment

10. Auxiliary services for machinery repairs

11. Postal, telephone, and telegraph services

The list is endless. Effectively, the planner must consider everything that would be necessary to persuade a Latin American peasant to move to a wilderness. A completely separate study would need to be made to determine exactly the persons on whom the planner is basing his plans. Age, family size, present income, attitudes, place of residence—city slum or rural hut—all would have to be determined. It is this human factor that planners have neglected—to their sorrow. Eventually all planning must be based on human reaction to change.

Benefits Compared to Costs

The report compared benefits to costs by means of a priority index that was defined as the average annual net return expressed as a percentage of the total initial cost.

The average annual net return was the addition to the gross national product occurring each year that was induced by the road construction. As an average, the tenth year was selected, that is, halfway to full permanent production. No allowance was made for the indefinite number of years in the future during which full production would proceed. The second line of Table 24.8 shows the average annual value of induced production. The annual cost of highway maintenance was subtracted from the average annual production value to arrive at the third line—average annual net product, which is the benefit portion of the priority index.

The cost portion of the priority index is the sum of the next two lines, the construction cost and the cost of development.

The priority index was calculated by dividing the average net production per year by the total first cost and multiplying by 100, which results in the last line of the table. The last line gives a priority list of sections 1, 3, 2, 4, 7, 6, 5.

The index represents something akin to the rate of return on an investment with a perpetual life, evaluated at half its real value, with no allowance made for the delay of 20 years between the inception of the project and its coming into full production.

Figure 24.1 shows the cash flow stream as it was assumed to exist by the planners. A simple method of handling is to calculate the ratio of the present worth of the benefits to the present worth of the costs, the traditional benefit/cost ratio, with the maintenance costs relegated to their more appropriate position in the denominator. Results of the calculation are surprising and totally due to the inclusion of that most

TABLE 24.8 Benefits Compared to Costs (000 pesos)

Section	1	2	3	4	5	6	7
Benefits							
Full development production/year	2156	692	1731	801	459	527	591
Average production/year	1078	346	866	401	230	264	296
Annual maintenance cost	26	28	46	54	38	46	44
Average net production/year (Benefit)	1052	318	820	347	192	218	252
Costs							
Construction	2720	4440	6440	5360	6180	4760	4560
Development	1360	1060	2920	1520	440	1900	1900
Total first cost (Cost)	4080	5500	9360	6880	6620	6660	6460
Priority index	25.8	5.8	8.8	5.0	2.9	3.3	3.9

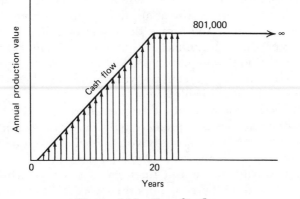

Figure 24.1 Benefits flow.

unavoidable condition of economic analysis, the opportunity cost of resources over time. I assume a 15 percent cost of resources, a not unusual figure for developing countries and on the fairly conservative side. The experiment is performed with section 4.

The benefit stream must be as shown in Figure 24.1. The equation appears in two parts. The first reduces the perpetual stream of benefits at full production to its present value. The second does the same for the growth phase of the first 20 years, assuming that the growth starts at the end of the first year.

$$PW_4 = \frac{(801,000)}{0.15} (P/F, 15, 20) + \frac{801,000}{20} (P/G, 15, 20)$$
$$= (5,340,000)(0.0611) + (40,050)(33.5822)$$
$$= 326,000 + 1,345,000$$
$$= 1,671,000$$

The costs are the construction cost of 6,880,000 plus the present worth of the perpetual cost of annual maintenance.

$$PW_4 = 6,880,000 + \frac{54,000}{0.15}$$
$$= 6,880,000 + 360,000$$
$$= 7,240,000$$

Using a standard measure, akin to the one used by our mythical consultants, the benefit/cost ratio is:

$$B/C = \frac{1,671,000}{7,240,000}$$
$$= 0.23$$

which is a miserable showing by section 4, because it is only a quarter of what it should be to qualify at all. Before proceeding, look back at the benefit calculation and notice the effect of a 15 percent present worth factor on those perpetual benefits—from 5,340,000 to 326,000. The 20-year postponement of full production when other projects that would have returned 15 percent per year could have been built in the country has had a remarkable effect.

It happens that the consultant's report cited a priority index of 5.0 as the dividing line between projects that would qualify and those that would not. One of the reasons given was that 5 percent was the approximate annual charge on a 40-year, 4 percent loan for an investment with no salvage value. But 4 percent is a low opportunity cost of capital. At 10 and 15 percent opportunity costs, the sections have benefit/cost ratios as shown in Table 24.9. The priority order is still the same, but only section 1 qualifies as a project.

One objection to a priority index such as the one I have presented here is that its usefulness is limited to ordering the priority of the sections themselves without providing any means of comparison with other projects within the country or among all the countries through which the project would pass. A measure such as the benefit/cost ratio does provide comparison with other projects, providing that we accept the assumption that the opportunity cost of all other inputs is zero.

This is the kind of project that must be evaluated a number of times as construction proceeds. Imagine that section 1 is built. It may have a salutary effect on the benefits for section 2 because the T of section 2 will connect with the existing T of section 1. Accessibility is thereby increased for section 2 over and above that existing before section 1 was constructed. Thus, the project should be restudied after each section is completed because of the possibility of higher benefit/cost ratios and increased predictability of benefits and costs after the experience of previous sections.

TABLE 24.9 B/C Ratio at 10 and 15 percent

Section	*B/C* Ratio	
	10%	15%
1	2.11	1.06
2	0.51	0.25
3	0.75	0.37
4	0.46	0.23
5	0.28	0.14
6	0.32	0.16
7	0.36	0.18

Finally, our assumed consultants conclude their report by noting that the benefits of the project have been greatly understated because of the following:

1. Industrial and mineral development in the area traversed by the new road has not been included in the benefit estimate.

2. Benefits to road users have not been considered. They will surely exist because of the increased ability of the user to choose routes, that is, there will be increased connectedness of the system.

3. Farm management was assumed to remain at its present low state of efficiency.

The non-quantifiable benefits of the project were as follows:

1. Increased national and international integration of economies and cultures for the countries involved.

2. The chance for further development of unknown resources that would not exist without the project.

3. Increased national security because guerrilla forces would have their operating area reduced and government military arms would achieve greater operating mobility. Whether these are benefits or costs depends on where one's political sympathies lie.

REFERENCES

Baumol, William J., *Economic Theory and Operations Analysis*, 3rd ed. Englewood Cliffs, New Jersey: Prentice-Hall, 1972, pp. 187–190, 531–532.

Carnemark, Curt, Jaime Biderman, and David Bovet, *The Economic Analysis of Rural Road Projects, World Bank Staff Working Paper No. 241*. Washington, D.C.: World Bank, 1976.

Dorfman, Robert, Paul A. Samuelson, and Robert M. Solow, *Linear Programming and Economic Analysis*. New York: McGraw-Hill, 1958.

Heggie, Ian G., *Transport Engineering Economics*. London: McGraw-Hill, 1972.

Seminario, Adan E., and Henry M. Steiner, *The Carretera Bolivariana Marginal de la Selva: An International Development Highway (A)*. Lima: ESAN, 1966.

Shaner, W. W., *Economic Evaluation of Investments in Agricultural Penetration Roads in Developing Countries: A Case Study of the Tingo Maria-Tocache Project in Peru, Report EEP-22*, Palo Alto, Calif.: Program in Engineering-Economic Planning, Stanford University, 1966.

Steiner, H. M., *Criteria for Planning Rural Roads in a Developing Country: The Case of Mexico, Report EEP-17*, Palo Alto, California: Program in Engineering-Economic Planning, Stanford University, 1965.

25

Economic Development by Hand

Recently the director of the National Center for Labor Information and Statistics of the government of Mexico, Geronimo Martinez Garcia, made a statement about the employment of unskilled labor in Mexico. He said that the economy of Mexico had demonstrated its incapacity to make productive use of its abundant labor supply. Neither agriculture nor industry had provided enough opportunities for work. Thus, the number of Mexicans who were obliged to undertake tasks that employed only a part of their time or that were degrading was increasing. This situation had developed in a growing economy. Martinez emphasized that technological development had mitigated against reducing the unemployment rate and that economic policy had favored the sectors that made little use of labor. Capital-intensive development was being encouraged. Even in agriculture, hand labor was being supplanted by machinery, resulting in a rise in the number of persons dependent on each employed person and thus a rise in poverty. From three persons per employed person in 1950, the ratio had risen to four persons per employed person in 1970. The ratio is projected for six to one in 1980. Martinez pointed out the necessity for more information about the lessening use of labor because of the indiscriminate acquisition of capital goods.

This statement, made in 1978, underlines the worry present in the minds of concerned persons throughout the world that rising birthrates, or even stable ones at high levels, plus the replacement of hand labor by machines, will bring about an intolerable social situation in much of the world. The result will surely be enormous social upheaval and violent change. We must all make an effort to bring about the necessary changes with the minimum of violence. This statement

336

sounds like one of those pious phrases so beloved of politicians. And it would be no more than that were it not that ways do exist to bring about fundamental change without world-shattering violence. These ways are discussed in this chapter. They relate directly to Martinez' statement that the indiscriminate acquisition of capital goods is one of the problems. One of the solutions is to change the attitudes of decision makers toward technology that makes use of the enormous supplies of labor present in the world today from one of disapproval to one of acceptance. Another solution is to approach the difficulty at the bottom level of society—through the impoverished villagers of the world—from whom change must come, by violent or peaceful means, by tyranny or reasonable persuasion. The problem is still there in the hinterlands, for it is from there that the rural people go to swell the cities and to there that they must return if the life of the ranches and farms can be made attractive once again.

LABOR-INTENSIVE METHODS

How does the acquisition of capital goods occur? The answer to this question is directly related to the attitudes of decision makers.

Let us say that a particular production can be accomplished by various combinations of labor and capital. We can imagine that we are sitting at the city planner's desk in a large city of the Third World. The planner draws the traditional production possibility curve (see Figure 25.1), with labor along the horizontal axis and capital along the vertical axis. It happens, however, that the planner has in mind a specific situation. He is trying to decide between two methods of sweeping the city's streets. The present method employs 5000 men with brooms and rubber-tired wheeled cans, which they push about the streets. Another method—and this is the method under consideration to replace the men, brooms, and cans—uses the large U.S.-made motorized street sweepers, with two wheels in front and a third steering wheel in back. One man can operate this machine. Two hundred and fifty of these machines will be required, along with a repair shop and parking lot. Two hundred and fifty skilled operators will be needed, as well as some 30 mechanics. All the rest of the administrative space and personnel are the same for the two street-cleaning systems. Thus, Figure 25.1 really has only two points on it. They are marked L for the labor-intensive method and M for the capital-intensive, or machine, method.

The labor-intensive method employs 5000 men at $1 per day for 300 days per year. About $100,000 of office overhead is allocated to record keeping—salary payments, sick leave, and the like. The employment of these men costs the city $1,600,000 per year. Their

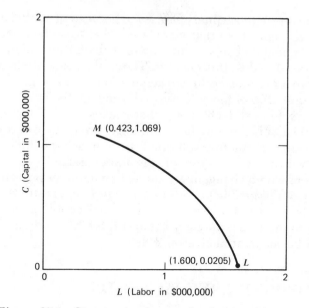

Figure 25.1   Street sweeping production combinations.

wheeled cans could be sold for perhaps $50,000, the planning engineer believes, to other more backward cities in the country. To keep them in use means an annual cost of:

$$A_L = (50,000) (A/P, 15, 20) = \$8000$$

given a life of 20 years and a social cost of capital of 15 percent. In addition, 5 percent of the cans need to be replaced each year at a cost of $50 each, or $12,500. The capital cost of this production combination is therefore about $20,500 annually.

The capital-intensive method employs the drivers at $5 per day for 300 days per year and the mechanics at $7 per day for the same number of days. In addition, overhead costs associated with their employment will be reduced to only $6000 per year. The labor cost for this method is therefore $423,000 annually. Capital costs are for 250 street sweeping machines at $25,000 each. Their estimated life is 15 years, and the cost of getting them off the books and scrapped will be about equal to their scrap value. The same 15 percent opportunity cost of capital applies.

$$A_M = (25,000) (250) (A/P, 15, 15) = \$1,069,000$$

The engineer plots the points and draws a curve between them, more for completeness than for information. The decision is now between annual costs of $1,492,000 for the machine sweepers and

$1,620,500 for the men. The nonmonetary factors are that some protests may be expected from the discharged sweepers; however, this is balanced by the fact that the management effort required to receive deputations to the mayor to protest working conditions and salaries will happily disappear forever. Machines do not form committees. Even more, and this appeals to the engineer, who was educated in the United States, an antiquated and in many ways ridiculous way of keeping the streets clean, reminiscent of Charlie Chaplin at his funniest, will be replaced by modern, brightly painted, submissive, monster machines not unlike great toys. The planning engineer chooses the machines. He has chosen a capital-intensive over a labor-intensive method.

The error—and it is a grave one—is to substitute accountants' costs, even suitably adjusted to reflect sunk costs plus interest on the investment, for social costs. For the truth is that the 5000 men are not going to find other work, or if they do, they will prevent an equal number of other men from finding a job. The country is not going to allow them to starve to death, so they and their families will continue to eat, although much less well. The result of this policy is that not even the food costs for them and their families will be saved on the national accounts. Their opportunity cost—their social cost—was really close to zero, not $1,500,000 per year.

The opportunity cost of the foreign exchange used to buy the mechanized street sweepers was probably greater than the price plus the insurance and freight that were paid for them in dollars. This further swings the balance in favor of retaining the men.

And then there are the shadier aspects of such a decision as actually made. The concessionaire will make a good profit on the machines, and this fact is often reflected in a hundred mirrors down the bureaucratic line. Labor leaders will loose power and money if the men are fired. This fact may also be taken into account in many subtle ways.

The other error is one of attitude. Because the engineer–planner was trained in the United States, his background dictates the use of machines. In fact, he has no figures on what men can do. None of the handbooks bother to cite production norms for hand labor any more. The technology—how to go about doing things by hand—is no longer taught in engineering schools in developed countries and has not been for 50 years. For example, a simple arch bridge in stone made from local materials would be difficult to design and build simply because the technique is almost unknown. Such a design could be constructed with hand labor. The usual steel or reinforced concrete bridge uses little hand labor by comparison and much machinery. Designs that use hand labor can be taught again as soon as the need for teaching them is recognized.

Planning decisions that replace hand labor with machines receive support from the citizenry of Third World countries because of the idea that mechanization means progress. The idea is 150 years old now, and it will be difficult to uproot.

When labor-intensive methods are mentioned, most of us tend to think of vast projects—dams in India, levees in China—that have been built by armies of people carrying baskets of earth on their heads. We do not think of the everyday decisions made by functionaries everywhere in relation to small projects. Yet is is in the latter context that the important gains of machines over men are made. The large projects in the Third World will no doubt continue to be built using hand labor and requiring immense organization to feed, house, and generally take care of such immense construction armies. But it is the small projects such as the back country road of the factual study of this chapter that make the real difference in the economy.

An attempt has been made over the past quarter century to call up from the people themselves the organization necessary to build small projects. This effort has been known as *community development.* Small roads, schools, water supply systems, and bridges are some of the projects built by community development organization. Hand labor is, of course, the method used. Community development provides the organization that allows the labor potential of the community to be brought to bear on the project. It is worth a discussion at length.

COMMUNITY DEVELOPMENT

In the sense that I use the term, a *community* is a small, organized, rural population center. The members of the community are bound together by tradition and codes of conduct bequeathed to them by their predecessors. A sense of solidarity exists because of common interests and common heritage. Generally, the group lives and works in a defined area inherited from its ancestors. In this area it satisfies its primary needs for food, clothing, housing, security, and care by using the community's own resources, or it develops the means to satisfy these needs from outside the community by selling or trading the products of its own industry. Each community is spontaneously organized in groups—a group to govern the community, for example—and may form new groups or subgroups to meet its needs better. In nearly all such communities a differentiation exists in the form of strata, or layers, within the population. These strata often operate with opposing and antagonistic interests, and this antagonism is beneficial in an important way, as we shall see.

No element, structure, or part of the community may change by itself or be studied independently; each must be considered in its relationship to the whole. The community is a system, with the whole and all its parts interrelated.

These small human groups are not found independent of their closest neighbors. There are ties among the different social centers that are more or less strong depending on the region and the historical and social conditions prevailing in the country.

According to the Economic and Social Council of the Social Affairs Committee of the United Nations, in the middle 1960s of this century there were 3 to 5 million rural communities in the world. They varied from nomadic tribes with 50 members to densely populated agricultural districts with thousands of inhabitants. About 80 percent of the developing world is composed of such groups. Governments in the developing countries have discovered that the most difficult social problems they face arise from farm communities. The economic, social, and technical changes that have recently taken place have not benefited these communities. Rather, they have upset them. The usual subsistence economy has been disturbed. The ties binding each group together have weakened. Population growth demanding more and more from inadequate agricultural resources, newly created wants for consumer products that stem from listening to the ubiquitous transistor battery-powered radio, the population movements resulting from increased ease of transportation, and greater opportunities for production for market rather than for subsistence have created the pressures that have broken down rural communities. The communities have not found within themselves the strength to oppose the changes but have often succumbed to them. Therefore, part of the problem—a vital part—is to build up the communities again and to cause them to discover new possibilities for helping themselves.

Community development may take two forms: the slow, traditional evolutionary process as the community adjusts itself to change, or the accelerated and planned process in which the social and natural resources of the community are used to greatest effect. The latter planned process is what is ordinarily meant by community development. It requires the conscious participation of the community for the purpose of establishing the conditions of economic and social progress. It also requires the confidence of the community in its own initiative. Thus, the prevalent cynicism among the community members must be dispelled. The development requires two antecedents; both must be present for the reaction to take place. The first is cooperation among the members of the community. Initiative must provide an opportunity to cooperate—they must have a project to cooperate *on*—and adaptation to the new conditions must also take place. The second antecedent is tools, not only physical objects to work with but techniques of using these elementary tools so that construction such as a road can come into being. These techniques need to be developed. Some have been forgotten; others must be invented.

To begin accelerated development, it is necessary to understand spontaneous development. All human groups have the ability to assimilate and adapt themselves to a new mode of living. But one must understand how any particular group accomplishes this. Normally, new procedures are substituted for old in the satisfaction of needs. This substitution does not come about easily. Mechanical imitation will not do, nor are the members of the community always unanimous in their acceptance of new ways. An internal struggle may develop between the group opposing and the group favoring the change. There is no room for apathy. Nor is it advisable to attempt to abolish habits, customs, and traditions that are opposed to the progress of the community. Such opposition would effectively destroy the community. Group life is composed of antagonistic elements.

Progressive ways, however, must win the battle. Development implies simultaneous destruction and construction, a bonding of the old to the new, with something more positive to substitute for what has been destroyed. The ideal goal, seldom reached, is to achieve the maximum welfare for the members of the community through their own confidence and active participation.

The Place of Government

A long-term rational program must be set up. Lasting benefits should be aimed at, not short-range immediacies. A constant and steady effort is required by the community, but this can never be achieved without the cooperation of the government, which is the only agency that can coordinate action among many communities. The government is the only entity that is aware of the needs of the nation and aware, therefore, of what kinds of production will be most in demand over the long haul. Social welfare programs must take place under established norms. For example, a community would find it impossible to set up a school without government help in the form of teachers, textbooks, and a program of study that would allow graduates of the school to continue their education in other places. Therefore, a central government agency is vital.

A community development program on a national scale requires personnel contracting and training, a place in the governmental hierarchy to allow it to operate efficiently, buildings and equipment, and most of all an organizational plan to permit it to do the research and experimentation necessary to discover the best methods of working toward its goals. Each nation must conceive its own program in keeping with its traditions.

Felt Needs

A felt need is the key to beginning a community development program. Any project undertaken should meet the expressed wishes of the community members. No programs should be imposed upon the community. (This is usually a great temptation for government, and it must be resisted from the start.) Studies of the needs of rural communities in several countries indicate that they are most interested in the following needs:

1. Land reclamation for agriculture.
2. Irrigation work.
3. Roads.
4. Health services and schools.

Any of these needs can form the starting point of a program. Once underway, a single project can serve as the springboard to a multiple-purpose program that must form the basis of long-range activity.

Community Development Benefits

The real benefits of a community development program lie not only in the material facilities produced but also in the change of attitude of the population. When people begin to think that they are improving their condition through their own efforts, the way is open toward continued progress. The old apathy and cynicism begin to break down. The change in attitude may then be channeled toward encouraging the population to participate more in local government and eventually to become citizens who actively participate in democratic government, locally and nationally. Local leaders will emerge in the process; this is an essential goal of such programs.

International organizations, both public and private, have been formed to aid community development because many community problems are common to the entire world. The United Nations has made important contributions through its technical aid programs, reports, and scholarship grants. The Agency for International Development of the government of the United States has also provided help, principally through the provision of foodstuffs under Public Law 480 (Food for Peace). These foodstuffs are provided as additional incentive for those who work as volunteers in development works.

In Peru, the site of the factual study that follows this brief discussion, the Food for Peace program provided food shipped from the United States to private charitable organizations that distributed it. At the time of the study (1966), Peace Corps volunteers were the actual distribution agents. The prerequisites for receiving the food were the following:

1. A community project approved by the government on which technical advice had been given.
2. A felt need for the project.
3. Sufficient volunteer labor to complete the project.
4. The material necessary to build the project.

The Food for Peace program was not without its drawbacks, however. The drawbacks arose from the distrust and the customs of the recipients. The members of many communities feared accepting the food because they believed that it was being provided by vested interests that would eventually exploit and dominate them. Customs entered the picture because the recipients came to consider the food as part of their pay. In some cases the recipients stopped work until the ration had been given them.

A MAJOR OBSTACLE

In back of the discussion in this chapter looms one of the massive economic principles—opportunity cost. We have discussed the idea of opportunity cost many times in this book but never in so important a guise as in this discussion of labor-intensive versus capital-intensive methods. All indications point to the lack of understanding of this principle on the part of those who make the important decisions in the developing world. These decision makers insist on taking the private sector point of view in public decisions, which means that they unconsciously accept the assumption that the price system is working perfectly. For countries with an enormous oversupply of labor—Mexico, for example—the assumption is nothing short of catastrophic. One wonders what Adam Smith would say if he could see how heavily his invisible hand lies on the Third World.

A FACTUAL STUDY

This study was made in Peru in 1966. A small road was built in the highlands—a kind of middle level between the coast and the Andean settlements—by labor-intensive methods. Because the workers were unpaid, the work was organized by community development methods. The study itself compared the social cost of building the road by pick, shovel, and dynamite to the cost of building it by the usual capital-intensive, heavily motorized methods.

Peruvian Community Development

Before 1959 Peru had in operation a Bureau of Indian Affairs under the Ministry of Labor. This organization provided legal advice to Indian communities in their never-ending battle to maintain ownership of land. Protection rather than promotion was the policy of this agency. When the National Plan for the Integration of the Indian Population was adopted in 1959, the policy was changed, in part owing to the experience gained in previous programs in Vicos and Puno, to one of promotion of Indian welfare. The Vicos and Puno programs had demonstrated that a multiple program including educational, health, social welfare, farm promotion, and communications plans for community development was the proper course. A special government agency was set up to handle the matter centrally. This agency was the Bureau of Communities in the Ministry of Labor.

In 1963 *Cooperacion Popular* was established. This was a move on the part of the government of Peru, then under President Fernando Belaunde Terry, to help the socioeconomic development of Peru by mobilizing the Indian communities in a cooperative effort to help themselves obtain the local infrastructure they needed. Schools, roads, water systems were to be built by the voluntary unpaid labor of community members. Technical direction was to be provided by personnel from the central office.

The usual bureaucratic structure was set up (nothing can be done without functionaries in Peru) the National Planning Institute on top, next the Basic, Intermediate, and Regional Offices, and at the bottom the Local Development Boards. Bureaucratic structures were nothing new in Peru, however. The Inca empire had a most detailed and efficient public administration.

Community labor existed in the Inca empire, but it was not voluntary. Each subject had to carry out obligatory labor in the cultivation of crops belonging to the Inca and the nobles as a form of tribute. When no work was needed in cultivation, the local labor was used for the construction and maintenance of the extensive system of roads in the empire.

After the Incas, road work was carried out through the levee system in which the government required farmers to keep up the roads in lieu of a tax.

It was hoped by the establishment of *Cooperacion Popular* that the best feature of the old system could be retained—the organization of local people to do road work. And it was hoped that the new feature of voluntary cooperation could be added, thus strengthening local self-government. The technical assistance had no doubt always been available, even in Inca times. Suspension bridges for which the Incan engineers were famous required considerable construction supervision. Roads were to be the most important product of community action. The isolation of many villages in jungles and mountains all over Peru was to be ended by pick-and-shovel roads.

The San Isidro—Limon Road

We will use the mythical road from San Isidro to Limon to illustrate the comparison on a socioeconomic level of local road construction by capital-intensive methods carried out by a state agency with the labor-intensive construction carried out through community action. The road itself does not exist, but it is representative of many of the roads built in Peru during those years.

The road was begun by volunteers from the town of San Isidro because San Isidro had no road connection with the town of Limon. Limon did possess a road to a main paved highway that led eventually to Lima. Limon had been established on a hillside above a river many years before because of its proximity to community-owned corn lands bordering the river. As population increased, more land was cultivated, of poorer and poorer grade, higher and higher on the hillside. San Isidro was founded above Limon at a point close to the higher fields. Thus, the small villages followed the stages of cultivation of the land.

The road was begun in October, 1965, at a point where construction had stopped 12 or 13 years before, after an unexplained interruption, 500 meters having been built. No volunteers from Limon participated in the construction because, as has been noted, Limon already had a road to the main highway. This illustrates the concept of "felt need." San Isidro's inhabitants felt a strong need for the road so that they could be connected to the rest of the world and thus were willing to work for it. The inhabitants of Limon felt no need to connect themselves with a village farther into the hinterlands than they were and thus did no work. Much advice was offered, however.

The distance to be covered was 12 kilometers (about 7.2 miles). The first 2 kilometers were used as a basis for costing the road by labor-intensive methods because that was the amount of construction that had been completed by the time the study was made. Fifty percent of the construction—a total of 12 kilometers—was in soft earth, 30 percent in hard earth, and 20 percent in rock.

Costs by Labor-Intensive Methods

The principal costs considered were the following:

1. Labor.
2. Materials and tools.

3. Management and supervision.
4. Machinery.
5. Crop loss.

Each of these costs is discussed in the following paragraphs.

Labor

San Isidro was composed of 50 families; a family averaged five members. When the members of the community were not engaged in farm labor, they worked at home—the women sewed, carried out voluntary jobs, or remained idle. When they worked in the fields, their schedule was about as follows:

6 to 7 AM Walking to work.

7 to 8 AM   *Chacchado* and *armado*. The leaf of the *coca* plant is widely used by Indians throughout the Andean region to drug themselves. To use the *coca* leaf, the Indian first forms a ball by chewing the *coca* and adding lime and salt. This is called the *chacchado*. He then continues mixing and sucking on the ball until he feels the effect of the drug, when he says that it has finally set—*armado*.

8 to 11 AM Effective work done.

11 to 1 PM Lunch, rest, *chacchado*, and *armado*.

1 to 4 PM   Effective work done.

4 to 5 PM   Return home.

The team of volunteers was made up of the mayor and members of the community, with about eight women handling the carrying and cooking of the common food, providing water, and so on. An average of 45 community members worked on any given day.

Work was carried out during October, November, December, and January—the summer months. An average of 11 days per month were worked.

The average wage for the region was 40 soles per day. At that time 26.80 soles(S) equaled one United States dollar. The 40 soles was made up of 25 soles in cash plus breakfast, lunch, supper, *coca*, and cigarettes. (By law, construction workers were supposed to receive 57 soles per day in that region with no additional benefits.) Of course, since the labor was voluntary, no one actually received any money for his work. The 25 soles was the opportunity cost of labor. The meals, *coca*, and cigarettes would have been consumed in any case and therefore were not differential cost items.

The length of road built during this time was 1500 meters. The labor cost was:

11 days/month × 4 months × 45 laborers/day × S/.25/man = S/.49,500

Materials and Tools

Dynamite was used for blasting in rock cut and was valued at about S/.600 for the whole working period.

The tools used were picks, shovels, and steel bars.

$$
\begin{array}{lll}
\text{30 shovels at S/.50 each} & = 1500\text{r} \\
\text{30 picks at S/.50 each} & = 1500 \\
\text{30 bars at S/.80 each} & = 2400 \\
\hline
& 5400
\end{array}
$$

If two years is taken as the useful life of such tools, the cost for four months came to S/.900. Total cost for materials and tools came to S/.1500.

Management and Supervision

Cooperacion Popular provided the services of a resident engineer for the area in which Limon and San Isidro were located. He made regular visits to the construction sites in his area. He did design and layout on the spot, trucked in materials, and demonstrated the government's interest and good will to the volunteers. He made four visits to the San Isidro–Limon site during the four months construction was in progress. His costs were:

$$
\begin{array}{ll}
\text{Salary} & \text{S/.300 daily} \\
\text{Travel expenses} & 250 \text{ daily} \\
\quad \text{(engineer and driver)} & \\
\text{Transportation} & 400 \text{ daily} \\
\hline
& 950
\end{array}
$$

Four visits cost 3800 soles.

Machinery

The machinery employed was a gasoline-powered Atlas-Copco drill with an original cost of S/.35,000, and a fuel consumption of one gallon per day at 6 soles per gallon. The operator cost S/.100 per day. The machine's life was five years. It was used 10 days during the four months.

$$
\begin{array}{ll}
\text{Labor} & \text{S/.1000} \\
\text{Fuel} & 60 \\
\text{Drill} & 140 \\
\hline
& 1200
\end{array}
$$

If the drill had not been used, the blasting holes would have been drilled by hand, using a sledge hammer. The gasoline drill made it easier, was available, and therefore was used. (For a historical comparison, depreciation is appropriately used even though it reflects sunk cost.)

Crop Loss

The social cost of the right of way for a road of this type is the agricultural production lost by taking the land out of crops. The width of the wearing surface plus shoulders for the road was 5.50 meters. A right of way width of 10 meters was needed. The land area per kilometer was therefore 10,000 square meters lost to right of way. It was assumed that potatoes—the crop in the area—yielded about 0.8 kilograms per square meter at a price of S/.2.50 per kilo. Total crop loss per kilometer was therefore 20,000 soles.

In fact, none of the land crossed by the road had to be purchased; it all belonged to the community. As anywhere else, land taken for public works was paid for by the government. This sort of compensation does not enter a social cost study that takes the viewpoint of an entire society because such compensations are transfer payments. The costs per kilometer of road are shown in Table 25.1.

Costs by Capital-Intensive Methods

Roads built in Peru by the Ministry of Development and Public Works used heavy equipment, much as would have been used in the United States at the same period. Engineers are trained to look at costs from the accountant's point of view. Social costs, or costs in the sense of opportunity costs, are not considered by them. Since construction decisions are normally made by engineers, least cost often appears as cost by capital-intensive methods.

The costs of roads in Peru during 1965 were obtained by dividing the total costs of the road by class by the total length built. Notice that

TABLE 25.1 Costs of San Isidro–Limon Road
(in soles)

	For 1,500 Meters	Per Kilometer
Labor	S/.49,500	S/.33,000
Materials	1,500	1,000
Supervision	3,800	2,533
Machinery	1,200	800
Crop Loss	30,000	20,000
		57,333

TABLE 25.2   Average Road Costs Per Kilometer
by Capital-Intensive Methods
(in soles)

Type	Leveling and Grading	Surfacing	Total
Third class[a]			
(joins small towns)	136,656	44,063	180,719
Third class			
(Joins provincial capitals)	472,599	42,626	515,225
Second class	389,653	151,054	540,707

[a] San Isidro–Limon type.

the figures in Table 25.2 do not include indirect costs and overhead of the Ministry of Development and Public Works.

CONCLUSION

A road comparable to the San Isidro–Limon road cost S/.180,000 per kilometer surfaced. Unsurfaced, as the San Isidro–Limon road was to be, the cost was about 137,000 soles per kilometer. By community development methods, the little road cost only about S/.57,000 per kilometer, somewhat less than half. True, the capital-intensive costs do not include opportunity costs. But these may be presumed to cancel out differences. The opportunity cost of the capital equipment probably more than balances the opportunity cost of labor, because unskilled labor, which might have an opportunity cost similar to that used for San Isidro's volunteers, forms only a small part of the cost when computing by capital-intensive methods. The machine operators probably had an opportunity cost at least equivalent to the actual wage they received because they were much in demand in Peru.

Overhead costs were not included in either analysis—if we neglect the fact that we included supervision costs in the labor-intensive summary. Major overhead costs for central office personnel were not included in either analysis. But the overhead costs of *Cooperacion Popular* were surely much less—probably a fraction—of the costs of an old leviathan like the Ministry of Development and Public Works.

A final objection and an answer to it close this chapter. You will have detected a flaw in the previous analysis or, rather, a lack of completeness. The San Isidrans will take about eight years to complete the road if they proceed at their present rate of advance of 1500 meters per season. The government could come in and complete the road in a few months, probably well within a single season. Benefits of the road, which we will assume are exactly the same no matter how the road is built, would not need to be deferred while the slow volunteers with their *coca* and six hours per day dawdle along.

The answer is in two parts. First, it is unlikely that the government is going to leap in and build a road like this tomorrow. Of this type of road, in all of 1965, only about 188 kilometers were built in Peru with its hundreds and thousands of communities like San Isidro. One of the reasons given for the interruption of construction 12 or 13 years before the villagers began to build their road again was that the government was going to build it for them. In desperation, sick of waiting for the bulldozers and wagon drills that never came, the villagers recommenced the work with bent backs and dynamite.

Let us assume some probabilities for the delay in construction by the government. We will then be able to evaluate the alternative construction methods including the delay factor. Assume that the probability of government construction beginning in two years is 0.1, in five years 0.2, in 10 years 0.7. The expected value of the delay in commencing construction is therefore about eight years, the same time that it will take the volunteers to finish their road. Let us assume also that the quality of the finished product will be the same. Figure 25.2 shows the cash flows associated with each construction method. Let us assume a 15 percent opportunity cost of capital in Peru over the

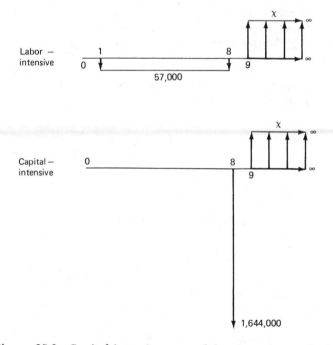

Figure 25.2 Capital-intensive versus labor-intensive methods.

next eight years. A present worth analysis follows:

$$PW_{L-I} = 57,000 \ (P/A, 15, 8) = (57,000)(4.487) = 256,000$$
$$PW_{C-I} = (137,000)(12)(P/F, 15, 8) = 1,644,000 (0.3269)$$
$$= 537,000$$

Capital-intensive construction will still cost over twice as much as the labor-intensive construction method. None of the external benefits of community construction will have been achieved, for example, the demonstration to the community members that good results can come from working together. Instead, they will have put themselves even more spiritually in pawn to the central government.

A government cannot have too much of the kind of activity which does not impede, but aids and stimulates, individual exertion and development. The mischief begins when instead of calling forth the activity and powers of individuals and bodies, it substitutes its own activity for theirs; when, instead of informing, advising, and upon occasion, denouncing, it makes them work in fetters, or bids them stand aside and does their work instead of them. The worth of a State, in the long run, is the worth of the individuals composing it: and a State which postpones the interests of their mental expansion and elevation to a little more of administrative skill, or of that semblance of it which practice gives, in the details of business; a State which dwarfs its men, in order that they may be more docile instruments in its hands even for beneficial purposes—will find that with small men no great thing can really be accomplished, and that the perfection of machinery to which it has sacrificed everything will in the end avail it nothing, for want of the vital power which, in order that the machine might work more smoothly, it has preferred to banish.

John Stuart Mill, On Liberty

REFERENCES

Institute for Economic Development, *Social Progress Through Community Development*. Washington, D. C.: Institute for Economic Development, 1964.

Lewis, W. Arthur, "Economic Development with Unlimited Supplies of Labor," *Manchester School* (May 1954).

Nurkse, Ragnar, *Problems of Capital Formation in Underdeveloped Countries*. New York: Oxford University Press, 1961.

Pozas, Arciniega Ricardo, *Community Development*. Mexico City: Universidád Nacionál Autónoma de Mexico, 1964.

Ruopp, Phillips, *Approaches to Community Development*, Ed. Phillips Ruopp. The Hague: W. Van Hoeve, 1953.

U.S., Agency for International Development, *Village Technology Handbook*. Washington, D. C.: U. S. Government Printing Office, 1963.

26

Judging Existing National Enterprises

Certain special applications of the principles set forth in this book are present when existing national enterprises are judged according to a social benefit/cost analysis. *National enterprises* are those whose continued existence or demise have important social consequences in a society. To continue production of coal in Great Britain or to shut down some mines and import oil was a decision on national enterprise. To continue steel production at a Mexican plant or import steel products from Japan and shut down the plant was a decision on national enterprise. Whether a grocery store in a small town stays open or closes is not of national moment and therefore is not a national enterprise decision in the sense of this discussion. However, a governmental decision at the national level on whether to subsidize small grocery stores and thus keep them open, or to allow chain supermarkets to take over their business is in point. To abandon railroad operations and carry goods and passengers by highway is a decision on a national enterprise if the railroad is an important part of the transportation system of the country. (The factual study that concludes this chapter is based on a situation of this kind.) In particular, government-owned enterprises are relevant—railroads, steel mills, hydroelectric plants, automobile factories.

The fundamental error in making judgments on national enterprises is treating them as though they were private businesses whose books of accounts furnished the last word on their economic health. Like the small-town grocery store, if the railroad does not show a profit, then it should be shut down. But what are we to substitute for the railroad? Many would answer, "The highway." (The facile nature of this answer will be evident after a review of the factual study that concludes this chapter.) The answer does reveal, however, that a choice between alternatives is involved, and therefore that there is a choice between differential costs and benefits. The books of accounts do not reveal the nature of the choice in national enterprises, that is, entities that supply goods or services for which no easy substitute exists. They obscure the fact that sunk costs and their reflection in depreciation are irrelevant to a decision about the future. They hide the fact that financing charges are not differential costs, since they must be paid, except in rare circumstances, whether or not the economic entity survives. Thus the "loss" shown in the accounts is not relevant to the choice at all.

It is always a matter of differential costs in national enterprises. If steel is not made within the country, it must be bought outside the country. The choice is not really whether the national plant should be shut down because it is losing money, but what the differential consequences are between producing steel nationally and buying it abroad. Which alternative offers the best prospects for the nation? The choice may really come down to one between two evils, and the question may be, "Which of the two choices offers the lesser loss?"

It may seem that I am denouncing the accounting conventions to the point of ignoring them entirely or that I am even revising the conventions until they reflect economic reality. I plan no such crusade in behalf of the "New Accounting." Custom dies hard, and accountants are a conservative group.

Social costs are always involved in national enterprise decisions. The essential question is, "What sacrifice will the society make in forgone goods and services if this resource is used or continues to be used in this way?" If the answer is, "None," then the cost of the resource is zero. If it is, "$20 per day per man," then this is the cost that should be used, not the wages actually paid. Once again, the books of accounts give us only the actual wage paid, but the resource must be valued in terms of its opportunity cost. How to determine this is not always so obvious, but there is no doubt about the principle.

The principle applies in the case of shortages of resources as well. Imagine that the price of natural gas is controlled by a central government within a country (see Figure 17.4, page 230). This is the price that will be recorded in the books of accounts by all enterprises using natural gas. But is it the price that an analyst taking the societal point of view should use? The answer is, "No." The opportunity cost of natural gas is higher than the controlled price. A free market would see its price raised immediately, thus reflecting the opportunities for its beneficial uses that are being forgone at the controlled price because there is not enough natural gas to go around. As the price of natural gas rises in response to the lifting of controls, its use where its marginal productivity is low is forsaken—other fuels are substituted or the project is abandoned—and its opportunity cost once again becomes its equilibrium price. Again, the determination of equilibrium price while controls still exist is no easy matter, but it is better to recognize the error of using the accountant's price and to attempt to determine the opportunity cost than to accept the accountant's figure and force the analysis into greater error.

Questions of subsidy sometimes arise. Imagine an enterprise so important to a society that it cannot be allowed to fail. Its cash flow deficit is therefore made up by the government. From the point of view of the society, this is a pure transfer payment that has no place in social cost calculations. The money, as money, that makes up the subsidy has no opportunity cost, at least not in any direct way. (Inflationary effects are being ignored because of the microeconomic nature of the analysis. Subsidy on a grand scale, such as was practiced in the United States in an attempt to relieve the depressed economy of the 1930s, is a macroeconomic phenomenon.)

Subsidies are often hidden because they exist as external benefits for which the firm does not recompense the society. The highway trucker in the factual study of this chapter does not pay taxes that cover his fair share of the cost of the road he uses. A misallocation of resources occurs as a result. More freight goes by truck than should be carried by that mode, and less by railroad. Thus, society pays a bigger freight bill than it ought to.

Subsidies can be open, as is the one to the maritime shipping industry of the United States. Again, a larger freight bill is paid by United States taxpayers but knowingly, in order that enough ships remain in American control so that in time of national emergency the ships would be immediately available. The subsidy is an open transfer payment, not a social cost.

THE RAILROAD EXAMPLE

Railroads are often existing national enterprises that are studied with a view to curtailing some or all of their operations. In the United States technological advances in transportation account for part of this morbid interest in them, for airlines have taken away almost all the railroads' long-distance passenger traffic, the automobile much of their short-distance passenger traffic, and the highway trucks their most valuable freight traffic. This situation does not obtain worldwide, however. The United States is the only country of the industrialized world in which passenger traffic on railroads has fallen (United Nations, 1977). In the United States, freight traffic has increased year by year, but the railroads' share has steadily decreased. Again, this has not occurred in the rest of the developed world. However, in the

Third World, the question of what to do about railroads that are not paying their way appears frequently. Thus, the factual study that follows is of particular interest to American readers even though it concerns a Latin American country.

Not all railroads are persecuted public servants, judged unfairly. In a certain Latin American country, the railroad has been rendered obsolete by a pipeline, a long-awaited highway bridge, and several highways. Even judged by the most lenient standards, the railroad has been technologically outstripped by its competitors. (There is no low economic density cargo in large amounts, such as iron ore, that would make the railroad's role technologically irreproachable.) Yet it resists abandonment tenaciously. A powerful railroad union is a strong political force because it is so well organized. Largely because of this, assisted by other, less obvious forces, the economically and socially indefensible railroad has survived. It has been calculated that it would be cheaper for the government to pay every single railroad employee his present salary for the rest of his life than to continue railroad operations!

A FACTUAL STUDY: THE NORTHERN RAILROAD

In 1978 in a certain Latin American country the newspapers and magazines with few exceptions called for the abandonment of the Northern Railroad, which had been losing money for years, more recently at an increasing rate. To many readers, it was apparent that the railroad was a swamp into which millions of pesos (which went to subsidize losses) sank out of sight every year. Its continuance was considered scandalous and attributable only to corrupt governmental influences.

The country had a transport system that consisted of all modes: airlines, railways, coastal and river steamships, a small high seas fleet, and highways. The railroads were both privately and publicly owned. They had been in existence for over 100 years. In the 1930s highway trucks and buses began to compete in a small way with the railroads. The competition had increased so that the railroads in the 1960s and 1970s were losing more and more freight traffic to the truckers. Railroads continued to abandon track that had become a liability because of lost passenger and freight service.

The privately owned Northern Railroad operated about a third of the trackage in the country. Along with the rest of the railroads, it lost money year after year. Its 1970–1975 performance is shown in Table 26.1. The losses were incurred in spite of the steady increase in

TABLE 26.1   Income and Expenses—The Northern Railroad
(in 000,000 pesos)

Year	1970	1971	1972	1973	1974	1975
Income	112.7	131.3	139.2	152.2	156.6	187.3
Expenses	120.3	135.5	152.8	178.3	202.6	201.7
Loss	7.5	4.2	13.6	26.0	46.0	14.4

revenue from both passenger and freight operations. It was these that caused the demand for the railroad's abandonment.

The most important reason for the loss each year was the competition of the truckers, which offered lower rates than the railroad because they were relatively unregulated as to schedules and safety. They rode on the public way, paying in taxes only a fraction of their share of its cost. That is, they were subsidized, whereas the railroad had to pay for the maintenance of its own right of way.

The next most important reason for the loss was the salary increases demanded and received by the politically powerful railroad labor unions. However, rate increases could not be authorized until salary increases had been granted. There was a considerable bureaucratic delay in granting the rate increases after retroactive salary raises had been authorized and paid. The result was a lag between revenue and expenses.

Finally, the highway held a natural advantage over the railroads. Trucks could travel the back roads where railroads did not go. They needed no large terminals. They were far more suited to the needs of illiterate people because shipments required no paper work. Their travel time was shorter because highways followed a more direct route in mountainous terrain than did railroads.

In 1978 data were published on railroad and highway operations. It is on these data that I have based the following analysis.

The viewpoint taken is that of the society. That is, a privately owned company is to be judged on the basis of social costs. Taxes are therefore excluded as are certain other nonopportunity costs. Because the study is a comparison of alternatives, only differential costs are relevant.

The study provides an answer to the question: "Is it desirable from a national point of view that the Northern Railroad be abandoned?" The man on the street often did not realize that abandoning the Northern Railroad meant that goods and people would have to be carried by another means. In this case, the alternative sure to be chosen was the highway with its trucks and buses. Thus, the following paragraphs trace the costs of the railroad and the highway modes as alternative means of carrying railroad traffic in 1975. At the end of the study, the assumptions are discussed and certain conclusions reached.

Railroad Mode Costs

The Northern Railroad experienced costs as shown in Table 26.2. The rest of this section deals with a conversion of these accountant's figures to social and differential costs.

The most important operating cost for the Northern Railroad is labor. Table 26.3 presents these costs. These salaries were paid to the personnel who worked for the departments shown in Table 26.4. The retired persons in Table 26.5 received pensions, also shown under operating costs, in the amounts presented in the second line of the table.

Reviewing these costs in reverse order, I begin with the pensions. They are certainly a cash flow from the railroad's point of view, but from the viewpoint of society, they are a transfer payment only. The pensions represent no loss in the production of goods and services, because these retired persons are unemployed. The pensions the Northern Railroad pays are much like a tax paid directly to individuals rather than one routed through the social security system. They do not represent an opportunity cost of resources and therefore are not a social cost.

Let us inspect the remainder of the payroll of Table 26.3. Its total builds over the five years shown while total personnel of Table 26.4 falls slightly. Wages have increased—and in all departments. Which of these are social costs? That is, which represent an opportunity cost of resources in the sense of the loss of a person's production because he or she is working for the railroad rather than in the next best employment to be found? This is a difficult question to answer in regard to those persons employed in the Tracks and Auxiliary Works Department. The country suffers from unemployment of labor—some figures suggest an unemployment rate as high as 50 percent for unskilled labor. If half this department's payroll is for unskilled labor of the type engaged in track maintenance, then a quarter of the payroll does not

TABLE 26.2 Northern Railroad Costs
(in 000,000 pesos)

Year	1971	1972	1973	1974	1975
Operating	108.2	122.8	144.5	144.5	154.7
Depreciation	18.4	19.5	21.3	21.3	26.2
Financing charges	8.9	10.5	12.5	17.7	20.8
Total	135.5	152.8	178.3	183.5	201.7

TABLE 26.3 Northern Railroad Payroll
(in 000 pesos)

Department	1971	1972	1973	1974	1975
Tracks and auxiliary works department	16,234	19,454	23,547	29,837	31,959
Mechanical department	12,182	13,865	15,523	18,082	18,664
Locomotives and traffic department	24,718	27,983	31,954	37,247	38,659
General administration	4,846	5,669	6,509	7,980	8,228
Total	57,980	66,971	77,533	93,146	97,570

TABLE 26.4 Northern Railroad Personnel

	1971	1972	1973	1974	1975
Tracks and auxiliary works department	1175	1223	1237	1371	1194
Mechanical department	511	521	548	536	500
Locomotives and traffic department	986	999	951	922	891
General administration	128	131	132	135	140
Total	2800	2874	2868	2964	2725
Employees	627	628	635	627	619
Laborers	2173	2246	2233	2337	2106

TABLE 26.5 Retired Pensioners

	1971	1972	1973	1974	1975
Number	231	23	243	256	287
Total pensions (in 000,000 pesos)	4.03	4.69	5.75	7.46	9.75

represent social cost because half the personnel would be unemployed were they not working for the railroad. Therefore, the payroll for the Tracks and Auxiliary Works Department may be lessened by a quarter. The Mechanical, Locomotive and Traffic, and General Administration Departments employ workers whose opportunity cost of labor is equal to their salaries. Therefore, the payroll for 1975 should be reduced by 31,959,000 × 0.25 = 7,989,750 pesos, which does not represent social cost.

Depreciation and financing charges should be considered in relation to Table 26.6, which shows the changes in inventory of rolling

TABLE 26.6   Rolling Stock Inventory

	1971	1972	1973	1974	1975
Locomotives					
Steam-driven	47	39	35	30	1
Diesel-electric	7	13	13	29	29
Switchyard units	14	12	12	10	3
Other Rolling Stock					
Coaches and baggage cars	67	70	70	70	70
Freight cars	677	677	646	672	795
Company service cars	45	47	46	50	63

stock from 1971 to 1975. The increase in depreciation charges reflects the retirement of steam locomotives, the acquisition of new diesel-electric units, new freight cars, and company service cars. The increase in financing charges from 8,900 pesos to 20,800,000 pesos per year occurred in response to the foreign loans negotiated in order to purchase the new equipment.

Depreciation is not a cash flow. It represents sunk cost and is therefore not a differential cost for the comparison of this analysis. It represents a social cost in the past.

The financing charges are a social cost that will continue until the loans they service are paid off. They are not, however, a differential cost for the alternatives of this analysis, because they must be paid whether or not the railroad is abandoned in favor of the highway mode.

Both depreciation and financing charges must be excluded from the analysis.

One cost must be added—the resale value of all equipment, buildings, inventory, rights of way, and so on of the railway. By continuing to use the railway, the society gives up the value in goods and services of the rolling stock and property. The rolling stock could be sold to another country or to other railroads in the same country. Buildings, shops, and land could be converted to other uses, or the same use by other entities. The difficulty lies in evaluating the Northern Railroad in this sense.

It is not the book value that is referred to here. The book value may be much more than the resale value of a company automobile, for example. The book value of a piece of prime urban land may be much less than its market value, which I will suppose represents its social cost.

A valuation survey indicated a resale value of 1000 million pesos in 1975. Weighted average life of all assets was 30 years, with 100 million

TABLE 26.7   Annual Cost of the Northern Railroad (1975) (in 000,000 pesos)

Total accountant's cost		201.7
Less pensions	9.8	
Less 25% of Tracks and Mechanical Department	8.0	
Less depreciation	26.2	
Less financing charges	20.8	
		64.8
		136.9
Plus annualized resale value		123.7
Total social, differential costs		260.6

pesos of resale or salvage value at the end of that time. Capital recovery cost at a social opportunity cost of resources of 12 percent is therefore:

$$CR = (1000 - 100) \, (A/P, 12, 30) + 100(0.12)$$
$$= 900(0.12414) + 12$$
$$= 111.726 + 12$$
$$= 123,726,000 \text{ pesos annually}$$

For 1975, therefore, costs of continuing the Northern Railroad in operation compared to transferring all its duties to the highway is computed as shown in Table 26.7. The total social, differential cost per year is 260,600,000 pesos.

Freight Calculations

To begin the analysis in 1978 of the freight carried by the railroad, I will choose to use as a base the year 1975, because this is that last year for which data are available. The case for a decision will rest on that year. The important assumption is that all years in the future will not significantly differ from 1975.

Table 26.8 presents the freight carried by the Northern Railroad in 1974 and 1975 by month. The month of heaviest traffic during 1975 is July, with 22,791,006 ton-km. To handle freight without unusual delay, this is the monthly capacity on which calculations should be based. Yearly capacity should be 273,492 thousand ton-km—that is, 12 × 22,791,006 ton-km.

We must also allow for leftover space in the trucks. They will not be filled to capacity because of the bulkiness of some of the freight

TABLE 26.8 Total Freight Traffic by Months (Net Ton-Km)

Month	1975	1974
July	22,791,006	20,439,448
August	21,400,820	21,335,942
September	20,918,179	18,367,839
October	20,867,045	22,965,965
November	21,185,749	18,681,050
December	19,654,778	20,954,603
January	22,301,817	20,167,346
February	20,873,163	17,693,340
March	21,025,249	18,423,467
April	22,274,072	20,969,037
May	21,734,358	19,656,194
June	22,293,329	22,343,357
Total	257,319,567	241,997,588

carried. A study estimates this at 10 percent waste capacity. We can allow for this by multiplying the freight demand by 1.10.

$$\text{Annual demand} = 273,492 \times 1.10$$
$$= 300,841 \text{ thousand ton-km}$$

Now we must estimate an average distance traveled during a year in order to determine how many trucks will be needed to satisfy the demand.

A study discovered that among $2\frac{1}{2}$-, 4-, 6-, and 8-ton trucks, the 6-ton truck had cheaper operating costs according to terrain, age of vehicle, distance traveled annually, and average speed. Therefore, I will use the 6-ton truck as a representative vehicle. We will remember that a mix of truck sizes would be present in any actual fleet. Choosing the lowest-cost vehicle biases the study in favor of the truck mode. For the moment, we will assume that the study conclusions will not be sensitive to this assumption.

Table 26.9 shows the data available from the study mentioned previously on 6-ton trucks aged three, six, and nine years. Unfortunately, the average age of a truck in the country was about 12 years. The lack of data was overcome by extrapolation of the three, six, and nine year figures for 60,000 kilometers. The latter figure was obtained by assuming a 25 km/hr speed for the highlands where the Northern Railroad was located, an eight-hour day, and a 300-day year, allowing for holidays and truck down-time for repairs and maintenance. The extrapolation is shown in Figure 26.1.

TABLE 26.9   Total Costs of a Six-Ton Truck
                 (in pesos/km)

Age and distance traveled in km/year	Coast		Highlands	
	Ave. Speed		Ave. Speed	
	High	Low	High	Low
(3 years)				
20,000	6.87	7.47	9.62	11.73
40,000	4.44	5.04	6.46	8.57
60,000	3.63	4.23	5.41	7.52
80,000	3.23	3.83	4.88	6.99
100,000	2.98	3.58	4.56	6.57
(6 years)				
20,000	5.33	5.93	7.11	9.22
40,000	3.67	4.27	5.21	7.32
60,000	3.12	3.72	4.57	6.68
80,000	2.84	3.44	4.25	6.36
100,000	2.67	3.27	4.06	6.17
(9 years)				
20,000	4.74	5.34	6.68	8.79
40,000	3.38	3.98	4.99	7.10
60,000	2.92	3.52	4.43	6.54
80,000	2.69	3.29	4.14	6.25
100,000	2.56	3.16	3.98	6.09

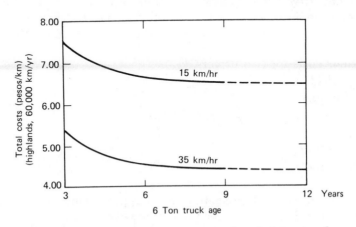

Figure 26.1   Operating costs extrapolated. 6 ton truck.

One 6-ton truck will carry 6 × 60,000 = 360,000 ton-km per year. Therefore, we will need 300,841,000 ÷ 360,000 = 836 of these vehicles to handle the freight presently being carried by the Northern Railroad.

Freight cost in pesos per kilometer for a 12-year-old truck, traveling at an average speed of 25 km/hr is:

$$4.40 + \frac{(6.50 - 4.40)}{2}$$

$$= 4.40 + \frac{2.10}{2}$$

$$= 5.45$$

Total freight cost per year is:

5.45 pesos/km × 836 vehicles × 60,000 km/yr
= 273,372 thousand pesos/yr

The result may be checked by the following calculation:

(300,841,000 ton-km ÷ 6T) × 5.45 pesos/km
= 273,264 thousand pesos/yr

The slight discrepancy with the previous figure arises because of the rounding of the number of trucks required.

Having arrived at this answer, we must now ask what expenses are accounted for in it, in particular whether or not the first cost of the vehicle is included. Costs included by the study were the following:

1. Labor costs for two drivers.
2. Repairs.
3. Insurance.
4. Interest and depreciation.
5. Fuel.
6. Lubricants.
7. Tires and tubes.

Item 4, interest and depreciation, is an approximation of the capital recovery cost. It must be recognized, however, that:

capital recovery ≠ depreciation plus interest

For a 6-ton truck, first cost was about 400,000 pesos in 1975, life was 20 years, salvage value was 5000 pesos, and interest was about 20 percent. On this basis,

$$\text{Annual capital recovery} = (P - L)(A/P, i, N) + Li$$

or
$$(400,000 - 5,000)(A/P, 20, 20) + 5,000(0.20)$$
$$= 395,000(0.20536) + 1000$$
$$= 81,117 \text{ pesos/yr}$$

The depreciation plus interest calculation gives:

$$\frac{400,000 - 5,000}{20} + 400,000(0.20)$$

$$= 19,750 + 80,000$$
$$= 99,750 \text{ pesos/yr}$$

which overstates the capital cost by 18,633 pesos/yr, but it is well within the accuracy of the assumptions. I need not include any further reflection of first cost.

Insurance costs may be assumed to represent the cost of accidents.

Passenger Calculations

In 1975 the Northern Railroad carried 722,600 passengers for a total of 86,349,000 passenger-km. This latter figure must now be translated into the cost of buses needed to take care of this demand and into a social cost per year.

Buses were of three types: the 50-passenger, long-distance bus of the Greyhound variety, a 35-passenger simpler bus much like the school buses of the United States, and a 15-passenger bus, which also carried cargo. The middle category was equivalent to a $2\frac{1}{2}$-ton truck in cost characteristics. Assuming the same distance traveled per year as in the freight case—60,000 km—the total costs are as shown in Figure 26.2.

The average age of a bus in the country was 15 years. I estimate that a bus traveled at a speed of 30 km/hr, slightly higher than the speed of a 6-ton truck over the same roads. The total cost per kilometer is, from extrapolated figures:

$$3.11 + \frac{4.17 - 3.11}{2}$$

$$= 3.64 \text{ pesos/km}$$

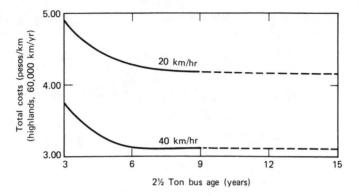

Figure 26.2   Operating costs extrapolated. 2½ ton truck.

Total cost of bus passenger travel is:

$$\frac{86,349,000 \text{ passenger-km}}{33 \text{ passenger/bus}} \times 3.64 \text{ pesos/km/bus}$$

$$= 9,524,556 \text{ pesos/yr}$$

No passenger time cost was included in these calculations because no data were available on passenger train speeds on the Northern Railroad. Nor did studies exist on the value of travel .time for the particular group of Peruvians who used the railroad and who would use the bus system. The railroad is the slower mode. The bias of the assumption that passenger time costs are equal between the modes, which is the implication of not treating travel time, is therefore in favor of the Northern Railroad.

Road Construction and Maintenance

Transfer of passenger and freight traffic from the Northern Railroad to the highway flanking it would mean an immense increase in traffic on the highway. The 300,841 thousand ton-km of freight per year averages to 300,841,000 ÷ 365 = 824,222 ton-km per day. An average daily run for a truck covering 60,000 km per year, using the 300-day year is 200 km. For 6-ton trucks, the increase in daily traffic is:

$$\frac{824,222 \text{ ton-km}}{200 \text{ km} \times 6\text{T/vehicle}}$$

$$= 687 \text{ trucks/day}$$

The passenger traffic, providing it all transferred to buses, is

86,349,000 ÷ 365 = 236,573 passenger-km per day. Buses carrying 35 passengers 200 km per day cause an increase of:

$$\frac{236,573}{20 \times 35}$$

$$= 338 \text{ buses/day}$$

The total traffic load is therefore 687 + 338 = 1025 vehicles/day. The heaviest traveled road along the route in 1974 carried 420 vehicles per day! The average daily traffic over the five sections of road that matched the Northern Railroad was 143 vehicles per day. Asphalt pavement covered about 12 percent of the route, or about 100 km. Approximately 800 km was gravel or earth road. The increase in traffic could be accommodated only by paving the existing road. Many studies showed that paving was justified at around 1000 vehicles per day. Paving costs in 1975 were about 600,000 pesos per kilometer. For the 800 km, paving would cost 480,000 thousand pesos. Capital recovery on the amount with a paving life of 10 years and an opportunity cost of capital of 12 percent in the public sector was:

$$\text{Annual capital recovery} = 480,000,000(A/P, 12, 10)$$
$$= 480,000,000(0.17698)$$
$$= 84,950,000 \text{ pesos/year}$$

Annual maintenance cost would run about 20,000 pesos per kilometer, or 16,000,000 pesos per year. Total new road cost because of moving all traffic to the roads from the railroad would be 100,950 thousand pesos per year.

This and preceding costs are shown in Table 26.10. Total cost for the highway mode is 383,900,000 pesos per year. For the railroad the total annual cost is 260,600,000 pesos. The difference, which rules overwhelmingly in favor of the railroad, is 123,300,000 pesos per year.

TABLE 26.10 Total Annual Costs by Mode
(in 000,000 pesos/year)

Truck and Bus	
Freight	273.4
Passenger	9.5
Road paving	101.0
	383.9
Railroad	260.6
Difference in favor of railroad	123.3

Assumptions

The most important assumption is a hidden one: that freight and passengers will travel the same distance on the highway as on the railroad. The number of passengers and the tonnage of freight will be the same in 1975—this is an assumption that is probably close to reality. (Some new traffic may occur because of the increase in trucks and buses and thus increased accessibility because of more frequent schedules, but this is an open question.)

The fact is that highways are more what might be called "terrain efficient" than are railroads. Because ordinary railroads are limited to a maximum grade of 1 percent (i.e., a one-foot rise or fall in every 100 feet of horizontal distance), they must follow a far longer route than does a highway, which has a maximum grade of 8 percent, to get from one point to another. Imagine a mountain range to be climbed by a highway and a railroad, and you will see in your mind's eye the long switchbacks of the railroad snaking up the mountain compared to the relatively short coils of the highway. Thus, time and distance are shorter by the highway mode. The passenger-km and ton-km figures on which the analysis was based should be reduced to the actual road distance each passenger and each ton would travel—and impossible task without a complete origin and destination study of the goods and passengers. The bias of this assumption is in favor of retaining the railroad. I do not believe that the assumption is critical because the margin in favor of the railroad is so large.

A less important assumption is that all freight presently carried by the railroad could be carried in 6-ton trucks. This is not entirely true because some freight—a D-8 bulldozer, for example—would have to be carried by a much larger tractor-semitrailer unit. Costs for the larger vehicles were higher and greater than proportionally so. This assumption favors the highway mode.

Passengers in $2\frac{1}{2}$-ton buses would not find every seat full. The load factor would be less than 100 percent. This assumption favors the highway mode.

Will the future differ greatly from 1975? The analysis assumes it will not. The relative increase in costs and rates for both modes will remain the same. Actually, the highway will draw more and more passengers and freight from the railroad so long as its subsidy will support the lower rates. The public will demand more and better roads. Unless taxes on passenger and freight-carrying highway vehicles are raised to a point at which these vehicles pay their fair share of the cost of construction and road maintenance, the subsidy will continue and the ostensibly poor performance of the Northern Railroad will worsen. The society suffers because goods and passengers will not be transported at their cheapest cost in resources.

CONCLUSION

The Northern Railroad should not be sold up. The man in the street and the editorial writers are wrong. Accounting costs are a poor guide for social decisions, either in private or public enterprises.

REFERENCES

Naciones Unidas, *El Transporte en América Latina*. New York: Naciones Unidas, 1965.

United Nations, *Statistical Yearbook, 1977*. New York: United Nations, 1978.

Appendix

Compound Interest Tables

Formulas for Calculating
Compound Interest Factors

Single Payment—Compound Amount Factor $\qquad\qquad (1+i)^n$

$\quad (F/P,\ i,\ n)$

Single Payment—Present Worth Factor $\qquad\qquad \dfrac{1}{(1+i)^n}$

$\quad (P/F,\ i,\ n)$

Sinking Fund Factor $\qquad\qquad\qquad\qquad\qquad \dfrac{i}{(1+i)^n-1}$

$\quad (A/F,\ i,\ n)$

Capital Recovery Factor $\qquad\qquad\qquad\qquad \dfrac{i(1+i)^n}{(1+i)^n-1}$

$\quad (A/P,\ i,\ n)$

Uniform Series—Compound Amount Factor $\qquad \dfrac{(1+i)^n-1}{i}$

$\quad (F/A,\ i,\ n)$

Uniform Series—Present Worth Factor $\qquad\qquad \dfrac{(1+i)^n-1}{i(1+i)^n}$

$\quad (P/A,\ i,\ n)$

1% Compound Interest Factors

	Single Payment		Uniform Series				
n	Compound Amount Factor F/P	Present Worth Factor P/F	Sinking Fund Factor A/F	Capital Recovery Factor A/P	Compound Amount Factor F/A	Present Worth Factor P/A	n
1	1.0100	0.9901	1.000 00	1.010 00	1.000	0.990	1
2	1.0201	0.9803	0.497 51	0.507 51	2.010	1.970	2
3	1.0303	0.9706	0.330 02	0.340 02	3.030	2.941	3
4	1.0406	0.9610	0.246 28	0.256 28	4.060	3.902	4
5	1.0510	0.9515	0.196 04	0.206 04	5.101	4.853	5
6	1.0615	0.9420	0.162 55	0.172 55	6.152	5.795	6
7	1.0721	0.9327	0.138 63	0.148 63	7.214	6.728	7
8	1.0829	0.9235	0.120 69	0.130 69	8.286	7.652	8
9	1.0937	0.9143	0.106 74	0.116 74	9.369	8.566	9
10	1.1046	0.9053	0.095 58	0.105 58	10.462	9.471	10
11	1.1157	0.8963	0.086 45	0.096 45	11.567	10.368	11
12	1.1268	0.8874	0.078 85	0.088 85	12.683	11.255	12
13	1.1381	0.8787	0.072 41	0.082 41	13.809	12.134	13
14	1.1495	0.8700	0.066 90	0.076 90	14.947	13.004	14
15	1.1610	0.8613	0.062 12	0.072 12	16.097	13.865	15
16	1.1726	0.8528	0.057 94	0.067 94	17.258	14.718	16
17	1.1843	0.8444	0.054 26	0.064 26	18.430	15.562	17
18	1.1961	0.8360	0.050 98	0.060 98	19.615	16.398	18
19	1.2081	0.8277	0.048 05	0.058 05	20.811	17.226	19
20	1.2202	0.8195	0.045 42	0.055 42	22.019	18.046	20
21	1.2324	0.8114	0.043 03	0.053 03	23.239	18.857	21
22	1.2447	0.8034	0.040 86	0.050 86	24.472	19.660	22
23	1.2572	0.7954	0.038 89	0.048 89	25.716	20.456	23
24	1.2697	0.7876	0.037 07	0.047 07	26.973	21.243	24
25	1.2824	0.7798	0.035 41	0.045 41	28.243	22.023	25
26	1.2953	0.7720	0.033 87	0.043 87	29.526	22.795	26
27	1.3082	0.7644	0.032 45	0.042 45	30.821	23.560	27
28	1.3213	0.7568	0.031 12	0.041 12	32.129	24.316	28
29	1.3345	0.7493	0.029 90	0.039 90	33.450	25.066	29
30	1.3478	0.7419	0.028 75	0.038 75	34.785	25.808	30
31	1.3613	0.7346	0.027 68	0.037 68	36.133	26.542	31
32	1.3749	0.7273	0.026 67	0.036 67	37.494	27.270	32
33	1.3887	0.7201	0.025 73	0.035 73	38.869	27.990	33
34	1.4026	0.7130	0.024 84	0.034 84	40.258	28.703	34
35	1.4166	0.7059	0.024 00	0.034 00	41.660	29.409	35
40	1.4889	0.6717	0.020 46	0.030 46	48.886	32.835	40
45	1.5648	0.6391	0.017 71	0.027 71	56.481	36.095	45
50	1.6446	0.60'0	0.015 51	0.025 51	64.463	39.196	50
55	1.7285	0.5785	0.013 73	0.023 73	72.852	42.147	55
60	1.8167	0.5504	0.012 24	0.022 24	81.670	44.955	60
65	1.9094	0.5237	0.011 00	0.021 00	90.937	47.627	65
70	2.0068	0.4983	0.009 93	0.019 93	100.676	50.169	70
75	2.1091	0.4741	0.009 02	0.019 02	110.913	52.587	75
80	2.2167	0.4511	0.008 22	0.018 22	121.672	54.888	80
85	2.3298	0.4292	0.007 52	0.017 52	132.979	57.078	85
90	2.4486	0.4084	0.006 90	0.016 90	144.863	59.161	90
95	2.5735	0.3886	0.006 36	0.016 36	157.354	61.143	95
100	2.7048	0.3697	0.005 87	0.015 87	170.481	63.029	100

1½% Compound Interest Factors

	Single Payment		Uniform Series				
	Compound Amount Factor	Present Worth Factor	Sinking Fund Factor	Capital Recovery Factor	Compound Amount Factor	Present Worth Factor	
n	F/P	P/F	A/F	A/P	F/A	P/A	n
1	1.0150	0.9852	1.000 00	1.015 00	1.000	0.985	1
2	1.0302	0.9707	0.496 28	0.511 28	2.015	1.956	2
3	1.0457	0.9563	0.328 38	0.343 38	3.045	2.912	3
4	1.0614	0.9422	0.244 44	0.259 44	4.091	3.854	4
5	1.0773	0.9283	0.194 09	0.209 09	5.152	4.783	5
6	1.0934	0.9145	0.160 53	0.175 53	6.230	5.697	6
7	1.1098	0.9010	0.136 56	0.151 56	7.323	6.598	7
8	1.1265	0.8877	0.118 58	0.133 58	8.433	7.486	8
9	1.1434	0.8746	0.104 61	0.119 61	9.559	8.361	9
10	1.1605	0.8617	0.093 43	0.108 43	10.703	9.222	10
11	1.1779	0.8489	0.084 29	0.099 29	11.863	10.071	11
12	1.1956	0.8364	0.076 68	0.091 68·	13.041	10.908	12
13	1.2136	0.8240	0.070 24	0.085 24	14.237	11.732	13
14	1.2318	0.8118	0.064 72	0.079 72	15.450	12.543	14
15	1.2502	0.7999	0.059 94	0.074 94	16.682	13.343	15
16	1.2690	0.7880	0.055 77	0.070 77	17.932	14.131	16
17	1.2880	0.7764	0.052 08	0.067 08	19.201	14.908	17
18	1.3073	0.7649	0.048 81	0.063 81	20.489	15.673	18
19	1.3270	0.7536	0.045 88	0.060 88	21.797	16.426	19
20	1.3469	0.7425	0.043 25	0.058 25	23.124	17.169	20
21	1.3671	0.7315	0.040 87	0.055 87	24.471	17.900	21
22	1.3876	0.7207	0.038 70	0.053 70	25.838	18.621	22
23	1.4084	0.7100	0.036 73	0.051 73	27.225	19.331	23
24	1.4300	0.6995	0.034 92	0.049 92	28.634	20.030	24
25	1.4509	0.6892	0.033 26	0.048 26	30.063	20.720	25
26	1.4727	0.6790	0.031 73	0.046 73	31.514	21.399	26
27	1.4948	0.6690	0.030 32	0.045 32	32.987	22.068	27
28	1.5172	0.6591	0.029 00	0.044 00	34.481	22.727	28
29	1.5400	0.6494	0.027 78	0.042 78	35.999	23.376	29
30	1.5631	0.6398	0.026 64	0.041 64	37.539	24.016	30
31	1.5865	0.6303	0.025 57	0.040 57	39.102	24.646	31
32	1.6103	0.6210	0.024 58	0.039 58	40.688	25.267	32
33	1.6345	0.6118	0.023 64	0.038 64	42.299	25.879	33
34	1.6590	0.6028	0.022 76	0.037 76	43.933	26.482	34
35	1.6839	0.5939	0.021 93	0.036 93	45.592	27.076	35
40	1.8140	0.5513	0.018 43	0.033 43	54.268	29.916	40
45	1.9542	0.5117	0.015 72	0.030 72	63.614	32.552	45
50	2.1052	0.4750	0.013 57	0.028 57	73.683	35.000	50
55	2.2679	0.4409	0.011 83	0.026 83	84.530	37.271	55
60	2.4432	0.4093	0.010 39	0.025 39	96.215	39.380	60
65	2.6320	0.3799	0.009 19	0.024 19	108.803	41.338	65
70	2.8355	0.3527	0.008 17	0.023 17	122.364	43.155	70
75	3.0546	0.3274	0.007 30	0.022 30	136.973	44.842	75
80	3.2907	0.3039	0.006 55	0.021 55	152.711	46.407	80
85	3.5450	0.2821	0.005 89	0.020 89	169.665	47.861	85
90	3.8189	0.2619	0.005 32	0.020 32	187.930	49.210	90
95	4.1141	0.2431	0.004 82	0.019 82	207.606	50.462	95
100	4.4320	0.2256	0.004 37	0.019 37	228.803	51.625	100

2% Compound Interest Factors

	Single Payment		Uniform Series				
	Compound Amount Factor	Present Worth Factor	Sinking Fund Factor	Capital Recovery Factor	Compound Amount Factor	Present Worth Factor	
n	*F/P*	*P/F*	*A/F*	*A/P*	*F/A*	*P/A*	*n*
1	1.0200	0.9804	1.000 00	1.020 00	1.000	0.980	1
2	1.0404	0.9612	0.495 05	0.515 05	2.020	1.942	2
3	1.0612	0.9423	0.326 75	0.346 75	3.060	2.884	3
4	1.0824	0.9238	0.242 62	0.262 62	4.122	3.808	4
5	1.1041	0.9057	0.192 16	0.212 16	5.204	4.713	5
6	1.1262	0.8880	0.158 53	0.178 53	6.308	5.601	6
7	1.1487	0.8706	0.134 51	0.154 51	7.434	6.472	7
8	1.1717	0.8535	0.116 51	0.136 51	8.583	7.325	8
9	1.1951	0.8368	0.102 52	0.122 52	9.755	8.162	9
10	1.2190	0.8203	0.091 33	0.111 33	10.950	8.983	10
11	1.2434	0.8043	0.082 18	0.102 18	12.169	9.787	11
12	1.2682	0.7885	0.074 56	0.094 56	13.412	10.575	12
13	1.2936	0.7730	0.068 12	0.088 12	14.680	11.348	13
14	1.3195	0.7579	0.062 60	0.082 60	15.974	12.106	14
15	1.3459	0.7430	0.057 83	0.077 83	17.293	12.849	15
16	1.3728	0.7284	0.053 65	0.073 65	18.639	13.578	16
17	1.4002	0.7142	0.049 97	0.069 97	20.012	14.292	17
18	1.4282	0.7002	0.046 70	0.066 70	21.412	14.992	18
19	1.4568	0.6864	0.043 78	0.063 78	22.841	15.678	19
20	1.4859	0.6730	0.041 16	0.061 16	24.297	16.351	20
21	1.5157	0.6598	0.038 78	0.058 78	25.783	17.011	21
22	1.5460	0.6468	0.036 63	0.056 63	27.299	17.658	22
23	1.5769	0.6342	0.034 67	0.054 67	28.845	18.292	23
24	1.6084	0.6217	0.032 87	0.052 87	30.422	18.914	24
25	1.6406	0.6095	0.031 22	0.051 22	32.030	19.523	25
26	1.6734	0.5976	0.029 70	0.049 70	33.671	20.121	26
27	1.7069	0.5859	0.028 29	0.048 29	35.344	20.707	27
28	1.7410	0.5744	0.026 99	0.046 99	37.051	21.281	28
29	1.7758	0.5631	0.025 78	0.045 78	38.792	21.844	29
30	1.8114	0.5521	0.024 65	0.044 65	40.568	22.396	30
31	1.8476	0.5412	0.023 60	0.043 60	42.379	22.938	31
32	1.8845	0.5306	0.022 61	0.042 61	44.227	23.468	32
33	1.9222	0.5202	0.021 69	0.041 69	46.112	23.989	33
34	1.9607	0.5100	0.020 82	0.040 82	48.034	24.499	34
35	1.9999	0.5000	0.020 00	0.040 00	49.994	24.999	35
40	2.2080	0.4529	0.016 56	0.036 56	60.402	27.355	40
45	2.4379	0.4102	0.013 91	0.033 91	71.893	29.490	45
50	2.6916	0.3715	0.011 82	0.031 82	84.579	31.424	50
55	2.9717	0.3365	0.010 14	0.030 14	98.587	33.175	55
60	3.2810	0.3048	0.008 77	0.028 77	114.052	34.761	60
65	3.6225	0.2761	0.007 63	0.027 63	131.126	36.197	65
70	3.9996	0.2500	0.006 67	0.026 67	149.978	37.499	70
75	4.4158	0.2265	0.005 86	0.025 86	170.792	38.677	75
80	4.8754	0.2051	0.005 16	0.025 16	193.772	39.745	80
85	5.3829	0.1858	0.004 56	0.024 56	219.144	40.711	85
90	5.9431	0.1683	0.004 05	0.024 05	247.157	41.587	90
95	6.5617	0.1524	0.003 60	0.023 60	278.085	42.380	95
100	7.2446	0.1380	0.003 20	0.023 20	312.232	43.098	100

2½% Compound Interest Factors

	Single Payment		Uniform Series				
	Compound Amount Factor	Present Worth Factor	Sinking Fund Factor	Capital Recovery Factor	Compound Amount Factor	Present Worth Factor	
n	F/P	P/F	A/F	A/P	F/A	P/A	n
1	1.0250	0.9756	1.000 00	1.025 00	1.000	0.976	1
2	1.0506	0.9518	0.493 83	0.518 83	2.025	1.927	2
3	1.0769	0.9286	0.325 14	0.350 14	3.076	2.856	3
4	1.1038	0.9060	0.240 82	0.265 82	4.153	3.762	4
5	1.1314	0.8839	0.190 25	0.215 25	5.256	4.646	5
6	1.1597	0.8623	0.156 55	0.181 55	6.388	5.508	6
7	1.1887	0.8413	0.132 50	0.157 50	7.547	6.349	7
8	1.2184	0.8207	0.114 47	0.139 47	8.736	7.170	8
9	1.2489	0.8007	0.100 46	0.125 46	9.955	7.971	9
10	1.2801	0.7812	0.089 26	0.114 26	11.203	8.752	10
11	1.3121	0.7621	0.080 11	0.105 11	12.483	9.514	11
12	1.3449	0.7436	0.072 49	0.097 49	13.796	10.258	12
13	1.3785	0.7254	0.066 05	0.091 05	15.140	10.983	13
14	1.4130	0.7077	0.060 54	0.085 54	16.519	11.691	14
15	1.4483	0.6905	0.055 77	0.080 77	17.932	12.381	15
16	1.4845	0.6736	0.051 60	0.076 60	19.380	13.055	16
17	1.5216	0.6572	0.047 93	0.072 93	20.865	13.712	17
18	1.5597	0.6412	0.044 67	0.069 67	22.386	14.353	18
19	1.5987	0.6255	0.041 76	0.066 76	23.946	14.979	19
20	1.6386	0.6103	0.039 15	0.064 15	25.545	15.589	20
21	1.6796	0.5954	0.036 79	0.061 79	27.183	16.185	21
22	1.7216	0.5809	0.034 65	0.059 65	28.863	16.765	22
23	1.7646	0.5667	0.032 70	0.057 70	30.584	17.332	23
24	1.8087	0.5529	0.030 91	0.055 91	32.349	17.885	24
25	1.8539	0.5394	0.029 28	0.054 28	34.158	18.424	25
26	1.9003	0.5262	0.027 77	0.052 77	36.012	18.951	26
27	1.9478	0.5134	0.026 38	0.051 38	37.912	19.464	27
28	1.9965	0.5009	0.025 09	0.050 09	39.860	19.965	28
29	2.0464	0.4887	0.023 89	0.048 89	41.856	20.454	29
30	2.0976	0.4767	0.022 78	0.047 78	43.903	20.930	30
31	2.1500	0.4651	0.021 74	0.046 74	46.000	21.395	31
32	2.2038	0.4538	0.020 77	0.045 77	48.150	21.849	32
33	2.2589	0.4427	0.019 86	0.044 86	50.354	22.292	33
34	2.3153	0.4319	0.019 01	0.044 01	52.613	22.724	34
35	2.3732	0.4214	0.018 21	0.043 21	54.928	23.145	35
40	2.6851	0.3724	0.014 84	0.039 84	67.403	25.103	40
45	3.0379	0.3292	0.012 27	0.037 27	81.516	26.833	45
50	3.4371	0.2909	0.010 26	0.035 26	97.484	28.362	50
55	3.8888	0.2572	0.008 65	0.033 65	115.551	29.714	55
60	4.3998	0.2273	0.007 35	0.032 35	135.992	30.909	60
65	4.9780	0.2009	0.006 28	0.031 28	159.118	31.965	65
70	5.6321	0.1776	0.005 40	0.030 40	185.284	32.898	70
75	6.3722	0.1569	0.004 65	0.029 65	214.888	33.723	75
80	7.2100	0.1387	0.004 03	0.029 03	248.383	34.452	80
85	8.1570	0.1226	0.003 49	0.028 49	286.279	35.096	85
90	9.2289	0.1084	0.003 04	0.028 04	329.154	35.666	90
95	10.4416	0.0958	0.002 65	0.027 65	377.664	36.169	95
100	11.8137	0.0846	0.002 31	0.027 31	432.549	36.614	100

3% Compound Interest Factors

	Single Payment		Uniform Series				
n	Compound Amount Factor F/P	Present Worth Factor P/F	Sinking Fund Factor A/F	Capital Recovery Factor A/P	Compound Amount Factor F/A	Present Worth Factor P/A	n
1	1.0300	0.9709	1.000 00	1.030 00	1.000	0.971	1
2	1.0609	0.9426	0.492 61	0.522 61	2.030	1.913	2
3	1.0927	0.9151	0.323 53	0.353 53	3.091	2.829	3
4	1.1255	0.8885	0.239 03	0.269 03	4.184	3.717	4
5	1.1593	0.8626	0.188 35	0.218 35	5.309	4.580	5
6	1.1941	0.8375	0.154 60	0.184 60	6.468	5.417	6
7	1.2299	0.8131	0.130 51	0.160 51	7.662	6.230	7
8	1.2668	0.7894	0.112 46	0.142 46	8.892	7.020	8
9	1.3048	0.7664	0.098 43	0.128 43	10.159	7.786	9
10	1.3439	0.7441	0.087 23	0.117 23	11.464	8.530	10
11	1.3842	0.7224	0.078 08	0.108 08	12.808	9.253	11
12	1.4258	0.7014	0.070 46	0.100 46	14.192	9.954	12
13	1.4685	0.6810	0.064 03	0.094 03	15.618	10.635	13
14	1.5126	0.6611	0.058 53	0.088 53	17.086	11.296	14
15	1.5580	0.6419	0.053 77	0.083 77	18.599	11.938	15
16	1.6047	0.6232	0.049 61	0.079 61	20.157	12.561	16
17	1.6528	0.6050	0.045 95	0.075 95	21.762	13.166	17
18	1.7024	0.5874	0.042 71	0.072 71	23.414	13.754	18
19	1.7535	0.5703	0.039 81	0.069 81	25.117	14.324	19
20	1.8061	0.5537	0.037 22	0.067 22	26.870	14.877	20
21	1.8603	0.5375	0.034 87	0.064 87	28.676	15.415	21
22	1.9161	0.5219	0.032 75	0.062 75	30.537	15.937	22
23	1.9736	0.5067	0.030 81	0.060 81	32.453	16.444	23
24	2.0328	0.4919	0.029 05	0.059 05	34.426	16.936	24
25	2.0938	0.4776	0.027 43	0.057 43	36.459	17.413	25
26	2.1566	0.4637	0.025 94	0.055 94	38.553	17.877	26
27	2.2213	0.4502	0.024 56	0.054 56	40.710	18.327	27
28	2.2879	0.4371	0.023 29	0.053 29	42.931	18.764	28
29	2.3566	0.4243	0.022 11	0.052 11	45.219	19.188	29
30	2.4273	0.4120	0.021 02	0.051 02	47.575	19.600	30
31	2.5001	0.4000	0.020 00	0.050 00	50.003	20.000	31
32	2.5751	0.3883	0.019 05	0.049 05	52.503	20.389	32
33	2.6523	0.3770	0.018 16	0.048 16	55.078	20.766	33
34	2.7319	0.3660	0.017 32	0.047 32	57.730	21.132	34
35	2.8139	0.3554	0.016 54	0.046 54	60.462	21.487	35
40	3.2620	0.3066	0.013 26	0.043 26	75.401	23.115	40
45	3.7816	0.2644	0.010 79	0.040 79	92.720	24.519	45
50	4.3839	0.2281	0.008 87	0.038 87	112.797	25.730	50
55	5.0821	0.1968	0.007 35	0.037 35	136.072	26.774	55
60	5.8916	0.1697	0.006 13	0.036 13	163.053	27.676	60
65	6.8300	0.1464	0.005 15	0.035 15	194.333	28.453	65
70	7.9178	0.1263	0.004 34	0.034 34	230.594	29.123	70
75	9.1789	0.1089	0.003 67	0.033 67	272.631	29.702	75
80	10.6409	0.0940	0.003 11	0.033 11	321.363	30.201	80
85	12.3357	0.0811	0.002 65	0.032 65	377.857	30.631	85
90	14.3005	0.0699	0.002 26	0.032 26	443.349	31.002	90
95	16.5782	0.0603	0.001 93	0.031 93	519.272	31.323	95
100	19.2186	0.0520	0.001 65	0.031 65	607.288	31.599	100

3½% Compound Interest Factors

	Single Payment		Uniform Series				
	Compound Amount Factor	Present Worth Factor	Sinking Fund Factor	Capital Recovery Factor	Compound Amount Factor	Present Worth Factor	
n	F/P	P/F	A/F	A/P	F/A	P/A	n
1	1.0350	0.9662	1.000 00	1.035 00	1.000	0.966	1
2	1.0712	0.9335	0.491 40	0.526 40	2.035	1.900	2
3	1.1087	0.9019	0.321 93	0.356 93	3.106	2.802	3
4	1.1475	0.8714	0.237 25	0.272 25	4.215	3.673	4
5	1.1877	0.8420	0.186 48	0.221 48	5.362	4.515	5
6	1.2293	0.8135	0.152 67	0.187 67	6.550	5.329	6
7	1.2723	0.7860	0.128 54	0.163 54	7.779	6.115	7
8	1.3168	0.7594	0.110 48	0.145 48	9.052	6.874	8
9	1.3629	0.7337	0.096 45	0.131 45	10.368	7.608	9
10	1.4106	0.7089	0.085 24	0.120 24	11.731	8.317	10
11	1.4600	0.6849	0.076 09	0.111 09	13.142	9.002	11
12	1.5111	0.6618	0.068 48	0.103 48	14.602	9.663	12
13	1.5640	0.6394	0.062 06	0.097 06	16.113	10.303	13
14	1.6187	0.6178	0.056 57	0.091 57	17.677	10.921	14
15	1.6753	0.5969	0.051 83	0.086 83	19.296	11.517	15
16	1.7340	0.5767	0.047 68	0.082 68	20.971	12.094	16
17	1.7947	0.5572	0.044 04	0.079 04	22.705	12.651	17
18	1.8575	0.5384	0.040 82	0.075 82	24.500	13.190	18
19	1.9225	0.5202	0.037 94	0.072 94	26.357	13.710	19
20	1.9898	0.5026	0.035 36	0.070 36	28.280	14.212	20
21	2.0594	0.4856	0.033 04	0.068 04	30.269	14.698	21
22	2.1315	0.4692	0.030 93	0.065 93	32.329	15.167	22
23	2.2061	0.4533	0.029 02	0.064 02	34.460	15.620	23
24	2.2833	0.4380	0.027 27	0.062 27	36.667	16.058	24
25	2.3632	0.4231	0.025 67	0.060 67	38.950	16.482	25
26	2.4460	0.4088	0.024 21	0.059 21	41.313	16.890	26
27	2.5316	0.3950	0.022 85	0.057 85	43.759	17.285	27
28	2.6202	0.3817	0.021 60	0.056 60	46.291	17.667	28
29	2.7119	0.3687	0.020 45	0.055 45	48.911	18.036	29
30	2.8068	0.3563	0.019 37	0.054 37	51.623	18.392	30
31	2.9050	0.3442	0.018 37	0.053 37	54.429	18.736	31
32	3.0067	0.3326	0.017 44	0.052 44	57.335	19.069	32
33	3.1119	0.3213	0.016 57	0.051 57	60.341	19.390	33
34	3.2209	0.3105	0.015 76	0.050 76	63.453	19.701	34
35	3.3336	0.3000	0.015 00	0.050 00	66.674	20.001	35
40	3.9593	0.2526	0.011 83	0.046 83	84.550	21.355	40
45	4.7024	0.2127	0.009 45	0.044 45	105.782	22.495	45
50	5.5849	0.1791	0.007 63	0.042 63	130.998	23.456	50
55	6.6331	0.1508	0.006 21	0.041 21	160.947	24.264	55
60	7.8781	0.1269	0.005 09	0.040 09	196.517	24.945	60
65	9.3567	0.1069	0.004 19	0.039 19	238.763	25.518	65
70	11.1128	0.0900	0.003 46	0.038 46	288.938	26.000	70
75	13.1986	0.0758	0.002 87	0.037 87	348.530	26.407	75
80	15.6757	0.0638	0.002 38	0.037 38	419.307	26.749	80
85	18.6179	0.0537	0.001 99	0.036 99	503.367	27.037	85
90	22.1122	0.0452	0.001 66	0.036 66	603.205	27.279	90
95	26.2623	0.0381	0.001 39	0.036 39	721.781	27.484	95
100	31.1914	0.0321	0.001 16	0.036 16	862.612	27.655	100

4% Compound Interest Factors

	Single Payment		Uniform Series				
	Compound Amount Factor	Present Worth Factor	Sinking Fund Factor	Capital Recovery Factor	Compound Amount Factor	Present Worth Factor	
n	F/P	P/F	A/F	A/P	F/A	P/A	n
1	1.0400	0.9615	1.000 00	1.040 00	1.000	0.962	1
2	1.0816	0.9246	0.490 20	0.530 20	2.040	1.886	2
3	1.1249	0.8890	0.320 35	0.360 35	3.122	2.775	3
4	1.1699	0.8548	0.235 49	0.275 49	4.246	3.630	4
5	1.2167	0.8219	0.184 63	0.224 63	5.416	4.452	5
6	1.2653	0.7903	0.150 76	0.190 76	6.633	5.242	6
7	1.3159	0.7599	0.126 61	0.166 61	7.898	6.002	7
8	1.3686	0.7307	0.108 53	0.148 53	9.214	6.733	8
9	1.4233	0.7026	0.094 49	0.134 49	10.583	7.435	9
10	1.4802	0.6756	0.083 29	0.123 29	12.006	8.111	10
11	1.5395	0.6496	0.074 15	0.114 15	13.486	8.760	11
12	1.6010	0.6246	0.066 55	0.106 55	15.026	9.385	12
13	1.6651	0.6006	0.060 14	0.100 14	16.627	9.986	13
14	1.7317	0.5775	0.054 67	0.094 67	18.292	10.563	14
15	1.8009	0.5553	0.049 94	0.089 94	20.024	11.118	15
16	1.8730	0.5339	0.045 82	0.085 82	21.825	11.652	16
17	1.9479	0.5134	0.042 20	0.082 20	23.698	12.166	17
18	2.0258	0.4936	0.038 99	0.078 99	25.645	12.659	18
19	2.1068	0.4746	0.036 14	0.076 14	27.671	13.134	19
20	2.1911	0.4564	0.033 58	0.073 58	29.778	13.590	20
21	2.2788	0.4388	0.031 28	0.071 28	31.969	14.029	21
22	2.3699	0.4220	0.029 20	0.069 20	34.248	14.451	22
23	2.4647	0.4057	0.027 31	0.067 31	36.618	14.857	23
24	2.5633	0.3901	0.025 59	0.065 59	39.083	15.247	24
25	2.6658	0.3751	0.024 01	0.064 01	41.646	15.622	25
26	2.7725	0.3607	0.022 57	0.062 57	44.312	15.983	26
27	2.8834	0.3468	0.021 24	0.061 24	47.084	16.330	27
28	2.9987	0.3335	0.020 01	0.060 01	49.968	16.663	28
29	3.1187	0.3207	0.018 88	0.058 88	52.966	16.984	29
30	3.2434	0.3083	0.017 83	0.057 83	56.085	17.292	30
31	3.3731	0.2965	0.016 86	0.056 86	59.328	17.588	31
32	3.5081	0.2851	0.015 95	0.055 95	62.701	17.874	32
33	3.6484	0.2741	0.015 10	0.055 10	66.210	18.148	33
34	3.7943	0.2636	0.014 31	0.054 31	69.858	18.411	34
35	3.9461	0.2534	0.013 58	0.053 58	73.652	18.665	35
40	4.8010	0.2083	0.010 52	0.050 52	95.026	19.793	40
45	5.8412	0.1712	0.008 26	0.048 26	121.029	20.720	45
50	7.1067	0.1407	0.006 55	0.046 55	152.667	21.482	50
55	8.6464	0.1157	0.005 23	0.045 23	191.159	22.109	55
60	10.5196	0.0951	0.004 20	0.044 20	237.991	22.623	60
65	12.7987	0.0781	0.003 39	0.043 39	294.968	23.047	65
70	15.5716	0.0642	0.002 75	0.042 75	364.290	23.395	70
75	18.9453	0.0528	0.002 23	0.042 23	448.631	23.680	75
80	23.0500	0.0434	0.001 81	0.041 81	551.245	23.915	80
85	28.0436	0.0357	0.001 48	0.041 48	676.090	24.109	85
90	34.1193	0.0293	0.001 21	0.041 21	827.983	24.267	90
95	41.5114	0.0241	0.000 99	0.040 99	1 012.785	24.398	95
100	50.5049	0.0198	0.000 81	0.040 81	1 237.624	24.505	100

4½% Compound Interest Factors

	Single Payment		Uniform Series				
	Compound Amount Factor F/P	Present Worth Factor P/F	Sinking Fund Factor A/F	Capital Recovery Factor A/P	Compound Amount Factor F/A	Present Worth Factor P/A	
n							n
1	1.0450	0.9569	1.000 00	1.045 00	1.000	0.957	1
2	1.0920	0.9157	0.489 00	0.534 00	2.045	1.873	2
3	1.1412	0.8763	0.318 77	0.363 77	3.137	2.749	3
4	1.1925	0.8386	0.233 74	0.278 74	4.278	3.588	4
5	1.2462	0.8025	0.182 79	0.227 79	5.471	4.390	5
6	1.3023	0.7679	0.148 88	0.193 88	6.717	5.158	6
7	1.3609	0.7348	0.124 70	0.169 70	8.019	5.893	7
8	1.4221	0.7032	0.106 61	0.151 61	9.380	6.596	8
9	1.4861	0.6729	0.092 57	0.137 57	10.802	7.269	9
10	1.5530	0.6439	0.081 38	0.126 38	12.288	7.913	10
11	1.6229	0.6162	0.072 25	0.117 25	13.841	8.529	11
12	1.6959	0.5897	0.064 67	0.109 67	15.464	9.119	12
13	1.7722	0.5643	0.058 28	0.103 28	17.160	9.683	13
14	1.8519	0.5400	0.052 82	0.097 82	18.932	10.223	14
15	1.9353	0.5167	0.048 11	0.093 11	20.784	10.740	15
16	2.0224	0.4945	0.044 02	0.089 02	22.719	11.234	16
17	2.1134	0.4732	0.040 42	0.085 42	24.742	11.707	17
18	2.2085	0.4528	0.037 24	0.082 24	26.855	12.160	18
19	2.3079	0.4333	0.034 41	0.079 41	29.064	12.593	19
20	2.4117	0.4146	0.031 88	0.076 88	31.371	13.008	20
21	2.5202	0.3968	0.029 60	0.074 60	33.783	13.405	21
22	2.6337	0.3797	0.027 55	0.072 55	36.303	13.784	22
23	2.7522	0.3634	0.025 68	0.070 68	38.937	14.148	23
24	2.8760	0.3477	0.023 99	0.068 99	41.689	14.495	24
25	3.0054	0.3327	0.022 44	0.067 44	44.565	14.828	25
26	3.1407	0.3184	0.021 02	0.066 02	47.571	15.147	26
27	3.2820	0.3047	0.019 72	0.064 72	50.711	15.451	27
28	3.4397	0.2916	0.018 52	0.063 52	53.993	15.743	28
29	3.5840	0.2790	0.017 41	0.062 41	57.423	16.022	29
30	3.7453	0.2670	0.016 39	0.061 39	61.007	16.289	30
31	3.9139	0.2555	0.015 44	0.060 44	64.752	16.544	31
32	4.0900	0.2445	0.014 56	0.059 56	68.666	16.789	32
33	4.2740	0.2340	0.013 74	0.058 74	72.756	17.023	33
34	4.4664	0.2239	0.012 98	0.057 98	77.030	17.247	34
35	4.6673	0.2143	0.012 27	0.057 27	81.497	17.461	35
40	5.8164	0.1719	0.009 34	0.054 34	107.030	18.402	40
45	7.2482	0.1380	0.007 20	0.052 20	138.850	19.156	45
50	9.0326	0.1107	0.005 60	0.050 60	178.503	19.762	50
55	11.2563	0.0888	0.004 39	0.049 39	227.918	20.248	55
60	14.0274	0.0713	0.003 45	0.048 45	289.498	20.638	60
65	17.4807	0.0572	0.002 73	0.047 73	366.238	20.951	65
70	21.7841	0.0459	0.002 17	0.047 17	461.870	21.202	70
75	27.1470	0.0368	0.001 72	0.046 72	581.044	21.404	75
80	33.8301	0.0296	0.001 37	0.046 37	729.558	21.565	80
85	42.1585	0.0237	0.001 09	0.046 09	914.632	21.695	85
90	52.5371	0.0190	0.000 87	0.045 87	1 145.269	21.799	90
95	65.4708	0.0153	0.000 70	0.045 70	1 432.684	21.883	95
100	81.5885	0.0123	0.000 56	0.045 56	1 790.856	21.950	100

5% Compound Interest Factors

	Single Payment		Uniform Series				
	Compound Amount Factor	Present Worth Factor	Sinking Fund Factor	Capital Recovery Factor	Compound Amount Factor	Present Worth Factor	
n	*F/P*	*P/F*	*A/F*	*A/P*	*F/A*	*P/A*	*n*
1	1.0500	0.9524	1.000 00	1.050 00	1.000	0.952	1
2	1.1025	0.9070	0.487 80	0.537 80	2.050	1.859	2
3	1.1576	0.8638	0.317 21	0.367 21	3.153	2.723	3
4	1.2155	0.8227	0.232 01	0.282 01	4.310	3.546	4
5	1.2763	0.7835	0.180 97	0.230 97	5.526	4.329	5
6	1.3401	0.7462	0.147 02	0.197 02	6.802	5.076	6
7	1.4071	0.7107	0.122 82	0.172 82	8.142	5.786	7
8	1.4775	0.6768	0.104 72	0.154 72	9.549	6.463	8
9	1.5513	0.6446	0.090 69	0.140 69	11.027	7.108	9
10	1.6289	0.6139	0.079 50	0.129 50	12.578	7.722	10
11	1.7103	0.5847	0.070 39	0.120 39	14.207	8.306	11
12	1.7959	0.5568	0.062 83	0.112 83	15.917	8.863	12
13	1.8856	0.5303	0.056 46	0.106 46	17.713	9.394	13
14	1.9800	0.5051	0.051 02	0.101 02	19.599	9.899	14
15	2.0789	0.4810	0.046 34	0.096 34	21.579	10.380	15
16	2.1829	0.4581	0.042 27	0.092 27	23.657	10.838	16
17	2.2920	0.4363	0.038 70	0.088 70	25.840	11.274	17
18	2.4066	0.4155	0.035 55	0.085 55	28.132	11.690	18
19	2.5270	0.3957	0.032 75	0.082 75	30.539	12.085	19
20	2.6533	0.3769	0.030 24	0.080 24	33.066	12.462	20
21	2.7860	0.3589	0.028 00	0.078 00	35.719	12.821	21
22	2.9253	0.3418	0.025 97	0.075 97	38.505	13.163	22
23	3.0715	0.3256	0.024 14	0.074 14	41.430	13.489	23
24	3.2251	0.3101	0.022 47	0.072 47	44.502	13.799	24
25	3.3864	0.2953	0.020 95	0.070 95	47.727	14.094	25
26	3.5557	0.2812	0.019 56	0.069 56	51.113	14.375	26
27	3.7335	0.2678	0.018 29	0.068 29	54.669	14.643	27
28	3.9201	0.2551	0.017 12	0.067 12	58.403	14.898	28
29	4.1161	0.2429	0.016 05	0.066 05	62.323	15.141	29
30	4.3219	0.2314	0.015 05	0.065 05	66.439	15.372	30
31	4.5380	0.2204	0.014 13	0.064 13	70.761	15.593	31
32	4.7649	0.2099	0.013 28	0.063 28	75.299	15.803	32
33	5.0032	0.1999	0.012 49	0.062 49	80.064	16.003	33
34	5.2533	0.1904	0.011 76	0.061 76	85.067	16.193	34
35	5.5160	0.1813	0.011 07	0.061 07	90.320	16.374	35
40	7.0400	0.1420	0.008 28	0.058 28	120.800	17.159	40
45	8.9850	0.1113	0.006 26	0.056 26	159.700	17.774	45
50	11.4674	0.0872	0.004 78	0.054 78	209.348	18.256	50
55	14.6356	0.0683	0.003 67	0.053 67	272.713	18.633	55
60	18.6792	0.0535	0.002 83	0.052 83	353.584	18.929	60
65	23.8399	0.0419	0.002 19	0.052 19	456.798	19.161	65
70	30.4264	0.0329	0.001 70	0.051 70	588.529	19.343	70
75	38.8327	0.0258	0.001 32	0.051 32	756.654	19.485	75
80	49.5614	0.0202	0.001 03	0.051 03	971.229	19.596	80
85	63.2544	0.0158	0.000 80	0.050 80	1 245.087	19.684	85
90	80.7304	0.0124	0.000 63	0.050 63	1 594.607	19.752	90
95	103.0357	0.0097	0.000 49	0.050 49	2 040.694	19.806	95
100	131.5013	0.0076	0.000 38	0.050 38	2 610.025	19.848	100

5½% Compound Interest Factors

	Single Payment		Uniform Series				
	Compound Amount Factor F/P	Present Worth Factor P/F	Sinking Fund Factor A/F	Capital Recovery Factor A/P	Compound Amount Factor F/A	Present Worth Factor P/A	
n							n
1	1.0550	0.9479	1.000 00	1.055 00	1.000	0.948	1
2	1.1130	0.8985	0.486 62	0.541 62	2.055	1.846	2
3	1.1742	0.8516	0.315 65	0.370 65	3.168	2.698	3
4	1.2388	0.8072	0.230 29	0.285 29	4.342	3.505	4
5	1.3070	0.7651	0.179 18	0.234 18	5.581	4.270	5
6	1.3788	0.7252	0.145 18	0.200 18	6.888	4.996	6
7	1.4547	0.6874	0.120 96	0.175 96	8.267	5.683	7
8	1.5347	0.6516	0.102 86	0.157 86	9.722	6.335	8
9	1.6191	0.6176	0.088 84	0.143 84	11.256	6.952	9
10	1.7081	0.5854	0.077 67	0.132 67	12.875	7.538	10
11	1.8021	0.5549	0.068 57	0.123 57	14.583	8.093	11
12	1.9012	0.5260	0.061 03	0.116 03	16.386	8.619	12
13	2.0058	0.4986	0.054 68	0.109 68	18.287	9.117	13
14	2.1161	0.4726	0.049 28	0.104 28	20.293	9.590	14
15	2.2325	0.4479	0.044 63	0.099 63	22.409	10.038	15
16	2.3553	0.4246	0.040 58	0.095 58	24.641	10.462	16
17	2.4848	0.4024	0.037 04	0.092 04	26.996	10.865	17
18	2.6215	0.3815	0.033 92	0.088 92	29.481	11.246	18
19	2.7656	0.3616	0.031 15	0.086 15	32.103	11.608	19
20	2.9178	0.3427	0.028 68	0.083 68	34.868	11.950	20
21	3.0782	0.3249	0.026 46	0.081 46	37.786	12.275	21
22	3.2475	0.3079	0.024 47	0.079 47	40.864	12.583	22
23	3.4262	0.2919	0.022 67	0.077 67	44.112	12.875	23
24	3.6146	0.2767	0.021 04	0.076 04	47.538	13.152	24
25	3.8134	0.2622	0.019 55	0.074 55	51.153	13.414	25
26	4.0231	0.2486	0.018 19	0.073 19	54.966	13.662	26
27	4.2444	0.2356	0.016 95	0.071 95	58.989	13.898	27
28	4.4778	0.2233	0.015 81	0.070 81	63.234	14.121	28
29	4.7241	0.2117	0.014 77	0.069 77	67.711	14.333	29
30	4.9840	0.2006	0.013 81	0.068 81	72.435	14.534	30
31	5.2581	0.1902	0.012 92	0.067 92	77.419	14.724	31
32	5.5473	0.1803	0.012 10	0.067 10	82.677	14.904	32
33	5.8524	0.1709	0.011 33	0.066 33	88.225	15.075	33
34	6.1742	0.1620	0.010 63	0.065 63	94.077	15.237	34
35	6.5138	0.1535	0.009 97	0.064 97	100.251	15.391	35
40	8.5133	0.1175	0.007 32	0.062 32	136.606	16.046	40
45	11.1266	0.0899	0.005 43	0.060 43	184.119	16.548	45
50	14.5420	0.0688	0.004 06	0.059 06	246.217	16.932	50
55	19.0058	0.0526	0.003 05	0.058 05	327.377	17.225	55
60	24.8398	0.0403	0.002 31	0.057 31	433.450	17.450	60
65	32.4646	0.0308	0.001 75	0.056 75	572.083	17.622	65
70	42.4299	0.0236	0.001 33	0.056 33	753.271	17.753	70
75	55.4542	0.0180	0.001 01	0.056 01	990.076	17.854	75
80	72.4764	0.0138	0.000 77	0.055 77	1 299.571	17.931	80
85	94.7238	0.0106	0.000 59	0.055 59	1 704.069	17.990	85
90	123.8002	0.0081	0.000 45	0.055 45	2 232.731	18.035	90
95	161.8019	0.0062	0.000 34	0.055 34	2 923.671	18.069	95
100	211.4686	0.0047	0.000 26	0.055 26	3 826.702	18.096	100

6% Compound Interest Factors

	Single Payment		Uniform Series				
n	Compound Amount Factor *F/P*	Present Worth Factor *P/F*	Sinking Fund Factor *A/F*	Capital Recovery Factor *A/P*	Compound Amount Factor *F/A*	Present Worth Factor *P/A*	*n*
1	1.0600	0.9434	1.000 00	1.060 00	1.000	0.943	1
2	1.1236	0.8900	0.485 44	0.545 44	2.060	1.833	2
3	1.1910	0.8396	0.314 11	0.374 11	3.184	2.673	3
4	1.2625	0.7921	0.228 59	0.288 59	4.375	3.465	4
5	1.3382	0.7473	0.177 40	0.237 40	5.637	4.212	5
6	1.4185	0.7050	0.143 36	0.203 36	6.975	4.917	6
7	1.5036	0.6651	0.119 14	0.179 14	8.394	5.582	7
8	1.5938	0.6274	0.101 04	0.161 04	9.897	6.210	8
9	1.6895	0.5919	0.087 02	0.147 02	11.491	6.802	9
10	1.7908	0.5584	0.075 87	0.135 87	13.181	7.360	10
11	1.8983	0.5268	0.066 79	0.126 79	14.972	7.887	11
12	2.0122	0.4970	0.059 28	0.119 28	16.870	8.384	12
13	2.1329	0.4688	0.052 96	0.112 96	18.882	8.853	13
14	2.2609	0.4423	0.047 58	0.107 58	21.015	9.295	14
15	2.3966	0.4173	0.042 96	0.102 96	23.276	9.712	15
16	2.5404	0.3936	0.038 95	0.098 95	25.673	10.106	16
17	2.6928	0.3714	0.035 44	0.095 44	28.213	10.477	17
18	2.8543	0.3503	0.032 36	0.092 36	30.906	10.828	18
19	3.0256	0.3305	0.029 62	0.089 62	33.760	11.158	19
20	3.2071	0.3118	0.027 18	0.087 18	36.786	11.470	20
21	3.3996	0.2942	0.025 00	0.085 00	39.993	11.764	21
22	3.6035	0.2775	0.023 05	0.083 05	43.392	12.042	22
23	3.8197	0.2618	0.021 28	0.081 28	46.996	12.303	23
24	4.0489	0.2470	0.019 68	0.079 68	50.816	12.550	24
25	4.2919	0.2330	0.018 23	0.078 23	54.865	12.783	25
26	4.5494	0.2198	0.016 90	0.076 90	59.156	13.003	26
27	4.8223	0.2074	0.015 70	0.075 70	63.706	13.211	27
28	5.1117	0.1956	0.014 59	0.074 59	68.528	13.406	28
29	5.4184	0.1846	0.013 58	0.073 58	73.640	13.591	29
30	5.7435	0.1741	0.012 65	0.072 65	79.058	13.765	30
31	6.0881	0.1643	0.011 79	0.071 79	84.802	13.929	31
32	6.4534	0.1550	0.011 00	0.071 00	90.890	14.084	32
33	6.8406	0.1462	0.010 27	0.070 27	97.343	14.230	33
34	7.2510	0.1379	0.009 60	0.069 60	104.184	14.368	34
35	7.6861	0.1301	0.008 97	0.068 97	111.435	14.498	35
40	10.2857	0.0972	0.006 46	0.066 46	154.762	15.046	40
45	13.7646	0.0727	0.004 70	0.064 70	212.744	15.456	45
50	18.4202	0.0543	0.003 44	0.063 44	290.336	15.762	50
55	24.6503	0.0406	0.002 54	0.062 54	394.172	15.991	55
60	32.9877	0.0303	0.001 88	0.061 88	533.128	16.161	60
65	44.1450	0.0227	0.001 39	0.061 39	719.083	16.289	65
70	59.0759	0.0169	0.001 03	0.061 03	967.932	16.385	70
75	79.0569	0.0126	0.000 77	0.060 77	1 300.949	16.456	75
80	105.7960	0.0095	0.000 57	0.060 57	1 746.600	16.509	80
85	141.5789	0.0071	0.000 43	0.060 43	2 342.982	16.549	85
90	189.4645	0.0053	0.000 32	0.060 32	3 141.075	16.579	90
95	253.5463	0.0039	0.000 24	0.060 24	4 209.104	16.601	95
100	339.3021	0.0029	0.000 18	0.060 18	5 638.368	16.618	100

7% Compound Interest Factors

	Single Payment		Uniform Series				
	Compound Amount Factor	Present Worth Factor	Sinking Fund Factor	Capital Recovery Factor	Compound Amount Factor	Present Worth Factor	
n	*F/P*	*P/F*	*A/F*	*A/P*	*F/A*	*P/A*	*n*
1	1.0700	0.9346	1.000 00	1.070 00	1.000	0.935	1
2	1.1449	0.8734	0.483 09	0.553 09	2.070	1.808	2
3	1.2250	0.8163	0.311 05	0.381 05	3.215	2.624	3
4	1.3108	0.7629	0.225 23	0.295 23	4.440	3.387	4
5	1.4026	0.7130	0.173 89	0.243 89	5.751	4.100	5
6	1.5007	0.6663	0.139 80	0.209 80	7.153	4.767	6
7	1.6058	0.6227	0.115 55	0.185 55	8.654	5.389	7
8	1.7182	0.5820	0.097 47	0.167 47	10.260	5.971	8
9	1.8385	0.5439	0.083 49	0.153 49	11.978	6.515	9
10	1.9672	0.5083	0.072 38	0.142 38	13.816	7.024	10
11	2.1049	0.4751	0.063 36	0.133 36	15.784	7.499	11
12	2.2522	0.4440	0.055 90	0.125 90	17.888	7.943	12
13	2.4098	0.4150	0.049 65	0.119 65	20.141	8.358	13
14	2.5785	0.3878	0.044 34	0.114 34	22.550	8.745	14
15	2.7590	0.3624	0.039 79	0.109 79	25.129	9.108	15
16	2.9522	0.3387	0.035 86	0.105 86	27.888	9.447	16
17	3.1588	0.3166	0.032 43	0.102 43	30.840	9.763	17
18	3.3799	0.2959	0.029 41	0.099 41	33.999	10.059	18
19	3.6165	0.2765	0.026 75	0.096 75	37.379	10.336	19
20	3.8697	0.2584	0.024 39	0.094 39	40.995	10.594	20
21	4.1406	0.2415	0.022 29	0.092 29	44.865	10.836	21
22	4.4304	0.2257	0.020 41	0.090 41	49.006	11.061	22
23	4.7405	0.2109	0.018 71	0.088 71	53.436	11.272	23
24	5.0724	0.1971	0.017 19	0.087 19	58.177	11.469	24
25	5.4274	0.1842	0.015 81	0.085 81	63.249	11.654	25
26	5.8074	0.1722	0.014 56	0.084 56	68.676	11.826	26
27	6.2139	0.1609	0.013 43	0.083 43	74.484	11.987	27
28	6.6488	0.1504	0.012 39	0.082 39	80.698	12.137	28
29	7.1143	0.1406	0.011 45	0.081 45	87.347	12.278	29
30	7.6123	0.1314	0.010 59	0.080 59	94.461	12.409	30
31	8.1451	0.1228	0.009 80	0.079 80	102.073	12.532	31
32	8.7153	0.1147	0.009 07	0.079 07	110.218	12.647	32
33	9.3253	0.1072	0.008 41	0.078 41	118.933	12.754	33
34	9.9781	0.1002	0.007 80	0.077 80	128.259	12.854	34
35	10.6766	0.0937	0.007 23	0.077 23	138.237	12.948	35
40	14.9745	0.0668	0.005 01	0.075 01	199.635	13.332	40
45	21.0025	0.0476	0.003 50	0.073 50	285.749	13.606	45
50	29.4570	0.0339	0.002 46	0.072 46	406.529	13.801	50
55	41.3150	0.0242	0.001 74	0.071 74	575.929	13.940	55
60	57.9464	0.0173	0.001 23	0.071 23	813.520	14.039	60
65	81.2729	0.0123	0.000 87	0.070 87	1 146.755	14.110	65
70	113.9894	0.0088	0.000 62	0.070 62	1 614.134	14.160	70
75	159.8760	0.0063	0.000 44	0.070 44	2 269.657	14.196	75
80	224.2344	0.0045	0.000 31	0.070 31	3 189.063	14.222	80
85	314.5003	0.0032	0.000 22	0.070 22	4 478.576	14.240	85
90	441.1030	0.0023	0.000 16	0.070 16	6 287.185	14.253	90
95	618.6697	0.0016	0.000 11	0.070 11	8 823.854	14.263	95
100	867.7163	0.0012	0.000 08	0.070 08	12 381.662	14.269	100

8% Compound Interest Factors

	Single Payment		Uniform Series				
	Compound Amount Factor	Present Worth Factor	Sinking Fund Factor	Capital Recovery Factor	Compound Amount Factor	Present Worth Factor	
n	*F/P*	*P/F*	*A/F*	*A/P*	*F/A*	*P/A*	*n*
1	1.0800	0.9259	1.000 00	1.080 00	1.000	0.926	1
2	1.1664	0.8573	0.480 77	0.560 77	2.080	1.783	2
3	1.2597	0.7938	0.308 03	0.388 03	3.246	2.577	3
4	1.3605	0.7350	0.221 92	0.301 92	4.506	3.312	4
5	1.4693	0.6806	0.170 46	0.250 46	5.867	3.993	5
6	1.5869	0.6302	0.136 32	0.216 32	7.336	4.623	6
7	1.7138	0.5835	0.112 07	0.192 07	8.923	5.206	7
8	1.8509	0.5403	0.094 01	0.174 01	10.637	5.747	8
9	1.9990	0.5002	0.080 08	0.160 08	12.488	6.247	9
10	2.1589	0.4632	0.069 03	0.149 03	14.487	6.710	10
11	2.3316	0.4289	0.060 08	0.140 08	16.645	7.139	11
12	2.5182	0.3971	0.052 70	0.132 70	18.977	7.536	12
13	2.7196	0.3677	0.046 52	0.126 52	21.495	7.904	13
14	2.9372	0.3405	0.041 30	0.121 30	24.215	8.244	14
15	3.1722	0.3152	0.036 83	0.116 83	27.152	8.559	15
16	3.4259	0.2919	0.032 98	0.112 98	30.324	8.851	16
17	3.7000	0.2703	0.029 63	0.109 63	33.750	9.122	17
18	3.9960	0.2502	0.026 70	0.106 70	37.450	9.372	18
19	4.3157	0.2317	0.024 13	0.104 13	41.446	9.604	19
20	4.6610	0.2145	0.021 85	0.101 85	45.762	9.818	20
21	5.0338	0.1987	0.019 83	0.099 83	50.423	10.017	21
22	5.4365	0.1839	0.018 03	0.098 03	55.457	10.201	22
23	5.8715	0.1703	0.016 42	0.096 42	60.893	10.371	23
24	6.3412	0.1577	0.014 98	0.094 98	66.765	10.529	24
25	6.8485	0.1460	0.013 68	0.093 68	73.106	10.675	25
26	7.3964	0.1352	0.012 51	0.092 51	79.954	10.810	26
27	7.9881	0.1252	0.011 45	0.091 45	87.351	10.935	27
28	8.6271	0.1159	0.010 49	0.090 49	95.339	11.051	28
29	9.3173	0.1073	0.009 62	0.089 62	103.966	11.158	29
30	10.0627	0.0994	0.008 83	0.088 83	113.283	11.258	30
31	10.8677	0.0920	0.008 11	0.088 11	123.346	11.350	31
32	11.7371	0.0852	0.007 45	0.087 45	134.214	11.435	32
33	12.6760	0.0789	0.006 85	0.086 85	145.951	11.514	33
34	13.6901	0.0730	0.006 30	0.086 30	158.627	11.587	34
35	14.7853	0.0676	0.005 80	0.085 80	172.317	11.655	35
40	21.7245	0.0460	0.003 86	0.083 86	259.057	11.925	40
45	31.9204	0.0313	0.002 59	0.082 59	386.506	12.108	45
50	46.9016	0.0213	0.001 74	0.081 74	573.770	12.233	50
55	68.9139	0.0145	0.001 18	0.081 18	848.923	12.319	55
60	101.2571	0.0099	0.000 80	0.080 80	1 253.213	12.377	60
65	148.7798	0.0067	0.000 54	0.080 54	1 847.248	12.416	65
70	218.6064	0.0046	0.000 37	0.080 37	2 720.080	12.443	70
75	321.2045	0.0031	0.000 25	0.080 25	4 002.557	12.461	75
80	471.9548	0.0021	0.000 17	0.080 17	5 886.935	12.474	80
85	693.4565	0.0014	0.000 12	0.080 12	8 655.706	12.482	85
90	1 018.9151	0.0010	0.000 08	0.080 08	12 723.939	12.488	90
95	1 497.1205	0.0007	0.000 05	0.080 05	18 701.507	12.492	95
100	2 199.7613	0.0005	0.000 04	0.080 04	27 484.516	12.494	100

9% Compound Interest Factors

	Single Payment		Uniform Series				
n	Compound Amount Factor F/P	Present Worth Factor P/F	Sinking Fund Factor A/F	Capital Recovery Factor A/P	Compound Amount Factor F/A	Present Worth Factor P/A	*n*
1	1.0900	0.9174	1.000 00	1.090 00	1.000	0.917	1
2	1.1881	0.8417	0.478 47	0.568 47	2.090	1.759	2
3	1.2950	0.7722	0.305 05	0.395 05	3.278	2.531	3
4	1.4116	0.7084	0.218 67	0.308 67	4.573	3.240	4
5	1.5386	0.6499	0.167 09	0.257 09	5.985	3.890	5
6	1.6771	0.5963	0.132 92	0.222 92	7.523	4.486	6
7	1.8280	0.5470	0.108 69	0.198 69	9.200	5.033	7
8	1.9926	0.5019	0.090 67	0.180 67	11.028	5.535	8
9	2.1719	0.4604	0.076 80	0.166 80	13.021	5.995	9
10	2.3674	0.4224	0.065 82	0.155 82	15.193	6.418	10
11	2.5804	0.3875	0.056 95	0.146 95	17.560	6.805	11
12	2.8127	0.3555	0.049 65	0.139 65	20.141	7.161	12
13	3.0658	0.3262	0.043 57	0.133 57	22.953	7.487	13
14	3.3417	0.2992	0.038 43	0.128 43	26.019	7.786	14
15	3.6425	0.2745	0.034 06	0.124 06	29.361	8.061	15
16	3.9703	0.2519	0.030 30	0.120 30	33.003	8.313	16
17	4.3276	0.2311	0.027 05	0.117 05	36.974	8.544	17
18	4.7171	0.2120	0.024 21	0.114 21	41.301	8.756	18
19	5.1417	0.1945	0.021 73	0.111 73	46.018	8.950	19
20	5.6044	0.1784	0.019 55	0.109 55	51.160	9.129	20
21	6.1088	0.1637	0.017 62	0.107 62	56.765	9.292	21
22	6.6586	0.1502	0.015 90	0.105 90	62.873	9.442	22
23	7.2579	0.1378	0.014 38	0.104 38	69.532	9.580	23
24	7.9111	0.1264	0.013 02	0.103 02	76.790	9.707	24
25	8.6231	0.1160	0.011 81	0.101 81	84.701	9.823	25
26	9.3992	0.1064	0.010 72	0.100 72	93.324	9.929	26
27	10.2451	0.0976	0.009 73	0.099 73	102.723	10.027	27
28	11.1671	0.0895	0.008 85	0.098 85	112.968	10.116	28
29	12.1722	0.0822	0.008 06	0.098 06	124.135	10.198	29
30	13.2677	0.0753	0.007 34	0.097 34	136.308	10.274	30
31	14.4618	0.0691	0.006 69	0.096 69	149.575	10.343	31
32	15.7633	0.0634	0.006 10	0.096 10	164.037	10.406	32
33	17.1820	0.0582	0.005 56	0.095 56	179.800	10.464	33
34	18.7284	0.0534	0.005 08	0.095 08	196.982	10.518	34
35	20.4140	0.0490	0.004 64	0.094 64	215.711	10.567	35
40	31.4094	0.0318	0.002 96	0.092 96	337.882	10.757	40
45	48.3273	0.0207	0.001 90	0.091 90	525.859	10.881	45
50	74.3575	0.0134	0.001 23	0.091 23	815.084	10.962	50
55	114.4083	0.0087	0.000 79	0.090 79	1 260.092	11.014	55
60	176.0313	0.0057	0.000 51	0.090 51	1 944.792	11.048	60
65	270.8460	0.0037	0.000 33	0.090 33	2 998.288	11.070	65
70	416.7301	0.0024	0.000 22	0.090 22	4 619.223	11.084	70
75	641.1909	0.0016	0.000 14	0.090 14	7 113.232	11.094	75
80	986.5517	0.0010	0.000 09	0.090 09	10 950.574	11.100	80
85	1 517.9320	0.0007	0.000 06	0.090 06	16 854.800	11.104	85
90	2 335.5266	0.0004	0.000 04	0.090 04	25 939.184	11.106	90
95	3 593.4971	0.0003	0.000 03	0.090 03	39 916.635	11.108	95
100	5 529.0408	0.0002	0.000 02	0.090 02	61 422.675	11.109	100

10% Compound Interest Factors

	Single Payment		Uniform Series				
	Compound Amount Factor	Present Worth Factor	Sinking Fund Factor	Capital Recovery Factor	Compound Amount Factor	Present Worth Factor	
n	F/P	P/F	A/F	A/P	F/A	P/A	n
1	1.1000	0.9091	1.000 00	1.100 00	1.000	0.909	1
2	1.2100	0.8264	0.476 19	0.576 19	2.100	1.736	2
3	1.3310	0.7513	0.302 11	0.402 11	3.310	2.487	3
4	1.4641	0.6830	0.215 47	0.315 47	4.641	3.170	4
5	1.6105	0.6209	0.163 80	0.263 80	6.105	3.791	5
6	1.7716	0.5645	0.129 61	0.229 61	7.716	4.355	6
7	1.9487	0.5132	0.105 41	0.205 41	9.487	4.868	7
8	2.1436	0.4665	0.087 44	0.187 44	11.436	5.335	8
9	2.3579	0.4241	0.073 64	0.173 64	13.579	5.759	9
10	2.5937	0.3855	0.062 75	0.162 75	15.937	6.144	10
11	2.8531	0.3505	0.053 96	0.153 96	18.531	6.495	11
12	3.1384	0.3186	0.046 76	0.146 76	21.384	6.814	12
13	3.4523	0.2897	0.040 78	0.140 78	24.523	7.103	13
14	3.7975	0.2633	0.035 75	0.135 75	27.975	7.367	14
15	4.1772	0.2394	0.031 47	0.131 47	31.772	7.606	15
16	4.5950	0.2176	0.027 82	0.127 82	35.950	7.824	16
17	5.0545	0.1978	0.024 66	0.124 66	40.545	8.022	17
18	5.5599	0.1799	0.021 93	0.121 93	45.599	8.201	18
19	6.1159	0.1635	0.019 55	0.119 55	51.159	8.365	19
20	6.7275	0.1486	0.017 46	0.117 46	57.275	8.514	20
21	7.4002	0.1351	0.015 62	0.115 62	64.002	8.649	21
22	8.1403	0.1228	0.014 01	0.114 01	71.403	8.772	22
23	8.9543	0.1117	0.012 57	0.112 57	79.543	8.883	23
24	9.8497	0.1015	0.011 30	0.111 30	88.497	8.985	24
25	10.8347	0.0923	0.010 17	0.110 17	98.347	9.077	25
26	11.9182	0.0839	0.009 16	0.109 16	109.182	9.161	26
27	13.1100	0.0763	0.008 26	0.108 26	121.100	9.237	27
28	14.4210	0.0693	0.007 45	0.107 45	134.210	9.307	28
29	15.8631	0.0630	0.006 73	0.106 73	148.631	9.370	29
30	17.4494	0.0573	0.006 08	0.106 08	164.494	9.427	30
31	19.1943	0.0521	0.005 50	0.105 50	181.943	9.479	31
32	21.1138	0.0474	0.004 97	0.104 97	201.138	9.526	32
33	23.2252	0.0431	0.004 50	0.104 50	222.252	9.569	33
34	25.5477	0.0391	0.004 07	0.104 07	245.477	9.609	34
35	28.1024	0.0356	0.003 69	0.103 69	271.024	9.644	35
40	45.2593	0.0221	0.002 26	0.102 26	442.593	9.779	40
45	72.8905	0.0137	0.001 39	0.101 39	718.905	9.863	45
50	117.3909	0.0085	0.000 86	0.100 86	1 163.909	9.915	50
55	189.0591	0.0053	0.000 53	0.100 53	1 880.591	9.947	55
60	304.4816	0.0033	0.000 33	0.100 33	3 034.816	9.967	60
65	490.3707	0.0020	0.000 20	0.100 20	4 893.707	9.980	65
70	789.7470	0.0013	0.000 13	0.100 13	7 887.470	9.987	70
75	1 271.8952	0.0008	0.000 08	0.100 08	12 708.954	9.992	75
80	2 048.4002	0.0005	0.000 05	0.100 05	20 474.002	9.995	80
85	3 298.9690	0.0003	0.000 03	0.100 03	32 979.690	9.997	85
90	5 313.0226	0.0002	0.000 02	0.100 02	53 120.226	9.998	90
95	8 556.6760	0.0001	0.000 01	0.100 01	85 556.760	9.999	95
100	13 780.6123	0.0001	0.000 01	0.100 01	137 796.123	9.999	100

11% Compound Interest Factors

	Single Payment		Uniform Series				
u	Compound Amount Factor F/P	Present Worth Factor P/F	Sinking Fund Factor A/F	Capital Recovery Factor A/P	Compound Amount Factor F/A	Present Worth Factor P/A	n
1	1.1100	0.9009	1.000 00	1.110 00	1.000	0.901	1
2	1.2321	0.8116	0.473 93	0.583 93	2.110	1.713	2
3	1.3676	0.7312	0.299 21	0.409 21	3.342	2.444	3
4	1.5181	0.6587	0.212 33	0.322 33	4.710	3.102	4
5	1.6851	0.5935	0.160 57	0.270 57	6.228	3.696	5
6	1.8704	0.5346	0.126 38	0.236 38	7.913	4.231	6
7	2.0762	0.4817	0.102 22	0.212 22	9.783	4.712	7
8	2.3045	0.4339	0.084 32	0.194 32	11.859	5.146	8
9	2.5581	0.3909	0.070 60	0.180 60	14.164	5.537	9
10	2.8394	0.3522	0.059 80	0.169 80	16.722	5.889	10
11	3.1518	0.3173	0.051 12	0.161 12	19.561	6.207	11
12	3.4984	0.2858	0.044 03	0.154 03	22.713	6.492	12
13	3.8833	0.2575	0.038 15	0.148 15	26.212	6.750	13
14	4.3104	0.2320	0.033 23	0.143 23	30.095	6.982	14
15	4.7846	0.2090	0.029 07	0.139 07	34.405	7.191	15
16	5.3109	0.1883	0.025 52	0.135 52	39.190	7.379	16
17	5.8951	0.1696	0.022 47	0.132 47	44.501	7.549	17
18	6.5436	0.1528	0.019 84	0.129 84	50.396	7.702	18
19	7.2633	0.1377	0.017 56	0.127 56	56.939	7.839	19
20	8.0623	0.1240	0.015 58	0.125 58	64.203	7.963	20
21	8.9492	0.1117	0.013 84	0.123 84	72.265	8.075	21
22	9.9336	0.1007	0.012 31	0.122 31	81.214	8.176	22
23	11.0263	0.0907	0.010 97	0.120 97	91.148	8.266	23
24	12.2392	0.0817	0.009 79	0.119 79	102.174	8.348	24
25	13.5855	0.0736	0.008 74	0.118 74	114.413	8.422	25
26	15.0799	0.0663	0.007 81	0.117 81	127.999	8.488	26
27	16.7386	0.0597	0.006 99	0.116 99	143.079	8.548	27
28	18.5799	0.0538	0.006 26	0.116 26	159.817	8.602	28
29	20.6237	0.0485	0.005 61	0.115 61	178.397	8.650	29
30	22.8923	0.0437	0.005 02	0.115 02	199.021	8.694	30
31	25.4104	0.0394	0.004 51	0.114 51	221.913	8.733	31
32	28.2056	0.0355	0.004 04	0.114 04	247.324	8.769	32
33	31.3082	0.0319	0.003 63	0.113 63	275.529	8.801	33
34	34.7521	0.0288	0.003 26	0.113 26	306.837	8.829	34
35	38.5749	0.0259	0.002 93	0.112 93	341.590	8.855	35
40	65.0009	0.0154	0.001 72	0.111 72	581.826	8.951	40
45	109.5302	0.0091	0.001 01	0.111 01	986.639	9.008	45
50	184.5648	0.0054	0.000 60	0.110 60	1 688.771	9.042	50
∞				0.110 00		9.091	∞

12% Compound Interest Factors

	Single Payment		Uniform Series				
	Compound Amount Factor	Present Worth Factor	Sinking Fund Factor	Capital Recovery Factor	Compound Amount Factor	Present Worth Factor	
n	*F/P*	*P/F*	*A/F*	*A/P*	*F/A*	*P/A*	*n*
1	1.1200	0.8929	1.000 00	1.120 00	1.000	0.893	1
2	1.2544	0.7972	0.471 70	0.591 70	2.120	1.690	2
3	1.4049	0.7118	0.296 35	0.416 35	3.374	2.402	3
4	1.5735	0.6355	0.209 23	0.329 23	4.779	3.037	4
5	1.7623	0.5674	0.157 41	0.277 41	6.353	3.605	5
6	1.9738	0.5066	0.123 23	0.243 23	8.115	4.111	6
7	2.2107	0.4523	0.099 12	0.219 12	10.089	4.564	7
8	2.4760	0.4039	0.081 30	0.201 30	12.300	4.968	8
9	2.7731	0.3606	0.067 68	0.187 68	14.776	5.328	9
10	3.1058	0.3220	0.056 98	0.176 98	17.549	5.650	10
11	3.4785	0.2875	0.048 42	0.168 42	20.655	5.938	11
12	3.8960	0.2567	0.041 44	0.161 44	24.133	6.194	12
13	4.3635	0.2292	0.035 68	0.155 68	28.029	6.424	13
14	4.8871	0.2046	0.030 87	0.150 87	32.393	6.628	14
15	5.4736	0.1827	0.026 82	0.146 82	37.280	6.811	15
16	6.1304	0.1631	0.023 39	0.143 39	42.753	6.974	16
17	6.8660	0.1456	0.020 46	0.140 46	48.884	7.120	17
18	7.6900	0.1300	0.017 94	0.137 94	55.750	7.250	18
19	8.6128	0.1161	0.015 76	0.135 76	63.440	7.366	19
20	9.6463	0.1037	0.013 88	0.133 88	72.052	7.469	20
21	10.8038	0.0926	0.012 24	0.132 24	81.699	7.562	21
22	12.1003	0.0826	0.010 81	0.130 81	92.503	7.645	22
23	13.5523	0.0738	0.009 56	0.129 56	104.603	7.718	23
24	15.1786	0.0659	0.008 46	0.128 46	118.155	7.784	24
25	17.0001	0.0588	0.007 50	0.127 50	133.334	7.843	25
26	19.0401	0.0525	0.006 65	0.126 65	150.334	7.896	26
27	21.3249	0.0469	0.005 90	0.125 90	169.374	7.943	27
28	23.8839	0.0419	0.005 24	0.125 24	190.699	7.984	28
29	26.7499	0.0374	0.004 66	0.124 66	214.583	8.022	29
30	29.9599	0.0334	0.004 14	0.124 14	241.333	8.055	30
31	33.5551	0.0298	0.003 69	0.123 69	271.292	8.085	31
32	37.5817	0.0266	0.003 28	0.123 28	304.847	8.112	32
33	42.0915	0.0238	0.002 92	0.122 92	342.429	8.135	33
34	47.1425	0.0212	0.002 60	0.122 60	384.520	8.157	34
35	52.7996	0.0189	0.002 32	0.122 32	431.663	8.176	35
40	93.0510	0.0107	0.001 30	0.121 30	767.091	8.244	40
45	163.9876	0.0061	0.000 74	0.120 74	1 358.230	8.283	45
50	289.0022	0.0035	0.000 42	0.120 42	2 400.018	8.305	50
∞				0.120 00		8.333	∞

13% Compound Interest Factors

	Single Payment		Uniform Series				
n	Compound Amount Factor F/P	Present Worth Factor P/F	Sinking Fund Factor A/F	Capital Recovery Factor A/P	Compound Amount Factor F/A	Present Worth Factor P/A	n
1	1.1300	0.8850	1.000 00	1.130 00	1.000	0.885	1
2	1.2769	0.7831	0.469 48	0.599 48	2.130	1.668	2
3	1.4429	0.6931	0.293 52	0.423 52	3.407	2.361	3
4	1.6305	0.6133	0.206 19	0.336 19	4.850	2.974	4
5	1.8424	0.5428	0.154 31	0.284 31	6.480	3.517	5
6	2.0820	0.4803	0.120 15	0.250 15	8.323	3.998	6
7	2.3526	0.4251	0.096 11	0.226 11	10.405	4.423	7
8	2.6584	0.3762	0.078 39	0.208 39	12.757	4.799	8
9	3.0040	0.3329	0.064 87	0.194 87	15.416	5.132	9
10	3.3946	0.2946	0.054 29	0.184 29	18.420	5.426	10
11	3.8359	0.2607	0.045 84	0.175 84	21.814	5.687	11
12	4.3345	0.2307	0.038 99	0.168 99	25.650	5.918	12
13	4.8980	0.2042	0.033 35	0.163 35	29.985	6.122	13
14	5.5348	0.1807	0.028 67	0.158 67	34.883	6.302	14
15	6.2543	0.1599	0.024 74	0.154 74	40.417	6.462	15
16	7.0673	0.1415	0.021 43	0.151 43	46.672	6.604	16
17	7.9861	0.1252	0.018 61	0.148 61	53.739	6.729	17
18	9.0243	0.1108	0.016 20	0.146 20	61.725	6.840	18
19	10.1974	0.0981	0.014 13	0.144 13	70.749	6.938	19
20	11.5231	0.0868	0.012 35	0.142 35	80.947	7.025	20
21	13.0211	0.0768	0.010 81	0.140 81	92.470	7.102	21
22	14.7138	0.0680	0.009 48	0.139 48	105.491	7.170	22
23	16.6266	0.0601	0.008 32	0.138 32	120.205	7.230	23
24	18.7881	0.0532	0.007 31	0.137 31	136.831	7.283	24
25	21.2305	0.0471	0.006 43	0.136 43	155.620	7.330	25
26	23.9905	0.0417	0.005 65	0.135 65	176.850	7.372	26
27	27.1093	0.0369	0.004 98	0.134 98	200.841	7.409	27
28	30.6335	0.0326	0.004 39	0.134 39	227.950	7.441	28
29	34.6158	0.0289	0.003 87	0.133 87	258.583	7.470	29
30	39.1159	0.0256	0.003 41	0.133 41	293.199	7.496	30
31	44.2010	0.0226	0.003 01	0.133 01	332.315	7.518	31
32	49.9471	0.0200	0.002 66	0.132 66	376.516	7.538	32
33	56.4402	0.0177	0.002 34	0.132 34	426.463	7.556	33
34	63.7774	0.0157	0.002 07	0.132 07	482.903	7.572	34
35	72.0685	0.0139	0.001 83	0.131 83	546.681	7.586	35
40	132.7816	0.0075	0.000 99	0.130 99	1 013.704	7.634	40
45	244.6414	0.0041	0.000 53	0.130 53	1 874.165	7.661	45
50	450.7359	0.0022	0.000 29	0.130 29	3 459.507	7.675	50
∞				0.130 00		7.692	∞

14% Compound Interest Factors

	Single Payment		Uniform Series				
n	Compound Amount Factor F/P	Present Worth Factor P/F	Sinking Fund Factor A/F	Capital Recovery Factor A/P	Compound Amount Factor F/A	Present Worth Factor P/A	n
1	1.1400	0.8772	1.000 00	1.140 00	1.000	0.877	1
2	1.2996	0.7695	0.467 29	0.607 29	2.140	1.647	2
3	1.4815	0.6750	0.290 73	0.430 73	3.440	2.322	3
4	1.6890	0.5921	0.203 20	0.343 20	4.921	2.914	4
5	1.9254	0.5194	0.151 28	0.291 28	6.610	3.433	5
6	2.1950	0.4556	0.117 16	0.257 16	8.536	3.889	6
7	2.5023	0.3996	0.093 19	0.233 19	10.730	4.288	7
8	2.8526	0.3506	0.075 57	0.215 57	13.233	4.639	8
9	3.2519	0.3075	0.062 17	0.202 17	·16.085	4.946	9
10	3.7072	0.2697	0.051 71	0.191 71	19.337	5.216	10
11	4.2262	0.2366	0.043 39	0.183 39	23.045	5.453	11
12	4.8179	0.2076	0.036 67	0.176 67	27.271	5.660	12
13	5.4924	0.1821	0.031 16	0.171 16	32.089	5.842	13
14	6.2613	0.1597	0.026 61	0.166 61	37.581	6.002	14
15	7.1379	0.1401	0.022 81	0.162 81	43.842	6.142	15
16	8.1372	0.1229	0.019 62	0.159 62	50.980	6.265	16
17	9.2765	0.1078	0.016 92	0.156 92	59.118	6.373	17
18	10.5752	0.0946	0.014 62	0.154 62	68.394	6.467	18
19	12.0557	0.0829	0.012 66	0.152 66	78.969	6.550	19
20	13.7435	0.0728	0.010 99	0.150 99	91.025	6.623	20
21	15.6676	0.0638	0.009 54	0.149 54	104.768	6.687	21
22	17.8610	0.0560	0.008 30	0.148 30	120.436	6.743	22
23	20.3616	0.0491	0.007 23	0.147 23	138.297	6.792	23
24	23.2122	0.0431	0.006 30	0.146 30	158.659	6.835	24
25	26.4619	0.0378	0.005 50	0.145 50	181.871	6.873	25
26	30.1666	0.0331	0.004 80	0.144 80	208.333	6.906	26
27	34.3899	0.0291	0.004 19	0.144 19	238.499	6.935	27
28	39.2045	0.0255	0.003 66	0.143 66	272.889	6.961	28
29	44.6931	0.0224	0.003 20	0.143 20	312.094	6.983	29
30	50.9502	0.0196	0.002 80	0.142 80	356.787	7.003	30
31	58.0832	0.0172	0.002 45	0.142 45	407.737	7.020	31
32	66.2148	0.0151	0.002 15	0.142 15	465.820	7.035	32
33	75.4849	0.0132	0.001 88	0.141 88	532.035	7.048	33
34	86.0528	0.0116	0.001 65	0.141 65	607.520	7.060	34
35	98.1002	0.0102	0.001 44	0.141 44	693.573	7.070	35
40	188.8835	0.0053	0.000 75	0.140 75	1 342.025	7.105	40
45	363.6791	0.0027	0.000 39	0.140 39	2 590.565	7.123	45
50	700.2330	0.0014	0.000 20	0.140 20	4 994.521	7.133	50
∞				0.140 00		7.143	∞

15% Compound Interest Factors

	Single Payment			Uniform Series			
	Compound Amount Factor	Present Worth Factor	Sinking Fund Factor	Capital Recovery Factor	Compound Amount Factor	Present Worth Factor	
n	*F/P*	*P/F*	*A/F*	*A/P*	*F/A*	*P/A*	*n*
1	1.1500	0.8696	1.000 00	1.150 00	1.000	0.870	1
2	1.3225	0.7561	0.465 12	0.615 12	2.150	1.626	2
3	1.5209	0.6575	0.287 98	0.437 98	3.472	2.283	3
4	1.7490	0.5718	0.200 26	0.350 27	4.993	2.855	4
5	2.0114	0.4972	0.148 32	0.298 32	6.742	3.352	5
6	2.3131	0.4323	0.114 24	0.264 24	8.754	3.784	6
7	2.6600	0.3759	0.090 36	0.240 36	11.067	4.160	7
8	3.0590	0.3269	0.072 85	0.222 85	13.727	4.487	8
9	3.5179	0.2843	0.059 57	0.209 57	16.786	4.772	9
10	4.0456	0.2472	0.049 25	0.199 25	20.304	5.019	10
11	4.6524	0.2149	0.041 07	0.191 07	24.349	5.234	11
12	5.3503	0.1869	0.034 48	0.184 48	29.002	5.421	12
13	6.1528	0.1625	0.029 11	0.179 11	34.352	5.583	13
14	7.0757	0.1413	0.024 69	0.174 69	40.505	5.724	14
15	8.1371	0.1229	0.021 02	0.171 02	47.580	5.847	15
16	9.3576	0.1069	0.017 95	0.167 95	55.717	5.954	16
17	10.7613	0.0929	0.015 37	0.165 37	65.075	6.047	17
18	12.3755	0.0808	0.013 19	0.163 19	75.836	6.128	18
19	14.2318	0.0703	0.011 34	0.161 34	88.212	6.198	19
20	16.3665	0.0611	0.009 76	0.159 76	102.444	6.259	20
21	18.8215	0.0531	0.008 42	0.158 42	118.810	6.312	21
22	21.6447	0.0462	0.007 27	0.157 27	137.632	6.359	22
23	24.8915	0.0402	0.006 28	0.156 28	159.276	6.399	23
24	28.6252	0.0349	0.005 43	0.155 43	184.168	6.434	24
25	32.9190	0.0304	0.004 70	0.154 70	212.793	6.464	25
26	37.8568	0.0264	0.004 07	0.154 07	245.712	6.491	26
27	43.5353	0.0230	0.003 53	0.153 53	283.569	6.514	27
28	50.0656	0.0200	0.003 06	0.153 06	327.104	6.534	28
29	57.5755	0.0174	0.002 65	0.152 65	377.170	6.551	29
30	66.2118	0.0151	0.002 30	0.152 30	434.745	6.566	30
31	76.1435	0.0131	0.002 00	0.152 00	500.957	6.579	31
32	87.5651	0.0114	0.001 73	0.151 73	577.100	6.591	32
33	100.6998	0.0099	0.001 50	0.151 50	664.666	6.600	33
34	115.8048	0.0086	0.001 31	0.151 31	765.365	6.609	34
35	133.1755	0.0075	0.001 13	0.151 13	881.170	6.617	35
40	267.8635	0.0037	0.000 56	0.150 56	1 779.090	6.642	40
45	538.7693	0.0019	0.000 28	0.150 28	3 585.128	6.654	45
50	1 083.6574	0.0009	0.000 14	0.150 14	7 217.716	6.661	50
∞				0.150 00		6.667	∞

16% Compound Interest Factors

	Single Payment		Uniform Series				
n	Compound Amount Factor F/P	Present Worth Factor P/F	Sinking Fund Factor A/F	Capital Recovery Factor A/P	Compound Amount Factor F/A	Present Worth Factor P/A	n
1	1.1600	0.8621	1.000 00	1.160 00	1.000	0.862	1
2	1.3456	0.7432	0.462 96	0.622 96	2.160	1.605	2
3	1.5609	0.6407	0.285 26	0.445 26	3.506	2.246	3
4	1.8106	0.5523	0.197 38	0.357 38	5.066	2.798	4
5	2.1003	0.4761	0.145 41	0.305 41	6.877	3.274	5
6	2.4364	0.4104	0.111 39	0.271 39	8.977	3.685	6
7	2.8262	0.3538	0.087 61	0.247 61	11.414	4.039	7
8	3.2784	0.3050	0.070 22	0.230 22	14.240	4.344	8
9	3.8030	0.2630	0.057 08	0.217 08	17.519	4.607	9
10	4.4114	0.2267	0.046 90	0.206 90	21.321	4.833	10
11	5.1173	0.1954	0.038 86	0.198 86	25.733	5.029	11
12	5.9360	0.1685	0.032 41	0.192 41	30.850	5.197	12
13	6.8858	0.1452	0.027 18	0.187 18	36.786	5.342	13
14	7.9875	0.1252	0.022 90	0.182 90	43.672	5.468	14
15	9.2655	0.1079	0.019 36	0.179 36	51.660	5.575	15
16	10.7480	0.0930	0.016 41	0.176 41	60.925	5.668	16
17	12.4677	0.0802	0.013 95	0.173 95	71.673	5.749	17
18	14.4625	0.0691	0.011 88	0.171 88	84.141	5.818	18
19	16.7765	0.0596	0.010 14	0.170 14	98.603	5.877	19
20	19.4608	0.0514	0.008 67	0.168 67	115.380	5.929	20
21	22.5745	0.0443	0.007 42	0.167 42	134.841	5.973	21
22	26.1864	0.0382	0.006 35	0.166 35	157.415	6.011	22
23	30.3762	0.0329	0.005 45	0.165 45	183.601	6.044	23
24	35.2364	0.0284	0.004 67	0.164 67	213.978	6.073	24
25	40.8742	0.0245	0.004 01	0.164 01	249.214	6.097	25
26	47.4141	0.0211	0.003 45	0.163 45	290.088	6.118	26
27	55.0004	0.0182	0.002 96	0.162 96	337.502	6.136	27
28	63.8004	0.0157	0.002 55	0.162 55	392.503	6.152	28
29	74.0085	0.0135	0.002 19	0.162 19	456.303	6.166	29
30	85.8499	0.0116	0.001 89	0.161 89	530.312	6.177	30
31	99.5859	0.0100	0.001 62	0.161 62	616.162	6.187	31
32	115.5196	0.0087	0.001 40	0.161 40	715.747	6.196	32
33	134.0027	0.0075	0.001 20	0.161 20	831.267	6.203	33
34	155.4432	0.0064	0.001 04	0.161 04	965.270	6.210	34
35	180.3141	0.0055	0.000 89	0.160 89	1 120.713	6.215	35
40	378.7212	0.0026	0.000 42	0.160 42	2 360.757	6.233	40
45	795.4438	0.0013	0.000 20	0.160 20	4 965.274	6.242	45
50	1 670.7038	0.0006	0.000 10	0.160 10	10 435.649	6.246	50
∞				0.160 00		6.250	∞

18% Compound Interest Factors

	Single Payment		Uniform Series				
n	Compound Amount Factor F/P	Present Worth Factor P/F	Sinking Fund Factor A/F	Capital Recovery Factor A/P	Compound Amount Factor F/A	Present Worth Factor P/A	n
1	1.1800	0.8475	1.000 00	1.180 00	1.000.	0.847	1
2	1.3924	0.7182	0.458 72	0.638 72	2.180	1.566	2
3	1.6430	0.6086	0.279 92	0.459 92	3.572	2.174	3
4	1.9388	0.5158	0.191 74	0.371 74	5.215	2.690	4
5	2.2878	0.4371	0.139 78	0.319 78	7.154	3.127	5
6	2.6996	0.3704	0.105 91	0.285 91	9.442	3.498	6
7	3.1855	0.3139	0.082 36	0.262 36	12.142	3.812	7
8	3.7589	0.2660	0.065 24	0.245 24	15.327	4.078	8
9	4.4355	0.2255	0.052 39	0.232 39	19.086	4.303	9
10	5.2338	0.1911	0.042 51	0.222 51	23.521	4.494	10
11	6.1759	0.1619	0.034 78	0.214 78	28.755	4.656	11
12	7.2876	0.1372	0.028 63	0.208 63	34.931	4.793	12
13	8.5994	0.1163	0.023 69	0.203 69	42.219	4.910	13
14	10.1472	0.0985	0.019 68	0.199 68	50.818	5.008	14
15	11.9737	0.0835	0.016 40	0.196 40	60.965	5.092	15
16	14.1290	0.0708	0.013 71	0.193 71	72.939	5.162	16
17	16.6722	0.0600	0.011 49	0.191 49	87.068	5.222	17
18	19.6733	0.0508	0.009 64	0.189 64	103.740	5.273	18
19	23.2144	0.0431	0.008 10	0.188 10	123.414	5.316	19
20	27.3930	0.0365	0.006 82	0.186 82	146.628	5.353	20
21	32.3238	0.0309	0.005 75	0.185 75	174.021	5.384	21
22	38.1421	0.0262	0.004 85	0.184 85	206.345	5.410	22
23	45.0076	0.0222	0.004 09	0.184 09	244.487	5.432	23
24	53.1090	0.0188	0.003 45	0.183 45	289.494	5.451	24
25	62.6686	0.0160	0.002 92	0.182 92	342.603	5.467	25
26	73.9490	0.0135	0.002 47	0.182 47	405.272	5.480	26
27	87.2598	0.0115	0.002 09	0.182 09	479.221	5.492	27
28	102.9665	0.0097	0.001 77	0.181 77	566.481	5.502	28
29	121.5005	0.0082	0.001 49	0.181 49	669.447	5.510	29
30	143.3706	0.0070	0.001 26	0.181 26	790.948	5.517	30
31	169.1774	0.0059	0.001 07	0.181 07	934.319	5.523	31
32	199.6293	0.0050	0.000 91	0.180 91	1 103.496	5.528	32
33	235.5625	0.0042	0.000 77	0.180 77	1 303.125	5.532	33
34	277.9638	0.0036	0.000 65	0.180 65	1 538.688	5.536	34
35	327.9973	0.0030	0.000 55	0.180 55	1 816.652	5.539	35
40	750.3783	0.0013	0.000 24	0.180 24	4 163.213	5.548	40
45	1 716.6839	0.0006	0.000 10	0.180 10	9 531.577	5.552	45
50	3 927.3569	0.0003	0.000 05	0.180 05	21 813.094	5.554	50
∞				0.180 00		5.556	∞

20% Compound Interest Factors

	Single Payment		Uniform Series				
	Compound Amount Factor	Present Worth Factor	Sinking Fund Factor	Capital Recovery Factor	Compound Amount Factor	Present Worth Factor	
n	F/P	P/F	A/F	A/P	F/A	P/A	n
1	1.2000	0.8333	1.000 00	1.200 00	1.000	0.833	1
2	1.4400	0.6944	0.454 55	0.654 55	2.200	1.528	2
3	1.7280	0.5787	0.274 73	0.474 73	3.640	2.106	3
4	2.0736	0.4823	0.186 29	0.386 29	5.368	2.589	4
5	2.4883	0.4019	0.134 38	0.334 38	7.442	2.991	5
6	2.9860	0.3349	0.100 71	0.300 71	9.930	3.326	6
7	3.5832	0.2791	0.077 42	0.277 42	12.916	3.605	7
8	4.2998	0.2326	0.060 61	0.260 61	16.499	3.837	8
9	5.1598	0.1938	0.048 08	0.248 08	20.799	4.031	9
10	6.1917	0.1615	0.038 52	0.238 52	25.959	4.192	10
11	7.4301	0.1346	0.031 10	0.231 10	32.150	4.327	11
12	8.9161	0.1122	0.025 26	0.225 26	39.581	4.439	12
13	10.6993	0.0935	0.020 62	0.220 62	48.497	4.533	13
14	12.8392	0.0779	0.016 89	0.216 89	59.196	4.611	14
15	15.4070	0.0649	0.013 88	0.213 88	72.035	4.675	15
16	18.4884	0.0541	0.011 44	0.211 44	87.442	4.730	16
17	22.1861	0.0451	0.009 44	0.209 44	105.931	4.775	17
18	26.6233	0.0376	0.007 81	0.207 81	128.117	4.812	18
19	31.9480	0.0313	0.006 46	0.206 46	154.740	4.844	19
20	38.3376	0.0261	0.005 36	0.205 36	186.688	4.870	20
21	46.0051	0.0217	0.004 44	0.204 44	225.026	4.891	21
22	55.2061	0.0181	0.003 69	0.203 69	271.031	4.909	22
23	66.2474	0.0151	0.003 07	0.203 07	326.237	4.925	23
24	79.4968	0.0126	0.002 55	0.202 55	392.484	4.937	24
25	95.3962	0.0105	0.002 12	0.202 12	471.981	4.948	25
26	114.4755	0.0087	0.001 76	0.201 76	567.377	4.956	26
27	137.3706	0.0073	0.001 47	0.201 47	681.853	4.964	27
28	164.8447	0.0061	0.001 22	0.201 22	819.223	4.970	28
29	197.8136	0.0051	0.001 02	0.201 02	984.068	4.975	29
30	237.3763	0.0042	0.000 85	0.200 85	1 181.882	4.979	30
31	284.8516	0.0035	0.000 70	0.200 70	1 419.258	4.982	31
32	341.8219	0.0029	0.000 59	0.200 59	1 704.109	4.985	32
33	410.1863	0.0024	0.000 49	0.200 49	2 045.931	4.988	33
34	492.2235	0.0020	0.000 41	0.200 41	2 456.118	4.990	34
35	590.6682	0.0017	0.000 34	0.200 34	2 948.341	4.992	35
40	1 469.7716	0.0007	0.000 14	0.200 14	7 343.858	4.997	40
45	3 657.2620	0.0003	0.000 05	0.200 05	18 281.310	4.999	45
50	9 100.4382	0.0001	0.000 02	0.200 02	45 497.191	4.999	50
∞				0.200 00		5.000	∞

25% Compound Interest Factors

	Single Payment		Uniform Series				
n	Compound Amount Factor F/P	Present Worth Factor P/F	Sinking Fund Factor A/F	Capital Recovery Factor A/P	Compound Amount Factor F/A	Present Worth Factor P/A	*n*
1	1.2500	0.8000	1.000 00	1.250 00	1.000	0.800	1
2	1.5625	0.6400	0.444 44	0.694 44	2.250	1.440	2
3	1.9531	0.5120	0.262 30	0.512 30	3.813	1.952	3
4	2.4414	0.4096	0.173 44	0.423 44	5.766	2.362	4
5	3.0518	0.3277	0.121 85	0.371 85	8.207	2.689	5
6	3.8147	0.2621	0.088 82	0.338 82	11.259	2.951	6
7	4.7684	0.2097	0.066 34	0.316 34	15.073	3.161	7
8	5.9605	0.1678	0.050 40	0.300 40	19.842	3.329	8
9	7.4506	0.1342	0.038 76	0.288 76	25.802	3.463	9
10	9.3132	0.1074	0.030 07	0.280 07	33.253	3.571	10
11	11.6415	0.0859	0.023 49	0.273 49	42.566	3.656	11
12	14.5519	0.0687	0.018 45	0.268 45	54.208	3.725	12
13	18.1899	0.0550	0.014 54	0.264 54	68.760	3.780	13
14	22.7374	0.0440	0.011 50	0.261 50	86.949	3.824	14
15	28.4217	0.0352	0.009 12	0.259 12	109.687	3.859	15
16	35.5271	0.0281	0.007 24	0.257 24	138.109	3.887	16
17	44.4089	0.0225	0.005 76	0.255 76	173.636	3.910	17
18	55.5112	0.0180	0.004 59	0.254 59	218.045	3.928	18
19	69.3889	0.0144	0.003 66	0.253 66	273.556	3.942	19
20	86.7362	0.0115	0.002 92	0.252 92	342.945	3.954	20
21	108.4202	0.0092	0.002 33	0.252 33	429.681	3.963	21
22	135.5253	0.0074	0.001 86	0.251 86	538.101	3.970	22
23	169.4066	0.0059	0.001 48	0.251 48	673.626	3.976	23
24	211.7582	0.0047	0.001 19	0.251 19	843.033	3.981	24
25	264.6978	0.0038	0.000 95	0.250 95	1 054.791	3.985	25
26	330.8722	0.0030	0.000 76	0.250 76	1 319.489	3.988	26
27	413.5903	0.0024	0.000 61	0.250 61	1 650.361	3.990	27
28	516.9879	0.0019	0.000 48	0.250 48	2 063.952	3.992	28
29	646.2349	0.0015	0.000 39	0.250 39	2 580.939	3.994	29
30	807.7936	0.0012	0.000 31	0.250 31	3 227.174	3.995	30
31	1 009.7420	0.0010	0.000 25	0.250 25	4 034.968	3.996	31
32	1 262.1774	0.0008	0.000 20	0.250 20	5 044.710	3.997	32
33	1 577.7218	0.0006	0.000 16	0.250 16	6 306.887	3.997	33
34	1 972.1523	0.0005	0.000 13	0.250 13	7 884.609	3.998	34
35	2 465.1903	0.0004	0.000 10	0.250 10	9 856.761	3.998	35
40	7 523.1638	0.0001	0.000 03	0.250 03	30 088.655	3.999	40
45	22 958.8740	0.0001	0.000 01	0.250 01	91 831.496	4.000	45
50	70 064.9232	0.0000	0.000 00	0.250 00	280 255.693	4.000	50
∞				0.250 00		4.000	∞

30% Compound Interest Factors

	Single Payment		Uniform Series				
n	Compound Amount Factor F/P	Present Worth Factor P/F	Sinking Fund Factor A/F	Capital Recovery Factor A/P	Compound Amount Factor F/A	Present Worth Factor P/A	*n*
1	1.3000	0.7692	1.000 00	1.300 00	1.000	0.769	1
2	1.6900	0.5917	0.434 78	0.734 78	2.300	1.361	2
3	2.1970	0.4552	0.250 63	0.550 63	3.990	1.816	3
4	2.8561	0.3501	0.161 63	0.461 63	6.187	2.166	4
5	3.7129	0.2693	0.110 58	0.410 58	9.043	2.436	5
6	4.8268	0.2072	0.078 39	0.378 39	12.756	2.643	6
7	6.2749	0.1594	0.056 87	0.356 87	17.583	2.802	7
8	8.1573	0.1226	0.041 92	0.341 92	23.858	2.925	8
9	10.6045	0.0943	0.031 24	0.331 24	32.015	3.019	9
10	13.7858	0.0725	0.023 46	0.323 46	42.619	3.092	10
11	17.9216	0.0558	0.017 73	0.317 73	56.405	3.147	11
12	23.2981	0.0429	0.013 45	0.313 45	74.327	3.190	12
13	30.2875	0.0330	0.010 24	0.310 24	97.625	3.223	13
14	39.3738	0.0254	0.007 82	0.307 82	127.913	3.249	14
15	51.1859	0.0195	0.005 98	0.305 98	167.286	3.268	15
16	66.5417	0.0150	0.004 58	0.304 58	218.472	3.283	16
17	86.5042	0.0116	0.003 51	0.303 51	285.014	3.295	17
18	112.4554	0.0089	0.002 69	0.302 69	371.518	3.304	18
19	146.1920	0.0068	0.002 07	0.302 07	483.973	3.311	19
20	190.0496	0.0053	0.001 59	0.301 59	630.165	3.316	20
21	247.0645	0.0040	0.001 22	0.301 22	820.215	3.320	21
22	321.1839	0.0031	0.000 94	0.300 94	1 067.280	3.323	22
23	417.5391	0.0024	0.000 72	0.300 72	1 388.464	3.325	23
24	542.8008	0.0018	0.000 55	0.300 55	1 806.003	3.327	24
25	705.6410	0.0014	0.000 43	0.300 43	2 348.803	3.329	25
26	917.3333	0.0011	0.000 33	0.300 33	3 054.444	3.330	26
27	1 192.5333	0.0008	0.000 25	0.300 25	3 971.778	3.331	27
28	1 550.2933	0.0006	0.000 19	0.300 19	5 164.311	3.331	28
29	2 015.3813	0.0005	0.000 15	0.300 15	6 714.604	3.332	29
30	2 619.9956	0.0004	0.000 11	0.300 11	8 729.985	3.332	30
31	3 405.9943	0.0003	0.000 09	0.300 09	11 349.981	3.332	31
32	4 427.7926	0.0002	0.000 07	0.300 07	14 755.975	3.333	32
33	5 756.1304	0.0002	0.000 05	0.300 05	19 183.768	3.333	33
34	7 482.9696	0.0001	0.000 04	0.300 04	24 939.899	3.333	34
35	9 727.8604	0.0001	0.000 03	0.300 03	32 422.868	3.333	35
∞				0.300 00		3.333	∞

35% Compound Interest Factors

	Single Payment		Uniform Series				
	Compound Amount Factor	Present Worth Factor	Sinking Fund Factor	Capital Recovery Factor	Compound Amount Factor	Present Worth Factor	
n	F/P	P/F	A/F	A/P	F/A	P/A	n
1	1.3500	0.7407	1.000 00	1.350 00	1.000	0.741	1
2	1.8225	0.5487	0.425 53	0.775 53	2.350	1.289	2
3	2.4604	0.4064	0.239 66	0.589 66	4.172	1.696	3
4	3.3215	0.3011	0.150 76	0.500 76	6.633	1.997	4
5	4.4840	0.2230	0.100 46	0.450 46	9.954	2.220	5
6	6.0534	0.1652	0.069 26	0.419 26	14.438	2.385	6
7	8.1722	0.1224	0.048 80	0.398 80	20.492	2.507	7
8	11.0324	0.0906	0.034 89	0.384 89	28.664	2.598	8
9	14.8937	0.0671	0.025 19	0.375 19	39.696	2.665	9
10	20.1066	0.0497	0.018 32	0.368 32	54.590	2.715	10
11	27.1439	0.0368	0.013 39	0.363 39	74.697	2.752	11
12	36.6442	0.0273	0.009 82	0.359 82	101.841	2.779	12
13	49.4697	0.0202	0.007 22	0.357 22	138.485	2.799	13
14	66.7841	0.0150	0.005 32	0.355 32	187.954	2.814	14
15	90.1585	0.0111	0.003 93	0.353 93	254.738	2.825	15
16	121.7139	0.0082	0.002 90	0.352 90	344.897	2.834	16
17	164.3138	0.0061	0.002 14	0.352 14	466.611	2.840	17
18	221.8236	0.0045	0.001 59	0.351 58	630.925	2.844	18
19	299.4619	0.0033	0.001 17	0.351 17	852.748	2.848	19
20	404.2736	0.0025	0.000 87	0.350 87	1 152.210	2.850	20
21	545.7693	0.0018	0.000 64	0.350 64	1 556.484	2.852	21
22	736.7886	0.0014	0.000 48	0.350 48	2 102.253	2.853	22
23	994.6646	0.0010	0.000 35	0.350 35	2 839.042	2.854	23
24	1 342.7973	0.0007	0.000 26	0.350 26	3 833.706	2.855	24
25	1 812.7763	0.0006	0.000 19	0.350 19	5 176.504	2.856	25
26	2 447.2480	0.0004	0.000 14	0.350 14	6 989.280	2.856	26
27	3 303.7848	0.0003	0.000 11	0.350 11	9 436.528	2.856	27
28	4 460.1095	0.0002	0.000 08	0.350 08	12 740.313	2.857	28
29	6 021.1478	0.0002	0.000 06	0.350 06	17 200.422	2.857	29
30	8 128.5495	0.0001	0.000 04	0.350 04	23 221.570	2.857	30
31	10 973.5418	0.0001	0.000 03	0.350 03	31 350.120	2.857	31
32	14 814.2815	0.0001	0.000 02	0.350 02	42 323.661	2.857	32
33	19 999.2800	0.0001	0.000 02	0.350 02	57 137.943	2.857	33
34	26 999.0280	0.0000	0.000 01	0.350 01	77 137.223	2.857	34
35	36 448.6878	. . . . . .	0.000 01	0.350 01	104 136.251	2.857	35
∞				0.350 00		2.857	∞

40% Compound Interest Factors

	Single Payment		Uniform Series				
	Compound Amount Factor	Present Worth Factor	Sinking Fund Factor	Capital Recovery Factor	Compound Amount Factor	Present Worth Factor	
n	F/P	P/F	A/F	A/P	F/A	P/A	n
1	1.4000	0.7143	1.000 00	1.400 00	1.000	0.714	1
2	1.9600	0.5102	0.416 67	0.816 67	2.400	1.224	2
3	2.7440	0.3644	0.229 36	0.629 36	4.360	1.589	3
4	3.8416	0.2603	0.140 77	0.540 77	7.104	1.849	4
5	5.3782	0.1859	0.091 36	0.491 36	10.946	2.035	5
6	7.5295	0.1328	0.061 26	0.461 26	16.324	2.168	6
7	10.5414	0.0949	0.041 92	0.441 92	23.853	2.263	7
8	14.7579	0.0678	0.029 07	0.429 07	34.395	2.331	8
9	20.6610	0.0484	0.020 34	0.420 34	49.153	2.379	9
10	28.9255	0.0346	0.014 32	0.414 32	69.814	2.414	10
11	40.4957	0.0247	0.010 13	0.410 13	98.739	2.438	11
12	56.6939	0.0176	0.007 18	0.407 18	139.235	2.456	12
13	79.3715	0.0126	0.005 10	0.405 10	195.929	2.469	13
14	111.1201	0.0090	0.003 63	0.403 63	275.300	2.478	14
15	155.5681	0.0064	0.002 59	0.402 59	386.420	2.484	15
16	217.7953	0.0046	0.001 85	0.401 85	541.988	2.489	16
17	304.9135	0.0033	0.001 32	0.401 32	759.784	2.492	17
18	426.8789	0.0023	0.000 94	0.400 94	1 064.697	2.494	18
19	597.6304	0.0017	0.000 67	0.400 67	1 491.576	2.496	19
20	836.6826	0.0012	0.000 48	0.400 48	2 089.206	2.497	20
21	1 171.3554	0.0009	0.000 34	0.400 34	2 925.889	2.498	21
22	1 639.8976	0.0006	0.000 24	0.400 24	4 097.245	2.498	22
23	2 295.8569	0.0004	0.000 17	0.400 17	5 737.142	2.499	23
24	3 214.1997	0.0003	0.000 12	0.400 12	8 032.999	2.499	24
25	4 499.8796	0.0002	0.000 09	0.400 09	11 247.199	2.499	25
26	6 299.8314	0.0002	0.000 06	0.400 06	15 747.079	2.500	26
27	8 819.7640	0.0001	0.000 05	0.400 05	22 046.910	2.500	27
28	12 347.6696	0.0001	0.000 03	0.400 03	30 866.674	2.500	28
29	17 286.7374	0.0001	0.000 02	0.400 02	43 214.343	2.500	29
30	24 201.4324	0.0000	0.000 01	0.400 02	60 501.081	2.500	30
31	33 882.0053	. . . . . .	0.000 01	0.400 01	84 702.513	2.500	31
32	47 434.8074	. . . . . .	0.000 01	0.400 01	118 584.519	2.500	32
33	66 408.7304	. . . . . .	0.000 01	0.400 01	166 019.326	2.500	33
34	92 972.2225	. . . . . .	0.000 00	0.400 00	232 428.056	2.500	34
35	130 161.1116	. . . . . .	. . . . . .	0.400 00	325 400.279	2.500	35
∞				0.400 00		2.500	∞

45% Compound Interest Factors

	Single Payment		Uniform Series				
	Compound Amount Factor	Present Worth Factor	Sinking Fund Factor	Capital Recovery Factor	Compound Amount Factor	Present Worth Factor	
n	F/P	P/F	A/F	A/P	F/A	P/A	n
1	1.4500	0.6897	1.000 00	1.450 00	1.000	0.690	1
2	2.1025	0.4756	0.408 16	0.858 16	2.450	1.165	2
3	3.0486	0.3280	0.219 66	0.669 66	4.552	1.493	3
4	4.4205	0.2262	0.131 56	0.581 56	7.601	1.720	4
5	6.4097	0.1560	0.083 18	0.533 18	12.022	1.876	5
6	9.2941	0.1076	0.054 26	0.504 26	18.431	1.983	6
7	13.4765	0.0742	0.036 07	0.486 07	27.725	2.057	7
8	19.5409	0.0512	0.024 27	0.474 27	41.202	2.109	8
9	28.3343	0.0353	0.016 46	0.466 46	60.743	2.144	9
10	41.0847	0.0243	0.011 23	0.461 23	89.077	2.168	10
11	59.5728	0.0168	0.007 68	0.457 68	130.162	2.185	11
12	86.3806	0.0116	0.005 27	0.455 27	189.735	2.196	12
13	125.2518	0.0080	0.003 62	0.453 62	276.115	2.204	13
14	181.6151	0.0055	0.002 49	0.452 49	401.367	2.210	14
15	263.3419	0.0038	0.001 72	0.451 72	582.982	2.214	15
16	381.8458	0.0026	0.001 18	0.451 18	846.324	2.216	16
17	553.6764	0.0018	0.000 81	0.450 81	1 228.170	2.218	17
18	802.8308	0.0012	0.000 56	0.450 56	1 781.846	2.219	18
19	1 164.1047	0.0009	0.000 39	0.450 39	2 584.677	2.220	19
20	1 687.9518	0.0006	0.000 27	0.450 27	3 748.782	2.221	20
21	2 447.5301	0.0004	0.000 18	0.450 18	5 436.734	2.221	21
22	3 548.9187	0.0003	0.000 13	0.450 13	7 884.264	2.222	22
23	5 145.9321	0.0002	0.000 09	0.450 09	11 433.182	2.222	23
24	7 461.6015	0.0001	0.000 06	0.450 06	16 579.115	2.222	24
25	10 819.3222	0.0001	0.000 04	0.450 04	24 040.716	2.222	25
26	15 688.0173	0.0001	0.000 03	0.450 03	34 860.038	2.222	26
27	22 747.6250	0.0000	0.000 02	0.450 02	50 548.056	2.222	27
28	32 984.0563	. . . . . .	0.000 01	0.450 01	73 295.681	2.222	28
29	47 826.8816	. . . . . .	0.000 01	0.450 01	106 279.737	2.222	29
30	69 348.9783	. . . . . .	0.000 01	0.450 01	154 106.618	2.222	30
∞				0.450 00		2.222	∞

50% Compound Interest Factors

	Single Payment		Uniform Series				
	Compound Amount Factor	Present Worth Factor	Sinking Fund Factor	Capital Recovery Factor	Compound Amount Factor	Present Worth Factor	
n	*F/P*	*P/F*	*A/F*	*A/P*	*F/A*	*P/A*	*n*
1	1.5000	0.6667	1.000 00	1.500 00	1.000	0.667	1
2	2.2500	0.4444	0.400 00	0.900 00	2.500	1.111	2
3	3.3750	0.2963	0.210 53	0.710 53	4.750	1.407	3
4	5.0625	0.1975	0.123 08	0.623 08	8.125	1.605	4
5	7.5938	0.1317	0.075 83	0.575 83	13.188	1.737	5
6	11.3906	0.0878	0.048 12	0.548 12	20.781	1.824	6
7	17.0859	0.0585	0.031 08	0.531 08	32.172	1.883	7
8	25.6289	0.0390	0.020 30	0.520 30	49.258	1.922	8
9	38.4434	0.0260	0.013 35	0.513 35	74.887	1.948	9
10	57.6650	0.0173	0.008 82	0.508 82	113.330	1.965	10
11	86.4976	0.0116	0.005 85	0.505 85	170.995	1.977	11
12	129.7463	0.0077	0.003 88	0.503 88	257.493	1.985	12
13	194.6195	0.0051	0.002 58	0.502 58	387.239	1.990	13
14	291.9293	0.0034	0.001 72	0.501 72	581.859	1.993	14
15	437.8939	0.0023	0.001 14	0.501 14	873.788	1.995	15
16	656.8408	0.0015	0.000 76	0.500 76	1 311.682	1.997	16
17	985.2613	0.0010	0.000 51	0.500 51	1 968.523	1.998	17
18	1 477.8919	0.0007	0.000 34	0.500 34	2 953.784	1.999	18
19	2 216.8378	0.0005	0.000 23	0.500 23	4 431.676	1.999	19
20	3 325.2567	0.0003	0.000 15	0.500 15	6 648.513	1.999	20
21	4 987.8851	0.0002	0.000 10	0.500 10	9 973.770	2.000	21
22	7 481.8276	0.0001	0.000 07	0.500 07	14 961.655	2.000	22
23	11 222.7415	0.0001	0.000 04	0.500 04	22 443.483	2.000	23
24	16 834.1122	0.0001	0.000 03	0.500 03	33 666.224	2.000	24
25	25 251.1683	0.0000	0.000 02	0.500 02	50 500.337	2.000	25
∞				0.500 00		2.000	∞

Factors To Convert a Gradient Series to an Equivalent Uniform Annual Series (A/G)

This table contains multipliers for a gradient G to convert the n-year end-of-year series 0, G, 2G, . . . (n — 1)G to an equivalent uniform annual series for n years.

n	1%	2%	3%	4%	5%	6%	7%	8%	10%	n
2	0.50	0.50	0.49	0.49	0.49	0.49	0.48	0.48	0.48	2
3	0.99	0.99	0.98	0.97	0.97	0.96	0.95	0.95	0.94	3
4	1.49	1.48	1.46	1.45	1.44	1.43	1.42	1.40	1.38	4
5	1.98	1.96	1.94	1.92	1.90	1.88	1.86	1.85	1.81	5
6	2.47	2.44	2.41	2.39	2.36	2.33	2.30	2.28	2.22	6
7	2.96	2.92	2.88	2.84	2.81	2.77	2.73	2.69	2.62	7
8	3.45	3.40	3.34	3.29	3.24	3.20	3.15	3.10	3.00	8
9	3.93	3.87	3.80	3.74	3.68	3.61	3.55	3.49	3.37	9
10	4.42	4.34	4.26	4.18	4.10	4.02	3.95	3.87	3.73	10
11	4.90	4.80	4.70	4.61	4.51	4.42	4.33	4.24	4.06	11
12	5.38	5.26	5.15	5.03	4.92	4.81	4.70	4.60	4.39	12
13	5.86	5.72	5.59	5.45	5.32	5.19	5.06	4.94	4.70	13
14	6.34	6.18	6.02	5.87	5.71	5.56	5.42	5.27	5.00	14
15	6.81	6.63	6.45	6.27	6.10	5.93	5.76	5.59	5.28	15
16	7.29	7.08	6.87	6.67	6.47	6.28	6.09	5.90	5.55	16
17	7.76	7.52	7.29	7.07	6.84	6.62	6.41	6.20	5.81	17
18	8.23	7.97	7.71	7.45	7.20	6.96	6.72	6.49	6.05	18
19	8.70	8.41	8.12	7.83	7.56	7.29	7.02	6.77	6.29	19
20	9.17	8.84	8.52	8.21	7.90	7.61	7.32	7.04	6.51	20
21	9.63	9.28	8.92	8.58	8.24	7.92	7.60	7.29	6.72	21
22	10.10	9.70	9.32	8.94	8.57	8.22	7.87	7.54	6.92	22
23	10.56	10.13	9.71	9.30	8.90	8.51	8.14	7.78	7.11	23
24	11.02	10.55	10.10	9.65	9.21	8.80	8.39	8.01	7.29	24
25	11.48	10.97	10.48	9.99	9.52	9.07	8.64	8.23	7.46	25
26	11.94	11.39	10.85	10.33	9.83	9.34	8.88	8.44	7.62	26
27	12.39	11.80	11.23	10.66	10.12	9.60	9.11	8.64	7.77	27
28	12.85	12.21	11.59	10.99	10.41	9.86	9.33	8.83	7.91	28
29	13.30	12.62	11.96	11.31	10.69	10.10	9.54	9.01	8.05	29
30	13.75	13.02	12.31	11.63	10.97	10.34	9.75	9.19	8.18	30
31	14.20	13.42	12.67	11.94	11.24	10.57	9.95	9.36	8.30	31
32	14.65	13.82	13.02	12.24	11.50	10.80	10.14	9.52	8.41	32
33	15.10	14.22	13.36	12.54	11.76	11.02	10.32	9.67	8.52	33
34	15.54	14.61	13.70	12.83	12.01	11.23	10.50	9.82	8.61	34
35	15.98	15.00	14.04	13.12	12.25	11.43	10.67	9.96	8.71	35
40	18.18	16.89	15.65	14.48	13.38	12.36	11.42	10.57	9.10	40
45	20.33	18.70	17.16	15.70	14.36	13.14	12.04	11.04	9.37	45
50	22.44	20.44	18.56	16.81	15.22	13.80	12.53	11.41	9.57	50
60	26.53	23.70	21.07	18.70	16.61	14.79	13.23	11.90	9.80	60
70	30.47	26.66	23.21	20.20	17.62	15.46	13.67	12.18	9.91	70
80	34.25	29.36	25.04	21.37	18.35	15.90	13.93	12.33	9.96	80
90	37.87	31.79	26.57	22.28	18.87	16.19	14.08	12.41	9.98	90
100	41.34	33.99	27.84	22.98	19.23	16.37	14.17	12.45	9.99	100

Factors To Convert a Gradient Series to an Equivalent Uniform Annual Series (A/G)

This table contains multipliers for a gradient G to convert the n-year end-of-year series 0, G, 2G, ... (n − 1)G to an equivalent uniform annual series for n years.

n	12%	15%	20%	25%	30%	35%	40%	45%	50%	n
2	0.47	0.47	0.45	0.44	0.43	0.43	0.42	0.41	0.40	2
3	0.92	0.91	0.88	0.85	0.83	0.80	0.78	0.76	0.74	3
4	1.36	1.33	1.27	1.22	1.18	1.13	1.09	1.05	1.02	4
5	1.77	1.72	1.64	1.56	1.49	1.42	1.36	1.30	1.24	5
6	2.17	2.10	1.98	1.87	1.77	1.67	1.58	1.50	1.42	6
7	2.55	2.45	2.29	2.14	2.01	1.88	1.77	1.66	1.56	7
8	2.91	2.78	2.58	2.39	2.22	2.06	1.92	1.79	1.68	8
9	3.26	3.09	2.84	2.60	2.40	2.21	2.04	1.89	1.76	9
10	3.58	3.38	3.07	2.80	2.55	2.33	2.14	1.97	1.82	10
11	3.90	3.65	3.29	2.97	2.68	2.44	2.22	2.03	1.87	11
12	4.19	3.91	3.48	3.11	2.80	2.52	2.28	2.08	1.91	12
13	4.47	4.14	3.66	3.24	2.89	2.59	2.33	2.12	1.93	13
14	4.73	4.36	3.82	3.36	2.97	2.64	2.37	2.14	1.95	14
15	4.98	4.56	3.96	3.45	3.03	2.69	2.40	2.17	1.97	15
16	5.21	4.75	4.09	3.54	3.09	2.72	2.43	2.18	1.98	16
17	5.44	4.93	4.20	3.61	3.13	2.75	2.44	2.19	1.98	17
18	5.64	5.08	4.30	3.67	3.17	2.78	2.46	2.20	1.99	18
19	5.84	5.23	4.39	3.72	3.20	2.79	2.47	2.21	1.99	19
20	6.02	5.37	4.46	3.77	3.23	2.81	2.48	2.21	1.99	20
21	6.19	5.49	4.53	3.80	3.25	2.82	2.48	2.21	2.00	21
22	6.35	5.60	4.59	3.84	3.26	2.83	2.49	2.22	2.00	22
23	6.50	5.70	4.65	3.86	3.28	2.83	2.49	2.22	2.00	23
24	6.64	5.80	4.69	3.89	3.29	2.84	2.49	2.22	2.00	24
25	6.77	5.88	4.74	3.91	3.30	2.84	2.49	2.22	2.00	25
26	6.89	5.96	4.77	3.92	3.30	2.85	2.50	2.22	2.00	26
27	7.00	6.03	4.80	3.94	3.31	2.85	2.50	2.22	2.00	27
28	7.11	6.10	4.83	3.95	3.32	2.85	2.50	2.22	2.00	28
29	7.21	6.15	4.85	3.96	3.32	2.85	2.50	2.22	2.00	29
30	7.30	6.21	4.87	3.96	3.32	2.85	2.50	2.22	2.00	30
31	7.38	6.25	4.89	3.97	3.32	2.85	2.50	2.22	2.00	31
32	7.46	6.30	4.91	3.97	3.33	2.85	2.50	2.22	2.00	32
33	7.53	6.34	4.92	3.98	3.33	2.86	2.50	2.22	2.00	33
34	7.60	6.37	4.93	3.98	3.33	2.86	2.50	2.22	2.00	34
35	7.66	6.40	4.94	3.99	3.33	2.86	2.50	2.22	2.00	35
40	7.90	6.52	4.97	4.00	3.33	2.86	2.50	2.22	2.00	40
45	8.06	6.58	4.99	4.00	3.33	2.86	2.50	2.22	2.00	45
50	8.16	6.62	4.99	4.00	3.33	2.86	2.50	2.22	2.00	50
60	8.27	6.65	5.00	4.00	3.33	2.86	2.50	2.22	2.00	60
70	8.31	6.66	5.00	4.00	3.33	2.86	2.50	2.22	2.00	70
80	8.32	6.67	5.00	4.00	3.33	2.86	2.50	2.22	2.00	80
90	8.33	6.67	5.00	4.00	3.33	2.86	2.50	2.22	2.00	90
100	8.33	6.67	5.00	4.00	3.33	2.86	2.50	2.22	2.00	100

Factors To Compute the Present Worth of a Gradient Series —Interest Rates from 1% to 50% *(P/G)*

This table contains multipliers for a gradient G to find the present worth of the n-year end-of-year series 0, G, 2G, ... (n — 1)G.

n	1%	2%	3%	4%	5%	6%	n
1	0.0000	0.0000	0.0000	0.0000	0.0000	0.0000	1
2	0.9803	0.9612	0.9426	0.9246	0.9070	0.8900	2
3	2.9215	2.8458	2.7729	2.7025	2.6347	2.5692	3
4	5.8044	5.6173	5.4383	5.2670	5.1028	4.9455	4
5	9.6103	9.2403	8.8888	8.5547	8.2369	7.9345	5
6	14.3205	13.6801	13.0762	12.5062	11.9680	11.4594	6
7	19.9168	18.9035	17.9547	17.0657	16.2321	15.4497	7
8	26.3812	24.8779	23.4806	22.1806	20.9700	19.8416	8
9	33.6959	31.5720	29.6119	27.8013	26.1268	24.5768	9
10	41.8435	38.9551	36.3088	33.8814	31.6520	29.6023	10
11	50.8067	46.9977	43.5330	40.3772	37.4988	34.8702	11
12	60.5687	55.6712	51.2482	47.2477	43.6241	40.3369	12
13	71.1126	64.9475	59.4196	54.4546	49.9879	45.9629	13
14	82.4221	74.7999	68.0141	61.9618	56.5538	51.7128	14
15	94.4810	85.2021	77.0002	69.7355	63.2880	57.5546	15
16	107.2734	96.1288	86.3477	77.7441	70.1597	63.4592	16
17	120.7834	107.5554	96.0280	85.9581	77.1405	69.4011	17
18	134.9957	119.4581	106.0137	94.3498	84.2043	75.3569	18
19	149.8950	131.8139	116.2788	102.8933	91.3275	81.3062	19
20	165.4664	144.6003	126.7987	111.5647	98.4884	87.2304	20
21	181.6950	157.7959	137.5496	120.3414	105.6673	93.1136	21
22	198.5663	171.3795	148.5094	129.2024	112.8461	98.9412	22
23	216.0660	185.3309	159.6566	138.1284	120.0087	104.7007	23
24	234.1800	199.6305	170.9711	147.1012	127.1402	110.3812	24
25	252.8945	214.2592	182.4336	156.1040	134.2275	115.9732	25
30	355.0021	291.7164	241.3613	201.0618	168.6226	142.3588	30
35	470.1583	374.8826	301.6267	244.8768	200.5807	165.7427	35
40	596.8561	461.9931	361.7500	286.5303	229.5452	185.9568	40
45	733.7038	551.5652	420.6325	325.4028	255.3146	203.1097	45
50	879.4177	642.3606	477.4804	361.1639	277.9148	217.4574	50

n	7%	8%	10%	12%	15%	20%	n
1	0.0000	0.0000	0.0000	0.0000	0.0000	0.0000	1
2	0.8734	0.8573	0.8264	0.7972	0.7561	0.6944	2
3	2.5060	2.4450	2.3291	2.2208	2.0712	1.8519	3
4	4.7947	4.6501	4.3781	4.1273	3.7864	3.2986	4
5	7.6467	7.3724	6.8618	6.3970	5.7751	4.9061	5
6	10.9784	10.5233	9.6842	8.9302	7.9368	6.5806	6
7	14.7149	14.0242	12.7631	11.6443	10.1924	8.2551	7
8	18.7889	17.8061	16.0287	14.4715	12.4807	9.8831	8
9	23.1404	21.8081	19.4215	17.3563	14.7548	11.4335	9
10	27.7156	25.9768	22.8913	20.2541	16.9795	12.8871	10
11	32.4665	30.2657	26.3963	23.1289	19.1289	14.2330	11
12	37.3506	34.6339	29.9012	25.9523	21.1849	15.4667	12
13	42.3302	39.0463	33.3772	28.7024	23.1352	16.5883	13
14	47.3718	43.4723	36.8005	31.3624	24.9725	17.6008	14
15	52.4461	47.8857	40.1520	33.9202	26.6930	18.5095	15

Factors To Compute the Present Worth of a Gradient Series
—Interest Rates from 1% to 50% *(P/G)*

This table contains multipliers for a gradient G to find the present worth of the n-year end-of-year series 0, G, 2G, . . . (n — 1)G.

n	7%	8%	10%	12%	15%	20%	n
16	57.5271	52.2640	43.4164	36.3670	28.2960	19.3208	16
17	62.5923	56.5883	46.5820	38.6973	29.7828	20.0419	17
18	67.6220	60.8426	49.6396	40.9080	31.1565	20.6805	18
19	72.5991	65.0134	52.5827	42.9979	32.4213	21.2439	19
20	77.5091	69.0898	55.4069	44.9676	33.5822	21.7395	20
21	82.3393	73.0629	58.1095	46.8188	34.6448	22.1742	21
22	87.0793	76.9257	60.6893	48.5543	35.6150	22.5546	22
23	91.7201	80.6726	63.1462	50.1776	36.4988	22.8867	23
24	96.2545	84.2997	65.4813	51.6929	37.3023	23.1760	24
25	100.6765	87.8041	67.6964	53.1047	38.0314	23.4276	25
30	120.9718	103.4558	77.0766	58.7821	40.7526	24.2628	30
35	138.1353	116.0920	83.9872	62.6052	42.3587	24.6614	35
40	152.2928	126.0422	88.9526	65.1159	43.2830	24.8469	40
45	163.7559	133.7331	92.4545	66.7343	43.8051	24.9316	45
50	172.9051	139.5928	94.8889	67.7625	44.0958	24.9698	50

n	25%	30%	35%	40%	45%	50%	n
1	0.0000	0.0000	0.0000	0.0000	0.0000	0.0000	1
2	0.6400	0.5917	0.5487	0.5102	0.4756	0.4444	2
3	1.6640	1.5020	1.3616	1.2391	1.1317	1.0370	3
4	2.8928	2.5524	2.2648	2.0200	1.8103	1.6296	4
5	4.2035	3.6297	3.1568	2.7637	2.4344	2.1564	5
6	5.5142	4.6656	3.9828	3.4278	2.9723	2.5953	6
7	6.7725	5.6218	4.7170	3.9970	3.4176	2.9465	7
8	7.9469	6.4800	5.3515	4.4713	3.7758	3.2196	8
9	9.0207	7.2344	5.8887	4.8585	4.0581	3.4277	9
10	9.9870	7.8872	6.3363	5.1696	4.2772	3.5838	10
11	10.8460	8.4452	6.7047	5.4166	4.4450	3.6994	11
12	11.6020	8.9173	7.0049	5.6106	4.5724	3.7842	12
13	12.2617	9.3135	7.2474	5.7618	4.6682	3.8459	13
14	12.8334	9.6437	7.4421	5.8788	4.7398	3.8904	14
15	13.3260	9.9172	7.5974	5.9688	4.7929	3.9224	15
16	13.7482	10.1426	7.7206	6.0376	4.8322	3.9452	16
17	14.1085	10.3276	7.8180	6.0901	4.8611	3.9614	17
18	14.4147	10.4788	7.8946	6.1299	4.8823	3.9729	18
19	14.6741	10.6019	7.9547	6.1601	4.8978	3.9811	19
20	14.8932	10.7019	8.0017	6.1828	4.9090	3.9868	20
21	15.0777	10.7828	8.0384	6.1998	4.9172	3.9908	21
22	15.2326	10.8482	8.0669	6.2127	4.9231	3.9936	22
23	15.3625	10.9009	8.0890	6.2222	4.9274	3.9955	23
24	15.4711	10.9433	8.1061	6.2294	4.9305	3.9969	24
25	15.5618	10.9773	8.1194	6.2347	4.9327	3.9979	25
30	15.8316	11.0687	8.1517	6.2466	4.9372	3.9997	30
35	15.9367	11.0980	8.1603	6.2493	4.9381		35
40	15.9766	11.1071	8.1625	6.2498			40
45	15.9915	11.1099	8.1631				45
50	15.9969	11.1108					50

Index